Cost-Benefit
Analysis

Cost-Benefit Analysis

Legal, Economic, and Philosophical Perspectives

EDITED BY
Matthew D. Adler
and Eric A. Posner

The University of Chicago Press
CHICAGO & LONDON

The essays in this volume originally appeared in *The Journal of Legal Studies*.

"The Discipline of Cost-Benefit Analysis" is © 2000 by Amartya Sen.

The University of Chicago Press, Chicago, 60637
The University of Chicago Press, Ltd., London
© 2001 The University of Chicago
All rights reserved. Published in 2001
Printed in the United States of America
ISBN: (cl)   0-226-00762-6
ISBN: (pa)   0-226-00763-4

05   04   03   02   01   5   4   3   2   1

Library of Congress Cataloging in Publication Data

Cost-benefit analysis : legal, economic, and philosophical perspectives / edited by Matthew D. Alder and Eric A. Posner.
    p. cm.
  Includes bibliographical references and index.
  ISBN 0-226-00762-6 (cloth) — ISBN 0-226-00763-4 (pbk.)
    I. Law and economics.   2. Cost effectiveness.   3. Distributive justice.   I. Adler, Matthew D.   II. Posner, Eric A.

K487.E3 C673
658.15′54—dc21

                                                                00-069065

The paper used in the publication meets the minimum requirements of American National Standard for Information Sciences—Permanence of Paper for Printed Library Materials, ANSI Z39.48.1984.

CONTENTS

Contents

INTRODUCTION

MATTHEW D. ADLER and ERIC A. POSNER*

THE contributions to this volume emerged from a conference on cost-benefit analysis held at the University of Chicago Law School in September 1999. The conference was motivated by the observation that cost-benefit analysis has become a very common tool of project evaluation in the federal government and indeed, as Robert Hahn's contribution shows, in state governments, but that the academic literature on the subject remains skeptical. The academic literature is also fragmented, and we believed that by bringing together prominent contributors from different disciplines—economics, philosophy, and the law—some progress could be made in understanding cost-benefit analysis. The contributions to this volume are cogently summarized and criticized in Richard Posner's comment. Rather than duplicate these labors here, we will make some general observations about the debate and about possible directions for future research.

General Observations about the (New) Debate about Cost-Benefit Analysis. There are already large philosophical, legal, and (especially) economic literatures on cost-benefit analysis dating back to the 1920s. Does this volume have anything to contribute to them? We think that it does.

First, it shows that cost-benefit analysis is a rich area for interdisciplinary work. Economists have defined the central cost-benefit methodology. They have also done a huge amount of crucial technical work in elaborating that methodology, for example, in determining how government should gather information about compensating variations, particularly where market prices are unavailable; in explaining how costs and benefits should be discounted over time; in adapting the methodology to areas where it first seemed inapplicable, for example, to governmental projects that cause death; and in illuminating the connections between cost-benefit analysis and other normative standards in economics like the Kaldor-Hicks standard. Economists still have much to say about cost-benefit analysis, as here evidenced by the contributions of Gary Becker, Robert Frank, Hahn, and W. Kip Viscusi. But philosophers should also be involved in the debate. For example, they can help illuminate the basic moral terrain (see the papers by

* University of Pennsylvania Law School and University of Chicago Law School.

[*Journal of Legal Studies,* vol. XXIX]

1

John Broome, Martha Nussbaum, and Amartya Sen), or specify alternative procedures different from those proposed within the economic literature (see Henry Richardson's paper). We do not mean to suggest that a philosophical perspective is the only noneconomic perspective of relevance to cost-benefit analysis. The papers by Viscusi and Cass Sunstein powerfully demonstrate that cognitive psychology can sharpen our understanding both of the justifiability of cost-benefit analysis and of its appropriate limits. And legal scholars have a critical role to play in answering legal and policy questions about cost-benefit analysis—for example, in debating the proper scope and content of Executive Order 12,866—by synthesizing economic, philosophical, psychological, and other relevant scholarship.

Second, we hazard to suggest that the new debate about cost-benefit analysis will be more empirical and pragmatic than the older literature. Most, perhaps all, of the contributors would apparently agree that if government agencies should employ cost-benefit analysis, then they should do so because it is a beneficial tool, not because the sum-of-compensating-variations test or any related test has basic moral weight. This conceptualization of cost-benefit analysis does not preclude theoretical work, as the Broome, Nussbaum, and Sen papers show. (We still need to know what the underlying moral criteria are.) But it also opens the door to a more concrete discussion of matters such as the following: the various types of cost-benefit methodologies that agencies and other governmental bodies might employ; the conditions under which cost-benefit analysis is relatively useful, or relatively unproductive (be they public choice conditions, cognitive-psychological conditions, or others); the conditions under which cost-benefit analysis is likely to be manipulated by agencies, or applied in relatively good faith; the policy areas in which, as a historical matter, cost-benefit analysis has proved to be a good, bad, or indifferent tool; the alternative tools that agencies might use; and the role of courts in reviewing cost-benefit studies conducted by agencies. Our optimistic prediction is that the new debate about cost-benefit analysis will bring to bear a more sophisticated philosophical and normative apparatus and use that apparatus as the framework for a detailed and empirically rich evaluation of cost-benefit analysis as a decisional tool. Older assumptions about the impossibility of interpersonal welfare comparisons, or the necessary equivalence of welfare and preference-satisfaction, will we hope be abandoned or at least be defended in new ways.

We turn now to some more concrete examples of the possible future directions of cost-benefit analysis.

Normative Justifications for Cost-Benefit Analysis: Boundary Conditions and Alternative Procedures. Even the proponents of cost-benefit analysis do not generally argue that it should be the sole decision procedure for administrative agencies and other governmental bodies. There may well be scenarios where it is welfare maximizing for agencies to employ some other procedure, such as QUALY-based assessment or (nonmonetized) multidimensional assessment. Similarly, if cost-benefit analysis is a procedure for implementing some normative criterion other than overall well-being, it could well be the case that—under certain conditions—alternative procedures implement that criterion better than cost-benefit analysis. Research remains to be done both (1) in specifying the details of these alternative procedures and (2) in specifying the boundary conditions under which agencies and other governmental bodies should switch from CBA to some alternative.

Normative Justifications for Cost-Benefit Analysis: Case Studies. An empirical (but normative) assessment of cost-benefit analysis would also be useful. One could take some set of actual agency choices and evaluate those choices using both cost-benefit analysis and whatever normative criterion cost-benefit analysis is supposed to implement. For example, it would be useful to collect the cost-benefit analyses published by federal agencies in the Federal Register, in the course of evaluating major rules, and then attempt to conduct a parallel assessment of those rule-making decisions in light of the appropriate normative criterion. What were the rule makings in which cost-benefit analysis produced the correct outcome—the outcome that (in the scholar's determination) is the outcome ranked highest by the proper normative criterion? What were the rule makings in which cost-benefit analysis produced a suboptimal outcome? An empirical study of this kind could be helpful in determining whether and how cost-benefit analysis should be modified (for example, through distributive weights) and in specifying the conditions under which agencies should employ some alternative procedure.

Normative Justification for Cost-Benefit Analysis: Feasibility. We agree with Becker that it is not sufficient to say that cost-benefit analysis is ''good enough'' and that the traditional derivation under a Social Planner model is not satisfactory. What is needed is a second-best model that explains why cost-benefit analysis might be desirable (if this is the case) given various constraints. What are these constraints? Certainly the cognitive limitations of the decision maker, but also constraints imposed by the political process. But if the government's behavior is entirely driven by public choice factors, it is idle to talk about whether various policy instruments are valuable or not.

Suppose, for example, that the public has no influence on political decision making and that all regulations are approved if and only if interest groups that benefit from them have more political power than interest groups that are harmed by them. Under these circumstances, it is hard to imagine a normative argument in favor of using cost-benefit analysis. The results of cost-benefit analysis performed by agencies would not influence their choice of regulations, and it's hard to see why any political actors would want agencies to use cost-benefit analysis in the first place.

Now suppose that the public imperfectly monitors regulations and punishes politicians who appoint or support agency chiefs who issue regulations that transfer resources from the general public to interest groups. If this is the case, the president and Congress might want agencies to use cost-benefit analysis as a way of overcoming agency costs. Cost-benefit analyses performed by agencies may disclose whether regulations transfer resources to interest groups from the public. When the president and Congress are apprised of regulations that violate the agencies' own cost-benefit analysis (or, more likely, are justified by transparently manipulated cost-benefit analysis), they will punish the agency chiefs responsible for the regulations. Fearing such punishment, the agency chiefs are deterred, at least partly, from succumbing to interest group pressures.

This account leaves a lot unexplained. Most important, it does not explain the connection between the public interest and cost-benefit analysis. There may be some connection, but surely it is weak. Members of the public will be most interested in regulations that affect them disproportionately (reproducing the public choice problem at the individual level). They may also be concerned about factors from which cost-benefit analysis abstracts, factors such as the distribution of wealth and the effects on minorities. Finally, the president and Congress do not necessarily support regulations that promote the public interest. They may not fear transfers to interest groups, just transfers to the *wrong* interest groups.

Positive Analysis of Cost-Benefit Analysis: Public Choice.   As far as we know, no one has tried to explain why Reagan, Bush, and Clinton have all endorsed the use of cost-benefit analysis by agencies. But it would be useful to have an explanation for the political fortunes of cost-benefit analysis— why it was relatively popular before and after the 1970s but was unpopular during that decade. Such an explanation would shed light on the constraints that one would have to take account of in normative analysis.

We can only speculate. It may not be a coincidence that cost-benefit analysis became popular at roughly the same time that deregulation did. It has been argued that deregulation resulted when the deadweight costs resulting from regulation became too high;[1] presumably, savings from deregulation could be used at least in part to compensate losers. Similarly, one might argue that cost-benefit analysis was used to identify regulations or potential regulations with high deadweight costs, so that these regulations could be

---

[1] See Sam Peltzman, The Economic Theory of Regulation after a Decade of Deregulation, Brookings Papers on Economic Activity: Microeconomics 1 (1989).

eliminated or avoided. But deregulation seems to be running out of steam, whereas cost-benefit analysis seems thoroughly entrenched in the federal bureaucracy.

Positive Analysis of Cost-Benefit Analysis: Public Relations. One interesting aspect of cost-benefit analysis is that it sparks strong emotions; one gets a sense that there is an ideological divide about cost-benefit analysis, with free-market conservatives on one side and liberal environmentalists on the other. But on closer inspection, the story becomes murkier. On the one hand, Clinton has carried through Reagan's cost-benefit initiative. On the other hand, it appears that Clinton's Office of Management and Budget (OMB) has not been as vigorous in enforcing cost-benefit analysis as Reagan's OMB was, particularly against the Environmental Protection Agency. A more telling point is that another initiative—creating markets in tradable pollution rights—has been rather popular, even among environmentalists. So it seems unlikely that the language of economics, or the mere use of the language of trade-offs, or monetization of incommensurables, can explain continuing opposition to cost-benefit analysis among academics and in public policy circles. Indeed, one might argue that the rhetoric of cost-benefit analysis is more powerful than the reality. Agencies seem to be less likely than in the past to say that cost-benefit analysis is undesirable or unsuitable, but that does not mean that they take it seriously.

One possibility is that tradable emission rights are always connected to particular programs in which deals are hashed out between the various interests, including environmental interests. Because of the efficiency of trading systems, business interests are more willing to agree to lower pollutant levels than they are for more conventional policies, and this makes the environmentalists happy. That is to say, if failure to agree to a tradable emission rights program would result in the imposition of a command-and-control system, it is easy to see why all parties would enthusiastically agree to the former, for it results in less pollution (for the environmentalists) at less cost (to business interests). By contrast, the cost-benefit analysis controversy has been about the use of an umbrella policy instrument to supervise all regulations (including regulations emerging from statutes that themselves were the product of interest group deals). We think that it would be valuable for scholars to analyze the relative popularity of tradable emissions rights programs and cost-benefit analysis.

Positive Analysis of Cost-Benefit Analysis: Does It Work? Much has been written about whether the cost-benefit analysis executive orders have actually influenced the behavior of agencies. Knowledgeable scholars in this area seem to doubt that the executive orders have had much influence. There are many reasons why these orders may not have. The enforcement of executive orders is not automatic, so enforcement can be subject to politics. Cost-benefit analysis requires a lot of data, and given cost constraints, speculation often is used in its place. And there is enough controversy over certain kinds of data—from valuations of life to discount rates—that an agency intent on pushing through a regulation may be able to rationalize almost anything.

If the executive orders have not affected agency behavior, if agency behavior remains subject to normal political pressures, then one must ask why anyone bothered with these orders in the first place. It may have been symbolic politics, but then why these symbols? And why use an economic symbolism that seems so unpopular among elites, and even among the lay public if it knows anything about it at all? Much more work can be done on these issues.

The conference and this volume were made possible through the generous financial support of the University of Chicago Law School and the John M. Olin Program in Law and Economics.

RISK EQUITY

*W. KIP VISCUSI**

ABSTRACT

Risk equity serves as the purported rationale for a wide range of inefficient policy practices, such as the concern that hypothetical individual risks not be too great. This paper proposes an alternative risk equity concept in terms of equitable trade-offs rather than equity in risk levels. Equalizing the cost per life saved across policy contexts will save additional lives and will give fair treatment to risks arising in a variety of domains. Equitable trade-offs will also benefit minorities who currently are disadvantaged by politically based inefficient policies.

I. INTRODUCTION

T HE equity consequences of risk regulations have become a formal component of governmental evaluations of risk and environmental policies. Policy concern with environmental justice and environmental equity is perhaps the most visible manifestation of a concern with risk equity. In 1994 President Clinton issued Executive Order No. 12,898,[1] which required agencies to "identify and address . . . disproportionately high and adverse human health or environmental impacts" on minority populations. In response to this order, the U.S. Environmental Protection Agency established a watchdog office within the agency, the Office of Environmental Equity, to monitor the effects of environmental policies on equity concerns. These developments were also mirrored in the emergence of a large literature dealing with environmental equity and related concerns.[2]

* John F. Cogan, Jr., Professor of Law and Economics, Director of the Program on Empirical Legal Studies, Harvard Law School. E-mail: kip@law.harvard.edu. Paper prepared for the University of Chicago Law School Cost-Benefit Analysis conference, September 17–18, 1999. Helpful comments were provided by Matthew Adler, Eric Posner, Judge Richard Posner, and conference participants.

[1] Exec. Order No. 12,898, 59 Fed. Reg. 7629 (1994).

[2] See, for example, Vicki Been, What's Fairness Got to Do with It? Environmental Justice and the Siting of Locally Undesirable Land Uses, 78 Cornell L. Rev. 1001 (1993); Vicki Been, Analyzing Evidence of Environmental Justice, 11 J. Land Use & Envt'l L. 1 (1995); Commission for Racial Justice, Toxic Wastes and Race in the United States: A National Report on the Racial and Socioeconomic Characteristics of Communities with Hazardous Waste Sites (1987); James T. Hamilton, Politics and Social Costs: Estimating the Impact of Collective Action on Hazardous Waste Facilities, 24 Rand J. Econ. 101 (1993); James T. Hamilton, Testing for Environmental Racism: Prejudice, Profits, Political Power? 14 J. Pol'y Analy-

While environmental equity has been the most salient concern, a variety of other forms of equity with respect to risk affect policies not only in the environmental area but across other types of risk regulations. What we mean by fair is more problematic and, in the extreme case, can lead to the ad hoc justification of any specific policy intervention, however expensive it might be. Is it, for example, fair to target a population group that has been disadvantaged for reasons other than risk, such as poor education, and to provide them with more protective risk regulations to compensate them for their disadvantaged status? Or should we attempt to provide some kind of equal protection irrespective of economic status, and, if so, what is it that we mean by equitable protection against risk? Fairness has no well-defined guidelines, and as a result, this article will explore a wide variety of potential fairness concepts, recognizing that there are quite diverse views as to what does in fact constitute an equitable risk policy.

My concern with risk equity will not be from the standpoint of moral criteria but rather social welfare maximization.[3] In particular, the emphasis is on decision procedures by government agencies, as these procedures function in practice. In a more idealized political world in which there was no use of equity concerns to mask self-interested efforts to tilt policies away from welfare-maximizing norms, the role of equity might be quite different. Thus, a driving force of much of what follows is that purported equity concerns often serve as the rationale for justifying bad policies.

My most direct experience with such notions of equity came with respect to the siting of the new landfill in Orange County, North Carolina, in the early 1990s. The previous landfill site, which was becoming full, was located in a rural area. To promote environmental equity, the policy decision was made to site the new landfill in a manner that would not affect farm uses in the rural areas of the county. The first recommended site was a tract of as yet undeveloped land bordering what was one of the most affluent suburban areas in Chapel Hill. This landfill site had the additional disadvantage that it was less than 500 yards from my house. While the neighborhood was successful in fighting this misguided notion of environmental equity, the site the county chose instead was not superior from an efficient policy standpoint. The county instead designated a section of the Duke Forest to be used as the landfill. In what was surely an outrageous environmental outcome, the county chose as its landfill site a pristine research forest and nature preserve of the Duke University School of the Environment. The envi-

sis & Mgmt. 107 (1995); Rae Zimmerman, Issues of Clarification in Environmental Equity: How We Manage Is How We Measure, 21 Fordham Urb. L. J. 633 (1994).

[3] This distinction parallels that in the paper by Matthew D. Adler & Eric A. Posner, Implementing Cost-Benefit Analysis When Preferences Are Distorted, in this issue, at 1105.

ronmental equity in this case was achieved by imposing substantial losses on an educational institution located in the neighboring Durham County and that consequently did not have as much political clout within Orange County as did the local farmers. In this instance, which is by no means unique, environmental equity provided the vaguely defined rationale for a thoroughly misguided and socially harmful policy driven by political interests.

The principal view I will advocate here is that risk equity concerns are almost invariably harmful to public welfare. Within the highly charged political context of policy development, it is almost always possible to conceive of some notion of risk equity to justify even the most inefficient policy interventions. The same kinds of problems are encountered in contexts of traditional economic regulation as, for example, one could justify milk price supports or other regulatory market distortions on the grounds that they provide equitable benefits to the milk producers. All government policies involve transfers of various kinds, some of which may be monetary and others of which may be in kind. Those who benefit invariably plead that equity demands that they receive the policy benefits. Risk regulation policies typically involve in-kind transfers, but they nevertheless raise the specter of rent seeking and attendant inefficiencies that one encounters whenever one departs from economic efficiency norms.

The particular equity reference point that I will advocate in Section II is the outcomes achieved by efficient markets. In particular, the outcomes in competitive market transactions involving risk will serve as the standard for what I will consider to be an equitable risk. Because markets for risk do not always exist, there are frequently regulatory interventions for which the efficiency test is benefit-cost analysis. I will explore this concept and its relationship to risk equity in Section III. What people mean by risk equity typically is neither market based nor linked to benefit-cost analysis but rather is linked to some other notion of what kinds of risks are fair and what kinds of risks are not. Section IV examines many diverse concepts along these lines and illustrates why departures from efficiency norms can lead to wildly ill-conceived government policies.

II. THE MARKET REFERENCE POINT

The functioning of efficient markets involving risk establishes what I will take as my reference point for equitable risks. Consider a market transaction in which risk attributes of a product are bundled with other product characteristics. Then if the consumer is willing to buy the product, the person's willingness to pay for it necessarily exceeds the cost of the product, taking into account all the effects of the product in terms of health and safety risks.

Similarly, in the case of jobs, the wages that workers are paid will either equal or exceed the amount that they require to bear the risk associated with the job. These decisions by consumers and by firms in turn create incentives for efficient levels of safety, the details of which have been explored elsewhere.[4] Because consumer and worker preferences in effect set the price of safety in the market place, the level of product safety and job safety will necessarily reflect these valuations, leading to an efficient level of risk.

Market outcomes have the additional feature that there is also a transfer to compensate individuals for bearing the risk. Purchasers of less crashworthy cars pay a lower price for these products.[5] Houses located near Superfund sites are priced lower than those in safer neighborhoods.[6] A substantial literature has documented the existence of compensating differentials for job risks.[7] Thus, a voluntary transaction necessarily improves the welfare of all participants in the market transaction, making them better off or indifferent with respect to their previous situation.

It is useful to link these market transactions to the basic principles of the Coase Theorem. For job risks and product risks in these market contexts, the individual bearing the risk must be compensated to incur the risk. For pollution situations in which property rights are assigned to the polluter, the outcome of Coasean bargains will provide for efficient levels of risk after the pollution victims pay the polluter sufficiently to decrease pollution levels.[8] While efficient in terms of risk, such situations are not comparable to my market ideal because they make the party bearing the risk worse off because they do not have the property rights and must pay to avoid the risk.

A distinctive feature of market transactions is that people make decisions reflective of their individual circumstances, and firms and other enterprises engaged in market transactions likewise make decisions on the basis of their

---

[4] See W. Kip Viscusi, Employment Hazards: An Investigation of Market Performance (1979), for a more complete description of the functioning of markets for hazardous jobs.

[5] See Scott E. Atkinson & Robert Halvorsen, The Valuation of Risks to Life: Evidence from the Market for Automobiles, 72 Rev. Econ. & Stat. 133 (1990); Mark Dreyfus & W. Kip Viscusi, Rates of Time Preference and Consumer Valuations of Automobile Safety and Fuel Efficiency, 38 J. Law & Econ. 79 (1995).

[6] Estimation of the value of life based on this relationship appears in Ted Gayer, James T. Hamilton, & W. Kip Viscusi, Private Values of Risk Tradeoffs at Superfund Sites: Housing Market Evidence on Learning about Risk, Rev. Econ. & Stat. (in press, 2000). Vicki Been & Francis Gupta, Coming to the Nuisance or Going to the Barrios? A Longitudinal Analysis of Environmental Justice Claims, 24 Ecology L. Q. 1 (1997), explores this relationship and its effect on environmental justice.

[7] For a review see W. Kip Viscusi, The Value of Life in Legal Contexts: Survey and Critique, Am. L. & Econ. Rev. (in press, 2000).

[8] Efficiency here is in terms of short-run efficiency in terms of pollution levels. Long-run incentives to enter the polluting industry will be too great if polluters are paid to reduce pollution.

economic situation. The essential element of markets is that they permit such heterogeneity to play an important economic role. Consider the case of firms with differing costs of providing safety. It is extremely costly to substantially reduce the risks in sawmills and for construction work, whereas making the health and safety risks to investment bankers very small is quite within the realm of economic feasibility. For any given price of safety set through consumer or worker preferences, we will observe higher risk levels at firms where safety is more costly to provide.

The risk heterogeneity of primary interest here is with respect to individuals. Discussions of risk equity typically focus on equity in the risks across people rather than equity in the risks across firms or other institutions. The three principal sources of heterogeneity that will be reflected in market transactions and that should be reflected to enhance economic efficiency are heterogeneity in individual riskiness, heterogeneity in individual willingness to incur risks, and differences in preferences for activities that pose risks. The decentralized individual decisions in the marketplace permit each of these sources of heterogeneity to be expressed in the market transaction and to be reflected in ultimate risk compensation outcome.

Consider first heterogeneity in individual riskiness. Individuals' susceptibilities to disease vary, as do their skills. Jobs that require heavy lifting, for example, will be more likely to pose injury for those who lack physical strength. Inspection of accident statistics suggests that there are many important personal characteristics that drive differences in accident rates. Some of these differences are by gender. Men suffer higher death rates for most causes of death, such as accidents and homicides, though women are more susceptible to pneumonia and risks of diabetes.[9] Age-related differences are consequential as well, as males aged 15–24 are particularly prone to being killed in motor vehicle accidents, and the elderly are particularly susceptible to deaths from falls.[10] Market outcomes exploit this heterogeneity in the riskiness across individuals by, for example, matching male workers in their twenties to physically demanding and risky employment.

A second source of heterogeneity is with respect to people's willingness to incur risk, in particular, their willingness to trade off money or other attributes for increases in the probability of some adverse outcome. Individual utility functions for different health states can differ just as can tastes for other goods. One of the most salient risk decisions people make is with respect to cigarette smoking. Not surprisingly, cigarette smokers differ in quite fundamental ways from nonsmokers. Consider the following results

---

[9] See National Safety Council, Accident Facts, 1998 Edition 10 (1998).
[10] *Id.* at 11–12.

for males from Joni Hersch and W. Kip Viscusi:[11] "Compared to non-smokers, male smokers are 16 percent less likely to wear their seatbelts, five percent less likely to check their blood pressure, and nine percent less likely to floss their teeth. They also are more likely to work on hazardous jobs and, for any given level of job riskiness, are more likely to be injured on these jobs. Moreover, they are more likely to be injured at home as well, incurring roughly double the home accident rate of nonsmokers. Quite simply, smokers are greater risk takers than are nonsmokers, and this willingness to bear risk is manifested across a wide range of personal activities."

A third source of heterogeneity is that people may have different preferences for activities or jobs associated with risks. Downhill skiing, driving long distances for one's job, and eating red meat all pose various hazards, but they also provide consumptive benefits wholly apart from the risk component that makes these consumption activities attractive to those who engage in them. Even in the case of cigarettes, which is perhaps the riskiest product consumed on a large scale, there is substantial heterogeneity in preferences. Estimates of the elasticity of demand for cigarettes typically cluster in the range from −0.4 to −0.7, indicating a fairly steeply sloping demand curve with some people willing to pay considerably more for cigarettes than the market price. Steepness in the product demand curve indicates substantial heterogeneity in the value consumers place on this product. Differences in the valuation of the consumptive benefits of cigarettes in turn will affect the amount of the health risk people are willing to incur in order to derive the pleasures associated with smoking cigarettes.

The role of heterogeneity is also manifested in situations in which there are differences in the risks that people take. A chief example is that of the labor market, in which workers who have self-selected into very high risk jobs have different attitudes toward risks in average risk jobs. For example, estimates of the implicit values of life based on labor market choices by Richard Thaler and Sherwin Rosen[12] focused on workers in comparatively high risk jobs that posed an annual fatality risk of one chance in 1,000. The implicit value of life for their sample was $1.0 million (1998:3 prices using the gross domestic product deflator). My comparable estimates of the value of life[13] for a broadly based sample in which workers faced an average risk

[11] Joni Hersch & W. Kip Viscusi, Smoking and Other Risky Behaviors, 28 J. Drug Issues 645 (1998).

[12] Richard Thaler & Sherwin Rosen, The Value of Saving a Life: Evidence from the Labor Market, in Household Production and Consumption (Nestor E. Terleckyj ed. 1976).

[13] W. Kip Viscusi, Wealth Effects and Earnings Premiums for Job Hazards, 60 Rev. Econ. & Stat. 408 (1978); Viscusi, *supra* note 4.

of death of one chance in 10,000 yielded estimates of the implicit value of life of $4.9 million. As I have also shown,[14] this heterogeneity across different groups in the labor market can be estimated explicitly, with the expected relationship that workers who gravitate to high-risk jobs exhibit lower values of life than those in comparatively less risky positions.

It is not appropriate to say these value-of-life numbers reflect monetary amounts of compensation to incur risk, whereas individual utility is a more fundamental concern. Value-of-life estimates are in fact reflections of individual preferences, and hence utility. More specifically, the marginal rate of trade-off between wages and fatality risk (that is, the value of life) equals the difference between the utility of money when alive minus the utility of money after death, where this difference is divided by the expected marginal utility of consumption. This division in effect normalizes the utility differences across people to reflect the rate of trade-off within their preference structure.

To focus not on trade-offs but on utility levels has no economic content under standard expected utility theory models. Utility functions are unique up to a positive linear transformation. The level of any person's utility can be scaled up or down arbitrarily. We cannot make valid interpersonal comparisons of utility levels, but we can draw conclusions within individuals. Moreover, greater risk-money trade-offs as reflected in a higher value of life show that within that person's preference structure safety is more highly valued. Social welfare functions could, of course, choose to weight people's valuations differently. However, my principal theme will be that greater attention to efficiency will foster greater equity than under the current regime in which various equity concepts are avowed concerns.

Heterogeneity in the value of life is also manifested in the correlation between the riskiness of individual jobs and the riskiness of one's other activities. Hersch and Viscusi[15] found that people who smoke cigarettes and who did not use seat belts while riding in cars exhibited lower implicit values of job injury than did their more safety-preferring counterparts. Evidence by Viscusi and Hersch[16] indicated that this relationship was extremely powerful. Indeed, smokers' greater willingness to bear risk as well as their greater riskiness for different activities leads them to accept ex-

[14] W. Kip Viscusi, Occupational Safety and Health Regulation: Its Impact and Policy Alternatives, in 2 Research in Public Policy Analysis and Management (John P. Crecine ed. 1981).

[15] Joni Hersch & W. Kip Viscusi, Cigarette Smoking, Seatbelt Use, and Differences in Wage-Risk Tradeoffs, 25 J. Human Resources 202 (1990).

[16] W. Kip Viscusi & Joni Hersch, Cigarette Smokers as Job Risk Takers (Working paper, Harvard Law Sch. 1999).

tremely risky jobs for which their total risk compensation is less than what nonsmokers receive for lower risks.

Other forms of heterogeneity in implicit values of life and injury are also well documented. Chief among these is the effect of age.[17] Workers exposed to risks on the job have different durations of life at risk, and, as one would expect, the greater the length of life at risk the higher the required compensation will be. Moreover, estimates for a number of data sets suggest that the implicit rate of discount that workers have with respect to years of life lost cannot be distinguished statistically from prevailing rates of interest.

Income levels are also consequential. Estimates of the income elasticity of the implicit value of job injuries by Viscusi and William Evans[18] suggest that the relationship is roughly proportional in much the same way as the present value of lost earnings in a wrongful death suit increases proportionally with one's income. Other personal characteristics, such as gender, also seem to be closely related to the willingness to bear risks, although the failure of many studies to find compensating differentials for job risks faced by female employees seems to be largely due to the failure of these earlier studies to use gender-specific job risk data. As shown by Hersch,[19] women face nonfatal injury risks just below those of men and have similar wage-risk trade-offs for injuries, but they are much less likely to be exposed to fatality risks on the job.

The magnitude of the risk involved also is influential. From a theoretical standpoint, as one's base risk changes, one's willingness to trade off money against health risks is altered as the opportunity cost of financial resources is reduced when the base-level mortality risk is higher. These base rate effects have been estimated explicitly by Viscusi and Evans,[20] who also explore the role of the magnitude of risk change. The money-risk trade-off rate is not a constant but in fact diminishes with the extent of the decline in risk for willingness to pay and increases with the extent of the increase in risk for the willingness to accept value.

All these different sources of heterogeneity have been documented empirically and are a reflection of the kinds of flexibility afforded by market outcomes. By matching individuals with risks suited to their preferences

---

[17] For estimates of the quantity-adjusted value of life, see Michael J. Moore & W. Kip Viscusi, The Quantity-Adjusted Value of Life, 26 Econ. Inquiry 369 (1988), and a series of sequels to this work, which are summarized in W. Kip Viscusi, Fatal Tradeoffs: Public and Private Responsibilities for Risk (1992).

[18] W. Kip Viscusi & William N. Evans, Utility Functions That Depend on Health Status: Estimates and Economic Implications, 80 Am. Econ. Rev. 353 (1990).

[19] Joni Hersch, Compensating Differentials for Gender-Specific Job Injury Risks, 88 Am. Econ. Rev. 598 (1998).

[20] Viscusi & Evans, *supra* note 18.

and capabilities, market outcomes exploit this heterogeneity in welfare that would be suppressed under the alternative situation in which individuals were constrained.

An immediate policy implication of this result beyond observing the benefits of market transactions is that regulatory interventions through informational regulations such as hazard warnings have much to recommend them. Such policies operate on a decentralized basis and, if the warnings efforts are designed appropriately, can be very effective in making people knowledgeable about risk and in assisting them in their discrete choices of risky activities (that is, why they take a particular job or buy a product) as well as with respect to the precautions they take within these particular activities or product uses.[21]

Consider the possibility of regulating asbestos exposure in the workplace. One possibility is to issue a governmental regulation that limits asbestos exposures in the workplace. Under that scenario, once firms comply with the regulation, asbestos exposures will be reduced to a lower level, but there will be no additional compensation to workers bearing the risk unless there is awareness of the asbestos exposure. If there had been such awareness previously, there would have been no need for the regulation since the market processes would have generated efficient risk levels in the absence of intervention.

An alternative to direct regulation of asbestos is to provide hazard warnings to workers. Table 1 indicates the effect of asbestos warnings provided to chemical workers who are told that asbestos would be the chemical with which they now work and that this is a carcinogenic substance. Before seeing the hazard warnings workers thought their annual risk of job injury was 0.09, and rated on the same probability risk scale workers roughly tripled their risk perceptions after receiving the asbestos warning. Some workers would leave the job after being given the warning irrespective of the wage rate they were paid, and two-thirds of them would quit if no wage increase was forthcoming. Only a small fraction of the workers would be willing to take the jobs again in the absence of a wage increase. Overall, these workers exhibit an implicit value of job injuries of $27,846, where this injury scale is with respect to nonfatal job injuries on the job and yields estimates comparable to those found in other studies for nonfatal job risks. What these results suggest is that the role of hazard warnings will lead workers who are particularly unwilling to bear health risks to leave their

---

[21] For evidence on the efficacy of hazard warnings policies and criteria for effective design of such efforts, see W. Kip Viscusi & Wesley A. Magat, Learning about Risk: Consumer and Worker Responses to Hazard Information (1987); Wesley A. Magat & W. Kip Viscusi, Informational Approaches to Regulation (1992).

TABLE 1

THE EFFECT OF HAZARD WARNINGS FOR ASBESTOS ON WORKER BEHAVIOR

Variable	Mean Value
Initial risk assessment before seeing the asbestos warning (0–1 probability scale)	.09
Risk assessment after receiving the asbestos warning (0–1 probability scale)	.26
Workers refusing to stay on the job at any wage after receiving the warning (fraction)	.11
Workers intending to quit if given no wage increase after receiving the warning (fraction)	.65
Workers who would take the job again if given no wage increase after receiving the warning (fraction)	.11
Additional wage premium for risk required (1995 $)	4,734
Implicit value of an injury (value per statistical injury) (1995 $)	27,846

SOURCE.—W. Kip Viscusi, Rational Risk Policy 117 (1998).

jobs, while those who remain will generate compensating differentials that will provide incentives for safety comparable to those for well-known non-fatal job injury risks.

It is useful to compare the market outcome under informational regulations with that achieved through regulatory standards. Each approach is successful in generating an efficient level of safety assuming, of course, that the risk communication effort is designed appropriately and leads to accurate perception of the risk. However, under the hazard communication approach there is also compensation of the individuals who bear the risk, whereas with regulatory standards in the absence of knowledge of the extent of the risk there will be no such compensation. Moreover, the informational approach provides for more efficient job matching by linking up workers willing to bear the health risks with these jobs with remaining asbestos exposures, whereas regulatory standards in a market in which workers are otherwise presumed to be ignorant will not have this effect. By generating efficient risk levels coupled with compensation for risks, informational regulations yield the two principal benefits of perfectly functioning markets.

To say that informational efforts are potentially beneficial policy interventions does not imply that all warnings policies are desirable.[22] Beneficial information efforts should provide new and accurate risk information in a convincing manner. Many informational efforts fall short on one or more

[22] See W. Kip Viscusi, Rational Risk Policy (1998), for a more detailed review of sound warnings principles.

dimensions. In some instances the apparent policy intent is not to inform but to deter certain kinds of behavior. Policies of persuasion that attempt to browbeat individuals into changing their behavior are often ineffective and are almost invariably undesirable from a policy standpoint. Excessive warnings stimulated by a desire to fend off liability burdens also may distort risk comparisons across products.

Informational efforts also impose costs, particularly in terms of their cognitive demands. As warnings efforts proliferate, problems of information overload may develop. Even within a particular warning difficulties may arise with respect to excessive information or label clutter. Warnings also have important externalities, as they may lower people's perceptions of the risks of products that did not receive a warning.

Warnings resulting from policy mandates have an additional potential disadvantage in that they may displace private efforts. However, informational policies represent a policy area in which diversity is not always desirable. Human hazard signal words such as "danger," "warning," and "poison" ideally should have comparable meanings across different risk contexts. Moreover, the most salient print size and the strongest warning are not always desirable, notwithstanding the pressures of tort liability suits to make warnings stronger. Excessive warnings distort across-product risk comparisons. What is needed is a standardized hazard warnings vocabulary, which in theory can result from governmental standards.

What these various caveats suggest is that while warnings policies can be constructive, they can also be flawed. Establishing a potentially beneficial governmental role provides no assurance that the actual intervention will necessarily be welfare enhancing. As with regulatory policies generally, the task is to design efforts that enhance efficiency.

III. BENEFIT-COST ANALYSIS

The principal economic efficiency norm for policy evaluation is to apply a benefit-cost test to policies. In particular, do the benefits of the policy to society exceed the costs? These benefits are conventionally measured by society's willingness to pay for the benefits, which in the case of risk reduction would be the willingness to pay for the small changes in risk resulting from the governmental policy effort. Market outcomes that generate the same risk levels as would benefit-cost analysis will differ in an important way in that those bearing the risk will receive some form of compensation in terms of higher wages or lower prices for the risk. In the situation of risk regulation coupled with a complete lack of information regarding the risk, there will be no associated compensation. The winners can only potentially compensate the losers under a benefit-cost regime, but in practice compensation is not actually paid. This lack of compensation is a long-standing issue that is prominent in critiques of benefit-cost analysis and whether it is necessarily compelling as a policy assessment framework.

Benefit-cost analysis has played a prominent role in establishing criteria for regulatory policies. Under Executive Order No. 12,291,[23] President Reagan mandated that agencies demonstrate that major regulations have benefits in excess of their costs, where this requirement is monitored by the U.S. Office of Management and Budget (OMB). Agencies are, however, not bound by this benefit-cost test in instances in which there is a conflict with the agency's legislative mandate, which is largely the norm among risk and environmental regulation agencies. President Clinton continued this approach through his Executive Order No. 12,866,[24] with the major change being that it was recognized that not all benefits can be quantified in monetary terms and that one should view benefits broadly to encompass all policy consequences of significance.

The experience under these benefit-cost regimes has been quite mixed and does not seem qualitatively different from the outcomes in the Carter administration, which did not have a benefit-cost test but instead quantified benefits, costs, and cost-effectiveness. As I indicated,[25] the OMB has never been successful in blocking a regulation with a cost per life saved below $142 million per life. This level is more than an order of magnitude greater than what is sensible based on implicit values of life reflected in market decisions. The result has been that many regulations promulgated have inordinately large costs per life saved.

Table 2 summarizes the costs per life saved for regulations of different regulatory agencies. Omitted from this group are governmental efforts that do not require the promulgation of formal regulations, such as the hazardous waste cleanup program known as the Superfund effort. This major program by the Environmental Protection Agency (EPA) generates a median cost per case of cancer across the cleanup sites of $6 billion per case, which would put it among the most expensive items in Table 2.[26]

What one should use as a cutoff for the appropriate cost per life saved depends on the methodological approach. Historically, government agencies had used the present value of lost earnings as the value-of-life measure,

[23] Exec. Order No. 12,291, 46 Fed. Reg. 13,193 (1981).
[24] Exec. Order No. 12,866, 58 Fed. Reg. 51,735 (1993).
[25] Viscusi, *supra* note 17.
[26] The source of this estimate is James T. Hamilton & W. Kip Viscusi, Calculating Risks? The Spatial and Political Dimensions of Hazardous Waste Policy (1999). Moreover, even this estimate understates the actual cost per cancer case since many risk and exposure assumptions are unrealistic.

or what agencies termed the "cost of death." In my 1982 analysis prepared to settle the dispute between the OMB and the Occupational Safety and Health Administration over the proposed hazard communication regulation, which had been appealed to then Vice President Bush, I introduced the value-of-life methodology based on the willingness-to-pay estimates derived from labor market behavior.[27] Since that time, agencies have widely adopted the value-of-life methodology, which has also been endorsed by the OMB, but the particular estimate of the value of life used by the agencies may differ. Most important, the value-of-life benefit estimate is not binding on policy judgments because of the restrictive nature of agencies' legislative mandates. Taking a $5 million value of life as a rough cutoff for cost-effective policies, in Table 2 all policies above the 1984 benzene emission standard costing $4.1 million per life saved would pass a benefit-cost requirement, and all policies beginning with the ethylene dibromide EPA regulation in 1991 costing $6.8 million per life saved would fail a benefit-cost test.

Asbestos is a particularly noteworthy target of regulatory action in that it has been subject to increasingly inefficient regulations as public pressures mounted in response to the wave of asbestos litigation stemming from exposures in the shipyards in World War II and thereafter. The cost per life saved for asbestos regulations rose from $9.9 million in 1972 to $88.1 million in 1986, with an even more expensive EPA regulation in 1989 at $131.8 million per case of cancer averted.

One quite reasonable notion of risk equity is that if society is homogeneous in its attitudes toward risk, then agencies should equalize the marginal cost per life saved across regulatory programs. Doing so will maximize the number of lives saved for any given cost amount. Table 2 presents average costs per life saved rather than marginal costs per life saved. Moreover, in some cases the policy benefits occur in discrete jumps, such as the deaths averted from aircraft floor emergency lighting, so that marginal trade-offs are not pertinent. However, if society wishes to treat exposures to risk equitably under the criteria specified above, it should attempt to spend up to the same marginal cost-per-life-saved amount for different agencies, where we abstract for the time being from the role of population heterogeneity. Thus, a more meaningful and compelling risk equity concept is to have equity in terms of the cost per life saved rather than equity in terms of risk outcomes. Equitable trade-offs consequently become the reference point for risk equity measurement.

---

[27] This analysis is discussed in Viscusi, *supra* note 17, and is based on W. Kip Viscusi, Analysis of OMB and OSHA Evaluations of the Hazard Communication Proposal (report prepared for Secretary of Labor Raymond Donovan, March 15, 1982).

TABLE 2

REGULATORY COSTS AND COST EFFECTIVENESS IN SAVING LIVES

Regulation	Year	Agency	Cost per Life Saved (1990 $Millions)	Cost per Normalized Life Saved (1995 $Millions)
Unvented space heater ban	1980	CPSC	.1	.1
Aircraft cabin fire protection standard	1985	FAA	.1	.1
Seat belt/air bag	1984	NHTSA	.1	.1
Steering column protection standards	1967	NHTSA	.1	.1
Underground construction standards	1989	OSHA	.1	.1
Trihalomethane in drinking water	1979	EPA	.2	.6
Aircraft seat cushion flammability	1984	FAA	.5	.6
Alcohol and drug controls	1985	FRA	.5	.6
Auto fuel system integrity	1975	NHTSA	.5	.5
Auto wheel rim servicing	1984	OSHA	.5	.6
Aircraft floor emergency lighting	1984	FAA	.7	.9
Concrete and masonry construction	1988	OSHA	.7	.9
Crane-suspended personnel platform	1988	OSHA	.8	1.0
Passive restraints for trucks and buses	1989	NHTSA	.8	.8
Auto side-impact standards	1990	NHTSA	1.0	1.0
Children's sleepwear flammability ban	1973	CPSC	1.0	1.2
Auto side-door supports	1970	NHTSA	1.0	1.0
Low-altitude windshear equipment and training	1988	FAA	1.6	1.9
Metal mine electrical equipment standards	1970	MSHA	1.7	2.0
Trenching and excavation standards	1989	OSHA	1.8	2.2
Traffic alert and collision avoidance systems	1988	FAA	1.8	2.2
Hazard communication standard	1983	OSHA	1.9	4.8
Trucks, buses, and MPV side-impact standards	1989	NHTSA	2.6	2.6
Grain dust explosion prevention standards	1987	OSHA	3.3	4.0
Rear lap/shoulder belts for autos	1989	NHTSA	3.8	3.8
Standards for radionuclides in uranium mines	1984	EPA	4.1	10.1
Benzene NESHAP (original: fugitive emissions)	1984	EPA	4.1	10.1
Ethylene dibromide in drinking water	1991	EPA	6.8	17.0
Benzene NESHAP (revised: coke by-products)	1988	EPA	7.3	18.1
Asbestos occupational exposure limit	1972	OSHA	9.9	24.7
Benzene occupational exposure limit	1987	OSHA	10.6	26.5
Electrical equipment in coal mines	1970	MSHA	11.1	13.3
Arsenic emission standards for glass plants	1986	EPA	16.1	40.2
Ethylene oxide occupational exposure limit	1984	OSHA	24.4	61.0
Arsenic/copper NESHAP	1986	EPA	27.4	68.4
Hazardous waste listing of petroleum-refining sludge	1990	EPA	32.9	82.1

TABLE 2 (*Continued*)

Regulation	Year	Agency	Cost per Life Saved (1990 $Millions)	Cost per Normalized Life Saved (1995 $Millions)
Cover/move uranium mill tailings (inactive sites)	1983	EPA	37.7	94.3
Benzene NESHAP (revised: transfer operations)	1990	EPA	39.2	97.9
Cover/move uranium mill tailings (active sites)	1983	EPA	53.6	133.8
Acrylonitrile occupational exposure limit	1978	OSHA	61.3	153.2
Coke ovens occupational exposure limit	1976	OSHA	75.6	188.9
Lockout/tag out	1989	OSHA	84.4	102.4
Asbestos occupational exposure limit	1986	OSHA	88.1	220.1
Arsenic occupational exposure limit	1978	OSHA	127.3	317.9
Asbestos ban	1989	EPA	131.8	329.2
Diethylstilbestrol (DES) cattle-feed ban	1979	FDA	148.6	371.2
Benzene NESHAP (revised: waste operations)	1990	EPA	200.2	500.2
1,2-Dichloropropane in drinking water	1991	EPA	777.4	1,942.1
Hazardous waste land disposal ban	1988	EPA	4,988.7	12,462.7
Municipal solid waste landfills	1988	EPA	22,746.8	56,826.1
Formaldehyde occupational exposure limit	1987	OSHA	102,622.8	256,372.7
Atrazine/alachlor in drinking water	1991	EPA	109,608.5	273,824.4
Hazardous waste listing for wood-preserving chemicals	1990	EPA	6,785,822.0	16,952,364.9

SOURCE.—W. Kip Viscusi, Jahn K. Hakes, & Alan Carlin, Measures of Mortality Risks, 14 J. Risk & Uncertainty 213, 228 (1997).

NOTE.—CPSC = Consumer Product Safety Commission; FAA = Federal Aviation Administration; NHTSA = National Highway Traffic Safety Administration; OSHA = Occupational Safety and Health Administration; EPA = Environmental Protection Agency; FRA = Federal Railroad Administration; MSHA = Mine Safety and Health Administration; FDA = Food and Drug Administration.

There are of course legitimate sources of heterogeneity, but agencies do not recognize them. Consider first the influence of the income of the person protected by the regulatory policy. More affluent individuals will have a greater willingness to pay for protection from health hazards. This issue arose with respect to a report I prepared for the Federal Aviation Administration (FAA) in 1991. The average passenger on a U.S. airline in 1989 had a median income level of $32,480, which is about 1½ times the average income level in a representative sample of workers in value-of-life studies at that time and double or more the income levels of workers confined to particularly high risk jobs. Should the FAA be permitted to use a higher value of life for airline safety policy than the rest of the U.S. Department of Transportation uses for valuing improved guard rails, automobile safety, and other matters? The rationale is that recognition of these income differences reflects the variations in individual willingness to pay for safety, with the counterargument being that this discrepancy creates a form of inequity in terms of the degree to which we are willing to protect people in different income groups. Recognition of these differences leads to a comparably higher willingness to pay for a statistical life saved through airline safety as opposed to other programs of the U.S. Department of Transportation. However, the FAA's use of a higher value of life was not a transfer to more affluent airline passengers. Mandating higher safety levels would boost airline costs and ticket prices. The Secretary of Transportation refused to recognize this heterogeneity that the FAA had sought and chose instead to treat all lives symmetrically, irrespective of differences in willingness to pay. This approach creates equity in terms of benefit valuation but in effect serves as a form of income redistribution to people who do not value the risk reduction policies as greatly.

The airline example becomes a bit more complicated if there is a mixture of income groups on the plane. Suppose that half the passengers value their lives at $8 million and half value their lives at $4 million. Use of an intermediate value of $6 million will lead the poorer passengers to pay more for safety than they would like and the richer passengers to buy less safety than they like. The outcome is efficient on average, but unfortunately airline safety policies do not permit recognition of such heterogeneity when all passengers face identical risks. A situation in which people pay more for safety than they might like individually is also not unique to this example. The bulk of the regulations in Table 2 impose costs well beyond what people would spend on these efforts if government officials chose policies reflecting their preferences instead of the excessive cost levels now being imposed by regulatory efforts.

Recognition of heterogeneity in benefit values can often prevent clearcut inefficiencies. Suppose that public parking facilities are valued greatly in urban areas, whereas improved erosion control is valued in rural areas. Few would suggest that it is sensible to spend as much per capita on parking structures in rural areas and that we spend the same amount on preventing soil erosion in all locales. Rather, public policy efforts are targeted where they benefit people to the greatest extent, where the value of these benefits is the willingness to pay for the benefit that, in the case of risk reduction policies, varies by income group.

An additional noteworthy feature of individual willingness to pay for risk reductions is that there is heterogeneity according to the length of life at risk. However, government agencies currently suppress this heterogeneity and value all lives equally. Such symmetry is a form of risk equity in terms of lives, but is one's remaining lifetime a sensible unit of measurement for equity? Current policies are not equitable with respect to the quantity of life at risk.

Controlling for the discounted expected remaining life-years is a useful measure to explore for lifesaving efforts, but it is not always compelling. Does, for example, a person's value of life peak at birth, or does education and training boost this value? Similarly, once many important lotteries of life are resolved, such as those affecting income level or societal contributions, the value of life may be quite different. Examining longevity effects is often instructive as policies benefiting people with only a few months to live are less attractive than those benefiting similarly situated people with greater lengths of life at risk.

Adjustments for the quantity of life often have a substantial influence. The final column of Table 2 presents the cost per normalized life saved. This normalization adjusts the lives lost to be equivalent in duration to the fatalities resulting from accidents based on the discounted loss in life expectancy. These efficacy numbers indicate that for health-oriented regulations, such as those affecting cancer for which there is a substantial latency period as well as less quantity of life saved when illnesses are prevented, there is a substantial increase in the cost per life saved. The asbestos occupational exposure limit in 1972, for example, had a cost per life saved of $9.9 million, but once the estimates are adjusted for the quantity of life saved, the cost rises to $24.7 million per accident equivalent life saved. This effect is more general throughout the table as the cancer-reducing policies greatly diminish in attractiveness compared to those preventing accidents.

The current practice of not making distinctions in terms of the kinds of lives saved creates major risk inequities. Lifesaving policies extend lives but do not confer immortality. The result is that efforts that save very little in terms of life expectancy divert resources from programs that could have a major life expectancy effect. A benefit-cost approach in which individual heterogeneity is explicitly recognized in determining benefit levels would prevent these inefficiencies, which are a form of inequity.

The principal counterargument to efficiency-based policy approaches is that they will penalize minorities. Indeed, the most salient risk equity concern has focused on environmental justice, which in turn has been stimulated by claims that hazardous waste sites disproportionately harm minorities. Whether this disproportionate harm actually occurs will be explored below, but the principal issue with respect to risk equity as I have defined it is not whether minorities face greater risk but whether they would fare particularly badly under a benefit-cost regime.

To explore this issue, James Hamilton and Viscusi[28] examined the conse-

[28] Hamilton & Viscusi, *supra* note 26.

TABLE 3

INTERACTION BETWEEN MINORITY POPULATION AND DIFFERENT
POLICY ANALYSIS ALTERNATIVES

	MEAN MINORITY POPULATION (as % of Site Population) IN ALL SITES IN SIMULATION	MEAN MINORITY POPULATION (as % of Site Population) IN ALL SITES WITH CLEANUP COSTS:		
		Over $5 Million	Over $5 Million and Cost per Cancer Case Averted under $5 Million	Over $5 Million and Cost per Cancer Case Averted under $100 Million
Sites with cleanup costs over $5 million:				
Current policy[a]	17	18	32	26
No ARARs[b]	17	17	39	25
Sites with cleanup costs under $5 million:				
Current policy[a]	17	14	17	12
No ARARs[b]	17	15	34	13

SOURCE.—James T. Hamilton & W. Kip Viscusi, Calculating Risks? The Spatial and Political Dimensions of Hazardous Waste Policy 234 (1999).

[a] All sites in risk sample.

[b] Sites with cumulative risks of at least 10^{-4}. ARAR = applicable or relevant and appropriate state or federal requirements.

quences of moving to a benefit-cost test for the cleanup of Superfund sites. At present, the mean minority percentage at the sites remediated under current policy practices is 17 percent. What would happen to the minority percentage if one applied a benefit-cost test requiring that the cost per case of cancer averted not exceed $5 million for the cleanup to be justified? Table 3 summarizes those policy consequences. For the reasonably significant sites with cleanup costs greater than $5 million (and consequently at least one expected case of cancer prevented if the site passes a benefit-cost test), the mean minority percentage at the site ranges from 32 to 39 percent depending on whether one recognizes other legislative constraints affecting cleanup decisions. For the very inexpensive site cleanups with a cleanup cost under $5 million, the mean minority percentage ranges from 17 to 34 percent. However, one obtains the low 17 percent figure only if one also imposes the influence of cleanup requirements relating to other environmental policies in the absence of a benefit-cost test. If one relied solely on benefit-cost analysis without any other legislative or regulatory constraints, the minority percentages affected by cleanup would be 39 percent for expensive cleanups and 34 percent for less expensive cleanups, where in each case the minority percentage whose welfare is improved by the policy is at least twice as great as the minority percentage affected by current cleanup actions. Note that with an inefficiently high cost per cancer case prevented cutoff of $100 million, the minority percentage in Table 3 drops.

These results are not an aberration. They can be traced to two sets of influences. First, what does in fact drive Superfund cleanup decisions is political power. Sites located in areas where there are influential populations are targeted for more vigorous and more expensive cleanup efforts than are areas with less political clout, which are disproportionately those where there are larger minority populations. Reliance on a benefit-cost test consequently equalizes the playing field across different population groups, enabling there to be true risk equity in terms of the cost per life saved rather than having policies driven by political power.

A second set of factors contributing to the disadvantaged status of minorities under current procedures is that a variety of risk equity notions have crept into policy design and evaluation. Risk analysis procedures throughout the federal government embody a variety of distortions that are all intended to reflect a kind of risk equity, but that push away from a benefit-cost norm and impose substantial losses on society, particularly on the minority groups who are most likely to be harmed by hazardous exposures. These influences will be explored below.

Minorities would benefit if policies gave benefits to that group the same weight as benefits to the white population. In effect, they would have the same willingness-to-pay value for benefits as nonminorities and consequently receive the same weight. In a more refined policy regime, policy makers might move beyond equalizing the cost per life saved across groups and policies but instead recognize that the value of life increases with one's income, lowering the benefit accorded to minorities. However, following the airline safety example, one might recognize the role of income differences only if people receiving more benefits pay for these additional benefits in some manner. This payment could be direct, as through airline ticket prices, or could be through a higher overall tax bill. Moreover, consistent with concerns arising with respect to Hicks-Kaldor compensation criteria, one could assess the entire spectrum of policies and the payments groups make toward government policies to assess their overall equity. In the absence of such distinctions, application of a uniform value of life will serve as an implicit form of income redistribution.

IV. Alternative Risk Equity Measures

Absolute Risk Levels

If one were to envision a risk-based measure of risk equity, perhaps the most natural measure would be the absolute risk that a person faced. Thus, for any given age level one would focus on the mortality risk. Taking a broader perspective in recognizing the effect of different activities on one's distribution of mortality risks over the lifetime, one might focus on one's incremental mortality risk at different ages or the total effect on life expectancy.

Cigarette smokers are certainly on the high end in terms of their current absolute risk levels. Smoking cigarettes imposes a lifetime risk of premature mortality from smoking of 0.18–0.36, and it shortens one's life expectancy by 3.6–7.2 years.[29] What would be the effect of recognizing that smokers already have very high risks to their lives from their smoking activity? Should these groups be given preference with respect to hazardous waste cleanup, job safety, and other practices? Alternatively, are we necessarily required to reduce smokers' risks to those of nonsmokers in a pursuit of risk equity? Must we ban smoking? If the latter prohibition is mandated, does it also extend to banning high-fat foods, mandating a daily exercise regimen, and driving large, crashworthy cars? Similarly, should we always give priority in risk regulation policies to those who live in high-crime areas because their residential exposures put them at the upper end of the personal risk spectrum?

Risk regulation policies have largely been unconcerned with absolute risk levels. The base mortality risk level of populations at risk seldom arises as a concern at all. What policy makers focus on instead is the incremental risk from a particular source of risk, whether it be the environment or hazardous products. Any meaningful notion of risk equity, however, presumably should be grounded in the absolute risk level of the individual rather than focusing on incremental risks since otherwise there will be clear-cut inequities in what is of consequence to people's lives, which is the total risk they face.

That having been said, it would not be wise to interfere with informed private choices to bear risk. The appropriate policy objective is maximization of expected individual welfare, not risk minimization. Ultimately, a concern with risk levels alone as the policy objective will divert attention from more fundamental welfare principles and lead to interference with economic decisions that should be unconstrained.

Incremental Risk Levels

The policy focus with respect to risk equity is almost invariably on the incremental risk associated with a particular risk exposure. In some in-

---

[29] For supporting data see W. Kip Viscusi, Smoking: Making the Risky Decision 70, 80 (1992).

stances, the emphasis is not even on a particular class of activities (for example, all pollution exposures) but rather on a specific source of risk (for example, risks from a single emissions source). While absolute risks may be a more sensible concern if risk-level equity is the policy objective, in practice it is particular incremental risks that drive policy.

Suppose our objective is to equalize risks from different sources so that we all face the same risks from consumer products, jobs, and types of environmental risks. Is this in fact feasible? Floods are more likely to affect the eastern states, with the most severe tallies of flood deaths over the past 2 decades being in the Appalachians, mid-Atlantic, Pennsylvania, West Virginia, Virginia, and northeast areas.[30] Do we really want to equalize the floods risk in these states with that faced by residents in arid states such as Arizona? Similarly, heat wave deaths in Chicago hold the fatality record, but would we want Chicago residents to face the same risk of death from heat waves as do people residing in Jackson Hole, Wyoming?[31] Hurricanes are much more likely to threaten residents on the Atlantic Coast, particularly in the southeast, than they are to affect the population of Kansas, which is more susceptible to tornadoes.[32]

Attempts to equalize the risk from different sources are no more sensible than trying to equalize these incremental risks from classes of natural disasters. The reason why it is not sensible to equalize risks from natural disasters any more than it is to equalize the risks from air pollution, hazardous waste, or job risks across different occupations is that there are different costs to reducing risk to low levels in these different contexts. Ultimately, any plausible objective for government policy must incorporate both costs as well as what is delivered for these costs, which are the risk reductions or the benefits achieved.

Focusing on incremental risks as the equity norm takes on additional irrationalities with respect to specific misguided notions of risk equity that have arisen. Within EPA hazardous cleanup efforts, the focus is on individual risks rather than population risks. Thus, any actual or hypothetical individual risk exposure to a cancer risk of at least one chance in 10,000 requires mandatory cleanup of the risk, and the agency has discretion to mandate a cleanup for risks up to a lifetime risk level of one in a million. The focus on individual risks rather than population risks stems from the risk equity notion that no particular individual should be exposed to an incremental lifetime risk exceeding a particular amount, in this case one in 10,000. What this seemingly innocuous risk equity requirement does is drastically distort

[30] These statistics on flood deaths are from National Safety Council, *supra* note 9, at 22.

[31] In 1995, 465 people died in a heat wave in Chicago. See *id.*

[32] For documentation, see The Wizard of Oz (1939).

policy practices. Risks where there is some potential hypothetical future exposure, which may or may not materialize, receive the same policy weight as do current risks to large populations. Indeed, under current policy practices the EPA does not even consider the size of the exposed populations. Moreover, empirically the population density has no statistically significant effect on Superfund cleanups.[33]

We are consequently faced with anomalies where EPA is mandating ambitious cleanups such as that noted by Justice Stephen Breyer:

Let me provide some examples. The first comes from a case in my own court, *United States v. Ottati & Goss,* arising out of a ten-year effort to force cleanup of a toxic waste dump in southern New Hampshire. The site was mostly cleaned up. All but one of the private parties had settled. The remaining private party litigated the cost of cleaning up the last little bit, a cost of about $9.3 million to remove a small amount of highly diluted PCBs and "volatile organic compounds" (benzene and gasoline components) by incinerating the dirt. How much extra safety did this $9.3 million buy? The forty-thousand-page record of this ten-year effort indicated (and all the parties seemed to agree) that, without the extra expenditure, the waste dump was clean enough for children playing on the site to eat small amounts of dirt daily for 70 days each year without significant harm. Burning the soil would have made it clean enough for the children to eat small amounts daily for 245 days per year without significant harm. But there were no dirt-eating children playing in the area, for it was a swamp. Nor were dirt-eating children likely to appear there, for future building seemed unlikely. The parties also agreed that at least half of the volatile organic chemicals would likely evaporate by the year 2000. To spend $9.3 million to protect non-existent dirt-eating children is what I mean by the problem of "the last 10 percent."[34]

Justice Breyer's experiences are not an outlier, as Superfund cleanup efforts are not grounded in protecting populations but in reducing individual risks, hypothetical or real. Risk equity in terms of reducing individual risks is the guiding principle, not total risk reduction benefits or benefit-cost trade-offs. This practice disproportionally harms minority populations. Minorities are particularly likely to be densely concentrated around hazardous waste sites. Indeed, for sites in which there are risks to existing populations from current risk exposures, 45 percent of the population within one-quarter of a mile of Superfund sites are minorities. Indeed, the main source of risk inequity to minorities is not that there are more hazardous waste sites located in minority neighborhoods. In fact, the average white population located within 1 mile of the Superfund site is actually greater than for minori-

---

[33] These and other descriptions of the operation of the Superfund program are based on the empirical analysis in Hamilton & Viscusi, *supra* note 26.

[34] See Stephen Breyer, Breaking the Vicious Circle: Toward Effective Risk Regulation 11–12 (1993).

ties. In particular, the average white population figure across all Superfund sites on the National Priorities List is 86 percent, which exceeds the minority population percentage of 80 percent.[35] However, when minorities are present they are often present in much greater numbers and are concentrated either directly on-site or particularly close to the Superfund sites. Somewhat incredulously, the EPA completely ignores the magnitudes of the population exposed and the total number of cancer cases to be prevented by any hazardous waste cleanup. It focuses instead on the risk equity concept of individual risks, which disadvantages existing populations who receive no weight for their greater numbers and no weight for the fact that these risk exposures now exist. Hypothetical risk exposures that may never exist and that are never discounted to present value receive the same weight as do current real risks. These individual risk equity practices consequently serve as one of the contributors to the neglect of minorities under current practices that nominally preach a commitment to environmental equity.

There is also inconsistency in terms of how the incremental risk levels are handled in reference to the policy targets. Suppose that a risk meeting the one in 10,000 lifetime risk is the trigger for cleanup. As part of the cleanup, the EPA may mandate extremely stringent policy options that reduce the postremediation risk to 10^{-8} or 10^{-9}. However, the result is that the postcleanup level of the risk will be much lower than the risk threshold of 10^{-6}, which the EPA has set as a cutoff where cleanup should not be pursued. If in fact risks greater than 10^{-4} require cleanup, risks between 10^{-4} and 10^{-6} can potentially be targets for cleanup, and risks smaller than 10^{-6} should never be addressed by EPA cleanup, will there not be substantial inequities created in terms of the incremental risk by reducing the risk level at sites receiving cleanup to levels 100 or 1,000 times safer than the risk cutoff at which the EPA stipulates that no cleanup should be undertaken? Quite simply, these individual risk policy guidelines that purport to be a form of risk equity are not a sensible basis for policy.

The concern with equity for hypothetical future generations of risk exposures becomes particularly problematic with respect to risks far into the distant future.[36] Recent studies of the storage of nuclear wastes indicate that there could be corrosive effects on the buried wastes beginning in the year 102,010, with potentially significant radioactive exposures for nearby farmers in the year 312,010.[37] Should risks at least 100,000 years from now

[35] See Hamilton & Viscusi, *supra* note 26, at 168.

[36] These issues are explored in detail by John Broome, Cost-Benefit Analysis and Population, in this issue, at 953.

[37] For supporting discussion, see John Christensen, New Questions Plague Nuclear Waste Storage Plan, N.Y. Times, August 10, 1999, at D1, D4.

merit the same concern as risks to current populations? As a policy matter, some federal agencies such as the EPA do not discount risk effects to present value so that deferred influences matter as much as current effects. From an economic standpoint, discounting is warranted because what is being discounted is society's willingness to pay for the benefits, not deaths. Coupling this lack of discounting with a practice of ignoring the size of populations affected creates a preposterous basis for policy in which the potential of future technologies to reduce these risks becomes less consequential than our current risk conservatism.

If our concern with incremental risk equity is real, should we not also have the same concerns across countries as well? Indeed, there have been some proposals espoused by labor unions and other groups that the United States not import any goods produced in a manner that does not conform with U.S. job safety and environmental standards and that the United States not export any goods that do not meet U.S. safety standards.[38]

Such notions of risk equity will engender substantial inefficiencies. Less developed countries have much lower income levels than in the United States, so that forcing them to adhere to U.S. safety and environmental practices will make these societies worse off, with their attendant adverse mortality effects. Is it, for example, realistic to require that China comply with current U.S. environmental pollution standards and that manufacturing production in Africa and Indonesia adhere to U.S. safety standards? It is only because of our greater affluence that we have been able to afford such efforts, as the preference for risk reduction increases substantially with societal income. Banning the import of these goods is little more than a form of disguised protectionism, as the main force that will promote economic well-being and ultimately the health of less developed countries will be international trade rather than embargoes on their products if they do not meet our lofty risk and environmental standards.

The prohibition of exports of hazardous goods is likewise ill conceived, except perhaps for situations in which there will be considerable misperceptions arising from goods made by U.S. companies that do not in fact meet U.S. safety standards. Requirements that U.S. exports meet U.S. safety standards create economic harms to U.S. workers. A salient case where these practices have been of concern is with respect to pharmaceutical products. Many drugs are approved for use in western Europe before approval is given in the United States by the Food and Drug Administration (FDA). By not permitting firms to manufacture and export goods that do not meet U.S. pharmaceutical safety requirements, the restrictions in effect force these op-

---

[38] For an academic advocacy of this position, see Nicolas Askounes Ashford, Crisis in the Workplace: Occupational Disease and Injury (1976).

erations overseas. Other countries with different medical establishments and different criteria for approval might legitimately choose to permit the use of the drug in that country even though it has not been approved by the FDA. Indeed, even with the United States there has been a long-standing complaint about the drug approval lag times. Policy efforts periodically attempt to accelerate drug approval times in recognition of the often tardy process by which lifesaving drugs reach the market.

Actual versus Perceived Risks

In promoting risk equity, should our concern be with the risks that people actually face or the risks that people perceive that they face? Put somewhat differently, should we equalize the mortality risk to individuals or their fears of these mortality risks? Let me make my biases clear at the outset. The objective of government policy in my view should be to reduce objective risks to populations and to generate actual improvements in health rather than foster illusory increases in well-being.

Policy discussions with respect to protecting populations, particularly with respect to hazardous waste exposures, often suggest that the emphasis should be on perceived risks rather than real risks. It is fear of hazardous waste that drives these programs, as hazards from chemical wastes rank first in the public's concerns for environmental risks even though the actual risks are quite small in most instances.

Suppose that the government had a choice between equally costing policy options for cleaning up wastes in two different towns. In Happyville there are no actual cases of cancer to be prevented but people believe that 100 cases would be prevented through a hazardous waste cleanup. In Blissville, people are completely ignorant of any risks, but hazardous waste cleanup efforts will reduce 100 cases of cancer. If cleanup efforts in each town have the same cost and if we could cleanup only one of the sites, which should we pick? Some scholars suggest that the choice is not clear-cut.[39]

The example discussed above is based on one that I developed as part of an exchange I had with Paul Portney on a panel at the American Economic Association meetings. Portney's example is Happyville, and my counter-example was Blissville. Current policy practices would support cleanup of Happyville. In my view, failure to clean up Blissville is a form of statistical murder in which lives are sacrificed to focus instead on illusory fears.

Proponents of promoting risk equity through addressing perceived risks

---

[39] See, in particular, Paul R. Portney, Trouble in Happyville, 11 J. Pol'y Analysis & Mgmt. 131 (1992).

rather than actual risks often defend their position by suggesting that in a democratic society the government should be responsive to the preferences of the citizenry. However, if these preferences stem from erroneous probabilistic beliefs, then they should be overridden. For much the same reason that we intervene when people underestimate the risk and buy products that are overly dangerous, we should also not succumb to irrational political pressures that lead us to institutionalize private irrationalities.

Current policies are affected by a curious asymmetry. If people underestimate the risk, policy makers rush to intervene to alleviate the market failure. If people overestimate the risk, creating pressures for wasteful interventions, policy makers defend their interventionist zeal by claiming that in a democracy citizen preferences must be respected. However, what is at stake is not preferences or the shape of individual utility functions. What is at issue is the underlying probabilistic beliefs that may be quite erroneous and should not receive deference when designing policies.

Is there nevertheless some set of circumstances in which the government should intervene, such as when alarmist responses to risk depress property values? In many instances all that is at stake is transfers across parties. Property owners will be made better off if a hazardous waste cleanup eliminates a feared, but nonexistent, risk. All that should count from an efficiency standpoint is the attendant efficiency loss from failing to develop the land to its best use.

Risk Characteristics

Often the policy concern is not with the overall risk or even the incremental risk but rather with the type of the risk. Thus, the risk equity notion is that there should be limits on particular classes of risks. The differing treatment of synthetic and natural chemicals is symptomatic of this concern with risk characteristics.[40]

Are synthetic chemicals in fact more dangerous? While some may be, as a general rule synthetic chemicals are not necessarily more dangerous. An examination of a large sample of 365 chemicals indicates that synthetic chemicals pose a lower risk as measured by the TD_{50} value, which is the amount of the chemical needed before 50 percent of the rats in the sample develop tumors as a result of exposure. Other measures of the carcinogenicity of synthetic and natural chemicals for the sample of 365 chemicals yield similar results. However, synthetic chemicals are much more likely to be regulated, particularly by the FDA. The nature of this bias stems from the bias against novel risks created by synthetic chemicals as opposed to ex-

[40] The data to be described below are drawn from Viscusi, *supra* note 22, at 86–88.

isting risks posed by natural chemicals. No measure of risk potency accounts for the differential regulatory bias, as the underlying risk equity concept driving policy is not even to equalize the risk in any meaningful sense but rather to eliminate the class of risks associated with synthetic chemicals.

Similar kinds of biases seem to arise with respect to health versus safety risks. As the data in Table 2 indicate, the cost per life saved is especially great for cancer reduction policies, where this bias is particularly strong once one adjusts for the length of life lost. To the extent that accidents are more familiar and often involve an element of volition, whereas the health outcomes are much more mysterious in terms of their cause, there may be a form of irrationality that creates pressures for health risk regulation. The relative inadequacy of market forces alone cannot explain this differential emphasis since one would be able to reduce health risks more cost effectively than safety risks if markets were more prone to failure for health hazards, which they may well be.

Another class of risks that has merited particular policy attention is with respect to involuntary risks as compared to voluntary risks. As noted in the discussion of market behavior, the self-selection of people into voluntary risks will lead the mix of individuals exposed to these risks to have a lower value of life. These values affect willingness-to-pay values and hence total benefit estimates. Some might suggest that we would go beyond these efficiency-related effects and place additional emphasis on eliminating involuntary risks. The stringent controls emerging throughout the country to limit exposures to environmental tobacco smoke indicate the substantial concern with involuntary risks as compared to risks that we knowingly incur. Voluntary risks have the additional advantage of providing some compensatory benefit, such as wages for a risky job, whereas involuntary risks do not. Striking an appropriate balance between the welfare of those affected by involuntary risks and the welfare of those who will be harmed by regulating such risks can be achieved by treating these effects symmetrically using benefit-cost analysis. Current policy practices often view the prevention of involuntary risks as a trump card that should dominate all other policy concerns.

V. The Costs of Risk Equity

The efficiency norm that serves as the point of departure for risk equity concerns can take on several different levels of refinement. At the most basic level one could equalize the marginal cost per life saved across different policies. People exposed to various sources of risk in different contexts would receive the same weight, unlike the current regime in which agencies differ quite starkly in the stringency of their risk regulations.

The first level of refinement would be to recognize that policies to extend life have quite different effects based on the quantity and quality of life at risk. While much remains to be done in refining these economic valuations, evaluating the cost per discounted life-year of policies would provide an index of some of the more salient policy concerns. The current approach of ignoring length-of-life issues creates inequities by valuing the life of a person with advanced respiratory disease and a 6-month life expectancy the same as a healthy person with a 40-year life expectancy.

Recognition of differences in willingness to pay based on income and attitudes toward risk would be the next level of refinement. Such recognition of heterogeneity in values might be most readily accepted in contexts for which there was an actual transaction in which the beneficiaries of the regulation pay for the benefits they receive. The closer the regulatory context can simulate a market structure, the more easily one can use a market efficiency reference point. If there is no payment extracted and some groups with high willingness to pay benefit disproportionately, the policy challenge is to ensure that the entire package of policies and taxes is equitable.

Risk equity as achieved through the operation of voluntary transactions in competitive markets leads to efficient safety levels as well as compensation of those bearing the risk. Hazard warnings that foster such market operations consequently rank very high in terms of their promotion of risk equity. More general regulatory policies grounded in benefit-cost criteria also achieve efficient levels of the risk and can recognize the kinds of diverse concerns to the economic benefits achieved by markets, including factors such as the heterogeneity in individual riskiness and differences in attitudes toward risk, as well as differences to the length of life that is at risk.

Even a simplified benefit-cost norm that abstracts from individual variations in willingness to pay is a more compelling equity rationale than that currently advocated under the guise of environmental equity. The efficiency norm is to equalize the marginal cost per life saved across all efforts, adjusting for factors such as the quantity of life at risk. All lives count equally. Moreover, lives saved by job safety policies count the same as those saved through safer highways or decreased pollution. People harmed by risks from a particular source would not receive differential policy emphasis, as they do now. The equity measure I advocate is to equalize benefit-cost trade-offs, not just risk levels. The cost-effectiveness equity measure recognizes that risk policies involve both benefits and costs. Current equity practices ignore costs altogether. Instead, they seek to equalize incremental risks, perceived risks, potential individual risks, or some other risk-based measure.

Analysis of the consequences of using benefit-cost tests for choosing hazardous waste site cleanups indicates that the trade-off between efficiency and equity is in fact a false dichotomy. Minorities would fare much better under a benefit-cost regime than under the current EPA cleanup policy strategy, which purports to advance environmental equity. Notwithstanding the agency's politically correct declarations, the driving force behind hazardous waste cleanup is the political clout of the affected populations. The powerless, the disenfranchised, and the less politically sophisticated fare much worse under the current regime than they would if policy choices were driven by evaluation of policy benefits and costs. Benefit-cost analysis equalizes the political playing field so that what has merit is the risk consequences of the policy, not the political power of those affected. Benefit-cost tests in effect endow minorities with equal standing that they do not otherwise have within the context of our current regime of politically driven risk regulation policies.

Notions of risk equity that permeate the federal regulatory regime include more than just an avowed concern with the well-being of minorities. For example, there are also efforts to ensure that no particular individual is exposed to too high a level of risk from a particular type of risk exposure. Equity in the sense of constraining risks not to be too great would seem to be an innocuous requirement. However, the policy emphasis on individual risks, many of which are hypothetical risks to speculative future populations, diverts our risk regulation resources away from actual risks to large populations. Since minorities tend to be more densely concentrated in more polluted areas, this policy emphasis creates a discriminatory bias against minorities.

More generally, exploration of the various risk equity concepts suggests that there is no salient risk equity measure to serve as a meaningful reference point. There is almost always some notion of risk equity that can be expounded to justify worthless risk regulations. We purportedly need to spend these funds to protect minorities, to ensure that farmers or those in high-risk locales are not at risk, or to eliminate the unfairness of involuntary risks. Ad hoc equity justifications can always be mustered because unlike efficiency norms there is no well-defined equity standard.

Consideration of a variety of risk equity approaches that are embodied in risk regulation policies suggests that there are often huge inefficiencies accompanying such misguided equity norms, the extent of which are reflected in the $6 billion median cost per case of cancer averted through hazardous waste cleanup efforts, which do not even advance the interests of minorities. More generally, almost all job safety and environmental policies have squandered our economic resources. The price that we pay for our equity illusions is thousands of lives that could be saved by basing regulatory policies on efficiency norms.

STATE AND FEDERAL REGULATORY REFORM: A COMPARATIVE ANALYSIS

*ROBERT W. HAHN**

ABSTRACT

This paper provides a comprehensive assessment of state efforts to eliminate or change burdensome regulations and to use economic analysis to produce more sensible results. More than half the states have undertaken initiatives of some kind to improve regulation, including oversight mechanisms and the use of cost-benefit analysis. However, the effectiveness of oversight and enforcement of regulatory reform initiatives in the day-to-day world of rule making is often doubtful. As in the case of the federal government, state agencies have devised ways to avoid doing what they do not want to do. Generally, regulatory reform initiatives are most effective when they have active political support, a strong, well-funded oversight mechanism, and states provide clear, specific guidelines to implementing agencies. While several states have sought to establish such a structure, most states have not. Until significant resources and political support are devoted to reform efforts, real-world progress in regulatory reform is not likely to be great.

I. INTRODUCTION

IN recent years, many states have recognized that overly burdensome regulations can adversely impact business and citizens.[1] In response to problems with excessive regulation, some states have initiated administrative reforms

* Director of the AEI-Brookings Joint Center for Regulatory Studies, Resident Scholar at the American Enterprise Institute, and Research Associate at the Kennedy School of Government, Harvard University. The author would like to thank Fumie Yokota, Petrea Moyle, Lisa Bustin, Elizabeth Cooper, Jonathan Siskin, and Amy Wendholt for their research support. The helpful comments of Bob King are gratefully acknowledged. The views in this paper reflect those of the author and do not necessarily represent the views of the institutions with which he is affiliated.

[1] There is no widely accepted definition of regulation. The Office of Management and Budget (OMB) defines regulation as a statement by an agency to implement, interpret, or prescribe law or policy or to describe the procedure or practice of an agency. See OMB, Report to Congress on the Costs and Benefits of Federal Regulation 24 (1997). The federal government and the states use similar definitions to establish requirements for the analysis and review of administrative rule making. Therefore, although regulations are generally perceived as agency rules that constrain the behavior of individuals or business, the legal definition of regulation also includes internal agency management. In this paper, the terms ''regulation'' and ''rule'' are used interchangeably.

[*Journal of Legal Studies*, vol. XXIX]

that expand the use of economic analysis to assess the impact of existing and proposed regulations.[2] While the economics literature deals extensively with the use of economic analysis as a mechanism to inform federal regulatory decision making, the literature does not emphasize comparable efforts at the state level. This is a serious oversight because states are often responsible for the implementation of federal regulation and pass many regulations based on their own laws.

This paper provides the first critical analysis of comprehensive reform initiatives at the state level.[3] It makes five important contributions to the existing literature. First, it reviews the evolution of comprehensive state and federal regulatory reform initiatives. Second, it examines several state reform efforts in detail, highlighting important characteristics of these efforts. Third, it evaluates the current application of economic analysis in federal and state regulatory decision making processes. Fourth, it analyzes the political forces shaping regulatory reform initiatives. Fifth, it offers some observations on the effectiveness of these reforms.

State governments use many different mechanisms to encourage agencies to identify rules that the agencies should repeal or modify and consequently reduce the regulatory burden. Nearly one-third of the states has initiated comprehensive reviews of all existing regulations. Some of these states conduct a page-by-page review of all regulations, similar to the federal government. Some states also have modified the administrative rule-making process to require analysis of the impacts of new regulatory activity and often strongly encourage the use of benefit-cost analysis and cost-effectiveness analysis. Over half of the states require agencies to assess the economic impact of all proposed rules. A legislative, executive, or independent entity reviews proposed rules in most states, and some of these entities must review the agency's analyses of the potential economic impacts. This paper explores the efficacy of these and other mechanisms in an effort to guide the regulatory reform efforts of decision makers.

The effectiveness of regulatory reform mechanisms varies from state to state, depending on the nature of statutory guidelines and requirements. If the statutory mandate is not clear, agencies may only superficially analyze the costs and benefits of regulations or may manipulate analyses to achieve political ends. To increase agency compliance, states have established over-

---

[2] Proposed regulations are new regulations or modifications of existing regulations.

[3] Some analysts have evaluated various attempts to reform specific types of state regulation, but no one has systematically examined comprehensive reforms. For example, Kristin Loerzel, State Regulatory Reform Initiatives (1996), and Alexander Volokh, Lynn Scarlett, & Scott Bush, Race to the Top: The Innovative Face of State Environmental Management (Policy Study No. 239, 1998), highlight recent attempts designed to reform state environmental regulation. Richard Whisnant & Diane DeWitt Cherry, 31 Wake Forest L. Rev. 693 (1996), reviews the use of economic analysis in selected states.

sight processes and increased the specificity of statutory requirements. A state may, for example, require agencies to balance costs and benefits. The impact of oversight processes and more stringent requirements varies greatly and is difficult to determine because funding for such improvements is often limited relative to the size of the task and because the requirements are generally new and relatively untested. Some states claim their regulations are more effective and less costly as a result of improvements to the regulatory process, but the analytical support for such claims is generally weak. Some states, however, appear to have made some progress.

Regulatory review activities at the federal and state level are examined in Section II. Section III describes the federal regulatory review process and analyzes examples of state-level regulatory review. Finally, Section IV summarizes the major conclusions of this study.

II. An Overview of Federal and State Regulatory Reform

This section examines federal statutes, state statutes, and executive orders that require analysis and/or review of rule-making actions by executive agencies. The purpose is to introduce the reader to the federal regulatory review process and provide an overview of comprehensive state regulatory reform efforts. Generally, comprehensive reform efforts introduce analysis and review requirements that apply to several regulatory agencies. Comprehensive reform efforts do not include reform efforts to overhaul specific agencies or deregulate specific industries.

No comprehensive source of state regulatory reform initiatives exists. I therefore interviewed state officials in all states, acquired and analyzed available state information, searched state web pages, and used survey data. State information includes administrative procedures acts, executive orders, and reports published by various agencies and legislative committees.[4] The primary source of survey data was the National Association on Administrative Rules Review (NAARR), which compiled information provided by state officials on current requirements and procedures for review of administrative rules.[5] In addition, I conducted a survey of 20 states for the purpose

---

[4] For an overview of state initiatives, see New York Governor's Office of Regulatory Reform, A Review of State Regulatory Initiatives (1995).

[5] See National Association on Administrative Rules Review, 1996–97 Administrative Rules Review Directory and Survey (1996). The survey was sent in May 1996 to 126 individuals across the 50 states and territories involved in some aspect of the rules review process. The NAARR received 60 usable responses, representing 49 states and Puerto Rico. Ten states provided multiple survey submissions, but in most cases only a single individual responded to the survey. Although most of the answers provided by individuals from the same state were identical, there were some discrepancies that the NAARR resolved by communicating directly with the respondents. The NAARR made no efforts, however, to validate the responses from states with individual respondents beyond calling the respondents for clarification of particular answers.

TABLE 1

SUMMARY OF ADMINISTRATIVE RULES REVIEW SURVEY RESULTS:
ANALYTICAL REQUIREMENTS

	NUMBER OF STATES EMPLOYING:		
	Benefit-Cost Analysis	Risk Assessment	Economic Impact Analysis
Application of review requirements:			
All rules	10	4	27
Selected rules	7	4	10
Rules with costs above dollar threshold	3	1	7
Rules from specific agencies	2	4	5
At the request of review entity	11	6	17
None of the above	28	37	9
Responsibility for requirements:			
Promulgating agency	28	12	36
Executive entity	5	3	9
Legislative entity	3	2	7
Reviewing entity	1	2	3
Other	2	2	1
None of the above	20	36	12

SOURCE.—National Association on Administrative Rules Review, 1996–97 Administrative Rules Review Directory and Survey (1996).
NOTE.—Columns do not sum to 50 because some states marked more than one answer in each; 49 states were surveyed.

of this analysis. The results of the NAARR survey are presented independent of the author's survey because of differences in the scope and methodology of the two surveys.

The NAARR survey, which includes information from all states except Rhode Island, shows that state regulatory reform initiatives follow some general trends. The survey also shows that the states employ a variety of mechanisms to achieve reform. The results of the survey are summarized in Tables 1 and 2. Table 1 shows that 27 states responded that they require economic impact analysis for all rules. Table 2 shows that 32 states report that agencies consider the adequate completion of economic and other technical analyses in the regulation process. In most states the promulgating agency is primarily responsible for conducting these analyses. Three-quarters of the states identified at least one government entity—legislative, independent, attorney general, or other—responsible for overseeing proposed rule making.

While states generally require agencies to analyze the economic impact of rules, most states shy away from more stringent requirements, such as benefit-cost analysis and risk assessment. According to Table 1, 10 states

TABLE 2

SUMMARY OF ADMINISTRATIVE RULES REVIEW SURVEY RESULTS: OVERSIGHT PROCEDURES

| | NUMBER OF STATES EMPLOYING: | | |
	Proposed Rules	Existing Rules	Veto Power
Oversight responsibility:			
Legislative committee	27	17	12
Independent review agency	8	2	6
Attorney general	13	5	9
Other	21	12	28
None of the above	13	26	10
Oversight considerations:			
Statutory authority	44		
Intent of legislature	40		
Clear unambiguous terms	35		
Reasonably necessary to fulfill statutory mandate	33		
Promulgated according to proper procedures	40		
Conflict with or duplicate existing statutes or rules	39		
Balancing of costs and benefits	23		
Adequate completion of analyses	32		

SOURCE.—National Association on Administrative Rules Review, 1996–97 Administrative Rules Review Directory and Survey (1996).

NOTE.—Columns do not sum to 50 because some states marked more than one answer in each category; 49 states were surveyed.

claimed to require benefit-cost analysis of all rules, and seven states require benefit-cost analysis of selected rules. Twenty-eight states did not use benefit-cost analysis. Only four states require risk assessment for all rules, and another four states require risk assessment for selected rules. Table 2 shows that states also seem hesitant to establish comprehensive oversight processes. While most states have some form of oversight entity, these entities are not typically responsible for review of the agency's economic analysis. Instead, the oversight entity generally focuses on issues related to the legality of the rule, such as statutory authority and adherence to proper procedures.

The NAARR survey data are sometimes misleading because they credit states for initiating potentially ineffective reform efforts. In Connecticut, for example, agencies use benefit-cost analysis to develop regulations without considering private-sector impacts, an egregious error because of the potentially large neglected costs.[6] Connecticut also requires agencies to consider modification of rules to reduce the adverse impact on small businesses but

---

[6] Conn. Gen. Stat. §§ 4-168, 4-168a (1999).

does not require agencies to quantify that burden. Finally, Connecticut does not require agencies to quantify or even identify the benefits of a rule. So, although the NAARR survey reports that Connecticut uses benefit-cost analysis, in practice Connecticut's efforts fall far short of widely accepted standards for such analysis. The NAARR survey is still useful, however, because it documents state-level requirements for review of existing regulations, analysis of proposed rule makings, and oversight of agency efforts.[7] Conclusions about state regulatory reform programs could not be drawn solely from the survey data, however, so the author conducted a more detailed survey of state efforts.

Analysis and Review of Proposed Regulation

Many states, as well as the federal government, require the analysis of proposed regulations, although they require varying amounts of detail. Table 3 presents the results of my survey of 20 states, chosen because of their significant statutory requirements for analysis and review of proposed regulation.[8] The table lists the various provisions mandated by statute or executive order and the different oversight mechanisms employed by the states.[9]

States consider and emphasize different regulatory reform initiatives. Some states are very specific about the content of analyses, while others are fairly open-ended. Many states have mechanisms to review the overall rule package, but very few seem to have an entity that conducts a review of the actual content of an agency's analysis. In almost all states, agencies are primarily responsible for preparation of the analysis. Nearly all states require some analysis of the rule's fiscal impact on state government and economic impact on the private sector and require agencies to assess the impact of the rule on small businesses and local governments. Less frequently, states require agencies to assess the impact of the rule on employment and on record-keeping and reporting responsibilities.

Some states require agencies to analyze the impact of all proposed regulations. The federal government, on the other hand, requires agencies to an-

---

[7] The NAARR survey may have overlooked some programs, but the major programs have been identified.

[8] The 20 states in the survey were chosen because significant reform efforts are underway in all of these states, whereas investigation of the other 30 states revealed little emphasis on regulatory reform. The author does not contend that his survey is exhaustive, however, as it was conducted without the methodological rigor necessary to make such an assertion. The author is confident, however, that he identified the major regulatory reform programs and has characterized them accurately.

[9] For more detailed information on individual states, see Robert W. Hahn, State and Federal Regulatory Reform: A Comparative Analysis (Working Paper No. 98-3, AEI-Brookings Joint Ctr. for Reg. Stud. 1998).

TABLE 3

	All Rules	Selected Rules
Statutory requirements (20 states surveyed):[a]		
Assess fiscal impact on state government	12	5
Assess economic impact on the private sector	11	8
Assess impact on small businesses	12	3
Assess fiscal impact on local government	11	3
Assess impact on state employment	5	0
Assess impact on paperwork burden[b]	5	2
Analyze alternatives[c]	5	3
Balance costs and benefits[d]	2	2
Ensure rules less strict than federal standards	1	3
Executive order requirements (five states surveyed):[e]		
Assess impact on state employment	1	0
Assess economic impact on the private sector	1	0
Analyze alternatives	4	1
Balance costs and benefits	3	0
Ensure rules less strict than federal standards	2	0
Oversight mechanisms (20 states surveyed):		
Executive branch guidelines	4	0
Standard form for presentation of analysis	3	0
Statutory review by independent entity	7	3
Executive order review by independent entity[f,g]	3	1

SOURCES.—State statutes, executive orders, government reports, and interviews with state officials. See Robert W. Hahn, State and Federal Regulatory Reform: A Comparative Analysis (Working Paper No. 98-3, AEI-Brookings Joint Ctr. for Reg. Stud. 1998).

NOTE.—Values given are number of states of those surveyed.

[a] The states surveyed are Arizona, California, Colorado, Connecticut, Florida, Illinois, Indiana, Iowa, Kansas, Kentucky, Maine, Massachusetts, Michigan, Nebraska, New Jersey, New York, North Carolina, Pennsylvania, Virginia, and Washington.

[b] The "paperwork burden" consists primarily of recordkeeping and reporting requirements.

[c] States are included in this category if they require the agency to analyze alternatives or to choose the "least burdensome" or "least onerous" alternative to a regulation, including nonregulatory alternatives such as economic incentives.

[d] A balancing test implies that the statute required the benefits to "justify," "outweigh," or "exceed" the costs. The three words imply different levels of stringency for cost-benefit tests, where "exceed" is the most stringent and "justify" is the least stringent. States that require agencies to "consider" or "assess" costs and benefits are not included in this category.

[e] Five states out of the 20 surveyed issued executive orders: Massachusetts, Michigan, New York, Pennsylvania, and Virginia.

[f] Five states surveyed.

[g] Two of the five states that issued executive orders created a separate Office of Regulatory Reform to review agency analyses, two rely on internal governmental offices to review analyses, and one did not establish an oversight mechanism.

alyze rules likely to have a significant economic impact, defined as rules that will cost the economy over $100 million. Only 4 percent of the rules analyzed by the federal government are designated "significant" because most federal rules pertain to daily operations, such as quarantine orders by the Department of Agriculture or government grant announcements.[10] Many states do not distinguish between significant and insignificant rules. States should not examine insignificant rules beyond supplying a concise statement of the objectives and a list of the likely benefits and costs, unless it is possible to improve such rules at low cost. More detailed analysis may consume resources that agencies could spend reviewing rules with larger economic impacts.

An agency may comply with the requirement to estimate the costs and benefits of a proposed rule, but nevertheless choose a policy that is less cost-effective or efficient than alternatives. States employ different mechanisms to address this problem. Eight states require agencies to analyze alternatives. Some of these states require an agency to review various policy options, choose the "least burdensome" alternative, and explain its decision if it does not choose the least burdensome alternative. Four states require agencies to balance the costs and benefits of a rule. Finally, four states require agencies to justify state standards that are more stringent than federal requirements to discourage agencies from promulgating more stringent rules that may not pass a benefit-cost test.

Furthermore, a mandate to analyze proposed regulations does not ensure that agencies will comply. Vague statutory language and a lack of oversight often allow agencies to comply only partially with requirements or not comply at all. A study in Virginia, for example, found that agencies complied with review requirements less than 20 percent of the time before recent reforms.[11] In addition, although 32 states claimed in the survey to consider whether the agency adequately completed an analysis when they review proposed rules, only 10 states established an independent entity to review the content of the analyses.

Most states have not attempted to increase compliance, but those that are trying to correct the problem employ a number of methods. These include the establishment of oversight processes, the use of executive orders to strengthen legislation, and the provision of specific guidelines for analysis. The extent to which states use each of these methods varies. The use of

---

[10] OMB, More Benefits, Fewer Burdens: Creating A Regulatory System That Works for the American People, A Report to the President on the Third Anniversary of Executive Order 12866, at A-1 (1996).

[11] Joint Legislative Audit and Review Committee, Review of Virginia's Administrative Process Act to the Governor and the General Assembly of Virginia (1993).

oversight processes is perhaps the best way to ensure compliance with review requirements. A few states have an independent oversight committee to review agency analyses, but most review analyses internally. Some states have an entity that ensures rules are consistent with statutory mandates, although these entities do not critique the methodology or content of analyses. Other states create oversight entities with the authority to delay the rule-making process if agency analyses are unsatisfactory, although none of them have the power to officially veto a rule. In short, most states need to develop more effective means through which to hold agencies accountable for their analyses.

More stringent statutory language or formal guidelines can also increase agency compliance. Five states out of the 20 in the survey use executive orders to strengthen statutory review requirements, while the rest rely solely on legislative efforts. Three of these five states require states to balance the benefits and costs, and all of the states require agencies to analyze alternatives to the proposed regulation. Two states require agencies to ensure the state regulations are less stringent than federal regulations. The executive orders also contain oversight provisions. Two of the five states create an Office of Regulatory Reform to review agency analyses. Two states give internal agencies the authority to review analyses, while one state does not provide an oversight mechanism. In addition, some states provide agencies with guidelines for analysis and/or standard forms for presentation of the analysis. California, New York, and Virginia provide a handbook with detailed instructions for analysis. California, Michigan, and Pennsylvania provide standard forms to summarize analyses. It appears that governors tend to use executive orders to supplement statutory requirements. Executive orders typically require analysis of alternatives or review of agency analyses, which are often not included in statutory review provisions.

Review of Existing Regulations

State- and federal-level review of existing regulation is a relatively recent addition to the regulatory process. At the federal level, President Bush and President Clinton established regulatory review requirements in 1992 and 1995, respectively. Similarly, at the state level only five states out of the 20 in the survey required review of existing regulation before 1994. Thirteen states required review after 1994. The other two states do not require review. States use a variety of approaches to review existing regulations, some of which differ significantly from federal requirements.[12] Although

[12] See Hahn, *supra* note 9, for additional information on individual states. It includes information on administrative procedures, entities primarily responsible for coordination, and the measurable results of the review.

some of these approaches seem comprehensive, the actual impact of state requirements is not clear because they are relatively untested and difficult to enforce and because most states do not consistently or accurately document the impact of the changes on the regulatory process.

States generally require agencies to identify regulations the agency should modify or repeal, similar to the federal government. The federal government requires a one-time review by executive order, while 10 states require a one-time review and nine states require periodic reviews.[13] Twelve states use executive orders and seven states rely on legislation to require reviews.[14] All states with legislative mandates require a periodic review, but most executive orders require a one-time review. Michigan, New Jersey, and Virginia, however, require periodic review by executive order. As is clear from these examples, states use an array of tools to review existing regulations.

States do not always comply with requirements for review of existing regulations. An Illinois statute, for example, requires agencies to review all rules at least every 5 years. Agencies have not, however, completed a review in over a decade. The legislative committee responsible for enforcement cited a lack of staff and funds as the reason for its negligence.[15] Options to improve compliance include stricter statutory language and the establishment of effective oversight mechanisms.

States can increase the stringency of requirements to review existing regulations in a number of ways, but the most common method is the sunset provision. A sunset provision requires the automatic expiration of a law or regulation after a designated amount of time. The legislature or agency must therefore review the regulation before they reinstate it. Indiana, New Jersey, and Tennessee currently have such sunset provisions. Tennessee and New Jersey enacted the provisions in 1982 and 1978, respectively, but Indiana only established the provision in 1996. Tennessee and New Jersey therefore provide some information about the effectiveness of the sunset provision. Indiana's first expiration deadline is not until 2002, so no information about the impact of the requirement is available at this time.[16] In

---

[13] The two categories do not add up to 18 because New York is counted in both categories. New York implemented a one-time review in 1995 and enacted a provision to require a periodic review in 1996.

[14] Again, the two categories do not add up to 18 because New York is counted in both categories. The governor of New York ordered a one-time review by an executive order, and the periodic review requirement is a statutory provision.

[15] Telephone interview by Fumie Yokota, research assistant, American Enterprise Institute, with Clare Eberle, Joint Committee on Administrative Rules (October 6, 1997).

[16] Ind. Code § 4-22-2.5-2 (1999). The legislature must review all rules in force as of December 31, 1995, in 2002.

Tennessee, the legislature routinely votes to eliminate the expiration date of the sunset provision, defeating its original purpose.[17] New Jersey requires the expiration of all rules within 5 years of adoption.[18] If an agency wishes to continue enforcement of the rule, it can reinstate it by complying with the extensive analysis and review requirements of the Administrative Procedures Act. New Jersey has not, however, assessed whether this requirement has increased the efficiency and efficacy of regulation. In practice, therefore, it is not clear whether sunset provisions encourage legislatures to vote periodically on the reinstatement of rules as intended. It seems, however, that sunset provisions may give legislators more opportunities to review rules critically than standard review requirements.

The establishment of effective oversight mechanisms may also increase compliance. Legislative committees, independent review agencies, and the office of the attorney general are among the entities to which states give oversight responsibility, although many states have no oversight mechanism at all. In addition, some states require agencies to report their findings to a coordinating office. These offices do not, however, necessarily review the agency's analysis. Agencies may therefore omit vital information from their analyses, make unnecessary mistakes, and overstate the benefits of a rule if it will help them achieve their political objectives. The establishment of an oversight process to review agency analyses would minimize these problems.

Determining which reform initiatives are most effective is difficult because states generally do not accurately document the impact of regulatory reform efforts. Most states and the federal government document the impact of initiatives by counting the number of rules or pages of regulation the government eliminates. Such a measure is not meaningful because the repeal of a rule may not change the behavior of regulators. The legislature, for example, may repeal a rule, and the agency may consolidate its requirements with existing regulations. Although the state reduces the absolute number of rules, the overall level of regulation remains the same. Florida, for example, defines a rule as a "rule section" of the Florida Administrative Code. Florida could, in theory, reduce the number of regulations by simply merging sections of the Administrative Code.[19] California, New

[17] In 1997, for example, the legislature allowed only seven rules adopted in 1996 to expire. Six of the rules were regulations regarding fees by various medical boards, and the seventh was a regulation of book-keeping procedures for the Registry of Election Finance. See 1997 Tenn. Pub. Acts 433, tit. 4, ch. 5 (1996).

[18] Exec. Order No. 66, N.J. Reg., 1978 N.J. Laws. The Order exempts rules the state adopted to comply with federal law and rules that contain requirements that would violate a state or federal law.

[19] See Section III for a more detailed discussion.

York, and Virginia are the only states that attempt to accurately document the economic impact of some regulatory changes. In particular, New York has made an effort to document the impacts of its reform program, but the quality of the analyses is suspect.[20] The analyses do not seem to identify a clear baseline, nor do they distinguish between transfers of wealth and actual efficiency gains.[21] The actual impact may therefore be much smaller than New York claims, although it seems the economy benefits from the changes. Still, the documentation provided by California, New York, and Virginia provides some useful information on the impact of reform measures.

Proponents of federal regulatory reform often advocate the use of oversight processes or other legal mechanisms to further reform efforts. Experience at the state level shows that a statutory review requirement is not necessarily sufficient to ensure ongoing review. Even when agencies conduct reviews, the results are often disappointing because the state does not require them to clearly document the effects of their actions. Further oversight or stricter statutory language is necessary to improve the review process. In short, some states have started down the road toward reform, but their current efforts are insufficient to achieve significant improvements.

III. REGULATORY REFORM: SOME INDIVIDUAL CASES

The general survey of state regulatory reform efforts presented in the first part of this paper suggests that states can improve analyses of proposed and existing regulations if they increase oversight of agency analyses, employ stricter statutory requirements, and document the impact of their efforts. The general survey does not, however, show conclusively that improved analyses will improve regulatory outcomes. One administrative law official in New Jersey suggested the quality of the analysis of proposed rules had improved since the state introduced a review requirement. The official has seen no evidence, however, that the requirement has had any substantive impact on the content of rules.[22] Politics, for example, can prevent decision makers from using information on costs, benefits, and alternatives to improve regulation. A distrust of economic analysis as a tool for decision making may also prevent the use of the results of such analysis. This section carefully examines state- and federal-level reform efforts, highlights

[20] See Section III for a more detailed discussion.

[21] These problems also arise at the federal level, but federal agencies generally treat them with more care (see, for example, Robert W. Hahn, Government Analysis of the Benefits and Costs of Regulation, 12(4) J. Econ. Persp. 201 (1998)).

[22] Telephone interview by Fumie Yokota, research assistant, American Enterprise Institute, with Anthony Miragliotta, New Jersey Office Administrative Law (October 6, 1997).

their strengths and weaknesses, and shows how political forces can influence reform initiatives. Although this section provides some useful information, additional research is necessary to develop a more complete theory
of the impact of politics on reform efforts.

A widely accepted view of regulatory politics is that Republicans want
to scale back regulation to ease the burden on industry and Democrats want
to increase regulation to help their preferred constituencies, including labor
and environmentalists. In the absence of detailed information about regulatory reform initiatives and their potential impact on the economy and social
welfare, the general public and the regulatory community will assume the
party advocating reform is motivated by these political agendas. The result
is often a lack of public support for reform initiatives or partisan wrangling
that stymies reform efforts. Ironically, some degree of public approval and
high-level political support are essential for the success of reform efforts.
Without them, significant reform initiatives will languish. A partial solution
to this problem is to increase the transparency of the regulatory process, so
politicians are held more accountable for the regulations that result from the
laws they pass. Transparency, coupled with stricter requirements for regulatory analysis and oversight, will help the public see how regulatory reform
can benefit society. States and the federal government can improve regulatory accountability if they recognize that transparency increases accountability and that accountability builds the public and political support necessary for effective reform.

Although politics is perhaps the most serious impediment to regulatory
reform, faith in the use of economics for regulatory decision making is another potential obstacle. While many states advocate the use of economic
analysis to review regulations, legislators and academics still hotly debate
the extent to which economics should influence decisions. Since economic
analysis is an emerging tool in the regulatory arena, it is still relatively untested. The general public and lawmakers are therefore often wary of requiring it because they fear it may be misused. The result, as the individual
case studies in this section make clear, is that states commit to varying degrees of economic analysis. Until the positive impact of economic analysis
is consistently and clearly documented, states will probably not enact comprehensive reforms.

California, Florida, New York, and Virginia are the focus of this section
because these states have initiated significant regulatory reform efforts in
recent years and have also documented some of their progress and results.[23]

---

[23] Other states, such as Arizona, Massachusetts, and Michigan, have noteworthy programs.
This paper does not review them because there was little or no information available on the
economic impact of their efforts, although assessments of the number of rules amended or

These four states, in addition to the federal government, provide excellent illustrations of the extent to which (1) politics can impede the use of agency analyses and (2) the distrust of economic analysis can result in varying analysis requirements.

Federal Government

When regulation represented only a small part of the activity of the federal government, there was no pressing need to evaluate its overall impact. Since the late 1960s, however, regulatory policy has played an increasingly important role in many areas of everyday life. To address the dramatic increase in regulatory activity, the last six presidents have introduced different analysis requirements and oversight mechanisms with varying degrees of success.

In 1971, President Nixon established a Quality of Life Review of selected regulations. The new initiative stemmed from concern that some recently enacted environmental regulations were ineffective or excessively costly. The Office of Management and Budget (OMB) administered the process and required agencies issuing health, safety, and environmental regulations to coordinate their activities. President Ford formalized and expanded the review process in Executive Order No. 11,821. The order required agencies to prepare, and the OMB to review, inflation impact statements for major rules, defined as rules whose annual impact typically exceeded $100 million.

In 1978, President Carter strengthened executive regulatory oversight by issuing Executive Order No. 12,044, which required agencies to conduct detailed regulatory analyses of proposed rule makings and required the OMB to review the analyses. In addition, he established two interagency groups. The Regulatory Analysis Review Group, composed of representatives from the Executive Office of the President and regulatory agencies, examined a limited number of proposed regulations expected to have substantial regulatory impact. The Regulatory Council, comprised of the heads of federal regulatory agencies, was asked to publish a *Calendar of Federal Regulations,* to summarize major regulations under development.[24]

The Reagan administration sought to further strengthen executive regulatory oversight. Just after entering office, President Reagan announced the formation of his interagency Task Force on Regulatory Relief chaired by

---

repealed were available. Florida lacks information on the economic impact as well, but Florida shows that the rule review process can lead to some undesirable results.

[24] The purpose of the *Calendar* was to point out regulatory overlap and provide information on the benefits and costs of proposed actions.

Vice President Bush. The task force reviewed existing regulations and would, in the president's words, "cut away the thicket of irrational and senseless regulations." President Reagan also issued Executive Order No. 12,291, requiring agencies to conduct benefit-cost analyses for all major rules. The OMB could not veto agency rules, but it could send the analysis back to the agency for improvement. A second executive order required annual publication of the *Regulatory Program of the United States,* a review of proposed regulations to determine whether they conformed to administration policy and priorities. The approach of the Reagan administration was unique because of the scope of the regulatory review and the formal requirement to estimate benefits for major rules. President Bush continued Reagan's policies, although he replaced the Task Force on Regulatory Relief with the Council on Competitiveness, headed by Vice President Quayle.

In 1993, President Clinton replaced the Reagan Executive Order No. 12,291 with Executive Order No. 12,886, which requires similar regulatory analyses but changed the standards for review and analysis. President Clinton also initiated a National Performance Review (NPR) to help "reinvent government."[25] The NPR, led by Vice President Gore, published a report with recommendations to improve the federal government, including cutting the federal work force by 252,000 employees, cutting internal management regulations in half, and requiring agencies to set customer performance standards.[26] President Clinton focused his attention on existing regulations in a memorandum to heads of departments and agencies in 1995.[27] The memorandum ordered each executive agency to conduct a page-by-page review of its existing regulations and to eliminate or modify rules in need of reform. During the 3-month review period, agencies identified 31,000 pages of the Code of Federal Regulation to modify and 16,000 pages of obsolete rules to eliminate.[28] The annual NPR reports identify cost savings from general reinvention, such as streamlining the executive branch bureaucracy, but offer no assessment of the economic effects of the regula-

[25] For a review of some efforts to "reinvent government," see Inside the Reinvention Machine: Appraising Governmental Reform (Donald F. Kettl & John J. DiIulio, Jr., eds. 1995).

[26] See Al Gore, Creating a Government That Works Better and Costs Less: Report of the National Performance Review (1993).

[27] See William J. Clinton, Regulatory Reinvention Initiative: Memorandum for Heads of Departments and Agencies (March 4, 1995). President Bush also asked agencies to review existing regulations and suggest methods to streamline them. See OMB, Regulatory Program of the United States Government: April 1, 1992–March 31, 1993, at 9–10 (1993).

[28] National Performance Review, The Best Kept Secrets in Government: A Report to President Bill Clinton 173 (1996).

tory reform initiatives. Therefore, it is not clear if these "reinventions" have increased the economic efficiency of regulations.

In spite of these executive efforts to reform regulation, dissatisfaction with the burdens of regulation persists. Following the Clinton initiatives, the 104th Congress made passionate pleas to design smarter, more efficient regulation. Unfortunately, the rhetoric fell short of the reality. Several comprehensive regulatory reform bills, which called for greater use of benefit-cost analysis and improved risk assessment, failed to pass—partly out of concern that the bills would "roll back" regulations designed to help protect health, safety, and the environment.[29] These reforms also failed because some lawmakers hesitated to support regulatory reform bills that applied to all statutes and superseded requirements already in place. After over 2 decades of command-and-control regulation, these lawmakers were simply not ready to support such seemingly dramatic changes in the regulatory process—even though they may have liked the idea of using economic analysis to improve regulation. As a result of such political factors, Congress settled for less far-reaching legislative reforms. Language was added to individual statutes to increase congressional oversight and provide more information on the benefits and costs of regulation. Table 4 summarizes the analysis and review requirements mandated by each piece of legislation. While the thrust of each piece of legislation differs, they share one common theme—the requirement that agencies use economic analysis to assess the benefits and costs of different kinds of regulations.

The incremental efforts to strengthen the influence of economic analysis on regulatory decision making fall into two categories: accountability mechanisms and analytical requirements. Both are designed to improve on the efficiency of the status quo. Accountability mechanisms include peer review, judicial review, sunset provisions, regulation budgets, and requirements to provide better information to Congress. Analytical requirements include benefit-cost analysis, cost-effectiveness analysis, and risk-risk analysis.[30] As is clear from Table 4, Congress created statutory requirements in both of these categories. In the accountability mechanism category, the

---

[29] See Risk Assessment and Cost-Benefit Act of 1995, H.R. 1022, 104th Cong., 1st Sess. (February 23, 1995); Comprehensive Regulatory Reform Act of 1995, S. 343, 104th Cong., 1st Sess. (February 2, 1995).

[30] By risk-risk analysis, I mean an evaluation of potential increases in health risks that may arise from efforts to combat a targeted health risk. Such an evaluation can help decision makers compare policies. See, for example, Lester Lave, The Strategy of Social Regulation (1981). Farmers, for example, may increase the use of an equally toxic alternative pesticide if use of the original pesticide is restricted or banned to prevent drinking water contamination. For more detailed examples of such trade-offs, see Risk vs. Risk: Tradeoffs in Protecting Health and the Environment (John D. Graham & Jonathan B. Wiener eds. 1995).

Small Business Regulatory Enforcement Fairness Act of 1996 requires agencies to submit final regulations to Congress for review. The Telecommunications Act of 1996 requires the Federal Communications Commission to conduct a biennial review of all regulations promulgated under the Act. The Regulatory Accountability provisions, discussed further later in this section, require the Office of Management and Budget to assess the benefits and costs of existing federal regulatory programs and recommend programs or specific regulations to reform or eliminate. While these statutes represent a step toward more comprehensive reform measures, they cover only a fraction of all regulations.

The addition of analytical requirements has generally received more attention than the addition of policy reforms, partly because of their prominence in the Reagan and Clinton executive orders and partly because of controversy regarding their impact. The Reagan executive order required agencies to promulgate regulations for which the benefits "outweigh" the costs, and the Clinton executive order superseded that requirement with language that the benefits must "justify" the costs. The variation of the language and the type of analysis required in each of the statutes listed in Table 4 reflect the results of the ongoing controversy regarding analytical tools, which takes place every time Congress debates requiring their use. Some statutes require only cost-effectiveness analysis, some require full-fledged benefit-cost analysis, and some combine a form of benefit-cost analysis with risk-risk analysis. The Unfunded Mandates Reform Act of 1995, for example, requires agencies to choose the "most cost-effective" alternative and to describe the costs and benefits of any unfunded mandate but does not require the benefits of the mandate to justify the costs. The Safe Drinking Water Amendments of 1996 require the administrator of the Environmental Protection Agency to determine whether the benefits justify the costs of a drinking water standard, but the administrator does not have to set a new standard if the benefits do not justify the costs.[31] Amendments in 1996 to the pipeline section of the Transportation Act, on the other hand, require the secretary of transportation to propose a standard for pipeline

---

[31] The Amendments also require some form of risk-risk analysis. They require the administrator of the Environmental Protection Agency to set maximum levels for contaminants in drinking water at a "feasible" level, defined as feasible with the use of the best technology and treatment techniques available, while "taking cost into consideration." The administrator must ignore the feasibility constraint if the feasible level would result in an increase in the concentration of other contaminants in drinking water or would interfere with the efficacy of treatment techniques used to comply with other national primary drinking water regulations. If the feasibility constraint does not apply, the administrator must set the maximum level to minimize "the overall risk of adverse health effects by balancing the risk from the contaminant and the risk from other contaminants." Safe Drinking Water Act (PHSA), 42 U.S.C.S. § 300g-1(a)(5)(B)(i).

TABLE 4

RECENT REGULATORY REFORM LEGISLATION

Legislation	Description
Unfunded Mandates Reform Act of 1995	Requires the Congressional Budget Office to estimate the direct costs of unfunded federal mandates with significant economic impacts. Requires agencies to describe the costs and benefits of the majority of such mandates. Requires agencies to identify alternatives to the proposed mandate and select the "least costly, most cost-effective, or least burdensome alternative" that achieves the desired social objective.
Small Business Regulatory Enforcement Fairness Act of 1996	Requires agencies to submit each final regulation with supporting analyses to Congress. Congress has 60 days to review major regulations and can enact a joint resolution of disapproval to void the regulation if the resolution is passed and signed by the president. Strengthens judicial review provisions to hold agencies more accountable for the impacts of regulation on small entities.
Telecommunications Act of 1996	Allows the Federal Communications Commission to grant exemptions from regulations in certain cases and requires the consideration of the costs and benefits of specific provisions. Allows the Commission to grant waivers to buy out prohibitions on local telephone companies if the anticompetitive effects are "clearly outweighed" by the benefits to the community of the transaction. Requires the Commission to conduct a biennial review of all regulations to determine whether any regulations are no longer necessary as a result of "meaningful economic competition" between providers.
Food Quality Protection Act of 1996	Eliminates the Delaney Clause of the Food, Drug, and Cosmetic Act, which set a zero-tolerance standard for pesticide residues on processed food. Establishes a "safe" tolerance level, defined as "a reasonable certainty of no harm." Allows the administrator of the Environmental Protection Agency to modify the tolerance level if use of the pesticide protects consumers from health risks greater than the dietary risk from the residue or if use is necessary to avoid a "significant disruption" of the food supply. Amends the Federal Insecticide, Fungicide, and Rodenticide Act by requiring a reevaluation of the safe tolerance level after the administrator determines during the reregistration process whether a pesticide will present an "unreasonable risk to man or the environment, taking into account the economic, social, and environmental costs and benefits of the use of any pesticide."

TABLE 4 (*Continued*)

Legislation	Description
Safe Drinking Water Act Amendments of 1996	Amends the procedure to set maximum contaminant levels for contaminants in public water supplies. Adds requirement to determine whether the benefits of the level justify the costs. Maintains feasibility standard for contaminant levels, unless feasible level would result in an increase in the concentration of other contaminants or would interfere with the efficacy of treatment techniques used to comply with other national drinking water regulations. Requires the administrator to set contaminant levels to minimize the overall risk of adverse health effects by balancing the risk from the contaminant and the risk from other contaminants in such cases.
Amended Gas Pipeline Safety Standards, 1996	Requires the secretary of transportation to consider the benefits and costs expected to result from implementation of a safety standard and to propose a standard only if the benefits justify its costs. The benefit and cost estimates are based on a risk assessment, for which the secretary must identify regulatory and nonregulatory options and must explain the selection of the standard in lieu of other options.
Regulatory Accountability Provision of 1996, 1997, and 1998	In separate appropriations legislation in 1996, 1997, and 1998, Congress required the Office of Management and Budget to submit an assessment of the annual benefits and costs of all existing federal regulatory programs to Congress for 1997, 1998, and 2000, respectively. The Office of Management and Budget already must review and approve analyses submitted by agencies estimating the costs and benefits of major proposed rules. The annual report provisions build on this review process.

safety *only* if the benefits justify the costs. Other statutes simply require the agency to ''consider'' costs and benefits.

Another significant difference between the requirements listed in Table 4 is the applicability of the requirements. Some of the statutes contain economic analysis provisions that apply only to specific provisions in the statute. The Telecommunications Act of 1996, for example, states that the Federal Communications Commission can grant waivers to buyout prohibitions on local telephone companies only if the anticompetitive effects are clearly outweighed by the benefits to the community. Similarly, other statutes are directed at specific safety standards, such as pipeline safety or clean drinking water. In contrast, statutes such as the Small Business Regulatory Enforcement Act and the Unfunded Mandates Reform Act contain economic analysis provisions that apply to all regulations under the jurisdiction of the legislation. These statutes are much more far-reaching in their approach to reform, as they pertain to large groupings of regulations instead of specific provisions or safety standards.

Perhaps the most significant recent step toward incorporating economic analysis into the regulatory process occurred in 1996, when the Congress showed a greater interest in requiring the OMB to assess the economic impact of regulation—partially because of new estimates that federal regulation costs several hundreds billion dollars annually.[32] In 1996 Senator Ted Stevens added an unprecedented amendment to the Omnibus Consolidated Appropriations Act, listed in Table 4 as the Regulatory Accountability Provision of 1996, that could significantly impact the assessment of regulations in the future. The amendment required the director of the OMB to provide Congress with estimates of the total annual benefits and costs of all federal regulatory programs as well as individual regulations.[33] The OMB produced its first report on the benefits and costs of regulation in response to the Stevens amendment in 1997[34] and published an improved second report in the fall of 1998.[35] The OMB will publish the third report in the year 2000. Congress will probably appropriate funding for additional reports, although it is unclear whether OMB will issue the reports on an annual or biennial basis.

Formal consideration of economic benefits and costs in regulatory decision making will likely persist, at least as long as the Republicans maintain a majority in Congress since they have incorporated regulatory reform into their policy agenda. As a result, an important concern is whether analysis and oversight actually affect policy decisions. It is difficult to determine, primarily because it is hard to predict the outcome of many regulations in the absence of oversight. More research may reveal the extent of the influence of the attempts to incorporate economic analysis into decision making sketched in Table 4. Nevertheless, it is clear that agencies could design many regulations more intelligently. Some regulations are even counterproductive. Research suggests more than half (57 percent) of the federal gov-

---

[32] See Thomas D. Hopkins, Cost of Regulation: Filling the Gaps, Report Prepared for the Regulatory Information Service Center (1992).

[33] Regulatory Accounting Provision—Stevens Amendment—was included in the Omnibus Consolidated Appropriations Act, 1997, Pub. L. No. 104-208 § 645 Stat. See Robert W. Hahn & Robert E. Litan, Improving Regulatory Accountability (1997), for a discussion of the implication of this provision.

[34] See OMB, Report to Congress on the Costs and Benefits of Federal Regulation 24 (1997).

[35] See OMB, Report to Congress on the Costs and Benefits of Federal Regulation (1998).

ernment's regulations would fail a strict benefit-cost test using the government's own numbers.[36] Moreover, ample research suggests that the government could significantly improve regulation to save more lives with fewer resources.[37] According to one study, a reallocation of mandated expenditures toward regulations with the highest payoff to society could save as many as 60,000 more lives a year at no additional cost.[38]

Some scholars have argued that the regulatory analysis and oversight have influenced policy outcomes.[39] In certain instances, such optimism is justified. One must, however, be careful about generalizations from a small sample.[40] At this point, knowledge about the effects of oversight and analysis is limited. In particular instances, oversight has made a difference. At the same time, it is not obvious how regulatory activities would have evolved in the absence of such oversight.

California

California has a long history of reform efforts.[41] In 1979, the legislature recognized the excessive burden imposed on business and individuals by regulation in the California Administrative Procedures Act (CAPA).[42] The CAPA requires agencies to assess the economic impact of rules and review proposed rules. In addition, Governor Pete Wilson issued executive orders to expand and supplement the CAPA analysis and review requirements and to create a means through which to obtain suggestions from the regulated community for reform of the rule-making process.

[36] Reviving Regulatory Reform: A Global Perspective § 11 (Robert W. Hahn ed. 2000, in press).

[37] See John F. Morrall, A Review of the Record, Regulation, November–December 1986, at 25–34; and W. Kip Viscusi, The Dangers of Unbounded Commitments to Regulate Risk, in Risks, Costs, and Lives Saved: Getting Better Results from Regulation (Robert W. Hahn ed. 1996).

[38] See Tammy O. Tengs & John D. Graham, The Opportunity Costs of Haphazard Social Investments in Life-Saving, in Hahn ed., *supra* note 37.

[39] See Economic Analyses at EPA: Assessing Regulatory Impact (Richard D. Morgenstern ed. 1997).

[40] Analysis is often used to justify political ends. See, for example, Janet Yellen, Testimony of Janet Yellen, Chair, Council of Economic Advisers, before the U.S. Senate Committee on Agriculture, Nutrition, and Forestry on the Economics of the Kyoto Protocol (Council of Economic Advisers, March 5, 1998).

[41] For a detailed review of California regulatory review initiatives, see California Trade and Commerce Agency, Regulation Review Unit, Improving Regulations and Rulemaking (1997).

[42] Cal. Gov't Code § 11340 (1999). In California, laws normally identified as "statutes" in other states are designated as "codes."

The original CAPA created the Office of Administrative Law (OAL) to conduct an "orderly review of adopted regulations" to reduce the number of regulations and improve the quality of adopted regulations.[43] The OAL can veto rules that violate the procedural requirements of the CAPA. According to the OAL, this review saves the state an estimated $500,000 to $2 million annually in avoided lawsuits.[44] The OAL serves an important function because it reviews the legality of rules, but it does not evaluate whether agencies select the most efficient method to achieve legislative goals. The office staff are mainly attorneys and paralegals who typically do not have the expertise to review a rule's economic impact. In the past, such expertise was unnecessary because the law did not require the analysis of economic effects of regulation. California law now, however, requires state agencies to assess significant adverse effects of regulations on business or individuals.[45] In the early 1990s, the legislature passed a series of amendments with detailed analysis requirements. In 1991, for example, the legislature passed a bill requiring agencies to assess the potential impact of regulation on small businesses,[46] the first state mandate to consider the economic effects of a regulation on the private sector. The legislature expanded the requirement to include all businesses in 1992 and later added other requirements, such as a 1993 provision to assess the impact of regulation on statewide employment and the competitiveness of California enterprises with businesses from other states.[47]

The California Administrative Procedure Act requirements generally apply to all rules, but there are some stricter requirements for certain agencies and certain types of rules. In 1993, the legislature added a provision to the Act to allow the California Environmental Protection Agency (Cal EPA), Resources Agency, and the Office of the Fire Marshall to adopt a regulation that is substantially different from federal requirements only if it is authorized by state law or the agency shows that the costs are justified by the benefits.[48] The CAPA does not require an agency to compare benefits and costs anywhere else in the statute. Another provision enacted in 1993 required the Cal EPA to evaluate, for all major rules, whether a less costly alternative exists that would achieve the same level of environmental pro-

---

[43] Cal. Gov't Code § 11340.

[44] See California Trade and Commerce Agency, *supra* note 41, at 20. The date and derivation of the cost-savings estimate is not documented.

[45] Cal. Gov't Code § 11346 (1999).

[46] 1991 Cal. Stat. 794.

[47] 1992 Cal. Stat. 1306; and 1993 Cal. Stat. 1038, 1063.

[48] 1993 Cal. Stat. 1046.

tection as the proposed policy.[49] The provision thus expanded the CAPA's existing requirement to describe alternatives for all rules.[50]

Since the Office of Administrative Law does not evaluate the economic impact of proposed rules, the legislature introduced a statutory oversight mechanism to ensure such analysis played a role in the regulatory process.[51] The bill established the secretary of trade and commerce as an advisor to the review process. It authorized the secretary to review an agency's evaluation of the impact of its proposed regulation and to submit written comments to the agency explaining any observed deficiencies. The Regulation Review Unit (RRU) of the Trade and Commerce Department performs these tasks. The unit helps agencies decide which information the agencies should use for their analyses and include in the final report and also is a resource to the agencies on the practical application of benefit-cost analysis.[52] The unit can help agencies conduct better analyses, but it cannot veto rules. If the analysis is deficient, the Regulation Review Unit can only communicate its concerns to the agency. Only the Office of Administrative Law can veto a regulation if it is not "acceptable." States must have oversight entities with the power to evaluate the economic analysis, as well as the legality, of a rule to truly achieve regulatory reform.

The Regulation Review Unit was established in December 1995, so it is too early to evaluate its long-term impact on the regulatory process. There are, however, some early examples of the unit's positive contributions to the process. In one case, the RRU identified an adverse annual impact of tens of million of dollars from a proposed rule to restrict the use of state property.[53] The agency intended the regulation to restrict vendors, such as hot dog stands and coffee carts. It would have prohibited other commercial activities, such as filming, on state property—an impact the promulgating agency did not originally consider. Subsequent to the RRU's comments, the agency modified the rule. This case illustrates that review by outside parties may help agencies correct many obvious, unintentional errors. Even if the monetary benefits of these interventions are somewhat overstated, the expe-

---

[49] 1993 Cal. Stat. 418.

[50] A major regulation is a rule with an impact on the private sector that exceeds $10 million. See 1993 Cal. Stat. 418 § 57,005 (a).

[51] 1993 Cal. Stat. 418.

[52] See California Trade and Commerce Agency, Regulation Review Unit, Bringing Economic Sense to Regulation: Impact Assessment Information and Criteria, Draft Report (1996); and California Trade and Commerce Agency, Regulation Review Unit, Economic Impact Statement Instructions: California State Administrative Manual § 6680 (1998).

[53] California Trade and Commerce Agency, Regulation Review Unit, Improving Regulations and Rulemaking 22 (1997).

rience in California illustrates the potential benefits of holding regulators accountable by assigning an oversight function to an entity with economic expertise.

Beyond the statutory mandates for analysis and review, Governor Wilson has signed numerous executive orders to encourage further regulatory reform. In 1995, he signed an executive order that required agencies to review each regulation and identify all rules suitable for repeal.[54] This process identified 3,900 regulations for repeal and 1,700 for modification.[55] As with all other states, there is no comprehensive assessment of the economic impact of these activities. A 1996 executive order required the formation of a regulatory review task force to conduct public meetings and make specific recommendations to further reform the regulatory process. The Governor's Office of Planning and Research coordinated regional hearings, collected comments and recommendations from more than 300 individuals, and presented 10 recommendations.[56] These recommendations ranged from the expansion of a one-stop permit program to better enforcement of existing regulations.[57]

The governor appeared to take the recommendations seriously. He addressed half of the recommendations from the regulatory review task force to some extent in an executive order issued in January of 1997.[58] To partially address the request for periodic sunset reviews, for example, the governor ordered a one-time sunset review of all existing regulation by 1999.[59] This is perhaps the most significant provision in the executive order because it states an explicit goal to reduce total compliance costs by 5 percent per year. The governor previously had ordered a review of all regulations with only a vague goal to reduce the excessive burdens from regulation.[60] Other

[54] Cal. Exec. Order No. W-127-95 (1995). In 1996, Governor Wilson issued another executive order to require agencies to submit all regulations the agency recommended for repeal or modification to the Office of Administrative Law for appropriate regulatory action (Cal. Exec. Order No. W-131-96 (1996)).

[55] Cal. Exec. Order No. W-131-96.

[56] California Governor's Office of Planning and Research, Recommendations from the Regulatory Review Roundtables (1996).

[57] Id.

[58] Cal. Exec. Order No. W-144-97 (1997).

[59] Other recommendations implemented by the executive order include the publication of a Consolidated Regulatory Program that expands the annual Regulatory Calendar to include information on the estimated costs of all proposed regulations, a review of all existing statutes and administrative provisions to help adjust the severity of fines for minor violations of regulations that do not endanger public health or safety, and customer service surveys implemented by each agency to ensure continuous feedback from the regulated community on how to improve the regulatory process.

[60] Cal. Exec. Order No. W-127-95.

states with a quantitative goal focus on the reduction of the total number of rules, which has an ambiguous effect on the regulatory burden because agencies can combine regulations to reduce the total number.[61] California is, therefore, the only state with an explicit goal that may reduce the regulatory burden.[62]

The criteria agencies must use to review existing regulations are similar to the California Administrative Procedures Act requirements for proposed regulations. The agencies must review the authority, necessity, and cost-effectiveness of rules,[63] update the fiscal and economic effects of the rules, minimize duplication and inconsistencies with federal and local regulations, and consider less burdensome alternatives to achieve regulatory goals. Each agency must also calculate cost savings from their efforts and show it has achieved a 5 percent reduction in compliance costs.[64] The results of the review are unclear since the process is still in progress. If the agencies comply with the requirements of the 1997 executive order, California will have an estimate of the total costs of state regulation. This data would be invaluable to decision makers attempting to assess the effectiveness and efficiency of existing regulatory programs and could help guide them toward economically efficient reform efforts in the future.

The executive order also requires agencies to provide an Economic and Fiscal Impact Statement as part of the rule-making record, a requirement that builds on previous efforts to incorporate a standard economic impact statement into the rule-making process. The Economic and Fiscal Impact Statement is not a substitute for the analyses and documentation required by the California Administrative Procedures Act, but a supplement designed to provide a clear and concise summary of the economic effects identified in the analyses.[65] California had a standard format for the Economic and Fiscal Impact Statement before the executive order but had no equivalent form for the economic impact assessment required by the CAPA. The Department

---

[61] For example, Florida has a goal to halve the number of rules in the Administrative Code. See the next case study for a detailed discussion.

[62] The executive order directs the agencies to change regulations by considering alternative approaches that are less intrusive or more cost-effective. This order does not explicitly require that rules maintain the same level of regulatory protection. Therefore, if a rule is modified to reduce compliance costs and the social benefits from the regulation are also reduced, the net effect may be to reduce economic efficiency.

[63] Specifically, agencies must show that the benefits from a different requirement exceed the additional costs of a more stringent state regulation.

[64] The executive order allows agencies to include the cost savings from actions taken under Cal. Exec. Order No. W-131-96.

[65] The Office of Regulatory Reform in Michigan and the Independent Regulatory Review Commission in Pennsylvania both require agencies to complete a similar form.

of Finance issued a four-page form for the new impact statement to help agencies comply with the requirement, and the Regulation Review Unit developed explicit instructions to help agencies fill out the form.[66]

A standard form forces California agencies to clearly state their findings about various types of economic effects. The new statement allows qualitative responses in some cases, but it does not allow responses such as "inapplicable" or "unknown" without further information to clarify the response.[67] One of the major problems with regulatory impact analysis at the federal level is a lack of consistency in the presentation of information.[68] Even if an agency develops a regulatory impact analysis, the process through which an agency arrives at its final calculations is often unclear. The agency also does not usually provide a concise summary statement of the findings from the analysis.[69] A standard form will allow the Regulation Review Unit, as well as other interested parties, to easily review an agency's economic impact estimates. If the Regulation Review Unit determines the analysis is deficient, it can provide comments that the agency must address in writing. The Economic and Fiscal Impact Statement therefore helps increase transparency and accountability in the regulatory process.

No documentation of the actual efficiency gains from the recent reform efforts currently exists. Evidence suggests, however, that California is moving in the right direction. Statutory requirements do not ensure compliance, but California has laid a solid foundation by amending the California Administrative Procedures Act to encourage agencies to analyze the economic effects of regulation and to improve oversight processes. Governor Wilson has complemented these efforts with several initiatives to increase the use of economic analysis for both proposed and existing regulations and has made an effort to incorporate suggestions from the regulated community on improving the regulatory process. The actual economic impact deserves further study as the changes begin to take hold.

[66] California Trade and Commerce Agency, *supra* note 52.

[67] It also discourages the use of vague descriptions such as "few," "minor," and "occasional" without further explanation. See *id.* at 1.

[68] For a detailed review of federal regulatory impact analyses, see Robert W. Hahn, Regulatory Reform: What Do the Government's Numbers Tell Us? in Hahn ed., *supra* note 37.

[69] For a summary of economic information contained in recent Federal Register notices and suggestions for improvement of the presentation and content of that information, see Robert W. Hahn, How Changes in the Federal Register Can Help Improve Regulatory Accountability (AEI-Brookings Joint Center for Regulatory Studies Working Paper No. 98-1, 1998).

Florida

Florida enacted the Florida Administrative Procedures Act (FAPA) with provisions for economic analysis in the early 1970s, but major efforts to overhaul the rule-making process did not occur until 1995.[70] Democratic Governor Lawton Chiles was noticeably silent on regulatory reform issues prior to his reelection in 1994. He made the issue a top priority with his inaugural speech in January of 1995, however, in part to build bridges with reform-minded Republicans who made major gains in the state legislature in the 1994 election. Governor Chiles identified two primary goals for the reform effort: (1) to reduce rules and regulations by 50 percent within 2 years and (2) to reduce the inflexibility of rules by increasing agency discretion in the rule-making process.[71]

To achieve his two goals, the governor signed two executive orders and the 1996 amendments to the FAPA into law. The two executive orders directed all agencies to conduct a page-by-page review of all rules and to eliminate and revise them as necessary.[72] The 1996 amendments, which the legislature passed after the governor vetoed less rigorous amendments in 1995, also furthered the effort to reduce the number of regulations because they contain provisions to hold agencies more accountable for the economic impact of regulations. The accountability provisions include language that requires agencies to choose the "least-cost" alternative subject to judicial and internal review, limitations on agency rule makings without explicit legislative authority, and a sunset provision for existing rules.[73] The amendments also shift the burden of proof to agencies if regulated parties challenge the rule. All of these provisions make it more difficult for agencies to promulgate regulations and therefore are consistent with the governor's commitment to reducing the number of Florida rules.

The 1996 amendments also reflect the governor's agreement with the sentiments of *The Death of Common Sense* by Philip Howard, who argued that government could constructively reform regulation through greater agency discretion.[74] The 1996 amendments contained a "waiver" provision to allow agencies to grant exceptions to rules and therefore supposedly increased the flexibility of agency rule making. The statute requires the

[70] Jim Rossi, The 1996 Revised Florida Administrative Procedure Act: A Rulemaking Revolution or Counter-revolution? 49 Admin. L. Rev. Am. U. 362 (1996).

[71] *Id.*

[72] Fla. Exec. Order Nos. 95-74 & 95-256 (1995).

[73] Rossi, *supra* note 70, at 353.

[74] See Phillip K. Howard, Death of Common Sense: How Law Is Suffocating America (1994).

agency to grant waivers when the rule creates a "substantial hardship" or when the purpose of the statute can be achieved by "other means."[75] The governor's personal frustration with government bureaucracy supported the waiver provision, as he frequently told the story of the red tape he encountered when he attempted to add a cook shack to his log cabin in the woods.[76]

Despite the amount of political muscle devoted to reform in Florida, it appears that the initiatives have had less substantive impact on policy than originally hoped for by the governor and other legislators. The governor's goal to reduce the number of rules by 50 percent has not resulted in the expected reduction in the regulatory burden, although agencies purged many outdated regulations from the record. Florida defines a rule as a rule section of the Florida Administrative Code.[77] As a result, Florida eliminated regulations in response to the governor's mandate by simply merging sections of the Administrative Code. Florida also repealed many procedural and technical rules that did not substantively affect the agency's original policies.[78] Florida repealed close to 10,000 rules and was in the process of repealing almost 500 more by mid-1997,[79] but it appears that few substantive changes to regulations have been made. The staff of the Committee on Governmental Rules and Regulations systematically reviewed 5 percent of the repealed rules to determine whether the policy followed by the agencies changed as a result of the repeals.[80] Of the 251 rules in the sample, agencies did not use 44 percent, integrated 26 percent into new or existing rules, and moved 6 percent to agency policy or procedure. Approximately 4 percent exist in some other form.[81] If this sample is any indication of all repealed rules, it is clear that the so-called repeal of rules did not necessarily result in the expected policy changes.

Although it is perhaps too soon to tell, the waiver provision and the accountability provisions in the 1996 FAPA amendments also may not work as intended. The legislature enacted the waiver provision to help agencies avoid difficulties stemming from inflexible regulation, similar to those en-

[75] Fla. Stat. § 120.54 (2) (1996).

[76] Lawton Chiles, Inaugural Address (Office of the Governor, State of Florida, January 3, 1995).

[77] Fla. Exec. Order No. 95-74.

[78] Personal communication by Petrea Moyle, Research Associate, AEI-Brookings Joint Center for Regulatory Studies, with Jim Rossi, Florida State University College of Law (November 23, 1998).

[79] Committee on Governmental Rules and Regulation, Rules Reduction Efforts in Florida: Florida House of Representatives, Government Responsibility Council 2 (1997).

[80] The staff ordered all of the repealed rules by their Florida Administrative Code chapter number and included every twentieth rule in the sample. See id. at 4.

[81] The status of over 20 percent of the rules could not be determined.

countered by the governor when he built his cook shack.[82] Interest groups may, however, influence the regulatory agency by exerting pressure for waivers, and the agency may mold policy using the waiver system to suit its own agenda. The agency could, for example, grant waivers for environmental projects because of internal agency bias toward environmental protection measures. These unintended effects of the waiver provision are in part possible because Florida did not create an oversight mechanism to hold the agencies accountable for their actions when it enacted the waiver provision. Moreover, the move to increase agency discretion is contrary to the original intent of Section 120.535 in FAPA, which was added in 1991 to reduce agency discretion because of the failure of agencies to publish rules they enforced.[83,84] The governor wanted the legislature to repeal this provision because he views such mandates as an "effort by the legislature to micromanage the whole government."[85] The legislature would not repeal the provision, so the governor eventually compromised and agreed to the waiver provision in the 1996 amendments.

Although some of the regulatory reform efforts in Florida appear unsuccessful, Florida is still ahead of other states in its drive to integrate economic analysis into the rule-making process. The 1996 FAPA amendments require a statement of estimated regulatory impact, which replaced the economic impact statement required in the original 1974 Act.[86] The FAPA encourages agencies to develop regulatory impact statements for almost all rules.[87] The agency must produce a regulatory impact statement when a "substantially affected" person submits a lower cost alternative that achieves the same statutory goal.[88] The statement must contain specific information, including the number of individuals and entities likely to be affected, budgetary costs to state and local government agencies, compliance costs to individuals and entities, and an analysis of the effects on small

---

[82] Rossi, *supra* note 70, at 354.

[83] Fla. Stat. § 120.54 (1)(a) (1996).

[84] Fla. Stat. § 120.54 (7) (1996).

[85] The governor vetoed a bill to revise the Administrative Procedures Act in 1995, criticizing the legislature for not repealing these provisions. See Veto Message from Governor Chiles to Hon. Sandra Mortham, Secretary of State (July 12, 1995), cited in Stephen T. Maher, The Death of Rules: How Politics Is Suffocating Florida, 8 St. Thomas L. Rev. 316, 340 (1996).

[86] The original Florida Administrative Procedures Act, passed in 1974, contained a requirement for agencies to prepare an economic impact statement for all proposed rules. The requirement was modified in 1992 to limit the coverage to rules agencies determine have a significant adverse impact or when the governor, a corporation, or at least 100 people filed a written request. See Rossi, *supra* note 70, at 362–63.

[87] Fla. Stat. § 120.54 (3) (b) (1996).

[88] Fla. Stat. § 120.54(1) (1996).

businesses, counties, and cities.[89] The agency also must show a rule is preferable to the proposed alternative.[90] The state may veto the rule if the agency does not choose the least-cost alternative that accomplishes the statutory goal.[91] Thus, although the FAPA does not mandate a benefit-cost test, it requires a cost-effectiveness test for which the agencies are accountable.[92]

No significant gains in economic efficiency are likely to result from the governor's efforts to reduce the number of rules and to increase agency flexibility because they are not coupled with adequate oversight to ensure that agencies reduce the regulatory burden. The state may, however, benefit from the recent changes to the FAPA that induce agencies to apply cost-effectiveness criterion as they develop regulations. Without an oversight entity to check an agency's regulatory impact statement for potential problems, however, the use of cost-effectiveness analysis may also not achieve desired improvements in the regulatory process.

New York

New York has long promoted regulatory reform and has increased the level of its reform efforts in recent years. The state first required a regulatory impact statement for certain rules in 1980 by an executive order and later incorporated it into the New York Administrative Procedures Act (NYAPA).[93] The legislature has expanded the analysis requirements in the NYAPA steadily over the past 2 decades to include specific considerations, such as regulatory flexibility analysis to reduce disproportionate effects on small businesses and localities.[94]

The central executive branch office has reviewed proposed rules since the early 1980s. The legislature created the Office of Business Permits in 1980 to serve as a central clearinghouse for information about the numerous state permit requirements, changed the name of the office to the Office of Busi-

---

[89] Fla. Stat. § 120.54(2) (1996).

[90] Fla. Stat. § 120.541 (1) (b) (1996).

[91] Fla. Stat. §§ 120.52 (8) (g), 120.541 (1) (c) (1996).

[92] For a detailed discussion, see Rossi, *supra* note 70, at 365–67.

[93] N.Y. Exec. Order No. 100 (1980); and New York State Administrative Procedures Act § 202-a (1999). For a detailed discussion of the New York State Administrative Procedures Act, see Patrick J. Brochers & David L. Markell, New York Administrative Procedure and Practice (1995).

[94] New York State Administrative Procedures Act § 202-b. Other requirements include rural area flexibility analysis for reducing disproportionate impact on rural areas and job impact analysis to assess the impact on employment. See New York State Administrative Procedures Act § 202-bb and § 201-a.

ness Permits and Regulatory Assistance,[95] and expanded its responsibilities to include the review of required regulatory analyses.[96] Changes to the NYAPA codified the regulatory review functions of the Office of Business Permits and Regulatory Assistance.[97] The NYAPA required the office to determine whether each rule (1) is clearly written; (2) is consistent with the legislative purpose, existing statutes, and existing rules; (3) is a duplication of an existing state statute, federal statute, or rule; and (4) has been analyzed adequately by the appropriate entity. The state did not require the Office of Business Permits and Regulatory Assistance to balance the benefits and costs of rules.

The state renamed the office again in 1993 to the Office of Regulatory and Management Assistance and expanded its functions. Governor Cuomo expanded the Regulatory Reform Program initiated in 1988 and designated the Office of Regulatory and Management Assistance as the coordinating office.[98] The Office of Regulatory and Management Assistance's functions were similar to those of the federal government's Office of Information and Regulatory Affairs in the Office of Management and Budget.[99] The Office of Regulatory and Management Assistance did not have veto power, but the NYAPA required agencies to respond to its comments and objections or the Office could force the agencies to withdraw the rule.[100]

Even with statutory requirements for analysis and review and gubernatorial initiatives to reform the regulatory process, the burdens of regulation in New York continued to grow. In response to the public's growing discontent with an unwieldy bureaucracy and burdensome regulatory requirements, Governor Pataki made regulatory reform a top priority upon taking office in 1995.[101] As one of his first actions as governor, he signed an executive order that placed a 90-day moratorium on new rules and directed state regulatory agencies to evaluate the economic effects of all existing regulations.[102] Later that year, he established the Governor's Office of Regulatory

---

[95] See N.Y. Exec. Law § 878 (1999).

[96] See N.Y. Exec. Order No. 131 (1989).

[97] See New York State Administrative Procedures Act § 202-c (1995). This section expired on December 31, 1995.

[98] See N.Y. Exec. Order Nos. 108 (1988) & 108.1 (1993).

[99] Brochers & Markell, *supra* note 93, at 105.

[100] See New York State Administrative Procedures Act § 202-c(6) (1995). This section expired on December 31, 1995.

[101] See, for example, George E. Pataki, Inaugural Address (Office of the Governor, State of New York, 1995).

[102] N.Y. Exec. Order No. 2 (1995). The moratorium was later extended by N.Y. Exec. Order No. 7 (1995).

Reform (GORR) as the central office to review the effects of proposed regulatory activities, taking over the function of the Office of Regulatory and Management Assistance.[103] He also expanded requirements for agencies to assess the economic impact of proposed rules.[104]

Some measurable outputs resulted from the executive orders and the GORR's efforts over the last 3 years. A database of "regulatory successes" shows that the GORR's intervention in the proposed rule-making stage of the process has led to annual compliance cost savings of over $200 million.[105] Table 5 summarizes four interventions by the GORR, two of which account for almost all of the cost savings. The first is an effort by the GORR and the Department of Environmental Conservation to overhaul the draft of a rule to implement a Clean Air Act regulation. The review reduced industry costs by $5.5 million compared to the original draft of the regulation. The second was the GORR's rejection of a proposed regulation to make buildings more earthquake resistant. The GORR rejected the rule twice because of a lack of adequate scientific data to support a stricter building code. The agency finally withdrew this rule, which would have increased new construction costs by $220 million annually.

The GORR may also have contributed to real cost savings totaling $600 million annually resulting from the review of existing regulations.[106] Table 6 summarizes 10 of these rules. The state repealed, for example, an archaic regulation restricting hearses from traveling on certain parkways. The regulation cost funeral home owners $8 million annually in increased transportation and travel time costs. The state also repealed a 1994 regulation requiring the installation of reflective signs on the *bottom* of hotel and dorm room doors to indicate the room number. The rule was a result of a suggestion from a concerned sixth grader who believed the signs would aid people crawling through the halls during an evacuation. The agency implemented the rule without any scientific evidence to show its dedication to improving safety. The repeal of this rule produced a one-time compliance cost savings of $340,000 and annual savings of $11,000.

---

[103] The statutory authority of Office of Business Permits and Regulatory Assistance/Office of Regulatory and Management Assistance expired on December 31, 1995. See N.Y. Exec. Law § 893 (1999).

[104] N.Y. Exec. Order No. 20 (1995). An amendment to the State Administrative Procedures Act in 1996 now requires that the state review all rules adopted after the effective date of the section every 5 years. See 1996 N.Y. Laws § 262, codified in New York State Administrative Procedures Act § 207.

[105] Governor's Office of Regulatory Reform's web page, Success Stories in Regulatory Reform, http://www.state.ny.us/gorr/success.html (August 3, 1997). A lack of formal documentation prevented the identification of the precise basis for the cost savings estimates.

[106] *Id.*

TABLE 5

EXAMPLES OF COST SAVINGS FROM NEW YORK'S REVIEW OF PROPOSED REGULATION

Regulation	Summary	Agency Action	Savings
Building Code	Proposed regulations to make buildings more earthquake resistant were twice rejected by Governor's Office of Regulatory Reform (GORR) for lacking adequate scientific evidence. The proposal was finally withdrawn.	Withdraw	The proposed regulation would have added 3%–4% to the cost of new construction, approximately $220 million a year.
Clean Air Act Regulation	A cooperative effort between GORR and Department of Environmental Conservation (DEC) overhauled a draft regulation to comply with federal Clean Air Act requirements.	Amend	The amendments saved industry $5.5 million.
Fishing	GORR worked with DEC to withdraw a proposed regulation requiring fisheries to tag every black bass. This regulation strove to curb trafficking of illegal bass. An effective but less burdensome alternative was the use of identifiable containers.	Withdraw	The proposed regulation would have caused each fishery operator $20,000 a year to comply.
Food-Processing Waste	DEC circulated a draft regulation imposing new restrictive permitting requirements for food-processing waste and sludge. Instead of implementing the regulation, regulators and stakeholders developed voluntary protocol for the beneficial use of these by-products.	Withdraw	N.A.

SOURCE.—Estimates are from the Governor's Office of Regulatory Reform's web page, Success Stories in Regulatory Reform, http://www.state.ny.us/gorr/success.html (August 3, 1997).
NOTE.—N.A. = not applicable.

TABLE 6

EXAMPLES OF COST SAVINGS FROM NEW YORK'S REVIEW OF EXISTING REGULATION

Regulation	Summary	Agency Action	Savings
Medicaid Reimbursement for Clozapine	This rule changes the cumbersome prior approval process for Medicaid reimbursement to allow easier access to the drug Clozapine. It allows more schizophrenic patients to avoid confinement in psychiatric centers.	Amend	Prior approval was required due to the high cost of Clozapine, but the avoided psychiatric center costs will save taxpayers at least $17 million a year.
Telephone Billing	The rule change proposed by the Department of Public Service allows telephone companies to validate proof of identity for applicants. It also requires phone bills to clearly list the name of the billing company and a contact number.	Amend	This rule allows phone companies to validate the identity of applicants, saving an estimated $12.5 million yearly in uncollected bills.
Licensing of Cosmetologists	The Department of State eliminated the requirement for cosmetologists to have a doctor's signature verifying that he/she has no communicable disease when renewing a license.	Amend	Removing this requirement saves $8.6 million a year in doctors' fees, in addition to the time saved.
Highway Travel Restrictions for Hearses	The Department of Transportation and the Governor's Office of Regulatory Reform (GORR) are working to eliminate a regulation that prohibits hearses from traveling on selected parkways.	Repeal	Elimination of this rule saves $8 million a year in added transportation costs.

Transfer of Foreign Nationals	The proposed changes create uniform procedures for the voluntary transfer of incarcerated foreign nationals.	Amend, repeal	This will create an annual savings to New York of $6.3 million.
Nursing Home Regulations	The Health Department is eliminating a rule that requires a 30-day notice before moving a resident to a different room.	Repeal	This change reduces delays in admitting new patients that could save them $1.5 million a year.
Hospital Volunteers	The Health Department proposes a less stringent medical check than currently required for people interested in volunteering.	Amend	The new requirement will save hospitals $1.6 million per year.
Newborn Foot Printing	The Health Department eliminated the requirement for all newborns to be foot printed and their mothers fingerprinted. Footprints were rarely used for identification and new technology makes this method obsolete.	Repeal	Repealing this requirement saves hospitals $1.5 million a year.
Termite Control	The proposed rule lowers the restrictions for the application of termite control chemicals.	Amend	The changes will produce a savings of $1.4 million per year for homeowners.
Hotel Room Signs	A 1994 regulation required the installation of reflective signs on the doors of hotel and dorm rooms. The rule was based on the suggestion of a sixth grader concerned about fire safety. The rule was repealed.	Repeal	The removal of the rule produced a one-time savings of $340,000 and an annual savings of $11,000.

SOURCE.—Estimates are from the Governor's Office of Regulatory Reform's web page, Success Stories in Regulatory Reform, http://www.state.ny.us/gorr/success.html (August 3, 1997).

The cost savings estimates must be interpreted carefully, however, for two reasons. First, many of these costs represent potential regulatory costs and not an actual reduction in a regulatory burden. Second, it is difficult to determine which policy the agency would have implemented absent the GORR's intervention. For example, the agency may have redesigned a rule with large compliance costs as a result of the notice and comment process. Although agencies do not seriously consider all comments during the notice and comment process, they do tend to incorporate suggestions from interested parties with significant political clout. The agency may therefore have switched to a less burdensome alternative during this process, even without the existence of the GORR.

New York's reform efforts show that analysis and review requirements do not necessarily result in cost-effective regulation. Even with the reform initiatives in place during the 1980s and early 1990s, agencies adopted rules like the requirement for reflective door signs. The New York Administrative Procedures Act and executive orders provide the necessary authority to implement a reform program, but it took a central agency with the political backing of the governor to have a noticeable impact.

Virginia

The Virginia Administrative Process Act (VAPA) has required agencies to assess the compliance costs of regulations since 1977,[107] but in the early 1990s agencies presented compliance cost estimates for less than 20 percent of rules in the state *Register*.[108] To improve compliance with statutory requirements, the legislature passed amendments to the VAPA to change the structure of the analysis and review process. In addition, newly elected governor George Allen signed executive orders to facilitate the implementation of these changes and called for the analysis and review of existing regulations.[109] These efforts led agencies to some improved documentation of regulatory benefits and costs.[110]

A 1994 VAPA amendment shifted the responsibility for conducting the

---

[107] Va. Code § 9-6.14:7.1 (1999).

[108] Since 1989, Virginia's Administrative Process Act has required the publication of a concise statement of estimated regulatory effects. See Va. Code § 9-614:7.1(C). The Joint Legislative Audit and Review Committee reviewed all 217 rules proposed in the 1990–91 regulatory year and found that only 16 percent of rules provided estimates of compliance costs to regulated entities. See Virginia General Assembly, Joint Legislative Audit and Review Committee, Review of Virginia's administrative Procedures Act: House Document No. 51, at 48–51 (1993).

[109] Va. Exec. Order Nos. 14 & 15 (1994).

[110] Virginia Dep't of Planning and Budget, A Comprehensive Review of Existing State Regulations 3 (1997).

economic impact analysis from individual agencies to the Department of Planning and Budget (DPB).[111] The DPB now coordinates with the agencies to prepare economic analyses for all rules. These analyses must contain information such as the projected costs to affected businesses and the projected number of affected businesses and local governments. The state further amended the VAPA in 1995 to require agencies to include an estimate of the fiscal impact on localities[112] and the impact on the use and value of private property.[113] The DPB reports that agencies' compliance with the cost-reporting requirements is now 100 percent, compared with 20 percent just a few years ago.[114]

Virginia is the only state that designates a central entity to review agency data and prepare an analysis of regulatory effects. To assess the quality of the state's completed analyses, copies of all economic impact analyses that the DPB produced from September of 1995 through April of 1997 were obtained. A database was then constructed that contains summary information about each of the rules along with the DPB's economic impact estimates if available. The database also scores each rule on whether the DPB assessed costs or cost savings, quantified benefits, and monetized benefits.[115] In addition, the database notes whether the DPB believed the rule would produce net benefits to the state.

Table 7 presents the scorecard for the DPB's preparation of economic impact analyses. In almost all cases, rules either affect very few firms or they change minor procedures and do not result in a significant change in compliance costs. Many rules actually have cost savings because they are modifications to existing regulations in response to Governor Allen's review of existing regulations discussed below. The DPB, however, presents estimates of costs or cost savings or states that there are no costs or cost savings in only 55 percent of the economic impact analyses. In 26 percent of the economic impact analyses, DPB found zero costs or cost savings. These rules represent nearly half of all rules for which DPB assesses the cost or cost savings. Only 5 percent of economic impact analyses quantified benefits, and only 4 percent monetized benefits.

In general, the analyses qualitatively describe the economic effects but

---

[111] 1994 Va. Acts ch. 938.

[112] This analysis requirement was added by 1995 Va. Acts ch. 790.

[113] This analysis requirement was added by 1995 Va. Acts ch. 677.

[114] Virginia Dep't of Planning and Budget, *supra* note 110, at 3.

[115] Costs include compliance costs experienced by the regulated entity or administrative costs to the regulator. Cost savings refer to a reduction in these compliance or administrative costs. Although cost savings can be viewed as a benefit, the economic impact analyses do not seem to consider them a benefit. Monetized benefits are quantified benefits converted to a dollar value.

TABLE 7

VIRGINIA'S REGULATORY SCORECARD

	Economic Impact Analyses
Costs or cost savings quantified:	
DPB found nonzero costs or cost savings	32 (29%)
DPB found zero costs or cost savings	29 (26%)
DPB did not state costs or cost savings	50 (45%)
Benefits quantified:	
DPB quantified positive benefits	6 (5%)
DPB found zero benefits	33 (30%)
DPB did not state benefits	72 (65%)
Benefits monetized:	
DPB monetized positive benefits	4 (4%)
DPB found zero benefits	33 (30%)
DPB did not state benefits	74 (67%)
DPB states the benefits are likely to exceed the costs[a]	50 (45%)

NOTE.—Values are based on author's review of 111 economic impact analyses (EIAs) prepared by the Department of Planning and Budget (DPB).

[a] An EIA qualified for this category if the DPB attempted to determine whether benefits exceed costs. Since the data are uncertain, the DPB expressed varying levels of confidence in their conclusions.

provide no quantitative support. Many analyses note that the cost of quantifying the effects would be prohibitively large. Only in a few cases are the estimated effects clearly presented in a tabular format. Often analyses use vague language and present a few numbers without putting these numbers in context or noting the most likely economic effects. The analyses often do not provide the base year for the impact, the year dollar for the cost estimates, or probabilities of the likelihood of the outcome. As these are basic components of a thorough economic impact analysis, it appears that no oversight entity critically reviewed the agency evaluations. The DPB's assertion that 45 percent of the regulations it assessed produce net benefits to the state is therefore questionable.

Although some of the DPB analyses are obviously inadequate, the information presented in many of the analyses seems sufficient given the purpose of the rules. Rules that change fees slightly or require a slightly different procedure for applying for a license, for example, may require only a concise statement of the objectives of the rules and the potential benefits and costs. It is not clear, however, that the state allocates enough resources for review of regulations with more significant effects.

Although analyses of more ''significant'' rules are generally longer than the analyses of rules with lesser economic impact, they do not appear much more sophisticated. Because the DPB has reviewed rules for only a few years, the quality of analysis will probably improve over time. The more important question is whether the analyses have had any impact on policy. The DPB states that the analyses have "been widely cited and have actively fueled public debate on specific regulatory initiatives,"[116] but the actual impact of the analyses is not well documented.

Governor Allen's 1994 executive order resulted in some documented savings because it directed agencies to review all existing regulations to reduce the regulatory burden.[117] Over a 3-year period, the agencies reviewed 1,457 regulations and recommended the elimination of 30 percent of the rules and the modification of 41 percent of the rules. The cost savings reported in many of the economic impact analyses resulted from these reforms. The DPB did not compile an aggregate savings estimate from its efforts in its report on the comprehensive review of existing regulations, but it did present examples of economic analyses prepared for rules modified under the direction of the executive order.[118] Only two of the 25 analyses estimated the expected cost savings, which combined account for close to $2 million annually. Although Virginia's documented cost savings do not compare to the cost savings claimed by New York, the review efforts have reduced the regulatory burden.

The Virginia example shows that a lack of oversight results in a lack of compliance. The state now has an independent agency conducting the economic analysis, which presumably presents a more balanced assessment than an agency would, although it is not clear to what extent it challenges the assumptions of the agency. The assessment of the economic analyses shows that agencies can improve the analyses, but the DPB is making progress.

IV. CONCLUSION

The examination of regulatory reform initiatives at both the federal and state level reveals their strengths and limitations. Efforts to improve regulation are least effective when requirements are vague and lack specific guidelines and when states do not establish adequate oversight mechanisms. Regulatory reform efforts are most effective when they have active political support and a strong, well-funded, central oversight mechanism exists. Practiced artfully, structured and careful analysis of regulations can help achieve desired social objectives at a lower cost. It can also help agencies

---

[116] Virginia Dep't of Planning and Budget, *supra* note 110, at 3–4.

[117] Va. Exec. Order No. 15 (1994).

[118] See Virginia Dep't of Planning and Budget, *supra* note 110, app. B.

compare the economic costs and benefits of different goals and objectives and will increase the accountability of regulators and lawmakers.

States use different reform mechanisms with varying degrees of effectiveness. All states, however, can improve upon current efforts. Few states assess the economic impact of most rules in detail, even when laws or executive orders encourage or require such analysis. Many states do not systematically review regulations at all. States with ongoing programs should improve them by using stricter statutory language, more detailed guidelines, and more comprehensive oversight mechanisms. States without programs should establish them. All states should carefully document the impact of reform measures to provide much needed information on the effectiveness of reform.

If analysis of the economic impact of rules plays a more prominent nationwide role in the regulatory process, the effectiveness of analytical requirements will most likely increase. As agencies take their analysis and review responsibilities more seriously because of increased oversight and stricter requirements, the quality of analyses will improve. Policy makers will therefore integrate the new information into the decision-making process faster and more willingly than if they suspect the analyses are academically weak or politically motivated. A transparent, well-designed review process will encourage regulators to pursue more efficient policies.

WHY IS COST-BENEFIT ANALYSIS SO CONTROVERSIAL?

ROBERT H. FRANK*

ABSTRACT

The cost-benefit principle says we should take those actions, and only those actions, whose benefits exceed their costs. For many, this principle's commonsensical ring makes it hard to imagine how anyone could disagree. Yet critics of cost-benefit analysis are both numerous and outspoken. Many of them argue that cost-benefit analysis is unacceptable as a matter of principle. I begin by noting why many find this argument largely unpersuasive. I then examine several conventions adopted by cost-benefit analysts that do appear to yield misleading prescriptions. Finally, I consider the possibility that the cost-benefit principle may itself suggest why we might not always want to employ cost-benefit analysis as the explicit rationale for our actions.

THE INCOMMENSURABILITY PROBLEM

THE cost-benefit principle says we should install a guardrail on a dangerous stretch of mountain road if the dollar cost of doing so is less than the implicit dollar value of the injuries, deaths, and property damage thus prevented. Many critics respond that placing a dollar value on human life and suffering is morally illegitimate.[1]

The apparent implication is that we should install the guardrail no matter how much it costs or no matter how little it affects the risk of death and injury.

Given that we live in a world of scarcity, however, this position is difficult to defend. After all, money spent on a guardrail could be used to purchase other things we value, including things that enhance health and safety in other domains. Since we have only so much to spend, why should we install a guardrail if the same money spent on, say, better weather forecasting would prevent even more deaths and injuries?

* Goldwin Smith Professor of Economics, Cornell University. This paper was prepared for presentation at the University of Chicago Law School conference Cost-Benefit Analysis, September 17–18, 1999. I thank William Schulze for helpful discussions.
[1] For an overview, see Robert Kuttner, Everything for Sale (1997).

[*Journal of Legal Studies*, vol. XXIX]

More generally, critics object to the cost-benefit framework's use of a monetary metric to place the pros and cons of an action on a common footing. They complain, for example, that when a power plant pollutes the air, our gains from the cheap power thus obtained simply cannot be compared with the pristine view of the Grand Canyon we sacrifice.

Even the most ardent proponents of cost-benefit analysis concede that comparing disparate categories is extremely difficult in practice. But many critics insist that such comparisons cannot be made even in principle. In their view, the problem is not that we do not know how big a reduction in energy costs would be required to compensate for a given reduction in air quality. Rather, it is that the two categories are simply incommensurable.

This view has troubling implications. In the eyes of the cost-benefit analyst, any action—even one whose costs and benefits are hard to compare—becomes irresistibly attractive if its benefits are sufficiently large and its costs are sufficiently small. Indeed, few people would oppose a new technology that would reduce the cost of power by half if its only negative effect were to degrade our view of the Grand Canyon for just one 15-second interval each decade.[2] By the same token, no one would favor adoption of a technology that produced only a negligible reduction in the cost of power at the expense of a dark cloud that continuously shielded North America from the rays of the Sun. We live in a continuous world. If the first technology is clearly acceptable, and the second clearly unacceptable, some intermediate technology is neither better nor worse than the status quo. And we should count any technology that is better than that one as an improvement.

Scarcity is a simple fact of the human condition. To have more of one good thing, we must settle for less of another. Claiming that different values are incommensurable simply hinders clear thinking about difficult trade-offs.

Notwithstanding their public pronouncements about incommensurability, even the fiercest critics of cost-benefit analysis cannot escape such trade-offs. For example, they do not vacuum their houses several times a day, nor do they get their brakes checked every morning. The reason, presumably, is not that clean air and auto safety do not matter, but that they have more pressing uses of their time. Like the rest of us, they are forced to make the best accommodations they can between competing values.

---

[2] The few who did object would likely invoke a variation of the "slippery-slope" argument, which holds that allowing even a single small step will lead to an inevitable slide to the bottom. Yet we move partway down slippery slopes all the time, as when we amend the laws of free speech to prohibit people from yelling "fire" in a crowded theater in which there is no fire.

GENERAL RESERVATIONS ABOUT CONSEQUENTIALIST ETHICS

Many critics of cost-benefit analysis fault it for being rooted in utilitarianism or some closely related form of consequentialist ethical theory.[3] Consequentialist theories hold that the right course of action is the one that leads to the best consequences, where ''consequences'' under the utilitarian variant means ''highest total utility.'' Critics often attack consequentialism by citing examples in which its purported conclusions clash with the reader's ethical intuitions. One popular example invokes the ''utility monster,'' someone who transforms resources into utility far more efficiently than anyone else. Critics argue that since utilitarianism says the best outcome is to give all resources to the utility monster, and since we know this to be an absurd conclusion, we must reject the ethical theory upon which cost-benefit analysis rests.

Consequentialist moral philosophers have attempted to show that their theories, properly construed, do not imply the conclusions suggested by such examples.[4] But even if these disputes are never fully resolved, we may note that the theories favored by the rival camps reach remarkably similar decisions regarding a broad range of ethical questions. As a practical matter, then, the mere fact that cost-benefit analysis is closely identified with consequentialist ethical theories would not seem to imply that its prescriptions are systematically misleading.

DISCOUNTING THE FUTURE

As traditionally implemented, cost-benefit analysis attempts to put all relevant costs and benefits on a common temporal footing. A discount rate is chosen, which is then used to compute all relevant future costs and benefits in present-value terms. Most commonly, the discount rate used for present-value calculations is an interest rate taken from financial markets.

Though some critics complain about this practice, use of a market interest rate to discount future monetary costs and benefits commands broad approval. After all, if the annual interest rate on financial deposits is 7 percent, one can cover a $1,000 cost 10 years hence by depositing only $500 today.

There is less widespread agreement about using a market interest rate to discount future subjective utility. As Stanley Jevons argued, for example, ''To secure a maximum benefit in life, all future pleasures or pains, should

---

[3] See, for example, Steven Kelman, An Ethical Critique of Cost-Benefit Analysis, 5 Regulation 33 (1981).

[4] See, for example, John Jamieson, Carswell Smart, & Bernard Williams, Utilitarianism: For and Against (1973).

act upon us with the same force as if they were present, allowance being made for their uncertainty . . . But no human mind is constituted in this perfect way: a future feeling is always less influential than a present one.''[5]

On this view, if failure to adopt more stringent air quality standards today means that respiratory illnesses will be more common a generation from now, those illnesses should receive roughly the same weight as if they were to occur today. Having been born later should not mean that one's enjoyment and suffering receive less weight in important policy decisions. Of course, a complete cost-benefit calculation would also want to make allowance for possible improvements in medical technology that would make the consequences of a given illness less severe in the future.

Whatever the ultimate merits of this position, it does not argue against the use of cost-benefit analysis as a matter of principle. If analysts agree that future experiences should receive roughly the same weight as current ones, the costs and benefits associated with any policy change can simply be calculated on that basis.

DISTRIBUTIONAL ISSUES

Distributional issues have long been a favorite target of critics of cost-benefit analysis. Their objection, in a nutshell, is that because willingness to pay is based on income, cost-benefit analysis assigns unjustifiably large decision weight to high-income persons. Implicit in this objection is the view that everyone's preferences regarding policy decisions should receive the same weight, irrespective of income.

Critics presumably have the interests of the poor in mind when they press this objection. Yet it is not clear that the poor themselves would want policy decisions to be made on some basis other than willingness to pay. Consider, for example, a community consisting of three voters—one rich, the other two poor. Up for decision is a proposal to switch the local public radio station from an all-music format to an all-talk format. The rich voter would be willing to pay $1,000 to see this change enacted, while the poor voters would be willing to pay $100 each to prevent it. If each voter's interests are weighted equally, the switch will not be adopted. Yet, in cost-benefit terms, failure to switch results in a net loss of $800.

Under the circumstances, little ingenuity is required to design a proposal that would command unanimous support. The switch could be made conditional, for example, on the rich voter making an additional $500 contribution to the public treasury, which could then be used to reduce the taxes of each poor voter by $250.

---

[5] Stanley Jevons, The Theory of Political Economy 72–73 (1941) (1871).

Critics may respond that although such transfers would be fine in principle, the poor lack the political muscle to assure they are carried out. In an imperfect world, they argue, we get better results by resolving such issues on a one-person, one-vote basis.

But this response simply will not do. If the poor lack the political power to bargain for compensation in return for supporting a policy that harms them, what gives them the power to block that policy in the first place? But if they have that power, they necessarily have the power to bargain for compensation. After all, any policy that passes the cost-benefit test but creates net losses for the poor can be transformed into a Pareto improvement by simply making the tax system more progressive.

Critics of cost-benefit analysis are correct that using unweighted willingness-to-pay measures virtually assures a mix of public programs that are slanted in favor of the preferences of high-income persons. But rather than abandon cost-benefit analysis, we have a better alternative. We can employ unweighted willingness-to-pay measures without apology, and use the welfare and tax system to compensate low-income families ex ante for the resulting injury. The compensation need not—indeed cannot—occur on a case-by-case basis. Rather, low-income persons could simply be granted the welfare and tax breaks required by distributive justice, plus additional concessions reflecting their expected loss from the implementation of cost-benefit analysis using unweighted willingness-to-pay measures.

My point in offering this defense of standard cost-benefit analysis is not that granting additional political power to the poor would be a bad idea. Rather, it is that abandoning cost-benefit analysis is a gratuitously wasteful way of trying to achieve that goal. Rich and poor alike have an interest in making the economic pie as large as possible. Any policy that passes the cost-benefit test makes the economic pie larger. And when the pie is larger, everyone can have a larger slice.

MEASUREMENT PROBLEMS

To discover whether an action satisfies the cost-benefit test, we must come up with concrete measures of its costs and benefits. Notwithstanding the logical difficulties raised by claims of incommensurability, this much is clear: constructing plausible measures of the costs and benefits of specific actions is often very difficult. In practice, analysts try to estimate costs and benefits either by using survey methods or by drawing inferences from market behavior. Both approaches, however, are fraught with difficulty.

SURVEY METHODS

How much is the preservation of a virgin redwood forest worth? Proponents of the contingent-valuation method generate estimates by asking people how much they would be willing to pay to see the forest preserved. Responses in such surveys are problematic for several reasons.

One difficulty is that the valuations are often implausibly large. For example, if the amount someone would pay to prevent a specific stretch of coastline from being fouled by an oil spill were applied to all coastlines worldwide, the resulting sum would typically far exceed his total wealth.[6] Responses in contingent-valuation surveys are also highly sensitive to how questions are phrased and to the format provided for responses.[7]

But perhaps the most troubling feature of contingent-valuation surveys is that respondents are often willing to pay more, by several orders of magnitude, to prevent a harmful effect than to undo a harmful effect that has already occurred. Richard Thaler coined the term "loss aversion" to describe this tendency.[8] Loss aversion means not just that the pain of losing a given amount is larger, for most of us, than the pleasure from gaining that same amount. It is much larger.

Thaler illustrates the asymmetry by asking students to consider the following hypothetical questions:

1. By attending class today, you have been exposed to a rare, fatal disease. The probability that you have the disease is one in a thousand. If you have the disease you will die a quick and painless death in one week. There is a cure for the disease that always works, but it has to be taken now. We do not know how much it will cost. You must say now the most you would be willing to pay for this cure. If the cure ends up costing more you won't get it. If it costs less, you will pay the stated price, not the maximum you stated. How much will you pay?
2. We are conducting experiments on the same disease for which we need subjects. A subject will just have to expose him or herself to the disease and risk a one-in-a-thousand chance of death. What is the minimum fee you would accept to become such a subject?[9]

In each scenario, respondents are asked, in effect, how much they value a one in 1,000 reduction in the probability of death. But whereas the first

[6] See I. Ritov & Daniel Kahneman, How People Value the Environment: Attitudes vs. Economic Values, in Psychological Approaches to Environmental and Ethical Issues in Management 33–51 (M. Bazerman et al. eds. 1997); and Daniel Kahneman & Jack Knetsch, Valuing Public Goods: The Purchase of Moral Satisfaction, 22 J. Envtl. Econ. & Mgmt. 57 (1992).

[7] William H. Desvousges, John W. Payne, & David A. Schkade, How People Respond to Contingent Valuation Questions (EPA Grant No. R824310 Final Report, April 1998).

[8] Richard Thaler, Toward a Positive Theory of Consumer Choice, 1 J. Econ. Behav. & Org. 39 (1980).

[9] Richard Thaler, Precommitment and the Value of a Life, in The Value of Life and Safety 178–79 (M. W. Jones-Lee ed. 1982).

scenario asks how much they would pay to eliminate a risk of death to which they have already been exposed, the second asks them how much they would have to be paid before exposing themselves to a similar risk voluntarily. The median responses were approximately $800 for the first question and $100,000 for the second.[10] Similar disparities between willingness to pay and willingness to accept are observed in contingent-valuation surveys that pose environmental questions.[11] Disparities in other domains are typically smaller, though few surveys find willingness-to-pay values that are more than half as large as the corresponding values for willingness to accept.[12] These disparities, needless to say, pose formidable hurdles for analysts who employ contingent-valuation methods.

HEDONIC METHODS

These and other problems inherent in survey methods have led many analysts to favor hedonic pricing models, which attempt to infer valuations from observable market behavior. In typical applications, analysts estimate the value of noise reduction by examining how residential housing prices vary with ambient noise levels, or the value of safety by examining how wages vary with workplace injury levels.[13]

Hedonic pricing models assume that the wage-safety gradient tells us how much workers value safety. Is this a tenable assumption? The argument in support of it is a simple application of invisible-hand theory. If an amenity—say, a guardrail on a lathe—costs $50 per month to install and maintain, and if workers value it at $100 per month, then firms that do not install one risk losing valued employees to a competitor who does. After all, if a competitor were to pay a worker $60 per month less than he earns from his current employer, it could cover the cost of the safety device with $10 to spare, while providing an overall compensation package that is $40 per month more attractive than his current employer's.

To this argument, critics respond that labor markets are not workably competitive in practice. Incomplete information, worker immobility, and other imperfections force workers to accept whatever conditions employers offer. But even if a firm were the only employer in a labor market, it would

[10] *Id.* at 179.

[11] Ritov & Kahneman, *supra* note 6.

[12] Rebecca Boyce *et al.,* An Experimental Examination of Intrinsic Values as a Source of the WTA-WTP Disparity, 82 Am. Econ. Rev. 1366 (1992).

[13] See, for example, Richard Thaler & Sherwin Rosen, The Value of Saving a Life: Evidence from the Labor Market, in Household Production and Consumption 265 (N. Terlekyj ed. 1976).

still have a clear incentive to install a $50 safety device that is worth $100 to the worker. Failure to do so would leave cash on the table.

Other critics suggest that workers often do not know about the safety devices they lack. But this claim is also troubling because firms would have strong incentives to call these devices to workers' attention. After all, both the firm and its workers come out ahead when a cost-effective safety device is adopted.

With respect to the charge that labor markets are not effectively competitive, critics of hedonic pricing models have failed to meet the burden of proof. Worker mobility between firms is high, as is entry by new firms into existing markets, and cartel agreements have always been notoriously unstable. Information is never perfect, but if a new employer in town is offering a better deal, word sooner or later gets around.

If, despite these checks, some firms still managed to exploit their workers by paying less than a competitive wage, we should expect these firms to have relatively high profits. In fact, however, we observe just the opposite correlation. Year in and year out, the firms paying the highest wages are most profitable.[14]

But even if labor markets are workably competitive, the same theory of revealed preference that makes hedonic models so attractive also sounds a cautionary note. It calls our attention to a related form of behavioral evidence, namely, the laws we choose to adopt. Scholars in the law and economics movement have long argued that laws tend to evolve in ways that maximize wealth.[15] This characterization presumably also applies to laws regulating health and safety in the workplace, which by now have been enacted by virtually all industrial democracies. These laws pose a challenge to the hedonic pricing model's assumption that safety risks are fully reflected in compensating wage differentials. If this assumption were correct, safety regulations would entail costs that exceed their benefits and therefore should not have been enacted in the first place. But although these regulations have often been criticized on practical grounds, they appear in no imminent political danger.

Does the political success of safety regulation suggest that hedonic pricing models are misleading? I believe it does, but not for the reasons usually given. In what follows I construct an example to illustrate an alternative rationale for safety regulation, one that is independent of market power and imperfect information.

---

[14] See Lawrence Seidman, The Return of the Profit Rate to the Wage Equation, 61 Rev. Econ. & Stat. 139 (1979), and numerous studies cited therein.

[15] See, for example, Richard A. Posner, Economic Analysis of Law (5th ed. 1998).

Sherwin

	Safe job @ $300/week	Unsafe job @ $350/week
Safe job @ $300/week	$400/week each	$300/week for Gary $450/week for Sherwin
Unsafe job @ $350/week	$450/week for Gary $300/week for Sherwin	$350/week each

Gary

FIGURE 1.—The effect of concerns about relative income on worker choices regarding safety.

POSITIONAL CONCERNS AND REVEALED PREFERENCE

Consider a hypothetical community with only two members, Sherwin and Gary. Each gets satisfaction from three things—from his income, from his safety on the job, and from his position on the economic ladder. Each must choose between two jobs—a safe job that pays $300 per week and a risky job that pays $350 per week. The value of safety to each is $100 per week, and each evaluates relative income as follows: Having more income than his neighbor provides the equivalent of $100 per week worth of additional satisfaction; having less income than his neighbor means the equivalent of a $100 per week reduction in satisfaction; and having the same income as his neighbor means no change in the underlying level of satisfaction. Will Sherwin and Gary choose optimally between the two jobs?

If we viewed each person's decision in isolation, the uniquely correct choice would be the safe job. Although it pays $50 per week less than the risky job, the extra safety it provides is worth $100 per week. So if we abstract from the issue of concern about relative income, the value of the safe job is $400 per week (its $300 salary plus $100 worth of safety), which is $50 per week more than the $350 value of the risky job.

Once we incorporate concerns about relative income, however, the decision logic changes in a fundamental way. Now the attractiveness of each choice depends on the job chosen by the other. The four possible combinations of choices and the corresponding levels of satisfaction are shown in Figure 1.

Suppose, for example, that Gary chooses the safe job. If Sherwin then chooses the unsafe job, he ends up with total satisfaction worth $450— $350 in salary plus $100 from having more income than Gary. Gary, for his part, ends up with only $300 worth of total satisfaction—$300 in salary plus $100 from safety minus $100 from having lower income than Sherwin. Alternatively, suppose Gary chooses the unsafe job. Then Sherwin again does better to accept the unsafe job, for by so doing he gets $350 worth of satisfaction rather than only $300. Since the payoff matrix is symmetric, each player's dominant strategy is to choose the unsafe job. Analysts equipped with the hedonic pricing model will conclude that these workers must value the extra safety at less than $50 per week.

But this inference is clearly wrong. Note that if each chooses a safe job, each will get $400 worth of total satisfaction—$300 of income, $100 worth of satisfaction from safety, and zero satisfaction from relative position. If each had instead chosen the unsafe job, each would have had $350 of income, zero satisfaction from safety, and each would again have had the same level of income, so again zero satisfaction from relative position. If we compare the upper-left cell of Figure 1 to the lower-right cell, then, we can say unequivocally that Sherwin and Gary would be happier if each took a safe job at lower income than if each chose an unsafe job with more income. By assumption, the extra safety is worth more than its cost.

The discrepancy arises because the job safety choice confronts workers with a Prisoner's Dilemma. If they could choose collectively, they would pick the safe job, an outcome they prefer to what happens when they choose independently. On this interpretation, safety regulation is attractive not because it prevents exploitation, but because it mitigates the consequences of consumption externalities.

Many modern disciples of Adam Smith appear reluctant to introduce concerns about relative position into normative economic models. Yet as Smith himself recognized, such concerns are a basic component of human nature:

Consumable commodities are either necessaries or luxuries. By necessaries I understand not only the commodities which are indispensably necessary for the support of life, but whatever the custom of the country renders it indecent for creditable people, even of the lowest order, to be without. A linen shirt, for example, is, strictly speaking, not a necessary of life. The Greeks and Romans lived, I suppose, very comfortably though they had no linen. But in the present times, through the greater part of Europe, a creditable day-labourer would be ashamed to appear in public without a linen shirt, the want of which would be supposed to denote that disgraceful degree of poverty which, it is presumed, nobody can well fall into without extreme bad conduct. Custom, in the same manner, has rendered leather shoes a necessary of life in England. The poorest creditable person of either sex would be ashamed to appear in public without them.[16]

As Smith clearly understood, concerns about relative income need not entail a desire to have more or better goods than one's neighbors. People with low relative income experience not just psychological discomfort but also more tangible economic costs.[17] A resident of a remote Indian mountain village has no need for a car, but a resident of Los Angeles cannot meet even the most minimal demands of social existence without one. A family that wants to send its children to a good school must buy a house in a good school district, yet such houses are often beyond reach for families with low relative income. Similarly, if only 10 percent of houses have views and everybody cares equally strongly about having a view, then only people in the top 10 percent of the income distribution will get one.

Measuring the social value of a consumption good by summing what individuals spend on it is similar to measuring the social value of military armaments by summing the amounts that individual nations spend on them. Both measurements are problematic because they ignore the influence of context on demand.

Consider a simple model in which individuals apportion their income between consumption (C) and workplace safety (S) and in which the representative individual's utility depends not only on her absolute levels of consumption and safety, but also on her relative consumption. For example, suppose the ith individual's utility is given by[18]

$$U_i = U_i[C_i, S_i, R(C_i)], \tag{1}$$

where $R(C_i)$ denotes her rank in the consumption distribution, $0 \le R(C_i) \le 1$. If $f(C)$ is the density function for the observed values of consumption in the population, then

$$R(C_i) = \int_0^{C_i} f(C)dc.$$

Let M_i denote the individual's income, P_c the price of the consumption good, and P_s the price of safety. If the individual takes $f(C)$ as given, the first-order condition for maximum utility is given by

---

[16] Adam Smith, An Inquiry into the Nature and Causes of the Wealth of Nations, bk. 5, ch. II, pt. II, art. 4 (1952) (1776).

[17] On this point, see especially Amartya K. Sen, The Standard of Living (1989).

[18] For a more detailed discussion of the model that follows, see Robert H. Frank, The Demand for Unobservable and Other Nonpositional Goods, 75 Am. Econ. Rev. 101 (1985).

$$U_{i1}/U_{i2} + [U_{i3}f(C_i)C]/U_{i2} = P_C/P_S, \qquad (2)$$

where U_{ij} denotes the first partial derivative of U_i with respect to its jth argument.

The second term on the left-hand side of equation (2) reflects the fact that when an individual buys an additional unit of the consumption good, her payoff is not just the direct utility it provides but also the utility from the implied advance in the consumption ranking. But other individuals also perceive this second reward, and when all respond to it, the resulting consumption ranking remains as before. As a result, consumers spend more on consumption and less on safety than is socially optimal.

Suppose consumers could agree collectively to ignore the effect of individual consumption changes on consumption rank—that is, suppose they could agree to assume that $R'(C) = f(C) = 0$. The first-order condition in equation (2) would then simplify to

$$U_{i1}/U_{i2} = P_C/P_S, \qquad (3)$$

which is the familiar first-order condition from models in which consumption rank does not matter. Suppressing the rank term would lead individuals to consume less and spend more on safety than before. Equation (3), not equation (2), defines the socially optimal allocation.

The driving force behind this market failure is that the utility from consumption is more context dependent than the utility from safety. If utility had been equally context dependent for each good, there would have been no distortion.

Is the extent to which satisfaction depends on context different in different domains? Sara Solnick and David Hemenway recently conducted a survey of graduate students in the public health program at Harvard University in an attempt to answer this question.[19] They began by asking each subject to choose between the following hypothetical worlds:

A: You earn $50,000 a year, others earn $25,000;

B: You earn $100,000 a year, others earn $200,000.

Fifty-six percent of subjects chose the first world. Solnick and Hemenway then asked each subject to choose between worlds in which their relative and absolute income levels were the same, but their relative and absolute vacation times differed:

C: You have 2 weeks of vacation each year, others have 1 week;

D: You have 4 weeks of vacation each year, others have 8 weeks.

This time only 20 percent chose the first world, less than half as many as

[19] Sara J. Solnick & David Hemenway, Is More Always Better? A Survey on Positional Concerns, 37 J. Econ. Behav. & Org. 373 (1998).

in the first question. On its face, this suggests that satisfaction from consumption is more strongly context dependent than satisfaction from vacation time.

Other important consumption categories also appear to be less sensitive than material goods consumption to interpersonal comparisons. Consider traffic congestion, whose adverse effects on health and psychological well-being are similar to those of prolonged exposure to loud, unpredictable noise.[20] The effect of such noise on subjects in the laboratory occurs independently of the amount of noise to which other subjects are exposed, suggesting that the demand for goods is more context sensitive than the demand for such environmental amenities as freedom from noise and traffic congestion.

Interpersonal comparisons also appear relatively unimportant for savings, at least in the short run. Thus, whereas most of us know what kinds of houses our friends live in and what kinds of cars they drive, we are much less likely to know how large their savings accounts are. But even if everyone's savings balance were on public display, at least some important individual rewards from current consumption would still depend more on context than those from saving. Many parents, for example, might gladly settle for a diminished standard of living in retirement if by saving less they could meet the payments on a house in a better school district.[21] And the same incentives would lead many parents to accept less safe, more regimented, but better paying, jobs. As before, however, the positional gains enjoyed by families that make such choices are offset by the corresponding positional losses experienced by other families.

How might a cost-benefit analyst adjust conventional estimates to counteract the biases introduced by concerns about relative consumption? One simple method would make use of surveys in which subjects are periodically asked to report how much additional income a family would need to maintain a constant level of subjective well-being in the face of a rise in the incomes of others. Using data collected in several European countries, B. M. S. van Praag and Arie Kapteyn estimate an elasticity of roughly

[20] For a survey of the relevant studies, see Robert H. Frank, Luxury Fever, ch. 6 (1999).

[21] Some object that a desire for high consumption rank cannot really explain low savings rates, since those who save too little now simply consign themselves to having low consumption rank in the future. Yet, as noted, having lower consumption rank in the future may be an acceptable price to pay for the ability to have high rank with respect to some forms of current consumption. What is more, to the extent that driving the right cars and wearing the right clothes function as signals of ability, and thereby help people land better jobs or more lucrative contracts, low savings now may not even entail reduced consumption rank in the future. But whereas this may be true from the perspective of each individual, it is surely not true for society as a whole. For when all of us spend more to signal our abilities, the relative strength of each signal remains unchanged.

0.6—that is, that a family would need about a 6 percent increase in its real income to compensate for a 10 percent increase in the incomes of all others in the community.[22] If we take this estimate at face value for illustrative purposes, we can employ it to construct a simple multiplier for adjusting willingness-to-pay values generated by hedonic pricing models.

Suppose, for example, that a study in which wages were regressed on mortality rates in the workplace found that individual workers are willing to give up 2 percent of their incomes each year in exchange for a one in 1,000 reduction in the probability of dying in a workplace accident. This estimate tells us that a worker earning $50,000 per year would be would be willing to pay $1,000 per year for the additional safety, even though the expenditure would reduce his relative consumption by 2 percent. The Kapteyn–van Praag estimate suggests that this worker would be willing to pay roughly $600 more for the same increment in safety if he could be assured that his relative income would be unaffected by the expenditure—as would be the case, for example, if everyone else made similar expenditures on safety.

An adjustment based on the van Praag–Kapteyn survey data would thus call an upward revision by 60 percent in the willingness-to-pay values inferred from hedonic pricing models. It would be easy to quarrel, of course, with an adjustment procedure based on survey responses like these. Other, more objective procedures might be pursued. Elsewhere, for example, I have argued that one can infer the value of relative income by examining the relationship between wages, local rank, and productivity among groups of coworkers.[23] In any event, the mere fact that an adjustment procedure may be flawed clearly does not imply that it yields worse estimates than we would get by simply ignoring concerns about relative consumption.

In sum, if demands for some goods are more highly context sensitive than demands for others, then individual spending decisions cannot be aggregated to estimate social valuations for cost-benefit analysis. In general, the sum of individual valuations will be smaller than social value for goods whose demands are relatively sensitive to context and greater than social value for those whose demands are relatively insensitive to context. And because contextual forces influence demands in powerful ways,[24] we have ample reason to be skeptical of hedonic pricing models, even those based on perfectly competitive markets with complete information.

As before, however, the implication is not that the cost-benefit approach

---

[22] B. M. S. van Praag & Arie Kapteyn, Further Evidence on the Individual Welfare Function of Income, 4 Eur. Econ. Rev. 33 (1973).

[23] Robert H. Frank, Are Workers Paid Their Marginal Products? 74 Am. Econ. Rev. 549 (1984).

[24] See Robert H. Frank, Choosing the Right Pond (1985); and Frank, *supra* note 20.

is invalid as a matter of principle. Rather, it is that, as currently implemented, its prescriptions may be substantially misleading. If so, the remedy is not to abandon cost-benefit analysis but to amend conventional estimating procedures.

IMPULSE-CONTROL PROBLEMS AND REVEALED PREFERENCE

Hedonic pricing models also assume that we can infer the values people place on future events by observing the choices they make. On this view, if a person accepts a one in 10 chance of contracting a serious illness 1 year from now in return for a payment of $100 now, then the cost of taking that risk, expressed as a present value, cannot be more than $100. Compelling experimental evidence, however, suggests grounds for skepticism.[25] Consider, for example, the pair of choices A and B:

A: $100 tomorrow versus $105 a week from tomorrow;
B: $100 after 52 weeks versus $105 after 53 weeks.

The rational choice model on which hedonic pricing models are based says that people will discount future costs and benefits exponentially at their respective rates of time preference. If so, people should always choose similarly under alternatives A and B. Since the larger payoff comes a week later in each case, the ordering of the present values of the two alternatives must be the same in both, irrespective of the rate at which people discount. When people confront such choices in practice, however, most pick the $100 option in A, whereas most choose the $105 option in B.

Substantial experimental evidence suggests that individuals discount future costs and benefits not exponentially, as assumed by the rational choice model, but hyperbolically.[26] The psychological impact of a cost or benefit falls much more sharply with delay under hyperbolic discounting than under exponential discounting. One consequence is that preference reversals of the kind just discussed are all but inevitable under hyperbolic discounting. The classic reversal involves choosing the larger, later reward when both alternatives occur with substantial delay, then switching to the smaller, earlier reward when its delay falls below some threshold. Thus, from the pair of alternatives labeled B above, in which both rewards come only after a relatively long delay, most subjects chose the larger, later reward, whereas from the pair labeled A, most chose the earlier, smaller reward.

---

[25] See, for example, the papers in Choice over Time (Jon Elster & George Loewenstein eds. 1993).

[26] For detailed summary of the relevant evidence, see George Ainslie, Picoeconomics (1992).

The tendency to discount future costs and benefits hyperbolically gives rise to a variety of familiar impulse-control problems and, in turn, to a variety of strategies for solving them. Anticipating their temptation to overeat, people often try to limit the quantities of sweets, salted nuts, and other delicacies they keep on hand. Anticipating their temptation to spend cash in their checking accounts, people enroll in payroll deduction savings plans. Foreseeing the difficulty of putting down a good mystery novel in midstream, many people know better than to start one on the evening before an important meeting. Reformed smokers seek the company of nonsmokers when they first try to kick the habit and are more likely than others to favor laws that limit smoking in public places. The recovering alcoholic avoids cocktail lounges.

Effective as these bootstrap self-control techniques may often be, they are far from perfect. Many people continue to express regret about having overeaten, having drunk and smoked too much, having saved too little, having stayed up too late, having watched too much television, and so on. The exponential discounting model urges us to dismiss these expressions as sour grapes. But from the perspective of the hyperbolic discounting model, these same expressions are coherent. In each case, the actor chose an inferior option when a better one was available, and later feels genuinely sorry about it.

Hedonic pricing models use observed choices to infer discount rates, which cost-benefit analysts then use to compute present values. To the extent that many important intertemporal choices are driven by hyperbolic discounting, conventional methods will give too little weight to future costs and benefits.

STATUS QUO BIAS

Opposition to cost-benefit analysis may also stem from the fact that the costs of a policy change are often far easier to quantify than its benefits, especially in the domains of environmental policy and health and safety policy. In both fields, consensus about how to measure benefits has proved especially elusive. The upshot is that policy decisions in these arenas tend to be driven primarily by cost considerations, resulting in a bias in favor of the status quo. This bias may help explain why advocates of change are overrepresented among opponents of cost-benefit analysis.

The fact that benefits are more difficult to measure than costs does not provide a compelling reason to abandon cost-benefit analysis, just as the fact that costs are easier to forecast than revenues does not provide a compelling reason for firms to abandon profit maximization. In each case, we do better to act on the best information available than to act on no information at all.

Concluding Remarks

From the preceding discussion, I draw two conclusions. One is that critics have failed to offer persuasive arguments that cost-benefit analysis is objectionable as a matter of principle. The other is that many of the methods used by cost-benefit analysts generate systematically biased prescriptions. Hedonic pricing methods overstate the value of goods and activities whose demands are relatively context sensitive. And they give too much weight to current costs and benefits, too little weight to those that occur in the future. These biases suggest an answer to the question posed in my title. Cost-benefit analysis as currently practiced may be controversial simply because it often generates misleading prescriptions.

I conclude by considering a more speculative explanation for opposition to cost-benefit analysis, one rooted in the distinction between consequentialist and deontological moral theories. The deontologists insist that immutable moral principles distinguish right conduct from wrong conduct, irrespective of costs and benefits. They insist, for example, that stealing is wrong not because it does more harm than good, but simply because it violates the victim's rights. The consequentialist resists such absolute prescriptions, confident that there could always be *some* conditions in which the gains from stealing might outweigh its costs.

Yet even the most committed consequentialists seem to recognize that statements like "Stealing is permissible whenever its benefits exceed its costs" are not rhetorically effective for teaching their children moral values. Indeed, like the deontologists, most consequentialists teach their children that stealing is wrong as a matter of principle. Elsewhere I have argued that once we acknowledge the strategic role of moral emotions in solving commitment problems, this posture is coherent, even in purely consequentialist terms.[27]

Yet a potentially more worrisome aspect of the consequentialist position remains, which is that people who view their ethical choices in cost-benefit terms must also construct their own estimates of the relevant costs and benefits. The obvious concern is that their estimates will be self-serving. More than 90 percent of all drivers, for example, feel sure they are better than average.[28] More than 99 percent of high-school students think they are above average in terms of their ability to get along with others.[29] Ninety-four percent of college professors believe they are more productive than

---

[27] See Robert H. Frank, Passions within Reason (1988). For a related discussion, see Eric A. Posner, The Strategic Basis of Unprincipled Behavior: A Critique of the Incommensurability Thesis, 146 U. Pa. L. Rev. 1185 (1998).

[28] See Thomas Gilovich, How We Know What Isn't So (1991).

[29] College Board, Student Descriptive Questionnaire (1976–77).

their average colleague.[30] The same forces that make us overestimate our skills can be expected also to distort the estimates that underlie our ethical judgments. And if these self-serving calculations lead some to disregard the common good, their example will make others more apt to do likewise.

Needless to say, people may also be prone to self-serving biases in their interpretations of deontological moral principles. In the end, which approach entails the greater risk is an empirical question. But it is at least possible that consequentialist thinking could lead to a worse outcome on balance. If this were shown to be so, consequentialists would have little choice but to endorse the deontological position (much as an atheist might support fundamentalist religious institutions on the view that threats of hell-fire and damnation are the only practical way to get people to behave themselves). They would have to view cost-benefit analysis as correct in principle yet best avoided in practice.

I hasten to add that critics of cost-benefit analysis have made no such showing. And unless they do, it seems certain that cost-benefit analysis will continue to play an important role in decision making. Under the circumstances, both friends and foes of cost-benefit analysis have a shared interest in trying to eliminate the biases that distort its prescriptions.

[30] P. Cross, Not *Can* but *Will* College Teaching Be Improved? New Directions Higher Educ., Spring 1977, at 1.

THE DISCIPLINE OF COST-BENEFIT ANALYSIS

*AMARTYA SEN**

ABSTRACT

Cost-benefit analysis is a general discipline, based on the use of some foundational principles, which are not altogether controversial, but have nevertheless considered plausibility. Divisiveness increases as various additional requirements are imposed. There is a trade-off here between easier usability (through locked-up formulae) and more general acceptability (through allowing parametric variations). The paper examines and scrutinizes the merits and demerits of these additional requirements. The particular variant of cost-benefit approach that is most commonly used now is, in fact, extraordinarily limited, because of its insistence on doing the valuation entirely through an analogy with the market mechanism. This admits only a narrow class of values, and demands that individuals be unconcerned about many substantial variations, ignored in the procedure of market valuation. The use, instead, of a general social choice approach can allow greater freedom of valuation and can also accommodate more informational inputs.

THE discipline of cost-benefit analysis—if discipline it is—has fearless champions as well as resolute detractors. It is, partly, a battle of giants, for there are heavyweight intellectuals on both sides, wielding powerful weapons of impressively diverse kinds. It is also, partly, a conversation between great soliloquists—very skilled in making their points, and somewhat less troubled than Hamlet ("To be," say some, and "Not to be," announce the others).

The main object of this paper is not so much to decide who is right but to identify what the issues are. However, that is not my only objective. I also have some personal views and assessments, which I shall not hesitate to present. But principally (and I believe, more importantly) I will try to isolate the questions that divide us. We can agree on the questions even when we do not agree on the answers. There are several difficult issues here, which must be addressed in one way or another.

* Master, Trinity College, Cambridge, and Lamont University Professor Emeritus, Harvard University. For helpful comments, I am most grateful to Eric Posner.

[*Journal of Legal Studies,* vol. XXIX]

I. The Themes and the Debates

I shall proceed gradually from some basic principles that characterize the foundations of the general approach of cost-benefit analysis. These elementary principles would be accepted by many but rejected by some who are not that way inclined at all. The latter group would, then, have reason to go no further (given their rejection of one or other of these foundational cost-benefit principles). However, those who are ready to live with these foundational principles will then have to consider what additional requirements they are willing to consider to make cost-benefit analysis more specific and pointed. Any such narrowing will, of course, also make the approach less ecumenical and permissive. Indeed, the mainstream approach of cost-benefit analysis uses a formidable set of very exacting requirements, and we have particular reason to examine these additional conditions. Indeed, the list of requirements considered here follows the mainstream approach quite closely, though I shall also briefly refer to alternative possibilities as we go along.

I shall divide these additional demands into three groups: structural demands, evaluative indifferences, and market-centered valuation. To give away my main theme at the very beginning (this is definitely not a detective story), let me list the main headings under which the principles will be considered, in the sections that follow the more general Section III.

III. Foundational Principles
    A. Explicit Valuation
    B. Broadly Consequential Evaluation
    C. Additive Accounting
IV. Structural Demands
    A. Assumed Completeness
    B. Full Knowledge or Probabilistic Understanding
    C. Noniterative and Nonparametric Valuations
V. Evaluative Indifferences
    A. Nonvaluation of Actions, Motives, and Rights
    B. Indifference to Intrinsic Value of Freedom
    C. Instrumental View of Behavioral Values
VI. Market-Centered Valuation
    A. Reliance on Willingness to Pay
    B. Sufficiency of Potential Compensation
    C. Disregard of Social Choice Options

There is, I fear, much ground to cover, but before I try to get on with it, I would like to make three clarificatory points. First, the term ''cost-benefit analysis'' has considerable plasticity and various specific procedures have been called by that name (by the protagonists and by others). There is nothing particularly wrong in this permissiveness, so long as terminological unity is not taken to be the same as conceptual congruence. It is indeed perfectly possible for someone to accept the foundational outlook of cost-benefit analysis and yet reject one or more of the requirements imposed by the structural demands, evaluative indifferences, and market-centered valuation that characterize the mainstream applications. While the literature is full of repeated applications of a very well-delineated method that incorporate all these demands, this should not, in itself, be taken to compromise the claims of other procedures or approaches to be seen as legitimate cost-benefit analysis.

Second, the acceptance or nonacceptance of the foundational principles themselves may, in some ways, be as useful a classificatory device as the divisions produced by the insistence on all the requirements invoked by the mainstream methodology. Indeed, there are analysts who see themselves as defenders of cost-benefit analysis and who accept the foundational principles of this approach, who nevertheless cannot but be intensely unhappy with the elaborate methodology of valuation hammered into the mainstream procedure. If there is room for them too, I should apply for accommodation.

Third, the subject has been in vogue for many decades now and has generated vast literatures, some more oriented toward analytical issues and others more concerned with problems of practical application (usually of the delineated mainstream methodology). Many conceptual issues have received attention, and with them I shall be, in one way or another, concerned in this paper (even though I shall not attempt to make this into a "survey paper" with references to specific publications). But cost-benefit analysis— or a collection of procedures bearing that general name—has also been used in many practical decisions, generating corresponding literatures. It would be nice to attempt a comparative assessment of the varieties of particular methods that have been used and to discuss their respective suitability—absolute and comparative—in handling diverse decisional problems in practice. Whether this is feasible at this time, I do not know. But I do know that I am not in a position to do this, given the monumental size of the literature and my own limited knowledge. While I shall not go in that direction, I mention it nevertheless, since I do believe that it may be quite useful as an exercise to go from practice to principles, rather than the other way round (as attempted in this paper). Understanding can come in different ways, and despite my using only one general line of investigation (based on assessing the principles involved), I do not intend to deny the relevance of other ways of getting at these questions.

II. Costs and Benefits in General Reasoning

The basic rationale of cost-benefit analysis lies in the idea that things are worth doing if the benefits resulting from doing them outweigh their costs. This is not, of course, by any means, noncontroversial, but before getting into the controversies, it is useful to see first that there is some intelligible reasoning here. Indeed, we may well puzzle a bit if someone were to tell us "This project has little benefit and much cost—let us do it!" We would think that we are entitled to ask "why?" (or, more emphatically, "why on earth?"). Benefits and costs have claims to our attention. Furthermore, it may even be argued, with some plausibility (though, I believe, not total certainty), that any "pro" argument for a project can be seen as pointing to some benefit that it will yield and any "anti" argument must be associated with some cost.

Indeed, the language of benefits and costs is used by many who would have nothing to do with cost-benefit analysis as it is standardly practiced. Consider, for example, the big political debate that is going on in India right at this time about the big irrigation project called the Narmada Dam, which will provide water to a great many people but will also drown the homes of many others (who have been offered what is seen as inadequate or unacceptable compensation). The decision to produce the dam (and to continue with the project despite the opposition it generated) was, of course, based on cost-benefit analysis. However, in arguing against the decision, the opponents of it also point to costs, sometimes called "human costs," that have been ignored or not adequately considered.[1]

The framework of costs and benefits has a very extensive reach, going well beyond the variables that get standardized attention in the usual techniques associated with the application of cost-benefit analysis. Indeed, the ordinary procedure of considering, in a general way, the benefits and costs associated with alternative possibilities and then assessing their respective advantages is usable in a wide variety of problems, from appraising economic development or the quality of life to scrutinizing the extent of inequality, poverty, or gender disparity.[2]

---

[1] For a powerful and strongly reasoned exposition of the case against the dam, see Arundhati Roy, The Greater Common Good: The Human Cost of Big Dams, 16 (11), Frontline, June 4, 1999.

[2] See, for example, Amartya Sen, On Economic Inequality (enlarged ed. 1997) (1973); A. B. Atkinson, Social Justice and Public Policy (1983); Keith Griffin & John Knight, Human Development and International Development Strategies for the 1990s (1990); The Quality of Life (Martha Nussbaum & Amartya Sen eds. 1993); Women, Culture and Development: A Study of Human Capabilities (Martha C. Nussbaum & Jonathan Glover eds. 1995); Development with a Human Face (Santosh Mehrotra & Richard Jolly eds. 1997).

III. FOUNDATIONAL PRINCIPLES

A. *Explicit Valuation*

Despite the sweeping reach of reasoning invoking costs and benefits, cost-benefit analysis as a distinct approach (or, more accurately, as a class of distinct but related approaches) imposes certain restrictions on evaluative rules and permissive procedures. Perhaps it is appropriate to see the demand of explicit valuation as the first general condition imposed by the discipline. This is a forceful demand for fuller articulation, which involves the rejection of a commonly adopted position hallowed by tradition, to wit, that we may know what is right without knowing why it is right. At the risk of oversimplification, explicit valuation is a part of the insistence on a rationalist approach, which demands full explication of the reasons for taking a decision, rather than relying on an unreasoned conviction or on an implicitly derived conclusion.

Despite its rationalist appeal, explicit valuation as a principle is not without its problems. If one were to insist on this in all personal decisions, life would be quite unbearably complicated. The making of day-to-day decisions would, then, take more time than would be available for it, and decisional defenses might look terribly pedantic (perhaps even pompous, in much the same way the wine experts' specialist recommendations tend to sound, invoking such notions as the wine's "melodic quality" or "big nose" or "innate cheerfulness").

However, public decisions have more need for explicitness than private choices or personal actions. Others not involved in the decision may legitimately want to know why exactly something—rather than another—is being chosen. The demands of accountability apply not merely to implementation but also to choices of projects and programs. There is, thus, a case for fuller articulation and more explicit valuation in public decisions than in private ones.

Here too there may be problems. What Cass Sunstein calls "incompletely theorized agreements" may be quite important for agreed public decisions.[3] A consensus on public decisions may flourish so long as the exact grounds for that accord are not very precisely articulated. Explicit valuation may, thus, have its problems in public decisions as well as private ones.

There is, nevertheless, a case for explicitness, if only to encourage the possibility of reasoned consent and to present some kind of a barrier against implicit railroading of unacceptable decisions that would be widely rejected if properly articulated. There are several conflicting issues of pragmatic

---

[3] See Cass R. Sunstein, Legal Reasoning and Political Conflict (1996).

concern as well as analytical clarity in the insistence on explicit valuation, but judged as a technique of analysis (as opposed to rhetoric of advocacy) this insistence does have some very basic merit. Also, diverse grounds for agreement on a particular policy judgment can be accommodated within a general approach of relying on the intersection of partly divergent rankings over policy alternatives (on which more later—in Section IV).[4]

B. Broadly Consequential Evaluation

A second basic principle of cost-benefit analysis relates to the use of consequential evaluation. Costs and benefits are evaluated, in this approach, by looking at the consequences of the respective decisions. Broadly consequential evaluation allows the relevant consequences to include not only such things as happiness or the fulfillment of desire on which utilitarians tend to concentrate, but also whether certain actions have been performed or particular rights have been violated. This inclusiveness is resisted by some. Since consequentialist thinking has been very closely linked with utilitarianism and related approaches, there is a long tradition of taking a very narrow view of what can count as consequences (roughly in line with what utilitarians wish to focus on).

As a result, many political theorists have argued against taking an inclusive view of consequentialism. It has been claimed, for example, that a performed action cannot be included among the consequences of that action. But one has to be quite a pure theorist to escape the elementary thought that an action that has been successfully undertaken must have resulted in that action's occurrence, no matter what other consequences it may or may not have (the main argument against asserting this may be the difficulty in stating something quite so obvious, without sounding rather foolish).[5]

Similarly, if recognized rights are violated by particular actions (for example, by the jailing of dissidents), there is no great difficulty in seeing that these actions have resulted in the violation of those rights. We do not even face a tremendous intellectual challenge in understanding such statements as, "1976 was a very bad year for civil rights in India, since there were

[4] On the use of intersection partial orderings, see also Sen, *supra* note 2; and Amartya Sen, Employment, Technology and Development (1975).

[5] There are interesting issues of agent-relative ethics that are sometimes thought to be incompatible with consequential reasoning. But even this rather more sophisticated claim is hard to entertain except through a slightly disintegrated attempt to get to agent-relative action judgments starting from agent-independent judgments on states. Once that bit of implicit schizophrenia is eschewed, the reach of broad consequential reasoning is correspondingly extended to permit agent relativity in evaluating actions as well as states; on this see Amartya Sen, Rights and Agency, 11 Phil. & Pub. Aff. 3 (1982); Amartya Sen, Well-Being, Agency and Freedom: Dewey Lectures 1984, 82 J. Phil. 169 (1985).

many violations of civil rights as a consequence of policies that were followed during the so-called 'Emergency period.''' The vast majority of the
Indian voters who defeated the proposed continuation of the Emergency (as
well as the government that had imposed it) did not have to manage without
consequential reasoning. Indeed, looking at consequences on rights and
freedoms—though allegedly alien to rights-based reasoning in some modern political theories—is not really a new departure, as anyone studying
Tom Paine's *Rights of Man* or Mary Wollstonecraft's *The Vindication of
the Rights of Women* (both published in 1792) can readily check.

Taking a broad view of consequential evaluation does not, however,
make it nonassertive. It wrestles against deciding on actions on grounds of
their "rightness"—irrespective of their consequences. This is a debate that
has gone on for a long time and remains active today. Those opposed to
consequential evaluation—even in its broadest form—have shared a common rejection of being guided by consequences (the "right" action may be
determined, in this view, simply by one's "duty"—irrespective of consequences). But they have often argued for very different substantive posi-
tions on deontological grounds. For example, Mahatma Gandhi's deontological insistence on nonviolence irrespective of consequences clashes
substantially with Krishna's deontological advocacy, in *Bhagavadgeeta,* of
the epic hero Arjuna's duty to take part in a just war. On the eve of the
great battle, as Arjuna rebels against fighting (on the grounds that many
people will be killed on both sides, that many of them are people for whom
Arjuna has affection and respect, and, furthermore, that he himself—as the
leading warrior on his side—would have to do a lot of killing), Krishna
points to Arjuna's duty to fight, irrespective of his evaluation of the consequences. It is a just cause, and as a warrior and a general on whom his side
must rely, Arjuna cannot, in Krishna's view, waver from his obligations.

Krishna's high deontology has been deeply influential in Indian moral
debates in the subsequent millennia. It is also eloquently endorsed, among
others, by T. S. Eliot, in a poem in the *Four Quartets.* Eliot summarizes
Krishna's view in the form of an admonishment: "And do not think of the
fruit of action. / Fare forward." Eliot explains: "Not fare well, / But fare
forward, voyagers." [6] Cost-benefit analysis, on the other hand, suggests that
we try to "fare well" and not just "forward." The "wellness" that results
must take note inter alia of the badness of violation of rights and duties (if
such things are admitted into consideration), but the decision cannot be reduced just to doing one's "duty, irrespective of consequences."

---

[6] T. S. Eliot, Four Quartets 31 (1944) (The Dry Salvages). I have discussed the issues
involved in this debate in Amartya Sen, Consequential Evaluation and Practical Reason, 97
J. Phil. (in press, 2000).

It should, thus, be clear that consequential evaluation as a principle does impose a demand with some cutting power. I would argue that the principle does make good sense, but I know that deontologists would not agree and would, no doubt, decide that they have overwhelming reasons to reject that approach (the world is full of "very strange and well-bred" things, to use William Congreve's perplexed phrase). The world of costs and benefits (which includes taking note of the badness of nasty actions and of violation of freedoms and rights) is quite a different decisional universe from the sledgehammer reasoning of consequence-independent duties and obligations.

C. Additive Accounting

Cost-benefit analysis not only bases decisions on costs and benefits, it also looks for the value of net benefits after deducting costs from benefits. While benefits can be of different kinds and are put together—to the extent that they can be—through a selection of weights (or ranges of weights), costs are seen as forgone benefits. Thus, benefits and costs are defined, ultimately, in the same "space."

The additive form is implicit in all this. When different kinds of benefits are added together, with appropriate weights, the framework is clearly one of addition. It may be wondered whether there is anything to discuss here, since many people are so exclusively familiar with the additive form of reasoning (compared with all other possible forms) that addition may appear to be simply the natural form—perhaps even the only form—for getting together diverse benefits and costs. However, multiplicative forms have also been used in the evaluative literature (for example, by J. F. Nash in what he called "the bargaining problem").[7] Other forms are possible too.

In fact, there is a strong case for using concave functions that respond positively to benefits (and thus negatively to costs) but do not have constant weights and a linear format. In fact, concavity is very often the most plausible shape of an objective function involving different good things and has been used to derive variable weights at different points and correspondingly variable shadow prices of resources (for example, through use of the so-called Kuhn-Tucker Theorem).[8] In fact, in general we would expect some strict concavity (or at least strict quasi concavity, corresponding to dimin-

[7] See John F. Nash, Jr., The Bargaining Problem, 18 Econometrica 155 (1950).

[8] See H. W. Kuhn & A. W. Tucker, eds., 1 & 2 Contributions to the Theory of Games (1950, 1953); Samuel Karlin, 1 Mathematical Methods and Theory in Games, Programming and Economics (1959). The relevance of concave—as opposed to strictly linear—programming for cost-benefit analysis in general and for shadow pricing in particular is discussed in Amartya Sen, Choice of Techniques (3d ed. 1968).

ishing marginal rates of substitution between different kinds of benefits), and in this sense, the additive form of cost-benefit analysis requires careful handling. One way of dealing with the problem is to confine attention to relatively marginal changes, so that the weights may not change very much and the framework may be approximately linear (some would refer to Taylor's Theorem and to local approximations, at this point). But many projects are relatively large, and the benefits may be so particularized (especially in a distribution-sensitive accounting) that the weights may have to change quite readily. In that case, there is no alternative—if one were to use the additive form of cost-benefit analysis—to taking note of the need for varying weights as the magnitudes of different kinds of benefits change. The exercise must then take the form of a conjoint determination of quantities of benefits and their weights. I shall not go further into the technicalities here, but it is important to recognize that the additive form that cost-benefit analysis adopts is chosen at the cost of some limitation and certainly calls for more simultaneous reasoning of quantities and values as substantial alterations are considered.

Even with all these qualifications (explicit valuation, broadly consequential reasoning, and additive accounting), general cost-benefit analysis is a very ecumenical approach. It is compatible, for example, with weights based on willingness to pay as well as some quite different ways of valuation (for example, through questionnaires), which may supplement or supplant that willingness-to-pay framework.[9] There is reasoning here of great generality (despite the qualifications and disclaimers already considered), and it is important to see the reach of the general approach before we go on—from this point onward—to adding more and more restrictive requirements that make the procedures more specific and particular, at the cost of reducing the wide freedom given by the general approach of taking decisions by cost-benefit reasoning.

IV. STRUCTURAL DEMANDS

A. Assumed Completeness

As it is standardly practiced, cost-benefit analysis tends to invoke completeness of evaluations. This requires not only that each consequence be identified and known (more on this presently) but also that the weights, at

---

[9] See Partha Dasgupta, Stephen Marglin, & Amartya Sen, Guidelines to Project Evaluation (prepared for UNIDO, 1972). See also Sen, *supra* note 8; I. M. D. Little & James Mirrlees, Manual of Industrial Project Analysis in Developing Countries (1968); Cost-Benefit Analysis (Richard Layard ed. 1972); Amartya Sen, Employment, Technology and Development (1975); P. S. Dasgupta & G. M. Heal, Economic Theory and Exhaustible Resources (1979).

the appropriate point, are definitive and unique. It is often presumed, without any explicit argument, that if we are evaluating benefits and costs, then every possible state of affairs must be comparable—and be clearly ranked—vis-à-vis every other. This presumed requirement has sometimes been seen by critics of cost-benefit analysis as being quite implausible. How can we always compare every alternative with every other, especially since so many considerations are involved, which incorporate imprecise measurement and ambiguous valuation? Can we always find a best alternative? What if we fail to rank some states of affairs vis-à-vis others?

Some see completeness as a necessary requirement of consequential evaluation, but it is, of course, nothing of the sort. A consequentialist approach does involve the use of maximizing logic in a general form, but maximization does not require that all alternatives be comparable and does not even require that a best alternative be identifiable. Maximization only requires that we do not choose an alternative that is worse than another that can be chosen instead. If we cannot compare and rank two alternatives, then choosing either from that pair will fully satisfy the requirement of maximization.

The term maximization is often used quite loosely, rather than in its mathematically well-defined form. Sometimes the term is used to indicate that we must choose a best alternative. This is, technically, better described as optimization.[10] The technical definition of maximization in the foundational literature on set theory and analysis (in the form of picking an alternative to which there is none better) captures all that needs to be captured for being able to choose systematically and cogently through pairwise comparisons. Maximization and optimization coincide if the ordering is complete, which it may or may not be. If, for example, it so happens that (1) there are two options A and B that cannot be ranked vis-à-vis each other, but (2) each of them is better than all the other alternatives, then maximization would require that one of those two—A or B—be chosen.[11]

The distinction can be illustrated with the old story of Buridan's ass, which saw two haystacks that it could not rank vis-à-vis each other.[12] Buridan's ass, as a vigorous optimizer and a great believer in complete order-

[10] On the nature of this requirement and its implications, see Amartya Sen, Collective Choice and Social Welfare, ch. 1* (North-Holland 1979) (1970).

[11] This is indeed the way maximality is defined in the mathematical literature, both in pure set theory (for example, in N. Bourbaki, Éléments de Mathématique (1939); and Nicholas Bourbaki, Theory of Sets (English trans. 1968)) and in axiomatic economic analysis (for example, in Gerard Debreu, Theory of Value (1959)). The axiomatic connections between maximality and optimality are discussed in Amartya Sen, Maximization and the Act of Choice, 65 Econometrica 745 (1997).

[12] There is a more popular but less interesting version of the story of Buridan's ass, according to which it was indifferent between the two haystacks and could not decide which to choose. However, if the donkey were really indifferent, then either haystack would,

ings, could not choose either haystack (since neither was shown to be clearly the best), and it thus died of starvation. It starved to death since it could not rank the two haystacks, but of course each would have generated a better consequence than starvation. Even if the donkey failed to rank the two haystacks, it would have made sense—good cost-benefit sense—for it to choose either rather than neither. Cost-benefit analysis does need maximization, but not completeness or optimization.

When a particular exercise of cost-benefit analysis ends up with a complete ordering and a clearly optimal outcome (or an optimal set of outcomes), then that may be fine and good. But if that does not happen, and the valuational ordering is incomplete, then maximization with respect to that incomplete ranking is the natural way to proceed. This may yield several maximal solutions that are not comparable with each other, and it would make sense to choose one of them. If the valuations come in the form of ranges of weights, we can also do sensitivity analysis of the effect of reducing the ranges of variations on extending the generated partial ordering.[13] The extent of imprecision can be reflected in the assessment, and the choices can be systematically linked to the valuational ambiguities.

However, in the literature, completeness is sometimes insisted on, which tends to produce arbitrary completion in terms of imperious valuational judgments or capricious epistemic assessments. The result often enough is to ignore the less exactly measured consequences or less clearly agreed values, even though they may be extremely important (of which we can be sure even without zeroing in on an exact weight—the entire range of acceptable valuational weights may speak clearly enough). The neglect of the so-called human costs relates partly to this despotic quest for complete orderings. These are cases in which a little more sophistication in the technical exercise can allow us to include many variables that some technocrats find too messy to incorporate.

B. Full Knowledge or Probabilistic Understanding

The presumption of full knowledge of the consequences involved is rather similar to that of complete availability of definitive and precise valuational weights. It is relevant to see the sources of epistemic ambiguity and their far-reaching effects. No less importantly, there is a need to consider

---

clearly, have been as good as the other, and even a resolutely optimizing ass would not have faced an impasse.

[13] The technical connections are discussed in Sen, *supra* note 10, ch. 7 & 7*; Amartya Sen, Interpersonal Aggregation and Partial Comparability, 38 Econometrica 393 (1970); and Sen, Employment, Technology and Development, *supra* note 4. See also the recent literature on the use of "fuzzy sets" and "fuzzy valuations."

ranges of values of factual variables (like that used for evaluative weights), which lead mathematically to similarly partial orderings of alternative proposals (on the basis of intersection of all the total orderings compatible with each set of values within the respective ranges).[14] Again, the discipline of maximization provides a much fuller reach than the usual insistence on optimization.

It is sometimes presumed that the problem can be avoided by looking at expected values, with probability-weighted valuations. Indeed, this can often work well enough. However, for it to make sense, the choice of probability weights needs justification, as does the axiomatically demanding framework of expected value reasoning. These issues have been extensively discussed elsewhere, and I shall not go further into them here.[15] The use of partial ordering and maximization can be sometimes supplemented by the device of probability distributions and expected value optimization, but the extension may be purchased at some real cost.

The helpfulness of assuming complete knowledge, or less demandingly (but demandingly enough) the usability of expected value reasoning, cannot be doubted. What is at issue is whether substantially important decisional concerns get neglected because of these presumptions. I flag the question as important but will not further pursue this issue here.

C.   Noniterative and Nonparametric Valuations

Valuational judgments we make can take various forms. One distinction relates to judgments that are basic in the sense that they are not parasitic on any underlying factual presumption (other than those which are part of the subject matter of the judgment itself). Nonbasic judgments may, however, draw on factual presumptions, often made in an implicit way, and thus remain subject to revision in the light of more knowledge—indeed even in the light of the results of applying these nonbasic judgments themselves.[16]

When dealing with nonbasic judgments, say, in valuational weights, we have to be aware that the valuational priorities may undergo alteration as the implications of the presumed weights become more fully known or un-

---

[14] The practical bearing of such variations is discussed in Sen, Employment, Technology and Development, *supra* note 4; and Amartya Sen, Resources, Values and Development, essays 12, 14, & 17 (1982).

[15] See Mark J. Machina, "Rational" Decision Making versus "Rational" Decision Modelling? 24 J. Mathematical Psychology 163 (1981); Daniel Kahneman, P. Slovik, & A. Tversky, Judgement under Uncertainty: Heuristics and Biases (1982). I have tried to discuss the issues involved in Amartya Sen, Rationality and Uncertainty, 18 Theory & Decision 109 (1985).

[16] The distinction between "basic" and "nonbasic" judgments is discussed in Sen, *supra* note 10, ch. 5 (1970).

derstood. For example, we may not fully seize the implications of choosing one set of values over another, until we see the results of using that set of values. This suggests the need for iterative exercises of valuation, for example, through the procedure of parametric programming. Rather than taking the weights given as unalterable entities, they could be offered as tentative values, which remain open to revision as and when the results of using those values become clear. Then, instead of having a one-way sequence of valuation, we could proceed from tentative values to the applied results and then rethink as to whether the weights need revising in the light of the generated rankings of alternatives.

In some cases we have clearer values on particular elements in the list of benefits than we have on overall assessments of total happenings. In other cases, however, the overall assessments may speak more immediately to us, in terms of the valuations that we may entertain. Examples are easy to give of both kinds of judgments from the recent literature on contingent valuation as applied to environmental interventions.[17] The format of cost-benefit analysis allows iterative valuation and parametric techniques, even though the mainstream applications go relentlessly in one direction only. Again, the pragmatic convenience of suppressing iterative determination of weights has to be balanced against the practical importance of two-way influences on the nature of elementary valuations and their integrated effects.

V.   EVALUATIVE INDIFFERENCES

A.   Nonvaluation of Actions, Motives, and Rights

In the context of discussing broad consequential evaluation, there was already an opportunity of commenting on the inclusiveness of consequential reasoning, such as taking note of the nature of actions and the fulfillment and violation of recognized rights. Motives too can come into the accounting, even though they are more important in personal decisions than in public choice.[18]

The neglect of these considerations in mainstream cost-benefit analysis does reduce the reach of the ethical analysis underlying public decisions. The literature on human rights brings out how strongly relevant—and closely related—some of these concerns are to what people see as important. These concerns remain potentially pertinent to cost-benefit evaluation

---

[17] See, among many other writings, Contingent Valuation: A Critical Assessment (Jerry A. Hausman ed. 1993); Daniel Kahneman & Jack L. Knetsch, Contingent Valuation and the Value of Public Goods, 22 J. Envtl. Econ. & Mgmt. 90 (1992); W. Michael Hanemann, Valuing the Environment through Contingent Valuation, 8 J. Econ. Persp. 19 (Autumn 1994).

[18] On this see Amartya Sen, On Ethics and Economics (1970).

even when people have no opportunity of expressing their valuations of these concerns in limited models of cost-benefit assessment (for example, in terms of market-price-based evaluations).

B. Indifference to Intrinsic Value of Freedom

The neglect of the freedoms that people enjoy is no less serious a limitation than the neglect of rights. Indeed, recognized rights often tend to take the form of claims on others for compliance—or even help—in favor of the realization of the freedoms or liberties of the persons involved. These entitlements may take the form of cospecified perfect obligations of particular individuals or agencies, or—more standardly in the case of many of the claims of human rights—imperfect obligations of people or agencies who are generally in a position to help.[19]

It is possible for consequential cost-benefit analysis to take note of the substantive freedoms that people have (formally this will require valuation of opportunity sets, and not merely of the chosen alternatives). This can be an important distinction. For example, a person who voluntarily fasts (rather than involuntarily starves) is rejecting the option of eating, but to eliminate the option of eating would make nonsense of the voluntariness of his choice. Fasting is quintessentially an act of choosing to starve, and the elimination of the option of eating robs the person of the opportunity of choice that makes sense of the ''sacrifice'' involved in fasting.

The case for consequential analysis based on comprehensive outcomes (taking note of processes used and freedoms exercised, as opposed to merely culmination outcomes) closely relates to this question and to the extensive reach of consequential reasoning.[20] Insofar as the restricted format of mainstream cost-benefit analysis neglects the importance of freedom, there is a manifest limitation here, and the contrast with a more general consequential approach is clear enough. On the other hand, the practical convenience of allowing that neglect may be very easy to see. It is not crucial that we agree on what exactly is to be done (whether to go for the more

[19] Both ''perfect'' and ''imperfect'' obligations are Kantian concepts, even though modern Kantians seem to focus much more on the former than on the latter. Indeed, the view that human rights may not be properly formulated ''rights'' of any kind seems to relate to the idea that rights must be matched by perfect duties and it is not adequate to link them to imperfect and more general obligations of others. See, for example, Onora O'Neill, Towards Justice and Virtue (1996). A contrary position is defended in Amartya Sen, Development as Freedom, ch. 10 (1999); and also in Sen, *supra* note 6.

[20] On this see Amartya Sen, Internal Consistency of Choice, 61 Econometrica 495 (1993); Amartya Sen, Maximization and the Act of Choice, 65 Econometrica 745 (1997); Amartya Sen, Freedom and Social Choice, in Freedom, Reasoning and Social Choice: Arrow Lectures and Other Essays (forthcoming).

inclusive but more difficult approach, or the opposite), but it is quite important to see what the debate is about (and indeed that there is a debate here to be faced, which many exponents of the limited mainstream methodology seem rather reluctant to acknowledge).

C. *Instrumental View of Behavioral Values*

Values influence our actions, and in assessing the consequences of public projects, valuational assumptions are standardly made. But it is also the case that substantial projects, particularly those involving cultural challenges and also movements of people from one cultural setting to another (for example, from rural to urban areas), may tend to lead to modification of values.[21] This opens up a big issue as to how such value modifications are to be assessed and, in particular, in terms of which values—the prior or the posterior beliefs—the evaluation should occur.

The issue, though enormously complicated, has received attention from some social analysts.[22] I do not have a great solution to offer here, but if a serious problem is neglected—even if for the excellent reason of our not knowing how to go about dealing with it—it is right that the neglect should be flagged. It may conceivably turn out to be rather relevant in our decisional analysis, even if only for the reason that it may make us more modest about insisting on the unquestionable excellence of the advocated decisions.

VI. MARKET-CENTERED VALUATION

A. *Reliance on Willingness to Pay*

In mainstream cost-benefit analysis, the primary work of valuation is done by the use of willingness to pay. This approach is, of course, based on the rationale of the discipline of market valuation. Indeed, the use of valuations based on a market analogy has some of the merits that the market allocation system itself has, including sensitivity to individual preferences and tractability of relative weights.

The basic limitations of this approach include those experienced also by market signaling. There is, for example, the neglect of distributional issues, both (1) in the form of attaching the same weight on everyone's dollars

---

[21] It is, however, important to distinguish between genuine changes in values and those that reflect alterations of relative weights because of parametric variations of the determining variables; on this see Gary S. Becker, Economic Approach to Human Behavior (1976); and Gary S. Becker, Accounting for Tastes (1996).

[22] See, for example, Jon Elster, Ulysses and the Sirens: Studies in Rationality and Irrationality (1979); and Jon Elster, Sour Grapes: Studies in the Subversion of Rationality (1983).

(irrespective of the poverty or the opulence of the persons involved), and (2) in the shape of not attaching any weight to distributional changes resulting from the project or program (since those changes, even if valued positively or negatively by the citizens, are not up for valuation as a private good in the market system).[23] There are also signaling difficulties when there are interdependences and externalities.

In addition to shared problems of (i) the actual market system and (ii) market analogy valuation, the latter has some additional problems as well. This applies particularly to public goods, where valuations based on market analogy have often been invoked. Getting people to reveal what they are really willing to pay is not all that easy, when the question is not followed by an actual demand for that payment. And when it is so followed, there are also strategic considerations that may distort the revealed willingness to pay, for various reasons, of which free riding is perhaps the most well known. There are, of course, proposed devices to deal with incentive compatibility in implementation, but no general surefire method has emerged.

Estimation of willingness to pay is particularly hard in the case of contingent valuation of existence values of prized components of the environment—a centrally important exercise for cost-benefit analysis. The contingent valuation (CV) procedure takes the form of posing hypothetical questions about how much people would be willing to pay to prevent the loss of some particular object.[24] In the legal context, dealing with damage caused by oil spillage and other such acts, the contingent valuation approach has tended to be used as both (1) a measure of the actual loss involved and (2) an indication of the extent of culpability of the party whose negligence (or worse) led to the event that occurred.

The actual use of the CV procedure in devised experiments has tended to yield results that seem to go contrary to what is standardly seen as rational choice.[25] One of the problems—the so-called embedding effect—is illustrated by the finding that the average willingness to pay to prevent 2,000 migratory birds being killed was much the same as the willingness to pay

---

[23] The weights are sometimes interpreted not directly in terms of their actual and immediate consequences, but in terms of their potential use, as reflected in compensations tests of one kind or another. I comment on this line of interpretation in the next section (Section VIB).

[24] The question can also be put in the form of how much one would accept as compensation for the loss. This should tend to exceed—for good "Hicksian" reasons—the willingness to pay to prevent the loss. But the actual margins of difference in the answers to the two sets of questions have tended to be much too large to be readily explainable in this way.

[25] See, for example, Kahneman & Knetsch, *supra* note 17.

for preventing the destruction of 20,000 or 200,000 birds.[26] Had those birds been a threatened species, this set of choices need not have been so hard to follow, since each option may be seen as containing the "valuable" thing of continuity of that species (the people involved are perhaps not valuing anything else). However, the birds in question were not of the threatened type. It is, in fact, hard to judge what choices are or are not consistent or irrational, without going in some detail into the way the choosers see the problem and what they think they are trying to achieve.[27] I shall return to this question presently when discussing the requirements of a social choice formulation of the problem, as opposed to a market analogy valuation.

B.   Sufficiency of Potential Compensation

It is possible to interpret aggregates of willingness to pay in terms of the potential possibility of redistribution, including the compensation of any loss that some people may suffer. Given certain assumptions, such compensational interpretations do indeed have some plausibility. The question, however, is the relevance and persuasive power of ethical reasoning based not on actual outcomes but on potential compensational possibilities that may or may not be actually used.

There is a real motivational tension in the use of the logic of compensation for reading social welfare. If compensations are actually paid, then of course we do not need the compensation criterion, since the actual outcome already includes the paid compensations and can be judged without reference to compensation tests (in the case of Kaldor-Hicks criterion, after compensations have been paid, the result will be a case of a simple Pareto improvement). On the other hand, if compensations are not paid, it is not at all clear in what sense it can be said that this is a social improvement ("Don't worry, my dear loser, we can compensate you fully, and the fact that we don't have the slightest intention of actually paying this compensation makes no difference; it is merely a difference in distribution"). The compensation tests are either redundant or unconvincing.[28]

The assistance that cost-benefit analysis has sought from compensation

[26] See William H. Desvousge *et al.,* Measuring Natural Resource Damages with Contingent Valuation: Tests of Validity and Reliability, in Hausman ed., *supra* note 17.

[27] On this see Amartya Sen, Internal Consistency of Choice, *supra* note 20; and Amartya Sen, Environmental Evaluation and Social Choice: Contingent Valuation and the Market Analogy, 46 Japanese Econ. Rev. 23 (1995).

[28] On this see Amartya Sen, The Welfare Basis of Real Income Comparisons, 17 J. Econ. Literature 1 (1979), reprinted in Sen, Resources, Values and Development, *supra* note 14.

tests has not been particularly well reasoned. This does not, however, obliterate the merits of the approach of willingness to pay (without the odd use of compensational logic). No matter how the requirements of efficiency are specified, there is need for sensitivity to individual preferences, and in this willingness to pay would have a role. If, in a case without externality, a person is willing to pay far less for A than for B, then to give that person B rather than A, when either can be given to her, would involve a loss. This much can be acknowledged even without addressing the distributional issue (since the Pareto criterion is adequate here), and such subchoices will be typically embedded in larger choices (incorporating distributional issues as well).[29] So the information involved in the willingness to pay has some relevance to efficiency, no matter how anemic may be the equity conclusions drawn from it through the hallowed compensation tests. We must not grumble against small mercies, but nor need we dress them up as large triumphs.

C. *Disregard of Social Choice Options*

It was discussed earlier that market-centered valuation has ambiguities especially when it comes to interpreting what people say they are ready to pay for public goods, including environmental preservation and existence values. In this context, it may be useful to ask what kind of social choice interpretation underlies the contingent valuation procedure.[30] The philosophy behind contingent valuation seems to lie in the idea that an environmental good can be seen in essentially the same way as a normal private commodity that we purchase and consume. The valuation that is thus expressed is that of achieving single-handedly—this is crucial—this environmental benefit. Consider, for example, a case in which it is inquired how much I would pay to save all the living creatures that perished as a result of the *Exxon Valdez* disaster, and I say $20. As interpreted in CV, it is now presumed that if $20 paid by me would wipe out altogether all these losses, then I am ready to make that payment. It is hard to imagine that this question and answer can be taken seriously by any practical person (with some idea of what the *Exxon Valdez* disaster produced), since the state of affairs I am asked to imagine could not possibly be true. (Indeed, if I were really to believe that my $20 can on its own clear up the mess created by the

---

[29] On this see Amartya Sen, Real National Income, 43 Rev. Econ. Stud. 19 (1976); reprinted in Amartya Sen, Choice, Welfare and Measurement (Harvard Univ. Press 1997) (1982).

[30] The discussion that follows draws on Sen, Environmental Evaluation and Social Choice, *supra* note 27.

Exxon Valdez disaster, then I am not sure any importance should be attached to what I do think.)

The condition of independence of irrelevant alternatives, formulated by Kenneth Arrow in *Social Choice and Individual Values,* states that in making choices over the relevant alternatives (that is, over the alternative states in the actual opportunity set), the social choice should not depend on our valuation of irrelevant alternatives (that is, the ones not in the opportunity set).[31] The imagined state of affairs in which I have paid $20 and all the losses from the *Exxon Valdez* spill are gone is certainly not a relevant alternative, since it is just not feasible, but somehow our valuation of that irrelevant alternative is being made here into the central focus of attention in choosing between actually feasible alternatives—relevant for the choice.

The very idea that I treat the prevention of an environmental damage just like buying a private good is itself quite absurd. The amount I am ready to pay for my toothpaste is typically not affected by the amount you pay for yours. But it would be amazing if the payment I am ready to make to save nature is totally independent of what others are ready to pay for it, since it is specifically a social concern. The "lone ranger" model of environmental evaluation—central to the interpretation of CV valuation—confounds the nature of the problem at hand. We have no escape from having to use valuations derived from other methods of information gathering, such as questionnaires that describe the social states more fully.

Some have argued, with considerable cogency, that even though the formal question in the CV questionnaire refers to what each would pay alone to save that bit of nature, the answers are best interpreted as if they had been asked how much they would contribute in a joint effort to achieve that result.[32] It does indeed require much less willing suspension of disbelief to answer this allegedly de facto question seriously than the question that is actually asked. But it raises other difficulties. What I am willing to contribute must, given the nature of the task, depend on how much I expect others to contribute. There could be effects in different directions. I may be willing to contribute something if others also do, making this an assurance game.[33] On the other hand, I may feel a less pressing need to do something myself if others are in any case going to do a lot and my own sacrifice could make little difference to the social object in question (this is one route toward free

[31] Kenneth J. Arrow, Social Choice and Individual Values (1951).

[32] See, for example, Daniel Kahneman *et al.,* Stated Willingness to Pay for Public Goods: A Psychological Perspective, 4 Psychological Sci. 310 (1993).

[33] On assurance games, see Amartya Sen, Isolation, Assurance and the Social Rate of Discount, 81 Q. J. Econ. 112 (1967); and Angus Deaton & John Muellbauer, Economics and Consumer Behaviour (1980).

riding). If the lone-ranger model of CV is tightly specified but incredible, the contribution model is credible but severely underspecified.[34]

How might we make better use of the social choice approach to interpret this valuational issue?[35] One requirement would be to make sure that the individuals consider the actual alternative states from which the social choice is to be made. Properly devised questionnaires can easily achieve that. This is where the market analogy is particularly deceptive, since the market does not provide specified social states to the individuals to choose from. Given the prices, I choose my basket of commodities, and you choose yours; neither has to look beyond our nose. There are many problems for which all this works extremely well, but environmental evaluation is not one of them. In order to get people's views on what is to be done, they have to be told what the real alternatives are, involving specification of what will be done by the others. This is not the language of market valuation, nor a part of its epistemic probe. It requires specification of particular proposals of actions to be undertaken, with articulation of the actions of others as well (including contributions to be made by them). Valuation of social states is a part of a standard social choice exercise, but not of a market valuation exercise. The market analogy is particularly deceptive in this case since it does not deal with social alternatives.

VII. CONCLUDING REMARKS

To conclude, cost-benefit analysis is a very general discipline, with some basic demands—expressed here in the form of foundational principles— that establish an approach but not a specific method. Even these elementary demands would be resisted by those who would like a different general approach, involving, say, implicit valuation (rather than explicit articulation) or the use of pure deontological principles (rather than broadly consequential evaluation). There are also technical issues in the strategic use of additivity (despite the plausibility of concave objectives). However, even with these various foundational demands (I have tried to defend them, up to a

[34] There is a further difficulty in using the willingness to pay for "existence value" because of a problem in interpreting why a person is willing to pay a certain amount in order to try and achieve the continued existence of a threatened object. As Eric Posner has pointed out to me, if the payment offered comes not from the person's own expectation of benefit but from a sense of "commitment" (a commitment she has to try to bring about the continued existence of the threatened object), then the logic of interpreting the sum total of willingness to pay by all who promise to pay cannot be easily seen as the aggregate benefit they receive altogether.

[35] On this issue see Sen, Environmental Evaluation and Social Choice, *supra* note 27. See also the papers included in Social Choice Re-examined (Kenneth Arrow, Amartya Sen, & Kotaro Suzumura eds. 1997).

point), the approach of cost-benefit analysis is rather permissive and can be adopted by many warring factions in the field of public decisions.

Divisiveness increases as additional requirements are imposed, including structural demands and evaluative indifferences. There are gains and losses—the gains mainly in convenience and usability and losses mainly in the reach of the evaluative exercise. I have tried to indicate what the pros and cons are. While the mainstream procedures tend to incorporate all these requirements, it is easy to see how some of these demands may be dropped in a particular procedure of valuation.

The mainstream approach of cost-benefit analysis not only takes on the foundational principles, the structural demands, and the evaluative indifferences, but also uses a very special method of valuation through direct use of, or in analogy with, the logic of market allocation. This market-centered approach is sometimes taken (particularly by its advocates) to be the only approach of cost-benefit analysis. That claim is quite arbitrary, but given the importance of this approach, I have devoted a good deal of this paper to scrutinizing that approach in particular.

The market analogy has merits in the case of many public projects, particularly in providing sensitivity to individual preferences, relevant for efficiency considerations (in one form or another). Its equity claims are, however, mostly bogus, even though they can be made more real if explicit distributional weights are introduced (as they standardly are not in the mainstream approach).[36] The use of compensation tests suffers from the general problem that they are either redundant or entirely unconvincing.

Even the efficiency claims of the mainstream approach are severely compromised in the case of many public goods, and much would depend on the nature of the valuations in question. There are particular difficulties with environmental valuations, especially existence values. In this case, the valuational demands of social choice are easy to see, but not easy to reveal through the device of willingness to pay. The specification of social states that is needed for intelligent valuation (including the identification of who will do what) is simply not provided by the market-based questioning (either in the form "How much would you pay, if you could single-handedly bring about the environmental change?" or in the form "How much would you contribute, assuming whatever you want to assume as to what others are doing?"). The spectacular merit of the informational economy of the market system for private goods ends up being a big drag when more information is needed than the market analogy can offer.

---

[36] See, however, Dasgupta, Marglin, & Sen, supra note 9, for examples of techniques that combine willingness to pay with distributional weights (as well as recognition of "merit goods" and general social concerns).

When all the requirements of ubiquitous market-centered evaluation have been incorporated into the procedures of cost-benefit analysis, it is not so much a discipline as a daydream. If, however, the results are tested only in terms of internal consistency, rather than by their plausibility beyond the limits of the narrowly chosen system, the glaring defects remain hidden and escape exposure. Daydreams can be very consistent indeed. Sensible cost-benefit analysis demands something beyond the mainstream method, in particular, the invoking of explicit social choice judgments that take us beyond market-centered valuation. The exponents of the mainstream need not face much questioning from the deontologists (who will not speak to them), but they do have to address the questions that other cost-benefit analysts raise. The debate may be, in a sense, ''internal,'' but it is no less intense for that reason.

COST-BENEFIT ANALYSIS AND POPULATION

*JOHN BROOME**

ABSTRACT

A cost-benefit analysis of an event must take account of the event's effect on population. Cost-benefit analysts traditionally ignore these effects because they think that changes in the population are ethically neutral: neither benefits or costs. Although this view is intuitively plausible, it is false for theoretical reasons. There can be only one neutral level of lifetime well-being. Adding to the population a person whose well-being would be below this level is bad. However, this single neutral level might be very vague, which means that over a large range of levels of well-being, adding a person at that level is neither determinately good nor determinately bad. This helps to restore the view that changing the population is generally ethically neutral. But neutrality of this sort turns out to have incredible implications for cost-benefit analysis.

I. COST-BENEFIT ANALYSIS AS VALUATION

WHAT is the purpose of cost-benefit analysis? I assume it is to make a valuation. Cost-benefit analysis may be applied to an act, an event, a policy, a project, or something else—for uniformity I shall speak of events. It is intended to assess the value of the event. That is to say, it is intended to assess how good or bad it is—I use "value" as a synonym for "goodness." An event may have various good features, which we call its "benefits," and various bad features, which we call its "costs," or the "harms" it does. To assess how good the event is, taken as a whole, we have to put together its costs and benefits. This is a process of aggregation or weighing, and it is the purpose of cost-benefit analysis.

This is the conventional view, but it is not the only one. Cost-benefit analysis may alternatively be seen as a procedure for making a decision. In a democratic country, it may be seen as a democratic procedure: as a procedure the community sometimes adopts in order to put its wishes into effect. Different members of the community will naturally have conflicting preferences about some of the acts the community might choose to do. To arrive

* University of St. Andrews. This paper was presented at the conference Cost-Benefit Analysis in Chicago, September 1999. I am very grateful to the participants—particularly Matthew Adler and Eric Posner—for their comments.

[*Journal of Legal Studies*, vol. XXIX]

in a democratic fashion at a decision whether or not to do some particular act, people's conflicting preferences may have to be aggregated or weighed against each other. That can be seen as the purpose of cost-benefit analysis. It makes cost-benefit analysis parallel to voting or a parliament. The community decides some issues by means of voting, some through their representatives in parliament, and some by means of cost-benefit analysis.

Under the first interpretation of cost-benefit analysis, a particular way of doing the analysis would have to be justified on the basis of the theory of value. We should have to ask just how particular benefits and costs come together to determine the overall value of an event. By contrast, under the second interpretation, a particular way of doing cost-benefit analysis would have to be justified on the basis of democratic theory. We should have to ask what is an appropriate democratic way of putting together people's conflicting preferences in order to arrive at a decision.

The practice of cost-benefit analysis fits the first interpretation better than the second. To be sure, in a democratic country, cost-benefit analysis is a component of the democratic process—what else could it be? But it cannot plausibly be seen as itself a democratic decision-making procedure. In practice, the outcome of a cost-benefit analysis is never a decision; it is always just an input into a broader decision-making process. This is exactly what we should expect if cost-benefit analysis is seen as an evaluation. An assessment of value should be part of a well-functioning democratic process. When they participate in the democratic process, people at all levels—the government, the voters, and their representatives—need information about the value of events they are concerned with. That is what cost-benefit analysis can supply.

In a democracy, a particular assessment of value should not determine a decision on its own. For one thing, it is not infallible, and the decision process needs to take into account how reliable it is. Second, the decision process may need to take into account considerations that are separate from value, such as the rights of property owners or minorities. Finally, it has to be a genuinely democratic process, and democracy cannot always be expected to make the best decision. For example, the vote may go against the outcome of a cost-benefit analysis, even if the analysis is a correct assessment of value. Still, in a democracy, the vote should decide.

I dare say we could institute a process of decision making by means of cost-benefit analysis, and it might be a genuinely democratic process. But that is not the role of cost-benefit analysis at present. As present, it is intended to be an evaluation, and that is how I shall take it.

If it is to be an accurate evaluation, it needs to estimate costs and benefits at their true value. Consequently, it needs to be founded on a theory of value, aimed at determining what costs and benefits truly are. Cost-benefit analysis is the practical end of valuing. We start from a theory of value, and we put it into practical effect by means of cost-benefit analysis.

In this paper, I shall investigate some aspects of the theory of value that underlies cost-benefit analysis, but I shall take some other aspects for granted. I shall take it for granted that a cost-benefit analysis of an event is a comparison. It compares how good things would be if the event took place with how good they would be if it did not take place. So it compares the goodness of two states of affairs. I shall also take it for granted that the goodness of a state of affairs depends only on which people exist in that state and how well off those people are. Briefly and roughly, the only good is the good of people. This assumption may be stated formally as something I call "the principle of personal good," but I do not need to state it formally here.[1] It means that when we assess the costs and benefits of an event, we may concentrate on the well-being of people only.

Once we recognize that cost-benefit analysis depends on a theory of value, a question arises. How should we do cost-benefit analysis if no credible theory of value can be found? I ask this as a genuine—not a rhetorical—question. I do not know the answer to it. It is an important question in practice. In an important domain of cost-benefit analysis, no credible theory of value seems available. Yet there are pressing decisions to be made. What should we do?

II.   KILLING DONE BY GLOBAL WARMING

The problem is very widespread, as I shall explain. But it is especially pressing, or at least especially conspicuous, in decision making about global warming. I shall use that as my example. Global warming will cause various harms and various benefits. Conversely, if we act to control global warming, we shall bring about various benefits and also suffer various costs. To weigh them, we evidently need cost-benefit analysis.

Among the harms that global warming will do is the killing of very many people. It will kill in three predictable ways. First, infectious tropical diseases will increase their range. Second, there will be more frequent and more devastating floods. Third, because temperatures are higher, there will be an increased number of deaths caused directly by heat waves. Of these causes, the first will almost certainly be the most important, but only the third has been quantified. One estimate is that this third cause will kill around 200,000 people per year by about 50 years from now.[2] Taking all

[1] See John Broome, Weighing Lives, ch. 6 (forthcoming, Oxford Univ. Press 2001).

[2] See the survey in D. W. Pearce et al., The Social Costs of Climate Change: Greenhouse Damage and the Benefits of Control, in Climate Change 1995: Economic and Social Dimensions of Climate Change 179–224 (James P. Bruce, Hoesung Lee, & Erik F. Haites eds. 1996).

three causes together, it would not be unreasonable to predict a figure of 1 million deaths per year by about 50 years from now, and this rate of killing might continue for centuries.

Taking a very conservative estimate of the number of killings and a very conservative valuation of each death, Samuel Fankhauser estimates the harm done by killing as 18 percent of the total harm of global warming. With a less conservative valuation of a death, his estimate rises to 38 percent.[3] Whatever we may think of these figures, killing is plainly one of the greatest harms that global warming will cause. Any cost-benefit analysis of global warming or of measures to control global warming will have to take account of it.

III.   THE VALUE OF EXTENDING OR SHORTENING LIVES: VALUE BASED ON PREFERENCES

The harm of death and the benefit of saving life have been incorporated into practical cost-benefit analysis for a long time. As it happens, they have been incorporated badly. This point is incidental to my argument, but I shall cause confusion if I say no more about it. So this section and the next, which are about the value of extending or shortening lives, are really an aside from my line of argument.

Cost-benefit analysts have been reluctant to acknowledge that a theory of value must underlie their work, and they have tried to keep theory out of their practice as much as they can. Economists are traditionally reticent people, and they do not like to impose their own theories of value on their work; instead, they prefer to leave valuations as much as possible to the individual preferences of the public. In particular, economists have tried not to commit themselves to any substantive theory about the value of a person's life. So when they value people's lives, they like to base their valuation on the people's own preferences about preserving their lives.

A person's preferences can be represented ordinally by a utility function. That is to say, numbers called "utilities" can be assigned to states of affairs in such a way that one state has a higher utility than another if and only if the person prefers the first to the second. If a cost-benefit analyst is to base values on preferences, she will have to use utility as her measure of value. She will have to take the value of an event to a person to be the increase or decrease in the person's utility that the event causes.

Preferences do not determine utilities uniquely. Given a person's preferences, there is always a wide range of utility functions that will represent

---

[3] See Samuel Fankhauser, Valuing Climate Change: The Economics of the Greenhouse (1995), reported in Pearce *et al., supra* note 2, at 197.

them ordinally. Consequently, a cost-benefit analyst who wishes to base values on preferences needs to choose one function out of the range to serve as the measure of value for the person. Since the analyst is dealing with many people, she must choose one function for each person. In doing so, she implicitly does two things. For each person, she treats a particular function as a cardinal utility function for that person, and she takes each person's cardinal function to be interval comparable with other people's. Less technically, she chooses a particular arithmetic scale to measure each person's preferences, and she fixes a particular basis for weighing one person's preferences against another's.

In practice, the particular utility function picked by most cost-benefit analysts for valuing lives is one known as "willingness to pay." It is one of a class of functions called "money-metric utilities." It bases the value of a person's life on the money she is willing to pay to reduce a risk to her life. If she is willing to pay $50 to reduce by one in 10,000 her risk of being killed in (say) a road accident, then her life is valued at $50 times 10,000: $500,000, that is. A person's willingness to pay to reduce risk is a feature of her preferences about risk and about money. So this method bases the value of a person's life on her preferences, as it is intended to do.

A person's willingness to pay is normally used in cost-benefit analysis to provide both a cardinal scale of value and a basis for interpersonal comparisons of value. The effect of using it for interpersonal comparisons is to treat a dollar as equally as valuable to one person as to any other person. However, a dollar is manifestly not equally as valuable to one person as it is to any other person. A dollar to a peasant in Bangladesh will sustain life for a while, whereas a dollar to an affluent American, who already has all the necessities of life, will buy nothing of significant value. Using willingness to pay as a measure of value can result in absurdity. In a cost-benefit analysis of global warming, willingness to pay would treat an American life as worth 10 or 20 Indian lives.[4] Since Americans are much richer than Indians, they are willing to pay 10 or 20 times as much for safety.

This absurd conclusion is not inherent in the project of basing values on people's preferences. It results from adopting a money-metric utility function to represent a person's preferences, rather than some other utility function. It is possible to use the same data of preferences in a better way, by making appropriate adjustments to money-metric utility.[5] Alternatively, a

[4] See Pearce et al., supra note 2, at 195–98. This consequence of the willingness-to-pay utility function caused justified consternation in meetings of the Intergovernmental Panel on Climate Change. See Intergovernmental Panel on Climate Change, Policymakers' Summary, in Bruce, Lee, & Haites eds., supra note 2, at 11.

[5] See Jean Drèze & Nicholas Stern, The Theory of Cost-Benefit Analysis, in 2 Handbook of Public Economics 909–89 (Alan J. Auerbach & Martin Feldstein eds. 1987). In Pearce

quite different utility function may be used. For example, one known as the "healthy-years equivalent" has been recommended for health economics.[6]

However, all these utility functions represent preferences, and there are separate reasons why preferences are an unsatisfactory basis for valuing lives. There is plenty of evidence that, in contexts involving risks, people's preferences are generally muddled and incoherent. They cannot be considered rational,[7] which means they cannot be taken as a sound basis for valuation. Moreover, they are particularly dubious as a basis for valuation when it comes to people's lives. The value of a life is a complex thing, involving the aggregation of well-being across time, as I shall explain in Section IV. It is a difficult theoretical problem to know how the value is determined. Few people have thought much about it, and it is implausible that most people's preferences reflect a proper valuation of their lives.

The aggregation of well-being across time calls for some theoretical analysis; we cannot expect to base it entirely on people's preferences. We need a theory about how well-being distributed over time throughout a life comes together to determine the overall value of the life. So we need a theory of value. Preferences may well play a part in the theory. For example, people's preferences are a plausible basis for determining the relative values of many current goods, such as different sorts of food. But we cannot escape the need for theory by trying to base all our valuations directly on preferences.

IV. THE VALUE OF EXTENDING OR SHORTENING LIVES: LIFETIME WELL-BEING

When a person's life is saved, she lives a longer life than she would have lived. The benefit to her is the difference between the goodness, or value, of her longer life and the goodness, or value, of the shorter life she would have lived. Conversely, if an event kills a person, the harm done her is the difference between the value of the longer life she would have lived and the value of the shorter life she actually lives.

So to do cost-benefit analysis properly, we need a theory about the value of a life. I shall propose one. I have no conclusive arguments for it, and

---

et al., supra note 2, at 206, Pearce *et al.* point out that weights can be used to adjust the willingness-to-pay valuations.

[6] See A. Mehrez & A. Gafni, Quality-Adjusted Life Years, Utility Theory and Healthy-Years Equivalents, 9 Med. Decision Making 142 (1989).

[7] For instance, see Amos Tversky & Daniel Kahneman, Rational Choice and the Framing of Decisions, 59 J. Bus. 250 (1986). An example that creates problems specifically for valuation appears in M. W. Jones-Lee, G. Loomes, & P. R. Philips, Valuing the Prevention of Non-fatal Road Injuries: Contingent Valuation vs Standard Gambles, 47 Oxford Econ. Papers 676 (1995).

indeed I recognize that it may well be wrong. It is only what I call a "default theory." It is a natural, plausible starting point, which I think we should accept unless we find good reason for departing from it. There are some arguments for it, but they are definitely not conclusive, and I shall not set them out in this paper.[8]

First of all, I shall assume that the goodness of a person's life depends only on how long it continues and on how well it goes at each time it is in progress. A person is born at some time and dies at some time, and at each time in between her life goes well (or badly) to some degree. I shall use the term "temporal well-being" for how well it goes at a particular time. I shall use the term "lifetime well-being" for the goodness of the life as a whole. My first assumption is that a person's lifetime well-being depends only on the length of her life and on her temporal well-being at all times in her life.

To put it another way, lifetime well-being is some sort of an aggregate of temporal well-being at all times in the life. What sort of aggregate? I assume as my default theory that it is simply the total. To find the value of a life, simply add up how well the life goes at each time. If a person's life is saved, the benefit to her is the increase in her lifetime well-being, which is the increase in the total of her temporal well-being. This "total theory" is my default.

I can simplify it a little more if I make the assumption that there is no backward causation of temporal well-being. Can events that occur later in a person's life affect her temporal well-being at earlier times? Imagine you write a book that later turns out to be influential. The event of its becoming influential may add value to all the earlier time you spent writing it, by making your work during all those times worthwhile. That is arguable at least, but for simplicity let us assume away this type of backward causation. Then we can say that the benefit of saving someone's life is the total temporal well-being that she goes on to enjoy in the rest of her life after she is saved. This is the simplified version of the total theory.

There are many other possibilities besides the total theory. For example, some authors think a life that starts badly but improves is better than one that starts well and deteriorates, even if both have the same total of temporal well-being.[9] Some authors discount well-being in later years compared with earlier years, which has the opposite effect. Another suggestion is that ups and downs are a bad thing, so a life of even tenor is better than a variable one.[10] Conflicting with this is the view that a good life must have a

---

[8] See Broome, *supra* note 1, chs. 14–16.

[9] For instance, David Velleman, Well-being and Time, 72 Pac. Phil. Q. 48 (1991).

[10] See Amartya Sen, Utilitarianism and Welfarism, 76 J. Phil. 463 (1979).

high peak: what really matters is the best time in life. One might think that
the goodness of a life is its average level of temporal well-being, rather than
its total. And so on. I find it hard to assess these views. I know no good
arguments for any of them; at best some of them seem intuitively attractive.
But since some of them conflict with others, we ought to be suspicious of
their intuitive attractions. There are some arguments for the total theory,
and it is at least a simple theory. I think it is well qualified to be the default.

It only makes proper sense after we have done some preliminary technical work. First, we need to make sure that temporal well-being is measured
on a cardinal scale. Second, we need to fix a zero of temporal well-being,
because the zero makes a difference when it comes to comparing lives of
different lengths. This means that the scale of well-being is actually more
than cardinal; it is a ratio scale. Third, we have to make sure that well-being
is comparable between different times in a person's life; it must actually be
fully comparable. My own approach to these conditions is not to rely on an
intuitive cardinal scale or an intuitive zero, but to define the scale and the
zero, and then to defend the default theory specifically on the basis of the
definitions.[11] I do not have to go into these technical matters here.

A theory similar to my default is regularly used to value lives in much
of health economics. Health economists often measure the benefit of a treatment in terms of qalys, or quality-adjusted life-years. If a person's life is
extended by some treatment, they take the benefit to be the total number of
years she afterward lives, adjusted by the quality of life in those years. This
is not quite the same as my default theory, since what health economists
mean by "quality of life" is not the same as temporal well-being. Still, it
is similar. At least health economics has the merit that it bases the value of
life on a plausible theory of value.

V.   THE VALUE OF ADDING OR SUBTRACTING LIVES

According to the simplified version of my default theory, which assumes
away backward causation, if a person's life is saved, the benefit that results
is the well-being that the person goes on to enjoy in the rest of her life.
Saving her life adds well-being to the world in this way, and that is why
we value it. But saving a life often adds well-being to the world in a different way too. If a young person is saved, she may well later have a child,
who would never have existed had this person not been saved. The child
will enjoy well-being during her life; her life will be good (or bad) to some
degree. Why should we not count the child's well-being as part of the bene-

---

[11] See Broome, *supra* note 1.

fit of saving the existing person's life, if we count the well-being of the person herself?

This is just to raise the question. Saving a life adds well-being to the world, and so does creating a life. Why should we value one and not the other? Nothing forces us to treat the two ways of adding well-being equivalently, but at least we need to think about the value of bringing a person into existence. If it does indeed have a value, we certainly should not ignore its value in cost-benefit analysis.[12] Cost-benefit analysis must rest on a theory of value, and the theory must account for population changes. Very many events lead to the existence of new people, and many prevent the existence of people who otherwise would have existed. For example, a change in the rate of income tax will influence people's decisions about having children. Global warming will undoubtedly affect the world's population, though it may not yet be clear what its effect will be. So if adding people to the world has value—either positive or negative—its value is bound to be significant in many cost-benefit analyses.

This point is independent of my particular default theory for the value of extending an individual life. However we value extending life, we need at least to consider whether adding a new life to the world has a value. It is perhaps easiest to see this if you think, as I do, that the value of extending a person's life is simply the value of increasing the person's well-being. My discussion of the value of extending life was simply intended to lead up to this point. Now I have made it, we can set aside the question of how to value extending life. The default theory is no longer needed. Let us simply take it for granted that each person who lives has some level of lifetime well-being, however that may be determined. Then we can press on to consider the value of adding a person to the world. Naturally, this value may well depend on the level of lifetime well-being that the added person enjoys.

My terminology may cause confusion. I have been speaking of the value of a person's life and have also called this value the person's lifetime well-being. If a person is added to the population, she will have some lifetime well-being; her life will have some value. You might think that this value must be the value of the person's living that life; it must be the benefit of her existence, which must be added into our cost-benefit calculation. Once we have a theory of the value of life, why is that not automatically a theory

---

[12] In M. W. Jones-Lee, The Economics of Safety and Physical Risk (1989), Jones-Lee suggests it may be permissible to ignore the value of adding people to the population when the effects on population are unpredictable. But in many cases, the effects are quite well predictable. For example, most people have children, so it is predictable that saving the life of a young person will commonly bring it about that she later has children.

of the value of adding a life to the world, as well as a theory of the value of saving a life? Why is there any question about it?

To clear this up, it may be helpful if I introduce a distinction. When I spoke of the value of saving a life, I meant its value to the person. It is the benefit to her of having her life saved. I shall call this its "personal" value. But when we consider the value of adding a person to the world, we are asking how valuable it is that this person lives. We are not asking for the value to the person herself, but the value "from the point of view of the universe," as Henry Sidgwick put it. I call this its "general" value. Nothing says that the general value of a person's life must be the same as its personal value to the person. My default theory is a theory of the personal value of a life; it leaves open the question of its general value. In other words, it leaves open the general value of a person's existence.

VI. The Intuition of Neutrality

Now let us face up to this question of general value. What is the value of adding a person to the world? I know of no cost-benefit analysis in practice that has taken account of this value. I think the reason is plain and understandable. I think cost-benefit analysts take it for granted that adding a person has no value. More exactly, they assume it has no value in itself. No doubt adding a person has value for other people. Parents are often benefited by having a child, and on the other hand, many people may be harmed by the demands made on the world's resources by an extra person. But these are externalities, and there is no doubt they should be included in a cost-benefit analysis. However, cost-benefit analysts assume that adding a person has no value in itself, apart from externalities. Apart from externalities, the value of adding a person is zero.

This is understandable because it is an extremely natural intuition shared by very many people. The intuition is that bringing a person into existence is not in itself either good or bad; it is ethically neutral; it has no ethical value. Many people think that, and there is this argument to support it: Doing something is surely only good if it benefits someone and bad if it harms someone. To benefit a person you must make her better off than she would otherwise have been, and to harm her you must make her worse off than she would otherwise have been. Bringing a person into existence does not make her either better or worse off than she would otherwise have been. Therefore, it neither benefits nor harms her. So it must be neither good nor bad in itself.[13]

---

[13] An argument like this appears in Jan Narveson, Utilitarianism and New Generations, 76 Mind 62 (1967).

Let me spell out a specific implication of this intuition. Take two possible states of affairs, *A* and *B*, which contain the same population, except that *A* contains an extra person who does not exist in *B*. I mean that, besides this one extra person, both states contain exactly the same people, not merely the same number of people. Suppose that each of these other people is equally as well off in *A* as she is in *B*. For example, if the extra person's parents are happy in *A* because they have a child, then they have some compensating happiness in *B*, where they do not have a child. I assumed in Section I that all value derives from people's well-being. So the relative value of *A* and *B* must depend on the well-being of the people who exist in both, or else on the extra person's well-being. Everyone who exists in both is equally well off in either; so far as these people's well-being is concerned, *A* and *B* are equally good. The intuition of neutrality tells us that the extra person's well-being has no value in itself. The upshot is that, according to the intuition, *A* and *B* are equally good.

The intuition is not affected by the level of well-being enjoyed by the extra person in *A*. Actually, that is not completely true. If the extra person has a life of unrelieved suffering, then most of us would think it a bad thing that she should exist; it would be better if she did not. Then we would think *B* is better than *A*. But provided the extra person's life is not a bad one, we would think *A* and *B* are equally good, whether her life is very good or only moderately good. At least for a wide range of levels of well-being, *A* and *B* are equally good. We might say there is a neutral range of well-being such that adding a person whose well-being is in this range is equally as good as not adding her. The range may be very wide, extending from very mediocre lives up to the best lives imaginable. Intuitions vary about the width of the range, but most people's intuitions agree that there is a neutral range of some extent.

VII.   A SINGLE NEUTRAL LEVEL OF WELL-BEING

I share this intuition, but I also know it must be false. To see why, think now of a third state, *C*, which contains all the same people as *A*—all the people in *B* plus one more. Everyone apart from the extra person is equally as well off in *C* as she is in *A* and in *B*. In both *A* and *C* the extra person is within the neutral range. But in *A* she is better off than she is in *C*: her well-being is higher up in the neutral range. Undoubtedly, *A* is a better state of affairs than *C*, because it equally as good as *C* for everyone apart from the extra person, and it is better for the extra person. But according to the intuition, *A* is equally as good as *B*, and *B* is equally as good as *C*, because adding a person within the neutral range is neutral. "Equally as good as" is a transitive relation. It therefore follows from the intuition that *A* is equally as good as *C*. But this is not so: *A* is better than *C*. So the intuition is false.

This argument shows there cannot be a neutral range. There can only be a single level of well-being such that adding a person at that level is equally as good as not adding her. There is only a single neutral level, we may say. Adding a person at a level of well-being above the neutral level is better than not adding her; it has a positive value. Adding a person below the neutral level is worse than not adding her; it has a negative value.

For all I have said so far, this neutral level may depend on the starting point. My example was concerned with adding an extra person to a state of affairs *B; B* constitutes the starting point. In it, a particular number of people exist, and each person has a particular level of well-being. Given this number of people and their levels of well-being, there is a single neutral level such that adding a person at that level is equally as good as not adding her. If we set out from a different starting point, there will still be only a single neutral level, but it may be a different one.

However, there are arguments to show, or at least strongly suggest, that the neutral level is in fact constant; it is independent of the starting point. This is not essential to my conclusions in this paper, so I shall not rehearse these arguments here.[14] But it is a convenience and I shall take it for granted; I shall assume there is a constant neutral level. Adding a person above this level is a good thing; adding a person below this level is a bad thing.

I shall make a further assumption that is not essential to the argument but is a great convenience. I shall assume that when we compare two states of affairs that have the same population, the one that has the greater total of people's lifetime well-being is better than the other. This is a utilitarian principle, applied only to a constant population. I do not assume it gratuitously. It can be supported by arguments that I find reasonably persuasive.[15]

From this constant-population utilitarian principle, together with a constant neutral level, it is easy to derive a specific formula for the value of a state of affairs.[16] I do not regard this formula as merely a default, because its two premises are supported by reasonably persuasive arguments. It is

$$(g_1 - v) + (g_2 - v) + \cdots + (g_n - v). \qquad (1)$$

[14] See Charles Blackorby, Walter Bosser, & David Donaldson, Intertemporal Population Ethics: Critical-Level Utilitarian Principles, 63 Econometrica 1303 (1995); and a similar argument in Broome, *supra* note 1, ch. 12.

[15] See John Broome, Weighing Goods (1991); and Broome, *supra* note 1, ch. 7.

[16] The derivation is in Broome, *supra* note 1, ch. 13.

In this formula, $g_1, g_2, \ldots, g_n$ are the lifetime well-beings of all the people who exist, and v is the neutral level. The theory of value represented in this formula was originally called "critical-level utilitarianism" by Charles Blackorby and David Donaldson.[17] I prefer to call it the "normalized total principle."[18] To value a state of affairs, it tells us first to calculate, for each person, the difference between her well-being and the neutral level. Then we take the total of all these differences. This total is the value of the state of affairs.

We may treat the zero of well-being as arbitrary. If we were to set it at the neutral level, then formula (1) would be simplified. It would be simply the total of people's well-being—hence my name the "normalized total principle." However, because I wish to treat the neutral level as vague, I cannot actually make this normalization. So I shall assume the zero of well-being is assigned arbitrarily. It has no significance.

VIII.   A Vague Neutral Level

The conclusion that there is only a single neutral level, whether constant or not, is strongly counterintuitive. What level of well-being could it plausibly be? Suppose it is at the level of a fairly good life. Adding someone whose life would be a little less good than this would be a bad thing. It would be worth some small sacrifice on the part of existing people to prevent the existence of a person at this level. Yet her life, if she lived it, would be a fairly good one. How could it be a bad thing that a person lives a fairly good life? Or suppose alternatively that the neutral level is at the level of a mediocre life. Adding a person whose life would be a little better than this would be a good thing. It would be worth some small sacrifice on the part of existing people—a small reduction in their well-being—to bring this person into existence. Yet her life would be mediocre. It is implausible that existing people's well-being should be sacrificed for the sake of creating a person whose life would be mediocre. Either high or low, it is hard to believe there is just a single neutral level. Besides all this, there remains the argument I mentioned in Section VI, that adding a person must generally be ethically neutral because it neither harms nor benefits anyone.

The argument is not conclusive. It rests on the assumption that an event is ethically neutral if it neither harms nor benefits anyone, and we could reject that assumption. Furthermore, we could conclude that our intuition

---

[17] Charles Blackorby & David Donaldson, Social Criteria for Evaluating Population Change, 25 J. Pub. Econ. 13 (1984).

[18] Broome, *supra* note 1, ch. 13.

about the value of adding people is unreliable. Not all intuitions are correct, and if they cannot be fitted into a coherent theory of value, they must be rejected. Still, intuitions are an important source for moral philosophy, and it would be unwise to give this one up without a struggle. It is worth seeing how far it can be accommodated in our theory of value.

Because the intuition is so powerful, a great deal of literature tries to make this accommodation. Larry Temkin argues that the relation "equally as good as" may not be transitive. This would refute the argument I set out in Section VII for the conclusion that there is only a single neutral level.[19] Partha Dasgupta rejects the whole idea of goodness "from the point of view of the universe," which the argument relies on. Dasgupta thinks that goodness must be understood in a relative way: goodness from the point of view of a particular population.[20] A third potential accommodation can be found in a notion of conditional goodness that may be drawn from Bernard Williams's notion of conditional desires.[21] I have investigated all these attempted accommodations and others and concluded that all but one of them are unsuccessful.[22]

One is moderately successful. It stems from an idea that can be found in Derek Parfit's *Reasons and Persons*.[23] It has been developed in one direction by Charles Blackorby, Walter Bossert, and David Donaldson.[24] I have developed it in a different direction in my *Weighing Lives*.[25] Here is an outline of my development.

I suggest there is indeed only one neutral level, but this level is vague. I favor the supervaluationist account of vagueness,[26] and I shall explain my suggestion in terms of that account. So first I need to outline supervaluationism.

According to supervaluationism, the meaning of a vague term such as

---

[19] Larry S. Temkin, Intransitivity and the Mere Addition Paradox, 16 Phil. & Pub. Aff. 138 (1987).

[20] Partha Dasgupta, Savings and Fertility: Ethical Issues, 23 Phil. & Pub. Aff. 99 (1994).

[21] Williams describes conditional desires in Bernard Williams, The Makropulos Case: Reflections on the Tedium of Immortality, in Problems of the Self 82 (1973). I developed the idea of conditional goodness and applied it to the problem of population in John Broome, The Value of a Person, in 68 Proc. Aristotelian Soc'y 167 (Supp. 1994).

[22] See Broome, *supra* note 21; and Broome, *supra* note 1, chs. 8–11.

[23] Derek Parfit, Reasons and Persons 43–42 (1984).

[24] Charles Blackorby, Walter Bossert, & David Donaldson, Quasi-Orderings and Population Ethics, 13 Soc. Choice & Welfare 129 (1996).

[25] Broome, *supra* note 1, ch. 10.

[26] See Kit Fine, Vagueness, Truth and Logic, 30 Synthese 265 (1975). Strong objections to supervaluationism appear in Timothy Williamson, Vagueness (1994). My own version of supervaluationism differs from Fine's in order to overcome Williamson's objections. Details appear in John Broome, Supervaluation Reconstructed (unpublished manuscript, Univ. St. Andrews 1997).

"bald" consists of a range of "sharpenings," each of which is a potential interpretation of the term. The sharpenings of "bald" include having fewer than 1,000 hairs on the head, having fewer than 1,001 hairs on the head, having fewer than 990 hairs on the head, and so on. According to super-valuationism, we may assert a statement if and only if it is true under every sharpening of its terms. For instance, we may say that Serge is bald if and only if Serge has fewer than 1,000 hairs on the head, fewer than 1,001, fewer than 990, and so on. Correspondingly, we may deny a statement if and only it is false under every sharpening. If a statement is true under some sharpenings and false under others, we cannot assert or deny it. If Serge has 999 hairs on his head, we cannot say he is bald; nor can we deny it.

Remember that the neutral level of lifetime well-being is the level such that if a person lives at that level, her existing is equally as good as her not existing. If a person lives at a higher level, it is better that she lives than that she does not. If a person lives at a lower level, it is worse that she lives than that she does not. I suggest that the term "neutral level" is vague. It has many sharpenings, each of which is a particular level of well-being. These sharpenings fall within some range. The range has a lower limit at some level of well-being and an upper limit at some higher level. I do not rule out the possibility that the upper limit might be infinite. Also, the limits themselves are likely to be vague, but I shall ignore that complication.

We may assert a statement if and only if it is true whatever level of well-being within the range we interpret as the neutral level. For example, we can assert that it is better that a person exists rather than not if and only if the person's level of lifetime well-being is above the entire range. We can deny it if the level is below the entire range. If the level lies somewhere within the range, we can neither assert nor deny this statement. Conversely, we can say it is worse that a person exists rather than not if and only if the person's level of lifetime well-being is below the entire range. We can deny it if the level is above the entire range. If it lies somewhere within the range, we can neither assert nor deny this statement.

I said earlier that intuitively there is a neutral range of levels of well-being, rather than a single neutral level. As I originally interpreted the neutral range, for each level of well-being within the range, if a person will live at that level, her living is equally as good as her not living. Neutrality was interpreted as equality of goodness. Now, with the idea that the neutral level is vague, I have constructed a different sort of a neutral range. There is only one neutral level, but the level is vague. Its vagueness is spread over a range, which we may call a neutral range. For each level of well-being within this range, if a person will live at that level, we cannot either assert or deny that it is better she should live rather than not, and we cannot either assert or deny that it is worse. This is a different sort of neutrality, but it goes some way toward accommodating the intuition. I believe it is the best that can be done to accommodate it.

IX. AN INCREDIBLE CONCLUSION

It does not accommodate it fully, however. This sort of neutrality is not really neutral enough for intuition. To make this point I shall use a little example.

Suppose the neutral range of well-being is between 0 and 10. If a person's well-being is 7, adding that person to the population is neutral in my reconstructed sense: we cannot say it is better that she is added, and we cannot say it is worse. Nor can we deny either of these things. Now suppose a person is added at level 7, and at the same time some harm is done to an existing person. Suppose the existing person's well-being is reduced by 5 units as a result. How do we evaluate this combined change?

Let us adopt the normalized total principle, expressed in formula (1), as our theory of value. It is easy to see that the overall increase in the normalized total is $(7 - v) - 5$. This is positive for values of v less than 2 and negative for values of v above 2. Now we are taking the neutral level v to be vague, we can assert a statement only if it is true under all sharpenings of "neutral level." That is to say, it must be true for all values of v from 0 to 10. But it is not true for all values of v from 0 to 10 that the combined change is beneficial overall; nor is it true that it is harmful overall. So we cannot conclude that this change is beneficial nor that it is harmful. It is neutral in our newly defined sense.

But this conclusion is not as it intuitively should be. The change is to add one person at 7 and reduce one person's well-being by 5 units. Adding a person at 7 is supposed to be neutral. Reducing a person's well-being by 5 units is a bad thing. So we are doing one neutral thing and one bad thing. Intuitively, the result should be a bad thing. But according to our theory, it is not: it is neutral. The neutral act of adding a person turns out to neutralize the definitely harmful act of harming a person. This is not how neutrality should behave intuitively. It is not neutral enough; a neutral event should not cancel out other definitely good or definitely bad events.

This is a major failing in practice. It means that whenever any event affects the world's population, cost-benefit analysts cannot justifiably ignore this effect. Traditionally, they do ignore it, and I suggested the reason they do so is that they assume that changes in population are ethically neutral. But even if changes in population are indeed ethically neutral, it turns out that they may neutralize other good or bad effects. This is because the only theoretically coherent account of neutrality is the one I gave in terms of vagueness, and that account allows neutrality to swallow up other good or bad effects. So changes in population cannot be ignored.

Take global warming again. As I said, global warming will kill many people; it will shorten many people's lives. I discussed how this harm might be evaluated and offered nothing more than a default theory for that purpose. But however we do the evaluation, the conclusion must be that the killing is unambiguously a bad thing. There are no doubt exceptions; some people suffer so much that a shorter life is better for them than a longer one. But for nearly everyone, it is a bad thing for their lives to be shortened. So there will be this one definite bad effect of global warming.

Another effect of global warming is that it will undoubtedly change the world's population. I mean "population" in a timeless way, to include all the people who ever live, at any time. When global warming kills someone, in one sense it directly reduces the population by one person, but not in this timeless sense. However, by killing people it does reduce the timeless population less directly, because some of the people it kills would later have had children, had they survived. Global warming will affect the population in other ways, too. It will alter many people's conditions of life in ways that will undoubtedly have demographic effects. Take one example. If global warming is not checked, large areas of Bangladesh will be drowned. Bangladeshis will have to move elsewhere in the world, and such a vast migration cannot conceivably happen without changes in the size of the population.

I shall not even try to predict whether global warming will increase or decrease the population; I predict only that it will alter the population. How should we evaluate this alteration? The intuition I have been pursuing is that we should value it at zero: adding people to the population of the world and subtracting people from it are both ethically neutral. I have explained that this intuition is hard to fit into a coherent theory because theoretical arguments show there can only be one neutral level. But we can go some way toward accommodating the intuition if we assume the neutral level is vague. So let us make that assumption.

Let us also assume that most people's level of lifetime well-being is within the neutral range. That is to say, it lies within the range of vagueness of the neutral level. We assume, then, that the neutral range is wide enough to encompass most lives that are lived. It cannot plausibly encompass every life. Some people's lives are so full of suffering that it would have been better if they had not lived. Lives at this level are below the neutral range. But we might plausibly assume that every other life is within this range. For none of these lives can we say it is better that they are lived rather than not, nor can we say it is worse that they are lived rather than not. They are neutral in this sense.

That is as far as we can go in accommodating the intuition that adding people is neutral. It allows us to assume that the changes global warming will bring to the world's population are neutral.

The killing that global warming will do is unambiguously bad, and the effect it has on population is neutral. That makes one bad effect and one neutral effect. We should expect these two effects taken together to be on balance bad. Indeed, since the effect on population is neutral, we should expect to be able to ignore it and concentrate on the killing only, when we do a cost-benefit analysis. But we cannot. Take a crude example again. Suppose the neutral range is between 0 and 10 units of well-being. Suppose global warming kills 100 million people, and on average the harm done these people by their death is 3 units each. Suppose global warming also causes the world's population to be reduced. Suppose it reduces the number of people who live at some time or other by 100 million. Suppose on average each of these people would have lived at level 5. The net harm done by these changes is 100 million times $(5 - v) + 3$, according to formula (1). This is positive for some values of v within the neutral range (between 0 and 8) and negative for others (between 8 and 10). So we cannot say the change is harmful. Nor can we say it is beneficial.

Yet intuitively it is harmful because it kills 100 million people. It seems obvious to me that we are entitled to say it is harmful, and a theory that does not yield this conclusion is incredible. Yet the only coherent theory of value that gives some respect to our intuitions does not permit us to draw this conclusion. So what are we to do?

Notice that the problem is very widespread. The example of global warming perhaps raises it more obviously than other problems for cost-benefit analysis. But it will infect the cost-benefit analysis of any event that alters the world's population. Bear in mind that any effect on population is likely to be very large in total. The world's population is not limited by some stable process that causes small changes to die out over time. Instead, any small change will persist for generations and perhaps forever. A few tens of extra people now will grow to a large number of extra people over the generations. It is true that the problem can be mitigated by discounting future harms and benefits, since many of the people added will not exist until far in the future. But discounting lives is an arbitrary device, with little to justify it.

I conclude there is a serious problem in the foundations of cost-benefit analysis. We can hope that more work in the theory of value will come up with a solution. In the meantime, I do not know what cost-benefit analysts should do.

THE STUPIDITY OF THE COST-BENEFIT
STANDARD

HENRY S. RICHARDSON*

ABSTRACT

Cost-benefit analysis (CBA) is often touted as providing not just an important base of information useful in evaluating government programs, but a general standard of public choice that will help insure the wise and intelligent use of our limited resources. This article argues that (wholly apart from its deficiencies in other respects) CBA cannot provide such a standard. Intelligent deliberation is shown to require a willingness and ability to refashion aims in light of new information that comes in. Cost-benefit analysis, both in general and as a possible standard of choice in the context of democratic lawmaking, makes no room for this crucial aspect of intelligent deliberation. Calling its standard "stupid" for this want of intelligence would be unwarranted if no more intelligent mode of political decision making were available, but there is. The article closes by sketching this superior mode.

The pragmatic theory of intelligence means that the function of mind is to project new and more complex ends—to free experience from routine and from caprice. Not the use of thought to accomplish purposes already given either in the mechanism of the body or in that of the existent state of society, but the use of intelligence to liberate and liberalize action, is the pragmatic lesson. Action restricted to given and fixed ends may attain great technical efficiency; but efficiency is the only quality to which it can lay claim. Such action is mechanical (or becomes so), no matter what the scope of the pre-formed end, be it the Will of God or Kultur. But the doctrine that intelligence develops within the sphere of action for the sake of possibilities not yet given is the opposite of a doctrine of mechanical efficiency. Intelligence as intelligence is inherently forward-looking; only by ignoring its primary function does it become a mere means for an end already given. The latter is servile, even when the end is labeled moral, religious, or esthetic. But action directed to ends to which the agent has not previously been attached inevitably carries with it

* Georgetown University. This paper was presented at the conference Cost-Benefit Analysis held at the University of Chicago Law School, September 17, 1999. I am grateful to the organizers, Matthew Adler and Eric Posner, for the opportunity and for their comments, and to others present for their criticisms.

[*Journal of Legal Studies*, vol. XXIX]

a quickened and enlarged spirit. A pragmatic intelligence is a
creative intelligence, not a routine mechanic.[1]

I. INTRODUCTORY

THOSE who urge the use of cost-benefit analysis (CBA) in public decision
making would have us use our limited resources intelligently and efficiently. It will be the argument of this paper, however, that CBA's underlying normative standard of choice makes no room for intelligent deliberation
about how best to use our resources. Hence, I will urge, CBA, taken seriously, defeats its own aims. The model of public choice that CBA holds
out is, I will argue, a stupid one.

In using this provocative term "stupid," I am anticipating the main lines
of my argument, which are simple to sketch. As John Dewey most clearly
recognized, an intelligent approach to practical problems, whether individual or public ones, requires above all a flexible willingness to remake one's
aims in light of new information, especially information about costs. Cost-
benefit analysis, however, models decision making in two unconnected
steps: first one collects willingness-to-pay information, which stands proxy
for individuals' ends or aims, and then one aggregates that information, in
the way of Nicholas Kaldor and John Hicks, by calculating the sum of compensating variations. This sum reflects how much money individuals affected by a project would be able to give up and remain indifferent with
the state they were in absent the project; it represents in one way the idea
of a hypothetical Pareto improvement.[2] This sum serves to index the project's social desirability. In this two-step approach, there is no room for the
application of what Dewey termed "practical intelligence," which encom-
passes the ability to reformulate ends and aims in light of what emerges
about the costs and benefits of proceeding with a project. But this sort of
reformulation is essential to using resources wisely and effectively. It is because CBA has no place for the use of practical intelligence in this sense
that it presents a stupid standard of public choice.

To be sure, as others have well argued, CBA also suffers other defects
as a standard of choice. First, if it ignores distributional issues it is unjust,
while if it attempts to incorporate distributional concerns by some scheme

[1] John Dewey, The Need for a Recovery of Philosophy, in The Political Writings 6–7
(Debra Morris & Ian Shapiro eds. 1993) (1917).

[2] As will become apparent, it will not matter, for the purposes of my argument, whether
the normative standard underlying CBA is put in terms of the sum of compensating variations, the sum of equivalent variations, or, for that matter, simply in terms of the Marshallian
demand curve. On these variations, see, for example, Yew-Kwang Ng, Welfare Economics:
Introduction and Development of Basic Concepts 87–90 (1983).

of weighting it is doomed to do so crudely and controversially. Issues of injustice arise directly from its hypothetical-compensation standard, which does not require that losers actually be compensated, and from the fact that a willingness-to-pay standard inherently gives more weight to those with bigger budgets. Second, as a standard of public choice, CBA lacks a compelling justification. Although sometimes defended on the basis of a concern with individual welfare,[3] CBA's core concept of willingness to pay has no direct connection to individual welfare.[4] When it is understood as a fundamental normative criterion, as opposed merely to representing a standard of choice that marks out a convenient evaluation procedure, CBA's recourse to preferences as expressed in market behavior more likely marks an unstable way station on the road to a more thorough normative skepticism. Third, by arraying all reasons for or against a project on a single scale, CBA rides roughshod over important incommensurabilities among reasons—incommensurabilities that emerge clearly once one puts aside the blinkers of value skepticism and considers what reasons for and against public projects there actually are.[5]

Hence, the stupidity of CBA as a standard of public choice needs to be laid alongside its injustice, its lack of compelling justification, and its Procrustean treatment of value. While I will be concentrating on just the one problem with CBA, I would not want the others to be forgotten.

There is a sense, however, in which CBA's failure to make room for practical intelligence represents its most fundamental defect. The other defects I have mentioned are visible only against the backdrop of a relatively rich set of normative assumptions—about justice, justification, and value. While I would endorse these assumptions, many of the defenders of CBA would not. Cost-benefit analysis's failure of intelligence, by contrast, is deplorable from the point of view from which such analysis is typically recommended, that of a basic concern with the wise use of limited resources and of careful instrumental reasoning in pursuit of one's projects. To recommend CBA on this basis, as we shall see, is to make a fundamental error about the nature of instrumental (or end-means) reasoning.

I seek to be as clear as possible about one point. I in no way mean to downgrade the importance of collecting information about the benefits and costs of alternative proposals. To the contrary, this is the first step in any intelligent process of deliberation. Furthermore, it clearly can be quite use-

[3] See, for example, *id.,* ch. 1.

[4] Amartya Sen, Rational Fools, in Choice, Welfare, and Measurement (Collected Papers) 84–106 (1982).

[5] See Elizabeth Anderson, Value in Ethics and Economics (1993).

ful to attempt to be quantitatively precise about the magnitudes of these costs and benefits. What I will be criticizing is, instead, using the cost-benefit standard as a way of ranking alternatives—whether because one thinks that so ranking them directly reflects the appropriate normative basis of public choice or because one believes that this procedure of public choice is justified more indirectly.[6] Thus, I am all for finding out about the likely effects of proposed policies; what I am against is the suggestion that ranking proposals according to the CBA standard provides a sensible basis for public choice.

Suppose that my main thesis is correct and that CBA represents a stupid standard for public choice. Does it follow that we should not bother to collect willingness-to-pay information about the likely effects of government actions? Not at all. On the one hand, putting one's quantitative information about costs and benefits into that form will make the use of the CBA standard highly tempting and hence will encourage the lazy use of a stupid approach. On the other hand, however, this information could be used in a more disciplined and productive way, one that does not presuppose the validity of CBA as a normative standard. Collecting willingness-to-pay information can provide a way to raise red flags about proposals. In this role, CBA functions neither as a fundamental nor as a derivative standard of choice, but merely as a useful heuristic. Similarly, willingness-to-pay information is often fruitfully used to raise prima facie questions about the consistency of government efforts: if we are willing to spend $x per life saved in one regulatory context and $100x in another, we probably need either to push for reform or to explain how the context appropriately affects how we interpret the aim (how we would specify it: see below).[7]

As useful heuristics not backed up by a sensible standard of public choice, these roles for willingness-to-pay information should, ideally, be balanced by the use of other, complementary heuristics that instead lay stress on environmental values, discrimination, justice, and so on. Certainly, however, these willingness-to-pay heuristics are of some use.[8] Finally, CBA incorporating willingness-to-pay information can serve as a useful account-

[6] On this distinction between two modes of viewing CBA as a standard of choice, see Matthew Adler and Eric Posner's contribution to this symposium: Matthew D. Adler & Eric A. Posner, Implementing Cost-Benefit Analysis When Preferences Are Distorted, in this issue, at 1105.

[7] This sort of consistency is a concern of Stephen Breyer, Breaking the Vicious Circle: Toward Effective Risk Regulation (1993), and of a number of the other contributors to this symposium.

[8] See Cass Sunstein's contribution to this symposium: Cass R. Sunstein, Cognition and Cost-Benefit Analysis, in this issue, at 1059. Sunstein persuasively argues that cost-benefit information can compensate for some common cognitive failings.

ing device that helps other agents (the Office of Management and Budget or the courts, for instance) maintain control over an unruly bureaucracy. In this role, it is used not to make decisions but to keep agencies in line. While I recognize the need for such an external check on agency action, what I will be insisting upon, below, is that we must, at the same time, strive to ensure that agency decisions reflect our democratic will in the first instance.

My effort to be clear that I am attacking CBA's use as a standard of choice and not as a mere heuristic or accounting device may be undermined by the variety of ways in which the term "cost-benefit analysis" is currently used. This distinction between the normative standard built into CBA and the mere collection and heuristic use of willingness-to-pay information (which is a mere prelude to the application of this standard) has been unintentionally obscured by some recent prominent discussions of CBA in the public arena. I am thinking, in particular, of the American Enterprise Institute (AEI) pamphlet, Benefit-Cost Analysis in Environmental, Health, and Safety Regulation: A Statement of Principles, co-signed by Kenneth Arrow, Robert Hahn, and a core of other prominent economists. Their recommendations are summed up in the following words "Benefit-cost analysis should be required for all major regulatory decisions, but agency heads should not be bound by a strict benefit-cost test. Instead, they should be required to consider available benefit-cost analyses and to justify the reasons for their decision in the event that the expected costs of a regulation far exceed the expected benefits."[9] I agree; and nothing I will argue here undercuts the importance of taking account of information about the benefits and costs of proposals, put quantitatively in terms of willingness-to-pay information in this heuristic way. While these authors use the term "cost-benefit analysis" (or "benefit-cost analysis") to refer mainly to the pedestrian and unexceptionable idea that it would be good to collect precise information about costs and benefits, others use it to refer to the controversial—and ultimately stupid—idea that potential Pareto improvement provides a reasonable and often sufficient normative standard for public choice. To navigate my way through this confusion, I have been speaking of "the normative standard implicit in, or underlying, CBA."

The latter, controversial idea, though rapidly being abandoned by sensible economists, is by no means a straw man. It is explicitly endorsed by some of the principal articulators of the methods of cost-benefit analysis.[10] Judge Posner has even suggested that the normative standard underlying

[9] Kenneth J. Arrow et al., Benefit-Cost Analysis in Environmental, Health, and Safety Regulation 3 (1996).

[10] For example, E. J. Mishan, Cost-Benefit Analysis: An Informal Introduction (1988); Ng, supra note 2.

CBA not merely is the appropriate one for assessing public projects but also provides the correct basis for morality as a whole.[11] It would be well to lay this sort of belief definitively to rest. Furthermore, examining in more detail the reasons why the normative standard underlying CBA is a stupid one will reveal important truths about the nature of practical reasoning, ones that point us in the direction of a better understanding of public practical intelligence.

I will present my argument in three waves. The first will make out a prima facie case for the stupidity of the standard underlying CBA by contrasting it with intelligent practical deliberation, as generally described for an individual deliberator. The second will spell out this lack of intelligence in more detail, elaborating four key uses of intelligence in deliberation and confirming that each of these is unavailable in using the CBA standard. Finally, to confirm that practical intelligence is really available at the political level, I describe its necessary use in generating reasonable compromise and confront the challenges to embodying it in democratic institutions.

II.   The General Case for a Want of Intelligence

The initial case for the stupidity of the standard underlying CBA may be made out by contrasting the general nature of intelligent deliberation with the assumptions underlying the theory of revealed preferences, which are the informational basis of CBA.

A.   Intelligent Deliberation in the Individual Case

The case against the intelligence of the model of deliberation underlying CBA is so fundamental that it is necessary to object to the basic building block of this approach, namely, that of an individual's revealed preference. I cannot even lucidly state the defects of this approach without shifting to a different vocabulary. In so doing, however, I will not be begging the question against my opponents. I will return to revealed-preference theory, in its own terms, in the following subsection.

To sketch an account of intelligent deliberation in general, I will start with individual deliberation, which is in some ways simpler than collective deliberation. (The later portions of the present essay will concentrate on the differences between individual and collective deliberation.) If we are to gain even an elementary understanding of intelligent individual deliberation, we must take several rapid steps away from the idea of rationality that has been built up around the idea of preferences. We must leave behind

---

[11]   Richard A. Posner, The Economics of Justice (1981).

both the axiomatic utility theory of John von Neumann and Oskar Morgenstern and the idea of maximizing expected utility that has been built on it and begin afresh. There are several reasons for this,[12] but the most simple and fundamental is that, as I have argued elsewhere, the account of rational preferences employed in standard economics cannot help us model deliberation because it presupposes that all the significant deliberation has already been done.[13] "Forming a preference as between options" is a flat description of what one does at the conclusion of a course of deliberation. This fact is dramatized by the way that preference theorists deal with the apparent violations of their axioms, such as seeming intransitivities or the Allais paradox. What these cases show, we are told, is not that there is anything deeply irrational about people or fundamentally wrong with preference theory but rather that in the case, as hitherto described, the options had not yet been finely enough described. If we are willing to get fine-grained enough, and recognize enough of the contextual interactions that seem to matter to people—if, in other words, we are able to do as John Broome suggests and individuate the options by taking account of all "justifiers" or relevant reasons[14]—then we will be able to save the preference theory. But in order to have generated these more fine-grained and more transparently consistent preferences, individuals will have to have already processed, in their deliberations, all of these nice relevant reasons. Whatever a theory may do that presupposes from the outset that individuals have taken fully into account all of the reasons relevant to decision and reflected on their implications for action, it does not provide an account of individual deliberation.[15]

To attain even a basic understanding of intelligent deliberation, then, we

[12] For a related, but distinct, set of criticisms, see Jean Hampton, The Failure of Expected Utility Theory as a Theory of Reason, 10 Econ. & Phil. 195 (1994).

[13] See Henry S. Richardson, Practical Reasoning about Final Ends § 15 (1994). Matthew Adler has pointed out to me that the argument that I make there does not transfer directly to CBA (or to the collective case, more generally): while it is a necessary truth that an individual will not have arrived at completely thought-through preferences without having settled all of the significant issues that might arise on deliberation (see the text, below, on "completely thought-through preferences"), it is conceivable that each individual could completely think through his or her preferences and then make them available to the cost-benefit analyst for aggregation. My argument here about the stupidity of the CBA standard, however, is a more pragmatic and empirical one and does not turn on an impossibility or inconceivability claim; instead, my argument will be that in practice and in fact, individuals' completely thought-through preferences about public issues are not available independently of the process of collective deliberation. Rather, in practice, they require interaction in a process of collective deliberation to help individuals begin to think their preferences through.

[14] John Broome, Weighing Goods: Equality, Uncertainty, and Time 104 (1991).

[15] Perhaps the theory will be helpful in modeling rational responses to uncertainty and risk; but since among the things that individuals care about, and hence among the things that count as relevant reasons, are various aspects of the nature of risks and uncertainties faced, even in this context the theory will do less work than its proponents might have hoped.

need to step away from the idea of preference satisfaction and take up a different set of basic concepts. For this purpose, the traditional vocabulary, and still the best vocabulary, is that of end and means. We may set aside two sorts of objection to the vocabulary of end and means. First, some may doubt that these terms can be given a precise sense; them I refer to earlier work in which I endeavor to do just that.[16] While I will be making use of my analysis in the following section, I will begin by laying out the prima facie case against the standard underlying CBA in a way that employs these terms simply in commonsensical ways. Second, as will become obvious, the concepts of end and means offend against the behaviorist strictures that had once made the theory of revealed preference seem particularly appealing. While Amartya Sen and others have raised important doubts as to whether it is really plausible to understand preferences simply in terms of behavior, eschewing irreducibly psychological concepts,[17] there is no doubt but that the hope of getting by on such an austere basis provided some of the historical impetus behind revealed-preference theory. The notions of means and end, by contrast, are frankly psychological. Behaviorism, however, is an opponent with which we need no longer struggle, as the philosophical background that had supported it has melted away. Accordingly, there is less reason than there once appeared for avoiding the categories of end and means. While a view of rational deliberation that incorporates these richer psychological concepts will operate with information that is difficult to gather empirically, it would be letting the tail wag the dog to allow the possibilities of convenient data collection sharply to delimit our conception of intelligent practical reasoning.

Once one sheds the past's prejudices against psychological concepts, there is little reason to stick with a notion as thin as that of preference. As Martha Nussbaum has well argued, the philosophical tradition has richer and more refined concepts to offer for the empirical analysis and the ideal reconstruction of practical reasoning.[18] At once the most powerful and the most commonsensical of these are the categories of end and means.

We need practical intelligence in the simplest end-means deliberation. One of the oldest and most common ideas about deliberation is that the deliberator seeks to determine means to her ends, where these means can either be causally instrumental (as breaking eggs is to an omelet) or else constitutive (as drawing a good inference is to making a good argument). Call reasoning that both starts from an initial end and is limited to settling means (of either type) ''instrumental reasoning.'' A striking and important fact

[16] Richardson, *supra* note 13, § 7.

[17] Amartya Sen, Choice, Welfare, and Measurement, *supra* note 4, at 54–73.

[18] Martha Nussbaum, Flawed Foundations: The Philosophical Critique of (a Particular Type of) Economics, 64 U. Chi. L. Rev. 1197 (1997).

about instrumental reasoning is that it resists formal characterization. There has been no lack of attempts, starting, apparently, with Aristotle. Either carried away by the success of his logic of propositions or else misunderstood by us in the same vein,[19] Aristotle writes about a "practical syllogism," in which the first or major premise states the end, the second or minor premise notes the available means, and the conclusion either is or designates the action to be taken. Yet inferences do not flow through practical syllogisms with the inexorability that they do in the case of theoretical (or ordinary, or "real") syllogisms. There are three nested reasons why not. First, we typically are satisfied with sufficient means to our ends and are seldom in a position of having to accept a means as strictly necessary. Here is one of Aristotle's best-known examples:

I need a covering,
a coat is a covering:
I need a coat.[20]

While this example does well capture a common kind of practical reasoning, there is clearly no necessity to using a coat as one's covering. A second reason that practical reasoning resists formalization flows directly from the first: since there are typically a number of alternative means that would be sufficient, we must (as Aristotle again says) select "the easiest and best."[21] There is obviously no simple formula, however, for determining which means is easiest and best. If one is trying to select a birthday present for one's spouse, say—even within a fixed budget—there is no substitute for exercising creativity and imagination to generate options or using what Rawls would call "deliberative rationality" and Dewey would call "practical intelligence" to reflect about their relative merits.[22] A third reason why practical reasoning cannot be formalized arises from the second: for if instrumental reasoning seeks the easiest and best means to given ends, sometimes it bumps up against the fact that all available means are either too hard or not good enough. Sometimes, in other words, consideration of the available means reasonably leads us to give up on our pursuit of the end from which we began deliberating. If the only available covering was poison ivy, I, for one, would feel justified in going naked.[23]

---

[19] See Sarah W. Broadie, Ethics with Aristotle 226 (1991).

[20] Aristotle, Movement of Animals 701a17–18.

[21] Aristotle, Nicomachean Ethics 1112b17.

[22] John Rawls, A Theory of Justice 560 (1971).

[23] The availability of poison ivy suggests that hypothermia is not likely to be an underlying concern. The existence of underlying concerns, or of more final ends for the sake of which we pursue the end in view, raises important complexities that I do not have space to enter into here. See Richardson, *supra* note 13, §§ 7 & 29. Dewey describes "the continuum of end-means" in John Dewey, Theory of Valuation, in 13 The Later Works, 1925–1953, § 6 (Jo Ann Boydston ed. 1988).

Corresponding to the three reasons that instrumental reasoning cannot be formalized are three indispensable modes in which practical intelligence is exercised. First, since we often face a plethora of potentially sufficient means to our ends, we must be able to refine or specify our characterization of those ends so as to start to narrow down among the potential alternatives. Second, since, as the phrase "easiest and best" indicates, we operate with an irreducible plurality of ends that are always in the background of any choice, we must be able to bring them to bear in some way both in refining the end in view (the one from which we began deliberating) and in assessing alternative means. Third, since we have to accept that some ends in view will turn out not to be reasonably achievable, we have to be able to decide when it is appropriate to abort incipient projects or give up on cherished plans. In suggesting that we have these abilities, I am not making any controversial claim. In particular, each of these three aspects of practical intelligence is compatible with instrumental rationality, as I have defined it.

I believe that we also have forms of practical intelligence that transcend the limitations of instrumental rationality. I will describe them below. For the purposes of showing the stupidity of the standard underlying CBA, however, it will suffice that practical intelligence requires the three abilities described in the last paragraph: to refine our ends, to assess alternative means in light of multiple ends or objectives, and to give up on pursuing an end when it seems appropriate to do so. There is no room even for these simple exercises of practical intelligence within CBA's model of choice.

Cementing this point will require taking a more careful look at the idea of revealed preference that underlies the economics of CBA. Only after we have done that will I be in a position to sketch the more dramatic possibilities of practical intelligence, those that extend beyond the bounds of the instrumental.

B. Implications for Revealed-Preference Theory

Economists, including the proponents of CBA, are not committed by virtue of their theories to much in the way of a theory of preference formation. Preferences might arise any which way, as far as their theories are concerned. This fact may generate the suspicion, therefore, that while practical intelligence is not accounted for in CBA (or other economic theories of practical reasoning), that is just because it is included in something that these economic theories take as exogenous input, namely, the preferences. If that is where practical intelligence comes in, it might be thought, then it need not be included in the account of how it is rational to proceed with the preferences one has. Now, in the last section I already indicated that it is a mistake to think of preferences as being fixed independently of deliberation. The need to refine and possibly reject ends crucially implies that they must be reformulated as one proceeds. Definitively to shut off this reply, which foists concern with practical intelligence off on an exogenous and phantom theory of preference formation, however, the easiest and best way to proceed is to examine the theory of revealed preference a bit more carefully.

The problem for the theory of revealed preference that the three necessary modes of practical intelligence raise is that of "incomplete thinking." This problem for revealed-preference theory is a third-person or observer's version of the gappiness of instrumental practical reasoning we have been noticing from the deliberator's first-personal perspective. The deliberator needs to exercise practical intelligence in dealing with the gaps resulting from the usual plethora of sufficient means, the multiplicity of standards relevant to sorting among them, and the possibility that it may turn out that no sufficient means to one's end is reasonable. Correspondingly, in trying to infer someone's preferences from their actual, revealed choices, the observer must rely upon a host of assumptions about the extent to which, and the ways in which, the individual has dealt with these gaps in linear and explicit assessment. Sen gives the following example: "I am inclined to believe that the chair on which you are currently sitting in this room was not chosen entirely thoughtlessly, but I am not totally persuaded that you in fact did choose the particular chair you have chosen through a careful calculation of the pros and cons of sitting in each possible chair that was vacant when you came in. Even some important decisions in life seem to be taken on the basis of incomplete thinking about the possible courses of action, and the hypothesis of revealed preference, as a psychological generalization, may not be altogether convincing."[24] These observations of Sen's suggest two kinds of difficulty for the theory of revealed preference, one more fundamental and relevant to my argument than the other. The less deep worry has to do with interpreting behavior. As Sen's case makes clear, it is always a dicey business trying to interpret behavior in psychological terms. We must make assumptions about what alternatives were salient for the individual and under which descriptions before we can with any confidence say what preference a given action reveals. But this problem is not unique to the theory of revealed preference; and in any case, that theory's application in CBA can perhaps get around this problem to some extent by relying on statistical data about a group of individuals, letting the relevant factors emerge empirically from econometric analysis.

The more fundamental and relevant problem of incomplete thinking is

---

[24] Sen, *supra* note 17, at 60–61.

also the one that emerges most straightforwardly from the reasons that practical intelligence must be exercised: since preferences as revealed at any
given time are inevitably the result of incomplete thinking about the pros
and cons, they are always liable to being overturned by more complete
thinking. Sometimes, indeed, this more complete thinking depends upon experience. Perhaps you had not considered the dimension of smell at all
when you chose your seat; but as soon as you realize that the person sitting
next to you must have had garlic soup for lunch, you may come to regret
your choice. "Be careful what you wish for," we are warned; but it is in
the nature of human life that our thinking can never be complete enough to
be sure to capture all the pros and cons in advance. Sometimes we have
actually to try something to see how it goes.[25] At least as commonly, new
kinds of pros and cons occur to us halfway through the process of planning
something to which we are already committed. For all these reasons, when
we later spurn a choice we had once revealed, it is often not because we
are simply fickle—though we are that, too—but because we had not
thought our choice through completely.

Modern economists, in employing the idea of revealed preferences, have,
as I understand it, tried out two contrasting responses to this problem of
incomplete thinking. These responses seem to represent the two available
moves. The first response, natural to those whose enterprise is spinning out
ideal conceptions of social choice, has been to assume the problem away.
Here Kenneth Arrow's pioneering work on social choice is exemplary.
Arrow well recognized that a complete consideration of pros and cons must
always take account of the issues of "interdependence of values" that will
multiply as dimensions of deliberative assessment multiply. Accordingly,
he suggested, we are led in the direction of postulating that "each decision
is effectively a choice among total life histories."[26] For the purposes of developing his impossibility theorem, it was perfectly acceptable simply to
stipulate that we have available each individual's ordering across total social histories. For the purposes of making public policy, however, the impossibility of generating an acceptable social welfare function is com-
pounded—or, depending on your point of view, made irrelevant—by the
fact that individuals' final orderings of this kind, even highly partial ones,
are, as a practical matter, simply not available.

This idealizing approach to preferences presupposes that all significant
deliberation has been completed prior to their formation. One sign of this
is the way complete thinking, of the kind Arrow postulates, squeezes out

---

[25] Elijah Millgram, Practical Induction (1997).

[26] Kenneth J. Arrow, Utilities, Attitudes, Choices: A Review Note, in Individual Choice
under Certainty and Uncertainty, in Collected Papers of Kenneth J. Arrow 57 (1984).

the relation between end and means. When something is preferred to some-thing else as a superior means to some third thing, the stated preferences rest on incomplete thinking. Completely thought-through preferences would factor out this relation of means to end and simply order alternatives in light of what the individual prefers to what intrinsically—taking, of course, the whole package into account.[27] Thus, if your choice of a particular chair is partly a means to hearing well and partly a means to avoiding garlic smell, completely thought-through preferences would be as between different chair-hearing-smell packages. Again, this line of thought is what pushes the preference theorist in the direction of the alternative life histories discussed by Arrow. And again, this tendency yields a theory that is useless in model-ing or helping practical reasoning because it in effect supposes that all of the significant practical reasoning has already taken place.

In light of the fact that preference orderings resting on complete thinking are not to be found, however, economists of a more practical bent have ar-gued that we should simply content ourselves with the preferences as re-vealed in the marketplace. Supply and demand information, they argue, while not a perfect or definitive basis for getting at individuals' preferences, still tells us more than any other source might. Taking this tack amounts simply to taking the problem of incomplete thinking on board and hoping that one can live with it. My point is that perhaps one could, if there were not a more intelligent way to think about policy deliberations—but there is. In order for me to be able to sketch it convincingly, I will need to explain how to undo the restrictions of the external, third-person perspective that came with the behaviorism that historically underlay the theory of revealed preference.

Defenders of the standard of choice underlying CBA thus face a di-lemma: either they must unrealistically require that preferences reflect com-plete thinking, in which case their theory will be practically useless, or else they must simply try to live with the fact that preferences do not reflect complete thinking, in which case they make no room for practical intelli-gence. Either way, the approach is doomed to stupidity.

III. TYPES OF PRACTICAL INTELLIGENCE: THE COSTS OF STUPIDITY

Is failing to make room for practical intelligence really that bad? In this section, I will show that it is, first by elaborating my account of deliberation (still sticking, for the moment, to the individual case) and then by listing four key ways in which the model of choice underlying CBA blocks the use of practical intelligence. In sketching the former, I start with the concepts of

---

[27] G. H. von Wright, The Logic of Preference 23 (1963).

end and means and then move to the crucial rational operations involving
them and the overall basis of rationality for these operations.

A.   Rational Refashioning of Ends in the Individual Case[28]

We may define the concepts of end and means, in good Aristotelian fashion, by reference to the more fundamental idea that one thing, x, is pursued
for the sake of another, y. When we pursue x for the sake of y, two related
claims are true of us: (i) we would pursue (or choose) x even if y were the
only good we expected to come of it; and (ii) we judge it appropriate or
acceptable to regulate the manner and extent of our pursuit of x by reference to y. If I decide to pursue a writing project for the sake of clearing up
my thoughts about some difficult subject, then it follows both that (i) I
would pursue it even if that clarification were all that I expected out of the
effort and (ii) I find it appropriate to regulate how much time I spend on
the project and the ways I research and write it by reference to what will
best contribute to my own clarity of understanding.

We can now define "end" and "means" by reference to this relation of
pursuing x for the sake of y. What we ordinarily think of as an end—which
is what Aristotle called a "final end"—is something we seek for its own
sake. This we can define using the "for the sake" relation just analyzed,
for it is just the case in which x equals y. Something is a final end for me
if (i) I would pursue it even if nothing else were thereby attained and (ii) I
find it appropriate to let this pursuit be self-regulating. A "means" in the
broad sense (embracing both causal or instrumental and constitutive means)
is an x that we pursue for the sake of some distinct (if possibly conceptually
related) y.[29]

While reasoning may operate with these categories in a number of important ways, one operation whose potential has not been fully realized is that
of specification.[30] We often start from ends that are vague and abstract: to
be successful, to combat air quality degradation, or to make transportation
available to the disabled. A crucial step in deliberation, often, is to come
up with more concrete and specific interpretations of these ends. This pro-

---

[28] I will here be summarizing some aspects of my account in Richardson, *supra* note 13,
§§ 7, 13, 26.

[29] Here I set aside complications that arise from the possibility that we pursue something
that we mistakenly believe will yield a result we value.

[30] Aristotle and Aquinas both emphasize the importance of specifying norms. In modern
times, see Aurel Kolnai, Deliberation Is of Ends, in Ethics, Value, and Reality: Selected Papers of Aurel Kolnai 44–62 (1978); and David Wiggins, Deliberation and Practical Reason,
in Essays on Aristotle's Ethics 221–40 (Amélie Oksenberg Rorty ed., Univ. California Press
1980) (1975–76). I define specification more precisely in Henry S. Richardson, Specifying
Norms as a Way to Resolve Concrete Ethical Problems, 19 Phil. & Pub. Aff. 279 (1990).

cess of specification has an interestingly ambiguous relation to ordinary causal-instrumental reasoning. Obviously, if ends are left too vague, it will not be sensible to launch a causal investigation into how to achieve them. Suppose you are advising someone who has simply told you that they want to be a success. True, you could do an empirical study of what the easiest way to attain success of any kind might be; but you would be a better adviser if you first asked your companion a bit more about how they would like to understand "success." Hence, specifying ends is often an important prerequisite to sensible causal investigation. Yet it is also true that the process of specification will often make significant causal investigation unnecessary. If I begin with a vaguely stated aim of having a nice meal tonight, and then specify that end more fully as a nicely prepared and ethereal neo-American meal utilizing only the freshest ingredients, it may become simply obvious that Charlie Trotter's is the only such place that I can get to by mealtime using subsonic means of transportation. Accordingly, specifying the ends can make serious efforts at causal-instrumental investigation effectively unnecessary.

An even more striking feature of specifying ends is that it can generate new ends in a way that transcends the bounds of instrumental rationality. Whereas instrumental rationality, as defined above, is limited to settling means to an initial end, specifying reasoning can give rise to new ends. As Dewey would say, all deliberation starts with an "end in view." That on which we initially set our sights, however, need not be a final end, sought only for its own sake. We may deliberate about how to get into law school, knowing full well that we view law school only as a stepping-stone. Schematically, then, we often deliberate about how to pursue some x that in turn we pursue only for the sake of some distinct y. As we specify x in our deliberations, however, two new stances can emerge. First, it can become clear from the various ways in which we settle the manner and mode in which we would pursue x that, in fact, we would pursue it irrespective of whether it contributes to y. Second, it can also become clear from the various specifications that we add that we cannot, in fact, any longer regard it as appropriate to regulate the mode and manner of our pursuit of x by reference to y and that, instead, we view x as sufficiently significant to be self-regulating. If we arrive at both these conclusions, then we have, through an ordinary process of deliberation, promoted x from being a mere means to being a new final end. For example, a figure skater may start taking ballet lessons simply as a means to improving her posture and line. In working out her practice schedule, however, she may eventually determine to stick with a ballet regimen that, in its extent and timing, even interferes with the skating somewhat, or she may pursue the ballet to a level beyond which it still contributes to the skating. Further, she may affirm, on reflection, that it is appropriate to give up regulating the mode and extent of the ballet by reference to the skating. If so, then, by specifying her pursuit of ballet, which was initially merely a means, she has promoted it to being a final end, sought for its own sake.

"All well and good," you may say. "John Stuart Mill and others have long noted that, by various psychological processes, new ends arise. But what makes this process of specification a rational one?" There is a lot to be said in response to this question; here let me outline three main points.[31] First, the process of specification is a central aspect of what almost everyone would regard as a case of practical reasoning, namely, instrumental reasoning that settles on constitutive means. Second, this process can be discursively set out: it relies upon no black box of intuition. Third, the specification that the agent settles upon may be justified, as against alternative specifications, on the basis of what we might call "practical coherence": on the basis of its fit and mutually supportive relationships, of various kinds, with the agent's other aims. These relationships of mutual support may, in turn, also be set out discursively.

My claim that the normative standard underlying CBA is stupid depends upon some, but not all, of the above claims about the possibilities of practical reasoning. Specifically, what I depend upon is the possibility of remaking one's aims intelligently and rationally. This possibility can be realized within the limitations of instrumental rationality by respecifying aims in ways that may be justified or defended on the basis of the resulting coherence of one's practical commitments. Given this possibility, a more intelligent approach to practical reasoning appears to be available (whether it is truly available depends upon the political-institutional questions addressed in Section IV below). It is not necessary for my main argument here, then, to insist that rational deliberation can transcend instrumental rationality. Nonetheless, in assessing the overall political importance of the unintelligence of CBA's standard, it will help to keep this more radical possibility in mind.

Before I turn to an overall assessment of the political possibilities, however, I want to return to an examination of CBA's failure of practical intelligence. Now that we have seen in slightly more detail what is involved in an intelligent approach to practical deliberation, we are in a better position to appreciate the kinds of move that CBA's kind of standard closes off.

B. *A More Detailed Look at the Stupidity of CBA's Normative Standard*

I have argued (in Section II) that an intelligent approach to practical reasoning requires a willingness and ability to refashion one's aims in light

---

[31] Here, again, I summarize arguments set out in Richardson, *supra* note 13, §§ 6–8.

of information that comes to one's attention about costs and benefits. With reference to individual deliberation, I have just sketched how this refashioning can be rational. These conclusions reinforce the importance of the distinction I drew at the outset between studying the costs and benefits of proposed projects, which I endorse, and accepting the normative standard underlying CBA—that of potential Pareto improvement—which I am here attacking. The stupidity of the latter standard arises from the fact that it takes its content from willingness-to-pay information that is empirically fixed and unresponsive to the analyst's conclusions about costs and benefits. In light of the foregoing account of intelligent practical deliberation, we can now give more detail about the kinds of move that CBA's kind of standard fails to allow for. Without by any means attempting to give an exhaustive list of the possibilities, I will highlight the following four: (1) failure to generate the new solutions that new specifications of the ends can suggest, (2) failure to allow for the kind of resolutions of practical conflict that coordinated specification of two competing ends can provide, (3) failure to discriminate adequately among the various distinct ends that all fall under the rubric of a single less specific one, and (4) failure to consider promoting certain aims to the status of final ends.

1. *Failure to Generate New Solutions.* We show our intelligence in practical reasoning largely in our ability to adapt our purposes to the means available. Sometimes, as we have seen, this requires giving up on a project entirely. More commonly, we respecify in some way our end in view. If that end in view was rather vague, the new specification may simply add a new emphasis and refinement that points us in new directions; if it was already specific, we may need to revise it—sometimes by differently specifying a more general end of which our initial end was another specification, and sometimes by specifying a more final end for the sake of which our initial end was sought. In any of these ways, we can free ourselves up to seek new and better solutions. For example, "to win the war" may become an end that seems practically unreachable. If we interpret it more specifically, however, as "to win the war in the sense of establishing a secure boundary between us and the insurgents," then we will be led in the direction of a negotiated solution. If even that proves too difficult, we may look to what our underlying concerns were and settle for "peace with honor," security of our oil pipelines, or providing a safe exit for those of a threatened ethnicity. Similarly, "to find a cure for cancer" turned out to have been a naively grandiose goal that would, pursued literally, bankrupt the nation; however, "to understand the mechanisms giving rise to the most common cancers so as to develop effective ways of treating them" is an achievable goal. Now, of course, if we imagined CBA being applied only after ends or goals have been completely thought through, then we could

simply say that it will take account of all of these refined and realistic specifications. We have seen, though, that stipulating complete thinking is radically unrealistic. The trouble, then, is that since CBA's willingness-to-pay
standard must take the ends as fixed from the outset, it lacks a provision
for this kind of intelligent reformulation of them.

2. *Failure to Resolve Conflicts.*   Another reason practical intelligence is
called for, besides our so often being stymied by circumstances, is, as we
have seen, that we have so many mutually incommensurable ends and values. Difficult policy decisions typically involve competing values that are
different in kind. As others argue, attempting to resolve these conflicts on
a single, willingness-to-pay scale does violence to our commitments in various ways.[32] While I agree with that, the point I want to emphasize here
about these conflicts is a different one. It is this: intelligent deliberation involving competing ends or values will often find ways of respecifying one
or all of them so as to relieve their conflict in the case at hand, yielding (pro
tanto) a more coherent overall set of commitments. For instance, promoting
resource conservation conflicts with the goal of economic growth; but it
does not conflict (at least not to the same extent) with the goal of sustain-
able economic growth. Adding that qualification makes for a more coherent
package of commitments.

3. *Failure to Discriminate among Ends.*   As I have noted, the preference theorist may hold that preferences based on complete thinking reflect
an optimal individuation of alternatives, one that treats options as distinct
whenever they reflect discernible advantages or disadvantages. This fine-
grained individuation of alternatives thus depends upon an ideally fine-
grained individuation of desiderata; and this, in turn, is pie in the sky. Intelligent deliberation, involving the explicit reformulation of ends, can at least
move in the direction of a finer discrimination among the things that we
care about. Cost-benefit analysis, by contrast, employs some fixed individuation of costs and benefits. Of course, if we can think of an example of
what distinctions might have eluded us, we can also claim that they would
not have escaped us. Still, examples of the kinds of discrimination that
might well elude us unless we are actively and intelligently engaged in
specifying ends in a context of deliberation are (*a*) the distinction between
an innocent person being shot and an innocent person being shot by a member of the police force (distinctions of agency) and (*b*) the distinction between that aspect of environmental aims that involves protecting wilderness
from human encroachments and that aspect which centers instead on protecting the ecological supports of human health and flourishing (distinctions

---

[32] See, for example, Anderson, *supra* note 5.

of interpretation within an abstract goal). Intelligent deliberation will be in a position to generate such discriminations in response to features of the circumstances of action; CBA is not.

4. *Failure to Consider Promoting Aims to Final Ends.* Promotion of a means to status as a final end adds to the list of desiderata that matter.[33] In the policy context, this possibility is often at issue with regard to what we might call "expressive" goods and evils. Take the example of the so-called patients' bills of rights currently being put forward. Of course, these involve important pros and cons in terms of quality of health care, degree of delay and inconvenience suffered, and so on. Once this proposal is on the table, however, it also raises the issue of the potential value of a declaration of such a right, just in itself. If you like, this would be an aspect of the government's expression of its commitment to the rights of all of its citizens to equal concern and respect; it would be a constitutive means to this overall expression. It might be thought, however, that it is a sufficiently indispensable important constitutive means thereto to count as an intrinsically valuable component thereof, worth promoting for its own sake. In an intelligent discussion of these bills of rights, this possibility of promoting them from being mere means (to effective and convenient care) into in part being ends in themselves will at least be broached. This kind of possibility of intelligently adding to the list of dimensions of goodness is not provided for by CBA's standard of decision.

In this section, I have elaborated on the relative stupidity of using a Kaldor-Hicks sort of potential-Pareto-improvement standard of public choice. I have distinguished and illustrated four kinds of intelligent refashioning of ends that are available to ordinary deliberation but foreclosed by any model of decision that takes as its contentful normative basis a given set of willingness-to-pay information. Since the focus of my attack is this fixity of CBA's informational base, the reader may feel that I have proved too much: for the actual Pareto-improvement standard has the same informational base. And surely I am not against actual Pareto efficiency?

In response to this objection, a few quick points. First, no one thinks that the standard of actual Pareto improvement is a sound one for making public policy. Sound public policy will typically require that there be some losers. So the real question, here, is whether I would find reason to oppose approving of projects that actually do offer Pareto improvement. Of course, if (*per impossibile?*) the individuation of goods and ills on which this determination is based reflected complete thinking, I would have little basis to object. If it does not, however, there is reason to worry that a finer discrimination

---

[33] That matter, that is, to the agent who so promotes the means. I come in the next section to a discussion of collective agency.

of goods and ills would upset the appearance of Pareto improvement. Independently and in addition, Sen's argument about the impossibility of the Paretian liberal gives us reason to doubt the sufficiency of Paretian endorsement of a policy.[34] Finally, I would emphasize and repeat that I am assessing the standard of choice embedded in CBA. I am not against utilizing information about costs and benefits. Doing so might reasonably have the effect of ruling some projects in and ruling others out. Since the actual Pareto standard is obviously and by the admission of all not generally useful as a standard of choice in the kinds of policy decision we actually face, the fact that it might be useful sometimes and in some special cases is hardly relevant to the kind of critical assessment I have undertaken here.

IV.   THE POSSIBILITY OF PRACTICAL INTELLIGENCE IN DEMOCRATIC POLITICS

I have criticized the stupidity of CBA's standard of choice, contrasting it with the more intelligent sorts of deliberation that are commonly exercised by individuals. In the contemporary political context, however, many seem attracted to CBA less by its abstract virtues as a normative standard of choice than by skepticism about the rational virtues of political institutions. To address this skepticism, I will sketch how intelligent deliberation may be realized in a democratic political structure and argue that CBA is no less dependent on officials' virtues than are its more intelligent alternatives.

A.   The Need for Principled Compromise

In setting out this constructive argument, I will need to deal carefully with the division of roles between citizens and officials. The imperviousness of CBA to practical intelligence results from its separating the analyst from the deliberator. As I have observed, it is a third-person model of deliberation, in which the economist simply collects and reports information about the preferences of individuals and then attempts to support a decision by aggregating that information. Intelligent deliberation, by contrast, must be understood in first-personal terms, allowing the persons who analyze information about pros and cons to refashion their ends in light of it. In light of the explicitly political and institutional perspective we are now taking up, however, insisting on this raises important questions about the relative roles of citizens and government officials. In addressing these roles, we must take up our understandings of the democratic ideal—which, at some level, the defenders of CBA share with me.

---

[34] Sen, Choice, Welfare, and Measurement, *supra* note 17, at 285–90.

In particular, I share with the defenders of the Kaldor-Hicks standard a commitment to an individualized conception of popular sovereignty.[35] This is the idea that governmental decisions should reflect what individual citizens want their government to do—that, other things equal, the mere fact that a citizen prefers an option does count in its favor. Defenders of CBA as providing a criterion of public choice could well view its potential Pareto standard as specifying this ideal of individualized popular sovereignty in the most attractive and plausible way. Following out this line of thought, they could say that the Kaldor-Hicks standard provides a basis of governmental decision that is entirely rooted in citizen preferences and, in its Pareto aspect, does indeed give each individual's preferences a prima facie importance. In my view, however, this is neither an attractive nor a plausible interpretation of popular sovereignty.

The foregoing arguments about the stupidity of the CBA standard provide a two-part explanation of why it yields an implausible interpretation of popular sovereignty. To begin with, its fixed willingness-to-pay basis provides a poor interpretation of what people want. As a general matter of interpreting what someone wants, the principle of charity (as Donald Davidson has long stressed) provides important guidance.[36] We typically have strong reason to avoid attributing stupid practical commitments to people. To adapt Dewey's famous example: if someone has said they want to roast some pork, and we know that the only way for them to roast pork will be for them to burn down their house, we still lack sufficient reason to attribute to them an intention to burn down their house. We know that, being intelligent people, they would almost surely change their plans if confronted with this cost. As a general matter of interpreting what people want, then, we need to take account of their practical intelligence, by which they regulate and revise their aims in light of information that surfaces about the pros and cons of courses of action. Because it shuts off practical intelligence, CBA's interpretation of what people want is accordingly implausible. This point about the defectiveness of the interpretation of wants built into the CBA standard supplements, of course, the more basic points already made about the practical stupidity of building plans on a set of preferences that is simply held fixed. For both these reasons, CBA provides an unappealing interpretation of popular wants.

So what is the alternative? In part, a more attractive and plausible interpretation of popular sovereignty will provide for the possibility that individ-

---

[35] For some further implications of individualized popular sovereignty, see Henry S. Richardson, Democratic Intentions, in Deliberative Democracy: Essays on Reason and Politics 349–82 (James Bohman & William Rehg eds. 1997).

[36] Compare Donald Davidson, Essays on Actions and Events (1980).

ual preferences change in light of political deliberation. This aspect of deliberative democracy has been highlighted by Cass Sunstein, among others.[37] To stop here, however, would be to omit the most valuable political aspect of practical political intelligence, namely, the generation of principled compromise.

To see the importance of principled compromise, consider how all too many cases of actual political deliberation have recently gone. After much deliberation, the Republicans decide they favor a big package of tax cuts that will turn back more money to the rich than to the poor. Also after deliberation, the Democrats decide that any such tax cut would be unacceptable. The Republicans' plan prevails in the Congress; the Democratic president vetoes the bill; and we are back to square one. Although there is much preference-changing individual deliberation in this picture, the nation's ability to form an acceptable policy plan is shown in this kind of example to be quite pathetic. We have seen this kind of failure again and again recently, with campaign finance reform, gun control, health care regulation, and on and on. Pundits bemoan the lack of bipartisan spirit. What is missing from this picture is a willingness and ability to arrive at mutually acceptable compromise.

Practical intelligence requires a willingness and ability to arrive at compromise for two kinds of reason: because we care about others and because, even if we did not, we need their help and cooperation. To start with the first of these reasons, consider a case in which marriage partners have clashing preferences: one wants a big-screen TV, while the other is adamant that the living-room decor not be ruined by plunking a huge console down in the middle of it. In a well-functioning marriage, these spouses will not simply deliberate about how best to achieve their several preferences; rather, they will consider (separately or, more likely, together) how they might arrive at a compromise. Perhaps they will decide to wait for the prices of flat-screen TVs to come down a little and put the big screen on the wall, thus leaving the living-room layout intact. Here we see a willingness on the part of at least one of them to refashion or modify an aim (from a standard big-screen TV now to a flat one later) because and on account of the preferences of the other, whom he or she cares about. Where such technical fixes are unavailable, the compromise must go deeper. Suppose one spouse wants to use joint vacation time to experience really challenging wilderness adventure by going on a strenuous canoe trip, while the other wants to use that time to relax and be lazy while being pampered at a tropical resort. If this couple settles on a somewhat adventurous and less than perfectly re-

---

[37] Cass R. Sunstein, Preferences and Politics, 20 Phil. & Pub. Aff. 3 (1991).

laxing vacation on a sailing yacht in the Caribbean, and if each truly comes to terms with this solution (as we say), then they also will be modifying the ends that underlay their separate, initial choices of means—from strenuous wilderness adventure to outdoor trip in a beautiful setting, for instance. This latter marital case is an instance of what we might call "principled compromise." A compromise in general I understand as a change in one's practical commitments that responds to the commitments of another person and is made partly in an effort to arrive at a fuller agreement with that other. Principled compromise is a change in one's support of policies—of implementing or constitutive means—that is accompanied and explained or supported by a change in one's ends that itself counts as a compromise. That is, a principled compromise builds a new policy position on an underlying compromise at the level of ends.

Transparently, I chose marital cases because we tend to presume that spouses care for each other; but what about citizens? I believe that in a well-functioning democracy, citizens do tend to care for one another to some degree, treating one another with at least a modicum of concern and respect. Further, as in a well-functioning marriage, individual citizens in a well-functioning democracy will share some common concerns, if only those limited to the survival of their country and its just constitutional regime. Hence, in a well-functioning democracy, shared concerns and mutual caring will provide at least some reason for practical intelligence to extend to the generation of principled compromises.

Well-known collective-action problems provide additional reason for employing practical intelligence in generating compromises. In an analysis of the significance of Prisoner's Dilemmas for revealed-preference theory, Sen argued that they show that individuals are activated by moral commitments as well as by preferences. Caring for others, of the kind that I was speaking about in the last paragraph, can, he notes, be easily modeled by the revealed-preference theorist, whereas moral commitments, as a limitation on the individual's pursuit of welfare, cannot—at least so long as the preference theorist holds on to some inherent link between individual preferences and individual welfare.[38] But things look different if we block the preference theorist's unrealistic stipulation that preferences reflect complete thinking and remember the importance of practical intelligence in dealing with the kind of difficulties these collective conflicts present. While, in the end, I agree with Sen about the difficulty of capturing moral commitments in terms of individual preferences, I am here more concerned to emphasize the kind of practical intelligence needed to generate sensible responses to

[38] Sen, *supra* note 17, at 64–65.

collective conflicts, whether or not that response could then be captured in terms of revised preferences. Prisoner's Dilemma problems, in particular, need the kind of frame-changing revision of aims exemplified by agreeing to accept a collective sovereign—or at least a cooperative mode of decision making for the one kind of case we find ourselves in.[39]

Hence, for my own reasons I agree with Sen's remark that "the philosophy of the revealed preference approach essentially underestimates the fact that man is a social animal and his choices are not rigidly bound by his preferences only."[40] This is true, I think, not—or not only—because an individual's choices are traceable to some other aspect of his or her practical commitments, such as his or her moral convictions, but because individuals' choices are, across a very wide range, worked out in dynamic compromise with the preferences of the many others with whom they interact.

Given these strong general reasons for utilizing our practical intelligence to work out reasonable compromises, we have correspondingly strong reason to understand governmental decision making as a matter of doing just that. Given the insistence on individualized popular sovereignty that I share with my cost-benefit opponents, however, we need to understand this collective decision making in a way that retains a tie between the collective will of all and the individual will of each. Analytically, as I have suggested elsewhere,[41] this link is well modeled by a certain understanding of a joint intention—where an intention may be understood as the embrace of a course of action for the sake of some end[42]—on which the jointness of the intention does not imply that the collectivity or the government is a superindividual subject, but instead reflects a relationship among the intentions of individuals. According to this suggestion, then, we should think about governmental decision making in terms of the intelligent formation of joint intentions. As my cases of marital compromise suggested, we should view this process as one in which we work together, exercising our practical intelligence in ways whereby individuals repeatedly adjust their aims and wants, and demands and concessions, by responding to those of the others with whom we are negotiating and deliberating, and thereby construct new joint intentions.

If we think about this joint revision of ends abstractly enough, we can recognize that the very same ways of building practical coherence that can support the rationality of individual revision of ends can also allow joint

---

[39] I am not here implying that Prisoner's Dilemma problems provide any reason for regarding the establishment of a collective decision-making entity as a final end.

[40] Sen, *supra* note 17, at 66.

[41] Richardson, *supra* note 35.

[42] Compare Broadie, *supra* note 19, at 226.

deliberation about ends to be rational. Consider the shift to a flat-screen TV in my first marital example. This is a reasonable revision because it specifies underlying ends in a way that promotes their mutual fit. Although the prima facie case for the rationality of this revision of the couple's joint intention makes no fundamental presupposition that "the couple" is a normatively significant entity distinct from the individuals in it, the argument would work in much the same way for a single individual faced with a conflict between this pair of wishes.[43]

As an example of how intelligent, principled compromise might proceed in politics, consider the issue, which was much debated in the 1970s and 1980s, of providing transportation assistance for the disabled, a saga that has been ably chronicled and analyzed by Robert A. Katzmann.[44] As Katzmann tells the tale of the actual process of policy formation, this was an example of institutional breakdown and obtuseness in the formation of public policy. Congress had passed a series of vague statutes demanding that "special efforts" be made to make transportation available to the disabled. The statutes did not define what was meant by "special efforts," leaving it to the agencies and the courts to attempt to sort this out. An intelligent approach would have begun with the recognition that the end of "making transportation available to the disabled" is too vague to serve as a basis for policy making and needed specification before decisions could reasonably be made or supported. Instead, according to Katzmann, what happened was that the debate polarized. An "efficiency" camp attached itself to the idea of handing out money to the disabled and letting them make their own choices among the existing modes of transportation (for example, hiring van drivers), and a "rights" camp demanded that the existing public systems be modified so as to be made accessible to the disabled. As Katzmann points out, the rights language made the second position quite unresponsive to issues of cost and hence unreceptive to an intelligent modification of aims in light of obstacles that arise. Equally, however, it was unintelligent for the friends of "efficiency" to put efficiency in service of such a vaguely stated congressional aim. We do want our public aims to be efficiently pursued, but first we need to work better than that at articulating them. A more intelligent approach to this problem, then, would have squarely faced up

[43] The importance of solidarity within the couple is, instead, an assumed feature of each of its member's commitments. For making the prima facie case for the reasonableness of a given compromise, this aspect of a married couple's commitments stands as part of the normal background for such assessments, much as an individual's concern for his or her own future and for each of his or her distinct commitments is part of the normal background for assessing the reasonableness of individual choices.

[44] Robert A. Katzmann, Institutional Disability: The Saga of Transportation Policy for the Disabled (1986).

to this vagueness in the initial aim and attempted to arrive at a principled compromise that would make the aim definite enough to guide policy formation. There are lots of ways this might have gone; being no expert on the issue, I certainly cannot defend a particular compromise as being the most reasonable. In light of some of the arguments that were made at the time, however, here is a path of principled compromise that seems reasonable: Congress had stated the vague end of making transportation available to the disabled. The disabled themselves, however, had an additional, separate concern. As Katzmann writes, the associations representing them "were very much influenced by the civil rights struggle; disabled Vietnam veterans who returned home from an unpopular war viewed themselves as suffering the same kind of discrimination and ostracism that minorities had endured and sought to overcome. Having responded to their country's call to service, they now demanded that the nation assure that they not be shunted aside."[45] The additional concern of at least many of the disabled, then, was that they not be "ostracised" or "shunted aside." Their argument is, on the face of it, a serious one. It is an argument the importance of which "we"—including those of us who are not disabled—can recognize and we can try to respect by seeking a principled compromise that takes it into account. If we care enough about the disabled to want to help them with transportation, we presumably also care about their potential ostracization. From here, it is not far to look for a reasonable principled compromise. One could fill out the vague initial goal as follows: "to make transportation available to the disabled in a way that avoids ostracizing them or shunting them aside." Since this is a goal for policy, and not a rights claim, consideration of costs and of efficient means would naturally be a part of its intelligent pursuit, as would potential further specification of its content.

To be sure, when such compromises are struck among many individuals, it immediately becomes a salient issue for us, in a way that it does not for conflicts within a single person's ends, how much influence each of the competing sides exercises over the outcome. In my view, this concern about the way in which the concerns and voices of many ought to affect collective decision cannot be settled by a theory of rationality. Instead, it needs to be addressed by a full-fledged theory of constitutional justice, which will work out the implications of the ideal of equal concern and respect as it factors through the design of institutions that foster and enable democratic deliberation. I obviously cannot even begin to sketch such views here; however, I would endorse the view shared by John Rawls and Jürgen Habermas that

---

[45] *Id.* at 110.

the democratic ideal of popular sovereignty cannot be properly interpreted or realized apart from a set of constitutional provisions that protect democratic process and fundamental individual liberties.[46]

From the point of view of my set-to with CBA, however, a more basic question about institutionally realizing rational joint deliberation is not whether it can be done justly and in a way that appropriately respects the ideal of equal concern and respect, but whether it can really be done intelligently. I will come to that in closing. Before I get to that, however, I want to address an objection that I am sure my opponents will be eager to press.

B. The Necessity of Trust

The objection is this: All this lofty talk about forming joint intentions within the framework of just institutions makes it sound as if "the people" can simply get together and negotiate reasonably. In fact, however, most of the policy decisions must be made by officials of one kind or another (elected and unelected), and they have their own agendas. Instead of seeking to respect the preferences of the people, they engage in their own "rent-seeking" behavior and end up selling policy to the highest bidder. Thus, it would be nice to let intelligent deliberation proceed through the layers of policy formation if there were a way to keep it in the hands of the people; but since there is not, it is safer, and more in accord with the democratic ideal of popular sovereignty, to let things simply be constrained by the preferences of individuals as expressed in the market.[47]

This paper's full response to this objection will involve sketching (in the next subsection) some ways in which the voice of the people may, in fact, be made more influential in the policy-making process. Before we come to that, however, it is important to see that the worries that this objection raises about intelligent public deliberation are also worries about the use of CBA. True, the abstract standard of hypothetical Pareto improvement does state a constraint that is, in principle, independent of these ways in which official decision can get distorted by greed and power. But we may similarly state an ideal standard of intelligent public deliberation: that public decisions must accord with the practical commitments worked out by citizens in fair processes of principled compromise and justified (or justifiable) by the relations of mutual support that hold among those commitments to which the citizens adhere upon due reflection. Simply demanding that pro-

---

[46] Jürgen Habermas, Reconciliation through the Public Use of Reason: Remarks on John Rawls's Political Liberalism, 92 J. Phil. 109 (1995); John Rawls, Reply to Habermas, 92 J. Phil. 132 (1995).

[47] See Posner, *supra* note 11, at 93.

cesses of public decision live up to either of these ideals rings hollow. Hegel would have derided either demand as a "mere ought."

If we turn from either of these ideals to how they might end up guiding policy making in practice, it immediately becomes apparent that each of them is sufficiently subject to manipulation to leave each of them somewhat vulnerable to being derailed by greed and power. The proposal to use CBA as a standard for making policy decisions (as opposed, again, to a mere heuristic or post hoc accounting device) is by no means immune from these difficulties. Certainly it is striking that on most major regulatory questions in fields such as the environment and health, those on opposite sides of the issues commission their own competing cost-benefit studies, which unsurprisingly yield contrasting implications. I do not claim that this situation could not be ameliorated. The AEI study to which I alluded earlier contains some ideas that would help at least produce some greater uniformity among cost-benefit analyses. My present point, however, is just that those same corrupt or venal officials who might derail intelligent public deliberation are equally in a position to derail the objective and nontendentious use of CBA. The point is one of parity: it is not that CBA sets no limits on tendentious decision making. Of course it does. Ten thousand dollars is not a reasonable valuation of a human life. Similarly, however, there are limits on the tendentious use practical intelligence. Building a power plant, as such, is not a way of preserving the environment. In the last paragraph, I noted that each conception states an ideal standard for public deliberation; now I am simply adding the negative corollary, that neither ideal is self-enforcing or immune from manipulative use. Rather, realizing either depends to an important degree upon the good will of the public officials who appeal to them. We have no choice, in other words, but to place some trust in our officials. That does not mean, however, that we should not try to redesign our public institutions so that this need for trust is minimized and the chances of the trust being fulfilled are enhanced. To these questions of institutional design I turn in closing.

C.   Instituting Intelligent Public Deliberation

My rather unrestrained attack on the stupidity of the normative standard underlying CBA depends upon a more intelligent approach to policy making being reasonably available to us. I have given some examples that indicate that policy is sometimes made more intelligently than CBA's standard allows for. I have also insisted, however, that a thorough grasp of the process of intelligent public deliberation, compatibly with our shared democratic ideals, requires sufficiently diminishing the distance between the people and the decision makers such that it becomes plausible to view policy decisions first-personally. We need to be able to view them as ones that we make, and this despite the dangers of official corruption—and deference to the powerful few—just mentioned.

In order to help convince you of the practical possibility of intelligent democratic deliberation, I want in this closing section to put forward three interlocking suggestions about how to envision the policy-making process: suggestions about dividing deliberative labor, progressively specifying ends, and opening each step of this specification to negotiation. None of these ideas necessarily implies any great reform of the way things are currently done in the United States. Rather, together these offer a way of understanding what is done that contrasts with the kind of picture that would naturally go with CBA. Let me begin by describing this last so as to place before you an alternative with which to contrast my own picture. Here we have to discuss the policy-making process in somewhat more detail than we have hitherto.

Significantly, most of those who currently are concerned to push the use of CBA in policy making limit it to the stage of assessing the regulations that administrative agencies publish in furtherance of the typically rather general statutes that authorize and command them to act. As the authors of the AEI pamphlet concede, since the legislative proposals themselves remain rather vague, any cost-benefit analysis that takes them to define alternatives will necessarily be relatively "rough."[48] For this and no doubt various other reasons, most recent debate has focused on whether agencies should be required to do cost-benefit analyses of the rules and regulations that they write in furtherance of the power delegated to them by statute.

This limitation of CBA's proposed role brings out a point that was implicit in some of my earlier discussion of practical intelligence, but not on the surface—namely, that practical intelligence has crucial roles to play in setting the agenda of decision and in generating alternatives for evaluation. The foregoing discussion of the relative stupidity of CBA's standard should lead us to be completely unsurprised that no one has tried to propose CBA as the sole basis of governmental decision at all levels, and that instead it is generally cast in the relatively narrow, reactive, and often negative role of evaluating specific proposals that have been developed by the agencies. Since no one has suggested that CBA can help with setting agendas or generating alternatives, this observation does not by itself pose an objection to CBA. Further, as I noted at the outset, it is perfectly appropriate to give CBA a negative and reactive role either as a heuristic that can raise red flags or as an after-the-fact accounting device.

[48] Arrow *et al.*, *supra* note 9, at 9.

When defenders of CBA put it forward as a standard of choice, however, its limitations as a constructive device make for a difficulty about reconciling it to the core democratic ideal of popular sovereignty, destabilizing the abstract accommodation that I noted earlier between their position and that ideal. My earlier suggestion was that these two could be reconciled by insisting that the preferences of individuals, as expressed in the market, be the sole and sufficient way in which the policy-making process takes account of the will of citizens. As CBA's obvious limitations as an agenda-setting and option-generating device indicate, however, that suggestion was too crude. Some role must be given to democratically elected legislatures in setting the evaluative framework within which CBA works. Here the defender of CBA as a normative standard faces a dilemma: if democratic legislatures are (at least minimally) legitimate and competent organs for setting collective ends, then these ends, as worked out in collective deliberation—and not individuals' preferences as revealed in the market or in contingent evaluation studies—should provide the crucial basis of evaluating alternatives. If not, then CBA is thrust back into a global, agenda-setting role that is impossible for it. In other words, if we should respect the deliberative work of democratic legislatures, we ought to depart from individual willingness to pay as our normative basis in favor of an objective function transformed by the legislative work; and if we should not, we are left without any workable or legitimate way to generate collective decisions. Hence, the first objection against the common use of CBA as a normative standard applying to agency decisions is that it fails adequately to respect the decisions of democratic legislatures. This conclusion makes the attempt to ground CBA in an abstract view of popular sovereignty seem either disingenuous or utopian, as there is no practical way of articulating the popular will except via a democratically elected legislature.

Suppose, though, that the defender of using CBA as a normative standard for agency decisions concedes this point, admitting the imperfect fit between its willingness-to-pay basis and the set of ends generated by legislative deliberation. "Still," the defender might say, "CBA represents the best available way of ensuring that the ends set by legislatures are efficiently carried out by agencies. In that way, CBA at least can further the legislative projects despite its principled basis being somewhat at odds with the legislature's judgments. After all, we have no simple way of articulating in a systematic way just what the ends are that legislatures have endorsed." My rebuttal is twofold: first, it would be stupid—in just the ways set out above—for agencies to proceed as if the ends have been adequately fixed by legislatures. Legislative decisions will always rest on incompletely thought-through conceptions of public aims, requiring a lot of interpretation and further refinement by the agencies.[49] Second, since a lot of important interpretation of public ends unavoidably gets done by the agencies, we need to concentrate on finding ways to ensure that this process of deliberation is adequately public and rational to be susceptible of democratic control. While CBA, as I have been saying all along, may provide a useful accounting tool for after-the-fact checking by courts or oversight committees, it does not provide a way of articulating the process of interpreting ends. Rather, it assumes that process away. Of the two parts of this rebuttal, the stupidity point is the more fundamental, and that about legitimacy depends upon it. Of course, a democratic legislature might legitimately decide to require agencies to decide solely on the basis of CBA how best to carry out legislative directives. My central point is that, given how vague legislative directives inevitably tend to be, this limitation on agencies' deliberative possibilities will be stupid: it will cut short our thinking our joint aims through in the political process. Agencies must continue the work of refining our joint intentions.

What we need, then, is an account of how intelligent political decision can carry through to the agency level. To sketch an alternative picture of policy making in light of a realistic understanding of the way responsibility is divided between legislatures and administrative agencies, I want to put forward three positive ideas that respond to the joint implications of two facts: first, that intelligent public deliberation requires constant openness to refashioning ends and prior conclusions; and, second, that it is nowhere near possible literally to gather the whole public for each step of this reconsideration process.

The first idea, then, is simply that we must recognize that the labor of public deliberation is divided into various steps. While we do aim to arrive at joint intentions about what to do, we delegate various aspects of working this out. How this works is highly complex and only partially subject to centralized oversight. For instance, an important feature of our division of policy deliberation is the way that we defer to public interest groups that we trust, from the American Civil Liberties Union to the Christian Coalition. The process of policy formation within the federal government can be viewed as a special case of this kind of division of deliberative labor in which the divisions are crucially ordered in a stepwise fashion. Thus, while the legislative directives that Congress enacts are indeed often vague, they are usually not vacuous. Rather, they represent an important step in the ar-

---

[49] I defend this claim in Henry S. Richardson, Democracy and Administrative Rationality (unpublished manuscript, Georgetown Univ. 2000). Here, I am heartened by the fact that readers of that paper have found the point too obvious to need much argument.

ticulation of the popular will.[50] Hence, it is important to benefiting from this kind of division of deliberative labor that the agencies, when they go to write rules to implement those statutes, are working within a set of decisions that the statute outlines.

The second idea, which arises naturally from the first, is that to model the ideal way rationally to constrain this kind of stepwise division of democratic deliberation, it is best to see it as a progressive process of specifying ends. The task of the agency is to specify the legislative directive. As I have argued elsewhere, legitimate rule making will confine itself to specifying the aims embodied in the legislation.[51]

The third idea is that, even so, negotiation directed at freshly working out compromises among competing interests and commitments is still importantly relevant to elaborating the content of the popular will, even at this lower or more specific stage of public deliberation. This third idea brings to bear our earlier discussion of the place of practical intelligence in refashioning aims. We saw that practical intelligence that refashions aims is crucial even if we stick within the confines of instrumental rationality and hence confine ourselves to finding causal means to given ends and to specifying those ends. This specifying stage still requires important substantive negotiations directed at working out our joint intentions more exactly. In the United States, this has been partially recognized by the institution of a practice of ''negotiated rule making,'' a relatively new mechanism in which interested parties are invited to get together, under agency supervision, in order together to draft the detailed regulations implementing a statutory provision.[52] Negotiated rule making is no panacea. As currently practiced by the federal government under the Negotiated Rulemaking Act of 1980, it allows too much sway to the focused and powerful interests, in contrast to the diffuse and unempowered public. Here, though, I would remind the reader of my view that no theory of public rationality can solve these problems by itself: that, in particular, standards of public justice need better to be met, in any case, for democratic deliberation to be more fully legitimate than it now is. Despite this caveat, however, use of negotiated rule making seems a step in the right direction. It allows for a better implementation of the thought that public policy needs to arise from an intelligent process of deliberation in which we attempt to work out a joint plan in a way that (a) remains continually open to being refashioned in light of new informa-

---

[50] Not the first step: I here bypass questions about the link between voters and their representatives.

[51] Henry S. Richardson, Administrative Policy-Making: Rule of Law or Bureaucracy? in Recrafting the Rule of Law: The Limits of Legal Order 309 (David Dyzenhaus ed. 1999).

[52] See id.

tion about pros and cons despite (*b*) maintaining a firm enough stepwise division of labor to be likely actually to converge on some decisions. The requirement that the process specify the relevant ends, rather than the requirement that the choice maximize consumers' surplus or promote Kaldor-Hicks efficiency, is the rational constraint appropriate to invoke both within this process and in judging it from the outside.

Together, these three related ideas suggest how to envision democratic policy making as a process of elaborating our joint will in an intelligent fashion. While much more would need to be said to flesh this picture out, I hope to have said enough to indicate how intelligent democratic deliberation might go.

V. CONCLUSION

The careful and precise study of the pros and cons of policy proposals that is a necessary aspect of a process of intelligent public deliberation will do best to leave the normative standard underlying CBA entirely aside. An intelligent process of public deliberation must depart from that standard, for it must not be caught up in the dangerous fiction that preferences reflecting "complete thinking" are in any way available to the policy analyst. Instead, intelligent policy analysis needs, for various reasons set out above, to be open to refashioning aims and remaking ends in light of new information about the pros and cons. While implementing this ideal of public intelligence in a full-scale democracy does face us with difficult questions about the formation of popular will, it turns out that CBA has difficulties of its own on this score. More positively, the connected trio of ideas just explained—division of deliberative labor, respect for the bounds of specification in a stepwise process of deliberation, and openness to freshly negotiated compromise within such a process—sketch how intelligent democratic deliberation might be structured. Hence, while the standard underlying CBA offers itself as simply being a sensible way of efficiently satisfying the preferences of individuals, in fact it is a stupid way of doing that, compared with a mode of joint deliberation that encourages those individuals to refashion their preferences in light of the information about pros and cons that comes to light.

THE COSTS OF TRAGEDY: SOME MORAL LIMITS OF COST-BENEFIT ANALYSIS

MARTHA C. NUSSBAUM*

ABSTRACT

In all situations of choice, we face a question that I call "the obvious question": what shall we do? But sometimes we also face, or should face, a different question, which I call "the tragic question": is any of the alternatives open to us free from serious moral wrongdoing? Discussing cases of tragic conflict from literature, philosophy, and contemporary life, I argue that it is valuable to face the tragic question where it is pertinent, because facing it helps us think how we might design a society where such unpalatable choices do not confront people, or confront them less often. Cost-benefit analysis helps us answer the obvious question; but it does not help us either pose or answer the tragic question, and it frequently obscures the presence of a tragic situation, by suggesting that the obvious question is the only pertinent question. I apply these reflections to thinking about basic entitlements of citizens, such as might be embodied in constitutional guarantees.

I. TRAGIC PREDICAMENTS[1]

CASE A. Arjuna stands at the head of his troops. A huge battle is about to begin. On his side are the Pandavas, the royal family headed by Arjuna's

* Ernst Freund Distinguished Service Professor of Law and Ethics, Law School, Department of Philosophy, Divinity School, and The College, The University of Chicago. I am grateful to Matthew Adler, Douglas Baird, Emily Buss, John Deigh, Richard Epstein, Jill Hasday, Andrei Marmor, Bernard Melzer, Eric Posner, Richard Posner, Henry Richardson, Cass Sunstein, Alan Sykes, and Adrian Vermeule for helpful comments on a previous draft. I am sure that I have not answered all of their questions. This paper was also presented at a symposium in honor of Philip Quinn at the American Philosophical Association Eastern Division Meeting on December 28, 1999; I am most grateful to Quinn for his helpful reply on that occasion and to Hilary Putnam for comments from the floor.

[1] I have written extensively about these predicaments, both in Martha Nussbaum, The Fragility of Goodness: Luck and Ethics in Greek Tragedy and Philosophy, chs. 2 & 3 (1986); and in Martha Nussbaum, Love's Knowledge: Essays on Philosophy and Literature (1990), especially in the essay Flawed Crystals, at 125; and, finally, in Martha Nussbaum, Tragic Conflicts, Radcliffe Quarterly, March 1989. Fragility, *supra,* contains a detailed account of the tragic dilemmas in Aeschylus' Agamemnon and Seven against Thebes and in Sophocles' Antigone, with many references both to scholarship on those works and to the contemporary philosophical literature on moral dilemmas. In the latter literature, I have found most helpful: Ruth Barcan Marcus, Moral Dilemmas and Consistency, 77 J. Philosophy 121 (1980); Bernard Williams, Ethical Consistency, in Problems of the Self 166 (1973); John Searle, Prima Facie Obligations, in Philosophical Subjects: Essays Presented to P. F. Strawson 238 (Z. van Straaten ed. 1980); Michael Stocker, Plural and Conflicting Values (1990); Michael Walzer, Political Action: The Problem of Dirty Hands, 2 Phil. & Pub. Aff. 160 (1973).

[*Journal of Legal Studies,* vol. XXIX]

eldest brother, legitimate heir to the throne. On the other side are the Kauravas, Arjuna's cousins, who have usurped power. More or less everyone has
joined one side or the other, and Arjuna sees that many on the enemy side
are blameless people for whom he has affection. In the ensuing battle he
will have to kill as many of them as possible. How can it be right to embark
on a course that involves trying to bring death to so many relations and
friends? How, on the other hand, could it possibly be right to abandon one's
own side and one's family duty?

Arjuna saw his closest kinsmen, related to him as father or grandfather, uncle or
brother, son or grandson, preceptor as well as companion and friend, on both sides.
Overcome by this sight, he said in sorrow and compassion, "O Krishna, when I
see my own people ready to fight and eager for battle, my limbs shudder, my mouth
is dry, my body shivers, and my hair stands on end. Furthermore, I see evil portents,
and I can see no good in killing my own kinsmen. It is not right and proper that
we should kill our own kith and kin, the Kauravas. How can we be happy if we
slay our own people? . . . O Krishna, how can I strike with my arrows people like
the grandsire Bhisma and the preceptor Drona, who are worthy of my respect?"
. . . Having said these words, Arjuna threw away his bow and arrows, and sat down
sorrowfully on the seat of his car.[2]

Arjuna poses himself not one but two questions. The first question, which
I shall call the obvious question, is the question of what he ought to do.
That question may be difficult to answer. It may also be difficult to identify
the best method for arriving at the answer. In this case, Arjuna and his advisor Krishna differ sharply about method, Krishna recommending a single-
minded pursuit of duty without thought for the unpleasant consequences,
Arjuna proposing a careful consideration of all the foreseeable consequences.[3] What is not difficult, however, is to see that it is a question that
has to be answered, since some action must be taken, and even inaction is,
in such a situation, a kind of action. In that sense, the question is obvious:
it is forced by the situation. Arjuna cannot be both a loyal dutiful leader of

---

[2] Mahabharata (c. 3d century B.C.). This passage is quoted from the translation by Chakra-
varthi V. Narasimhan (1965), which translates only selections from the work, but renders
fully those passages it does select (whereas many shortened translations are also reworkings).
Van Buitenen's definitive unedited translation (Mahabharata (J. A. B. van Buitenen trans.
1973)) remains incomplete because of his death and did not progress as far as this passage.
The passage cited is from bk. 6, ch. 23.

[3] In the passage that has since become famous as the Bhagavad-Gita, Krishna advises Arjuna that he has "a right to action alone, but not to the fruits of action." Consequences
should not be taken into account at all in choosing a course of conduct. "[M]en attain the
highest good by doing work without attachment to its results" (Mahabharata, bk. 6, ch. 23).

his family and at the same time a preserver of lives of friends and relations on the other side. He has to choose.

The other question is not so obvious, nor is it forced by the situation. It might easily have eluded Arjuna. I shall call this the "tragic question." This is, whether any of the alternatives available to Arjuna in the situation is morally acceptable. Arjuna feels that this question must be faced, and that when it is faced, its answer is "no." Krishna, by contrast, either simply fails to see the force of the question altogether or recommends a policy of deliberately not facing it, in order the better to get on with one's duty.

The tragic question is not simply a way of expressing the fact that it is difficult to answer the obvious question. Difficulty of choice is quite independent of the presence of moral wrong on both sides of a choice. In fact, in this case as in many tragic dilemmas, it is rather clear what Arjuna should do: much though he is tempted to throw away his arrows, that would accomplish nothing, resulting simply in the deaths of many more on his own side, and possibly the loss of their just cause, while countless lives will still be lost on the other side. So he should fight. Similarly, in nontragic cases, the obvious question may frequently be very difficult, if two or more (nontragic) alternatives are equally balanced. The tragic question registers not the difficulty of solving the obvious question but a distinct difficulty: the fact that all the possible answers to the obvious question, including the best one, are bad, involving serious moral wrongdoing. In that sense, there is no "right answer."

How does Arjuna determine that the answer to the tragic question is "no"? Not, clearly, by weighing up costs and benefits. That he has done already in considering what he ought to do. (That was, in effect, his method, a quite reasonable one in the circumstances.) To answer the tragic question, he appears to consult an independent account of ethical value, according to which murdering one's own kin, especially when they are blameless, is a heinous wrong; but deserting one's family when one is their leader and essential supporter is also morally wrong. Ethical thoughts independent of the "what to do" question, thoughts about respect, kinship, and the right, enter in to inform him that his predicament is not just tough, but also tragic.

I shall argue in this paper that the tragic question is important for us all, when we evaluate our choices, and especially important in situations of public choice. I shall argue that while cost-benefit analysis offers an attractive way of approaching the obvious question, it offers no good way at all of registering the force of the tragic question or of representing a situation in which the answer to that question is "no." (I shall define what I mean by cost-benefit analysis below, in Section III.) Too much reliance on cost-benefit analysis as a general method of public choice can therefore distract us from an issue of major importance, making us believe that we have only one question on our hands, when in fact we have at least two. But to understand why the tragic question might have a bearing on public choice, we need to return to our tragic cases.

The answer to the tragic question is not always as clear as it is in Arjuna's situation on the battlefield. To put it another way, it is not always easy to tell whether we have a tragic situation on our hands, or simply a situation in which it is hard to answer the obvious question. Consider another choice Arjuna faces earlier in the poem. The Pandava brothers are living happily in their kingdom, when a certain poor man's cattle are stolen by thieves. He asks the help of the Pandavas, his rulers. The appeal naturally falls on Arjuna, the gifted warrior. This appeal makes Arjuna very unhappy, because he realizes that he is on potentially tragic ground (case B):

Arjuna thought wretchedly, "The wealth of this poor brahmin is being carried off, and it is certain that his tears must be dried. The king will suffer a great breach of Law by negligence, if I do not protect this man who is weeping at the gate. If I fail to protect, the impiety of us all with regard to protection will be established in the world, and we shall suffer a breach of Law . . . [But if I take steps to protect him] I must live in the forest.[4] Either a great breach of Law, or death in the forest! But Law wins out, even over the death of one's body."[5]

Arjuna initially faces the choice with gloom, both because of the risk of life it appears to require of him and also because he senses that the answer to the tragic question may be "yes." The failure of a leader to protect an impoverished subject is a gross violation of moral law.[6] (Twenty-three hundred years ago in India, this point was clearly understood.) On the other hand, forfeiting one's own life also looks unacceptable. It seems, however, that in thinking the choice through Arjuna comes to a different conclusion: hard though the choice is, it is not tragic. One of the choices would involve serious moral wrongdoing, but the other would not. Morality is squarely and unequivocally on the side of protecting, and the other side is just facing his own death, which is unpleasant but not morally blameworthy. The typi-

---

[4] The reason for this is that the protection will require Arjuna to go to see his older brother the king; but the brothers have all taken a vow that if any of them disturbs the other while he is with Draupadi (the common wife of all five), he must go and live like a hermit in the forest for 12 months.

[5] van Buitenen, Mahabharata, *supra* note 3, vol. I, p. 399: bk. I (16) 205.

[6] Law, *Dharma,* is a broad notion, encompassing an idea of universal moral requirement and something like natural law.

cal tragic attitude that says, "Which of these is without evils?"[7] never quite materializes: it drops away in favor of a decisive, even cheerful, acceptance of the risky alternative. Once again, it would seem that an independent ethical account has intervened to inform Arjuna: risking or even forfeiting one's own life is just not one of the things that is morally unacceptable.

What is the point of the tragic question? When we think about our two situations of choice, and particularly situation A, it might easily seem that Krishna has a point. The real question is the obvious question, and the tragic question is just a useless distraction. "O Arjuna," he says, "why have you become so depressed in this critical hour? Such dejection is unknown to noble men; it does not lead to the heavenly heights, and on earth it can only cause disgrace." Quite right, one may think: when one has seen where one's duty lies, one ought to get on with it, without tragic moaning and groaning. We do not want military leaders who self-indulgently wring their hands about the blood they are about to shed, or throw away their arrows to sit sorrowfully on the seats of their cars. It does no good for them to think this way, and it may well do harm, weakening their resolve and that of their troops.

On the other hand, one can argue that Arjuna is a better model of deliberation than Krishna: even in a case like this, where the tragedy does not look like one that could have been avoided by better political planning, there is a point to the tragic question. It keeps the mind of the chooser firmly on the fact that his action is an immoral action, which it is always wrong to choose. The recognition that one has "dirty hands" is not just self-indulgence: it has significance for future actions. It informs the chooser that he may owe reparations to the vanquished and an effort to rebuild their lives after the disaster that will have been inflicted on them. When the recognition is public, it constitutes an acknowledgment of moral culpability, something that frequently has significance in domestic and international politics.[8] (Michael Walzer writes eloquently about Hiroshima in this regard.) Most significantly, it reminds the chooser that he must not do such things henceforth, except in the very special tragic circumstance he faces here. Slaughtering one's kin is one of the terrible things that it is always

---

[7] Aeschylus, Agamemnon, 206–11: "A heavy doom is disobedience, but heavy, too, if I shall rend my own child, the adornment of my house, polluting a father's hands with streams of slaughtered maiden's blood close by the altar. Which of these is without evils?"

[8] Indeed, we might say that the main importance of reparations, too, is expressive. Obviously the fact that my grandmother-in-law received a regular income from the German government did nothing to bring back the family members who had perished during the Holocaust. Although the financial support was not negligible, its primary significance was as a public expression of wrongdoing and the determination to do things differently in the future.

tragic to pursue. In that way, facing the tragic question reinforces moral commitments that should be reinforced, particularly in wartime.

Asked to lecture on tragic dilemmas to the undergraduates at West Point, I had one of the best classroom discussions I have ever had, because these students knew that tragedy was not just a myth, it was their own future. And they recognized that the tragic question should be faced, again and again. Most of them thought that not deadening one's mind to the fact that (for example) one was taking an innocent life was among the first virtues of a good military leader. Clearly the officers in charge of the ethics program thought this as well: that was why the program was there, and I was invited to address this topic. The topic of Lieutenant Calley kept recurring in my informal conversations with the officers. One might say that they saw the purpose of the ethics program as the prevention of such unthinking acts of brutality. Not only higher-ups, but all officers, should have a sense of tragedy.

Many moral philosophers, among them some distinguished ones,[9] have insisted that tragic conflicts are conflicts of prima facie obligations only: there can be only one right choice, and once that choice is arrived at the conflicting obligation drops away, no longer exerting any claim. Or, to put it in Cicero's way, a fine-tuned casuistry will show us that the rule we were applying to one of the alternatives has an exception, and this case is it. The difficulty with this idea is that it makes morality the handmaiden of fortune—the sheer fact that obligation A happens to collide with obligation B brings it about that A (or, as the case may be, B) is no longer binding. And it allows agents to wriggle out of commitments that should be regarded as binding over a complete life. Someone who loves his family, as does Arjuna, and who thinks killing one's kin abhorrent, should not shift with the winds of chance and decide that it is after all all right, at least here. Such a picture of morality yields an unacceptable picture of the moral agent, as lacking principled commitments, as able to improvise his moral identity freely at any time. Sartre, at least, knew what he was up to when he took his line on moral dilemmas, which supported and was supported by the entirety of his philosophy. In essence I am saying that the failure to recognize genuine moral dilemmas commits us to something like an existentialist view of moral personality, in which we boldly take credit for choices that we make, undeterred by remorse for the wrong that we thereby have done. Sartre's Oresetes, however, is a scary figure, in his ability to sever himself

---

[9] Among the targets of my earlier writings on this topic are Aquinas, Cicero, Kant, W. D. Ross, R. M. Hare, and Jean-Paul Sartre; I do not say here which of these I take to be "distinguished."

from any moral tie at all. We do not want our soldiers, our politicians, or ourselves, to be like that.

In my two examples, the person who has the tragic choice before him is also the one who correctly poses and answers the question. (Similarly, the West Point cadets thought of themselves as preparing to face potentially tragic circumstances themselves, and to choose well in them.) But this, of course, is not always the case. Not all deliberators are as alert as Arjuna. And anyone who sees the case has a right to pose the question. In many such cases, the involved agent fails to see the tragedy in which he is implicated, while an onlooker sees clearly. (The Chorus of Aeschylus' Agamemnon see their king's tragic choice in a way that the deluded king does not. Lieutenant Calley did not see the nature of his situation, but the court, and the American public, saw more clearly.) Thus tragic dilemmas are not just occasions for one involved person's pondering: they are occasions for public deliberation, as we seek to get the best account of a situation that has large public consequences.

Obviously enough, the sense of tragedy should inform decent moral choice, rather than substituting for it. We all know too many people who think that if they wring their hands enough they can do anything they like. We should insist that decent emotion does not absolve the actor: that is why, even when the best choice has been made from among tragic alternatives, the person with a sense of tragedy should make reparations, not simply express guilt and sorrow.

When we consider the second case, we see the point of the tragic question even more clearly. For it is an important source of moral clarity to see that moral obligations are qualitatively different from the natural desire one has to preserve one's own life. In asking himself whether both alternatives are unacceptable, Arjuna has learned something about the difference between self-interest and moral commitment, something that might not have been learned had he approached the case simply in terms of the obvious question.

But there is a further way in which the tragic question brings illumination. Thinking about the second case, we see the further point already: for the reader is likely to think that the Pandavas have made a very foolish arrangement for governing their kingdom, and that it is this foolish arrangement that has caused a possibly tragic situation to materialize. How on earth could they have decided that the king must not be interrupted when he was with his wife?[10] Did they not foresee that sometimes someone else in the

---

[10] See note 4 *supra*.

family might need to get the king's attention? Stepping one step back from tragedy, and asking about its genesis, we ask how a different arrangement of the relevant values might have prevented disaster.

Consider Sophocles' *Antigone* (case C).[11] Creon tells the entire city that anyone who offers burial to the traitor Polynices is a traitor to the city and will be put to death. Antigone cannot accept the edict, because it asks her to violate a fundamental religious obligation to seek burial for her kin. As Hegel correctly argued, each protagonist is narrow, thinking only of one sphere of value and neglecting the claim of the other. Creon thinks only of the health of the city, neglecting the "unwritten laws" of family obligation. Antigone thinks only of the family, failing to recognize the crisis of the city. We may add that for this very reason each has an impoverished conception not only of value in general but also of his or her own cherished sphere of value. As Haemon points out, Creon fails to recognize that citizens are also members of families, and that therefore a protector of the city who neglects these values is hardly protecting the city at all. Antigone fails to note that families also live in cities, which must survive if the survival of the family is to be ensured. A person who thought well about Antigone's choice would see that it is genuinely a tragedy: there is no "right answer," because both alternatives contain serious wrongdoing. Burying a traitor is a serious wrong to the city, but for Antigone not to bury him involves a serious religious violation. Because neither sees the tragedy inherent in the situation, because neither so much as poses the tragic question, both are in these two distinct ways impoverished political actors.

And this makes a huge difference for the political future. The drama depicts a very extreme situation, which is unlikely to occur often. In this extreme situation, where the city has been invaded by a member of its own ruling household, there may be no avoiding a tragic clash of duties. But a protagonist who faced the tragic question squarely would be prompted to have a group of highly useful thoughts about governance in general. In particular, noting that both the well-being of the city and the "unwritten laws" of religious obligation are of central ethical importance, he or she would be led to want a city that makes room for people to pursue their familial religious obligations without running afoul of civic ordinances.[12] In other

---

[11] My interpretation is defended with a lot of textual detail and full discussion of the scholarly literature in Nussbaum, Fragility, *supra* note 1, ch. 3.

[12] In Fragility (*id.*) I note that this interpretation is shared by a number of critics, including I. M. Linforth, Antigone and Creon, 15 U. Cal. Publications Classical Philology 183, 257 (1961); Matthew Santirocco, Justice in Sophocles' "Antigone," 4 Phil. & Lit. 180, 182, 194 (1980); Charles Segal, Tragedy and Civilization: An Interpretation of Sophocles 205 (1981). Linforth: "For all Athenians, the play offers a powerful warning to see to it that the laws they enact are not in conflict with the laws of the gods." Segal: "Through its choral song, the *polis* arrives at self-awareness of the tensions between which it exists. Embodying these

words, he or she would want a city such as Pericles claims to find in democratic Athens, when he boasts that public policy shows respect for unwritten law. Just as Americans believe that we can create a public order that builds in spaces for the free exercise of religion, in which individuals are not always tragically torn between civic ordinance and religious command, so ancient Athens had an analogous antitragic thought—as a direct result, quite possibly, of watching tragedies such as Sophocles' *Antigone*.

It was here, indeed, that Hegel found, plausibly, the political significance of tragedy. Tragedy reminds us of the deep importance of the spheres of life that are in conflict within the drama and of the dire results when they are opposed and we have to choose between them. It therefore motivates us to imagine what a world would be like that did not confront people with such choices, a world of "concordant action" between the two spheres of value. In that sense, the end of the drama is written offstage, by citizens who enact these insights in their own constructive political reflection: "The true course of dramatic development consists in the annulment of *contradictions* viewed as such, in the reconciliation of the forces of human action, which alternately strive to negate each other in their conflict."[13]

Now in one way Hegel's approach to tragedy is too simple. For it ignores the possibility that some degree of tragedy is a structural feature of human life.[14] Many distinct spheres of value claim our attention and commitment. As Greek polytheism expresses the insight, there are many gods, all of whom demand worship. But the gods do not agree. Therefore the contingencies of life make it almost inevitable that some disharmony will materialize among our many commitments. The only alternative to the permanent possibility of tragedy would appear to be a life so impoverished in value that it neglects many things that human beings should not neglect. And of course such a life does not really avoid tragedy: it just fails to see the tragedy involved in its own neglect of genuine values. Relations within the family—and between the family and the public sphere—are one area where we might expect a permanent possibility of tragedy, no matter how well we arrange things.

In another way, however, Hegel gives us the best strategy to follow, es-

---

tensions in art, it can confront them and work towards their mediation, even though mediation is not permitted to the tragic heroes within the spectacle itself. The play in its social and ritual contexts achieves for society what it refuses to the actors within its fiction. Its context affirms what its content denies."

[13] Extract from 4 G. W. F. Hegel, The Philosophy of Fine Art (P. B. Osmaston trans. 1920) (1835), reproduced in Hegel on Tragedy 68, 71 (A. Paolucci & H. Paolucci eds. 1975).

[14] This was the emphasis of my reading of the *Antigone;* a similar view is defended in Nussbaum, Flawed Crystals, *supra* note 1, where I call moral dilemmas a secular analogue of original sin: you cannot live a fully pure life, a life in which you are false to no value.

pecially in political life. (Readers of my previous discussions will notice that my own attitude to the problem of moral dilemmas has become more Hegelian over time, in part because I have increasingly focused on public and political choice.) For we really do not know whether a harmonious fostering of two apparently opposed values can be achieved—until we try to bring that about. Many people in many places have thought that a harmonious accommodation between religion and the state is just impossible. Athens tried to prove them wrong. Modern liberal states—grappling with the even thornier problem of the plurality of religions, and of secular views of the good—all in their own ways try to prove them wrong. To a great extent, a political regime like ours does enable citizens to avoid Antigone-like tragedies. That is what is meant by saying—as the Court said until *Smith,* and as Congress said in passing the Religious Freedom Restoration Act—that the state may not impose a "substantial burden" on an individual's free exercise of religion without a "compelling state interest."[15] Creon, presumably, had such an interest, and so too will quite a few other state actors. Consequently, there will be a residuum of tragedy left even in the Hegelian nation. But we proclaim that we do our best to keep tragedy at bay. We do so because we understand the force of the tragic question: understand, that is, that to require an individual to depart from a religious commitment is not just to impose an inconvenience, it is to ask something that goes to the heart of that person's being. It is to deprive them of a sphere of liberty to which, as citizens, they have an entitlement based upon justice.

Often we do not know what arrangements we are capable of making, until we have faced the tragic question with Hegel's idea in view. Consider one more example, a true modern story (case D). Its content is more mundane than that of my mythic examples; in many ways, given that the harms done are smaller and possibly not irreparable, it will look less tragic. But it has a similar structure, and it raises similar Hegelian questions. Tragic cases, recall, are defined by the presence of serious wrongdoing on both sides; the wrongdoing does not always involve killing people; it may only involve neglect of some important obligation.

When I began teaching as an assistant professor at Harvard, philosophy department colloquia always began at 5 P.M., exactly when child care centers closed. Those of us who had child care obligations, consequently, faced many difficult choices. One problem we had was deciding what to do on each occasion. But I felt that we had another problem as well: for, often,

---

[15] Employment Div., Oregon Dep't Human Resources v. Smith, 482 U.S. 342 (1990); Religious Freedom Restoration Act (RFRA), H.R. 1308, 103d Cong. (1993). For my own discussion of the cases, and a proposal based on the language of the RFRA, see Martha Nussbaum, Women and Human Development: The Capabilities Approach, ch. 3 (2000).

neither of the alternatives looked morally acceptable. Either we would be deserting our duty to our colleagues or we would be deserting our duty to and love of our young children. The tragic question kept rearing its head, and frequently its answer was "no."

Obviously enough, this string of minitragedies was the result of obtuseness. The arrangements my colleagues had made about colloquia were no more sensible than the arrangements made by the Pandava brothers about visiting the king. Because it had never dawned on most men of that generation to think that a person ought to be able to be both a good primary caretaking parent and a good colleague, they had never bothered to think what very simple changes in the daily arrangements might be made to remove the problem. Nobody could talk about this; nobody could draw attention to it. I recall the day when this changed. At an important lecture by a major visiting philosopher, held as usual at 5 P.M. and (implicitly) mandatory for junior faculty, we reached the question period (by now it is after 6—I have gotten a sitter to pick my daughter up from child care). Robert Nozick stood up and said, with the carefree subversiveness of which only the tenured are capable, "I have to go now: I have to pick up my son from hockey practice."

This was a moment of Hegelian *Aufhebung*: the first public acknowledgment that there was a tension between two spheres of value and that we had not been managing that tension very well. By coming out as a parent, Nozick had posed the tragic question to us all, challenging us to think better about it. It was unclear whether Nozick thought that his own case had the structure of a tragic dilemma: as a tenured person, and a remarkably independent one at that, he might not have thought he had any duty to attend the colloquium. But he drew attention to the predicament of others who were more vulnerable and who had similar family obligations.[16]

By now, nonobtuse thinking on these issues is much more common, though by no means ubiquitous. (The world of legal practice, it seems, has been slower to seek "the annulment of contradictions" than has the humanities world, or the legal academy.) What the incident revealed was that many tragedies are produced not by natural necessity or by anything about the character of the contending values, but simply by habit and tradition, treated as natural and inevitable. Colloquia have to be at 5 P.M. The junior faculty seminar led by Burton Dreben has to be from 6 P.M. until 10 P.M. That is just the way life is, and it cannot be otherwise.

---

[16] Later, he also made a formal protest against the nighttime seminar held by Burton Dreben that was (again implicitly) mandatory for junior faculty, pointing out that it was a hardship for those who had children. He did not succeed—the response was simply to say, of course it is not mandatory, but of course it was, and remained so. But the intervention showed that his remark about hockey was no chance matter.

I think that whenever we are inclined to say this about any clash of values, we should always pause and ask Hegel's question: is there a rearrangement of our practices that can remove the tragedy? In this case rearrangement was straightforward; in many other cases, including many involving conflicts between work and child care, solutions are difficult and also costly: we need to think about public support for child care, about policies of parental leave. All this is much more radically subversive of tradition, and more threatening to entrenched preferences (in part because it is costly), than changing the time of the colloquium. But we need to imagine such alternatives—if only to inform ourselves about the real structure of our situation. Tragedy is rarely just tragedy. Most often, behind the gloom is stupidity, or selfishness, or laziness, or malice.[17]

Let me recapitulate. In all four of our cases, people face questions about what they should do, which may be more or less difficult. They also face a question of methodology: how shall they go about answering the question about what they should do? This methodological question, too, may be easier or harder. But all four people face, as well, a second and distinct question: the tragic question. There are times when it is not worth pausing very long over the tragic question—if, for example, it is obvious that there is at least one available course that involves no serious wrongdoing. But in all four of these cases the issue of serious wrongdoing is not obvious. Eventually Arjuna answered it in the negative in case B, for the alternative of his own risk of death. But our three other cases seem to involve genuinely tragic dilemmas—at varying levels of gravity and irreparability.

It is useful to pose the tragic question for four reasons. First, to do so clarifies the nature of our ethical alternatives, informing us about important

---

[17] Some might hold that if we do not find any of these human causes lurking in the background, the tragic case is just bad luck, and not tragedy in the moral sense. That is, we should not hold agents morally responsible for what mere luck, with no admixture of human error, has brought their way. With Bernard Williams, I dispute this: a murder of a family member is a murder of a family member, no matter how unfortunate the chain of events leading up to that. Clearly we will not blame Arjuna in precisely the same way as we would blame someone who walked out one fine morning and murdered his cousins; but we should feel that his moral life is irrevocably altered, and that he owes not only regret, but also remorse and reparative commitments, to the defeated. Another way of putting this was suggested to me by Philip Quinn: we may borrow Aquinas' distinction between dilemmas *secundum quid*—dilemmas an agent gets into through some personal fault—and dilemmas *simpliciter,* which Quinn calls ''no-fault dilemmas.'' These are not the result of previous wrongdoing. We would then deny Aquinas' contention, namely, that there are no real dilemmas *simpliciter.* Quinn further divides the class of ''no-fault'' dilemmas into those that are corrigible by some rearrangement of circumstances and those that are not corrigible. I accept (and indeed insist on) that division, but I doubt that it is ever easy to tell whether a dilemmas is or is not corrigible in advance of prolonged attempts to correct the circumstances that give rise to it.

differences between self-interest and commitment, prudential and moral values. Second, to recognize the existence of a tragic dilemma, in those cases where the answer to the tragic question is "no," reinforces commitments to important moral values that should in general be observed. Third, to recognize tragedy and our own "dirty hands" motivates us to make appropriate reparations for conduct that, while in a sense inevitable, was also unethical.[18] Finally, the Hegelian point, the recognition of tragedy leads us to ask how the tragic situation might have been avoided by better social planning; tragedy thus provides a major set of incentives for good social reflection.

Notice that our examples reveal a persistent human tendency to neglect the tragic question in favor of the more straightforward obvious question, a question that can hardly be avoided if action is in the offing. Krishna gives advice that is deeply equivocal in the context of the epic, where he is portrayed as a deceiver, and not at all a simply admirable character. Nonetheless, a lot of people like this advice, as evidenced by the fact that the *Bhagavad-Gita* (the section of the poem in which Krishna gives his advice) has acquired a life of its own, becoming one of the most influential texts of the history of philosophy, while Arjuna's very sensible response to his dilemma is not revered in this way or, frequently, even considered part of the same discussion. Again, Creon and Antigone prefer the simple focus on issues of choice and action to a more complex reflection on the plurality of conflicting values and the need to arrange things so that they conflict less tragically. Focusing on the moment of choice requires only some decision strategy, and one can always choose in an arbitrary way if a sounder decision strategy does not suggest itself. Asking the tragic question requires, first of all, assuming a possible burden of guilt and of reparative effort, something people, and especially leaders, do not always enjoy doing. Asking it in the Hegelian way requires more: a systematic critical scrutiny of habit and tradition, in search of a reasonable *Aufhebung* of the contending values. And this scrutiny requires of us nothing less than a comprehensive account of justice and central human goods. For these reasons it would not be surprising if technicians of choice avoided the tragic question in favor of the obvious question.

Our tragic examples show us one thing more that is highly pertinent to our modern-day alternatives. It is that there is a persistent tension between recognizing a plurality of commitments and the avoidance of tragedy. Creon and Antigone both see this clearly: indeed, I have argued that the

---

[18] See Walzer, *supra* note 1; and Stocker, *supra* note 1.

strategy of both is to recognize only a single commitment, precisely in order not to have troublesome dilemmas on one's hands. Fanaticism yields happy choice making. But the play shows us something else: such fanaticism is blind to genuine value. There is more in the world than can be seen by either of these obtuse protagonists. Greek polytheism expresses the view that if one recognizes all the things that are valuable, and pays them sufficient heed, one will not be able to count on avoiding tragedy. Judaeo-Christian monotheism recognizes the same issue by insisting that the commandments are 10 and not one—although not all Judaeo-Christian thinkers have drawn what I take to be the appropriate inference from this fact, namely, that there can be genuine moral dilemmas.[19]

What this means, in modern political terms, is that the more entitlements a society recognizes as basic and inalienable, the more the specter of tragedy will rear its head, and, therefore, the more delicate the political designing that will need to be done. In that sense, the libertarian state might seem the most rational, in the sense that it is the least likely to saddle us with tragedy. But Hegel did not conclude that Creon and Antigone were right to pursue, each of them, a fanatical course that avoided all tragedy. He concluded that they were blind and obtuse—because they refused to recognize values that should rightly be recognized. We cannot come to a similar conclusion about the libertarian state without extensive argument. Neither, however, can the libertarian state claim an advantage in point of tragedy avoidance. As Creon's story shows, one does not avoid tragedy simply by saying that one does—for there may be other legitimate claims that are being ignored. Probably there is a limit as to how many intrinsic values a reasonable private or public ethical system can recognize. If a system generates tragic tensions every day, despite the wisest and best planning over a long period of time, it might be safe to conclude that it has recognized too much or set the level too high. In that sense, Creon's program of simplification was not the dead opposite of what one should do. But his fanaticism is clearly unacceptable—as he himself acknowledges, calling it "the errors

---

[19] Aquinas, famously, took the line that at most one of the conflicting obligations could be valid. Saint Gregory the Great, by contrast, recognized the existence of genuine moral dilemmas, but ascribed their genesis to the devil (see Alan Donagan, Consistency in Rationalist Moral Systems, 81 J. Philosophy 291, 298 (1984)); Josef Stern has argued (in unpublished work) that something like this is Maimonides' view about Abraham's sacrifice of Isaac: namely, that the heavenly voice is not really from God, but is a diabolical deception. For extensive exploration of the role of moral dilemmas in Christian thought, see Philip Quinn, Moral Obligation, Religious Demand, and Practical Conflict, in Rationality, Religious Belief, and Moral Commitment (Robert Audi & W. J. Wainwright eds. 1986); Philip Quinn, Tragic Dilemmas, Suffering Love, and Christian Life, 17 J. Religious Ethics 151 (1989); Philip Quinn, Agamemnon and Abraham: The Tragic Dilemma of Kierkegaard's Knight of Faith, J. Literature & Theology 4 (1990).

of my ill-reasoning reasoning (*phrenôn dusphronôn*), harsh and death-dealing.''[20] And the Chorus sums up the issue in the play's final lines: ''Good reasoning (*to phronein*) is by far the most important part of a well-lived life. One must not dishonor any of the spheres protected by the gods. The big speeches of arrogant people receive big blows as their payment, and these blows teach good reasoning in old age.''[21]

II.   THE TWO QUESTIONS IN CONTEMPORARY POLITICAL DELIBERATION

All contemporary liberal democratic societies ask the obvious question all the time. That is no news: so too do all people. But it is also clear that all contemporary liberal democratic societies ask the tragic question, implicitly at any rate. That is, they commit themselves to a menu of certain social goals, and among those goals they single out some as having a special centrality, holding that they are things to which every citizen is entitled, things that each one has a right to demand. Sometimes the menu of such protected areas of value is relatively narrow, encompassing only the so-called first-generation rights, meaning the political and civil rights. Sometimes the menu is broader, taking in a group of economic and social rights. And all such nations have some account, however elastic or indefinite or disputed, of where the threshold falls with respect to each of these entitlements: what deprivation of liberty, or of property, is so unacceptable as to be a violation of a basic constitutional (or otherwise protected) norm. Thus our Bill of Rights carves out certain areas of entitlement that are held to be fundamental to our society. Usually their importance is understood in moral terms: these are things it is morally bad for citizens to lack. Thus most Americans would think that certain limits on freedom of the press, on the right to vote, or on liberty of conscience are not just big costs to be borne, but costs of a very particular kind, costs that consist in being made to bear a burden that no citizen should have to bear, costs that are not just disadvantageous, but wrong. We differ, of course, in many ways about where the line falls between permissible though disadvantageous and morally impermissible deprivations in these areas. Thus, Americans differ about whether the burden faced by the Native Americans when they were denied the right to use peyote in their religious ceremony is a violation of a fundamental moral entitlement. They differ even more intensely about whether the impediment to publishers of pornography that would be created by the MacKinnon/Dworkin civil damage ordinance is or is not an impermissible burden on the freedom of speech. But all would agree that there is some

[20] Sophocles, Antigone, 1262–64.
[21] *Id.* at 1347–53.

such class of morally central entitlements and that violating one of these is different in kind, not just in degree, from depriving someone of some advantage or service. They agree, that is, that in a case of putative conflict between two public goals, where one goal seems likely to be sacrificed, the tragic question must be posed: we must ask whether one or more of the values in question is among the fundamental entitlements of all citizens. For if it is, then any choice made against it involves an especially tragic type of cost, a cost that should be avoided if at all possible and that should be lamented if not avoidable.[22]

Because I myself have a view about which human entitlements should be politically central, which I have recommended as a basis for the formulation of fundamental constitutional principles, it seems wise to introduce it now, so that we can pursue the issues further using an account that gives definite answers to some of the theoretical questions before us, rather than arguing endlessly over the proper understanding of the U.S. Constitution and its various parts, as we would otherwise be likely to do. But it should be remembered that I introduce this view for the sake of having a discussable example. It is no part of my intention in this paper to defend the view, or even to explain it more fully. The arguments of this paper can be applied to any theory of fundamental entitlements one likes.

In my view, then, all citizens of any modern state are entitled, as a matter of basic minimum justice, to the following capabilities:[23]

---

[22] This issue is clearly seen by John Finnis, Natural Law and Natural Rights (1980). Although I disagree with a great deal in his more detailed formulation of his position, on this matter, and on the difference between the pursuit of basic rights and the pursuit of efficiency, he seems to me entirely correct.

[23] I defend this approach at greatest length in Nussbaum, *supra* note 15. Capabilities are conceived of as abilities of persons that combine internal preparation (education, and so on) with suitable external circumstances. My reasons for putting these particular items on the list cannot be given here, but I hope it will seem like a plausible list. For earlier discussions, see Martha Nussbaum, Nature, Function, and Capability: Aristotle on Political Distribution, in Oxford Studies in Ancient Philosophy 145–84 (Suppl. Vol. 1 1988); Martha Nussbaum, Aristotelian Social Democracy, in Liberalism and the Good 203–52 (R. B. Douglass *et al.* eds. 1990); Martha Nussbaum, Non-relative Virtues: An Aristotelian Approach, in The Quality of Life (M. Nussbaum & A. Sen eds. 1993); Martha Nussbaum, Aristotle on Human Nature and the Foundations of Ethics, in World, Mind and Ethics: Essays on the Ethical Philosophy of Bernard Williams 86–131 (J. E. J. Altham & Ross Harrison eds. 1995); Martha Nussbaum, Human Functioning and Social Justice: In Defense of Aristotelian Essentialism, 20 Pol. Theory 202 (1992); Martha Nussbaum, Human Capabilities, Female Human Beings, in Women, Culture, and Development 61 (M. Nussbaum & J. Glover eds. 1995); Martha Nussbaum, The Good as Discipline, the Good as Freedom, in Ethics of Consumption: The Good Life, Justice, and Global Stewardship 312 (David A. Crocker & Toby Linden eds. 1997); Martha Nussbaum, Women and Cultural Universals, ch. 1 in Martha Nussbaum, Sex and Social Justice 29 (1999); and Martha Nussbaum, Capabilities and Human Rights, 66 Fordham L. Rev. 273 (1997).

The Central Human Capabilities

1. Life. Being able to live to the end of a human life of normal length; not dying prematurely, or before one's life is so reduced as to be not worth living.
2. Bodily Health. Being able to have good health, including reproductive health; to be adequately nourished; to have adequate shelter.
3. Bodily Integrity. Being able to move freely from place to place; to be secure against violent assault, including sexual assault and domestic violence; having opportunities for sexual satisfaction and for choice in matters of reproduction.
4. Senses, Imagination, and Thought. Being able to use the senses, to imagine, think, and reason—and to do these things in a "truly human" way, a way informed and cultivated by an adequate education, including, but by no means limited to, literacy and basic mathematical and scientific training. Being able to use imagination and thought in connection with experiencing and producing works and events of one's own choice, religious, literary, musical, and so forth. Being able to use one's mind in ways protected by guarantees of freedom of expression with respect to both political and artistic speech, and freedom of religious exercise. Being able to have pleasurable experiences and to avoid nonbeneficial pain.
5. Emotions. Being able to have attachments to things and people outside ourselves; to love those who love and care for us, to grieve at their absence; in general, to love, to grieve, to experience longing, gratitude, and justified anger. Not having one's emotional development blighted by fear and anxiety. (Supporting this capability means supporting forms of human association that can be shown to be crucial in their development.)
6. Practical Reason. Being able to form a conception of the good and to engage in critical reflection about the planning of one's life. (This entails protection for the liberty of conscience and religious observance.)
7. Affiliation:
   A. Being able to live with and toward others, to recognize and show concern for other human beings, to engage in various forms of social interaction; to be able to imagine the situation of another. (Protecting this capability means protecting institutions that constitute and nourish such forms of affiliation, and also protecting the freedom of assembly and political speech.)
   B. Having the social bases of self-respect and nonhumiliation; being able to be treated as a dignified being whose worth is equal to that of others. This entails provisions of nondiscrimination on the basis

of race, sex, sexual orientation, ethnicity, caste, religion, national origin.
8. Other Species. Being able to live with concern for and in relation to animals, plants, and the world of nature.
9. Play. Being able to laugh, to play, to enjoy recreational activities.
10. Control over One's Environment:
    A. Political. Being able to participated effectively in political choices that govern one's life; having the right of political participation, protections of free speech and association.
    B. Material. Being able to hold property (both land and movable goods), and having property rights on an equal basis with others; having the right to seek employment on an equal basis with others; having the freedom from unwarranted search and seizure. In work, being able to work as a human being, exercising practical reason and entering into meaningful relationships of mutual recognition with other workers.

The capabilities list goes well beyond the U.S. Constitution in its explicit recognition of material entitlements; yet it is offered in a similar liberal spirit, and it has at times been argued that the U.S. Constitution should be understood to make similar commitments to a meaningful level of welfare.[24] In any case, the idea is that the acceptable political goal is not the actual functioning of citizens—for they may well choose not to avail themselves of one or most of these capabilities, in accordance with their comprehensive view of life and their own conscience—but the capability to choose the functioning (or not to choose it) in each area. (Thinking of the "free exercise of religion," and why the Constitution puts the entitlement that way, rather than specifying a definite preferred type of functioning, should help to make this point clear.) The reason for making capability, not functioning, the goal is grounded in respect for persons. Except in areas involving harm to others, and areas involving the health and education of children, we extend options to citizens, rather than dragooning them into a definite mode of life, because we respect their ability to design and lead a life.

That same respect, however, requires that we do not rest content with removing government interference from people's lives: the capabilities approach demands affirmative support, in such a way that the person really is

---

[24] See Frank Michelman, States' Rights and States' Roles: The Permutations of "Sovereignty" in National League of Cities v. Usery, 86 Yale L. J. 1165 (1977); Lawrence Tribe, Unraveling National League of Cities: The New Federalism and Affirmative Rights to Essential Government Services, 90 Harv. L. Rev. 1065 (1977); Owen Fiss on access to the political process; Rawls on the fair value of the political liberties, and so on.

able to do the thing in question. A society that gives women the vote on paper, and then does nothing to protect them from private intimidation and harassment when they attempt to get involved in the political process, has not secured to women the capabilities involve in citizenship.

The capabilities approach is a moral conception. It is a partial moral conception, because it specifies very little of what people's lives should include, and leaves to them a great deal of latitude in determining what goals to pursue. But (very much like the principles defended in John Rawls's political liberalism) it has a definite moral content. It asks citizens to sign on to this list not just as a list of efficient means to promote wealth or contentment, but as a set of basic entitlements of persons, required by human dignity itself.

This moral understanding of the list entails that there is always a potential for tragedy to arise, whenever citizens are pushed beneath the threshold on any one of the 10 capabilities. Thus not to have the freedom of speech (as specified further in the nation's constitutional tradition) is always a tragedy, not to be made up for by the presence of other items on the list, such as material well-being and health and even bodily integrity. Much further work must go into specifying the acceptable threshold level of each capability. I have left things deliberately vague at this point, in the belief that the most appropriate way for the threshold to be more precisely set—at least in liberal democratic societies—is by the citizens of each nation, as they elaborate and refine their constitutional traditions. Both legislation and, where there is a written constitution, a tradition of judicial interpretation will be involved in this process. Once some determination of the threshold level is made, however, the tragic question comes into play: for wherever we find citizens beneath the threshold on any one of these, social justice has not been done and people are incurring a particular kind of cost, a cost that no human being ought to have to bear, a cost implicated in the idea of human dignity itself.

In a modern state, two kinds of situations require us to raise the tragic question. First is the situation typified by my Nozick example: institutional actors are not directly involved, but we notice that citizens are facing an unusually high degree of tragic choosing, in ways that seem to implicate fundamental entitlements. In terms of my theory, it would appear that they are being forced to choose all the time between values of affiliation and employment-related capabilities; let us suppose that it is clear that the society agrees these capabilities are both important, and at the level raised by the example. Then the ubiquity of tragic choices demands Hegelian rethinking of our arrangements: how can we bring it about that citizens do not face such tragic choices all the time? A second way in which the tragic question may arise is when an institutional actor has a choice to make that seems as if it might involve choosing between two fundamental entitlements of citizens—as might be the case, for example, when religious claims appear to clash with values of sex equality. In both cases, institutional actors will have to get involved ultimately; but in the first case, because they are not involved already, it is easier to miss the fact that there is an institutional tragedy in the works.

Armed with the tragic question, a decision maker approaches a complex situation of choice. What does my approach urge her to do? First, she must examine all the available alternatives, holding them up against the account of basic entitlements, together with her society's current specification of them. She must get very clear about whether any of the alternatives involves violation of a fundamental entitlement. If none of them does, then she may proceed with the obvious question—which may frequently, of course, be very difficult to answer. If one or more involves violation of a fundamental entitlement and the others do not, then there is an extremely strong case for striking the tragedy-bearing alternatives off the list; indeed, it would be hard to know what could make one keep them on the list, other than a suspicion that the list had been badly constructed, or the levels of entitlements set too high. Then, having eliminated the morally unacceptable alternatives, she may, again, proceed with the obvious question, using whatever techniques she has at her disposal to answer it.

It is important to notice that many questions faced by administrative agencies will come into one of these categories: either the risk involved is not one that basic entitlements forbid or at least one of them is not of that character. An economic loss, for example, will not make a case into a tragedy, unless it is related to capability in the way I have described, pushing citizens beneath the threshold of capability in some area. Thus asking the tragic question will commonly not disable the use of cost-benefit analysis as it is standardly used by administrative agencies, as described, for example, in Cass Sunstein's work on "risk-risk" trade-offs. Even if our nation did recognize a basic health right, as I think it should, the level of that right should not be set so high that any cancer risk or any pollution at all is a violation.[25]

If, however, the answer to the tragic question is "no"—both or all of the alternatives involve violation of a basic entitlement—then Hegelian thinking must come into play. In addition to choosing as well as she can in the immediate case—posing the obvious question as wisely as she can—

---

[25] For the way health rights have been understood under international human rights law, see Brigit C. A. Toebes, The Right to Health as a Human Right in International Law (1999). Basic child health and equal access to available health services are among the salient points stressed in such documents.

the institutional decision maker will also acknowledge that this is a really bad situation. Both cases have unacceptable costs, and long-range planning had better begin immediately, to make sure that we do not face choices like this in the future.

My approach entails, then, answer to the tragic question will be "no" only when we find that we cannot get citizens above the capability threshold in one area, without pushing them below it in another area. (For example, that we cannot get all children in a nation educated without making their parents suffer economic losses that push them below the threshold—as is currently the case in India.) Such cases are tragedies, according to my definition; they will be regarded as blots on a decent society, and we will be on Hegelian notice that we should do everything in our power to arrange things so that we are not confronted with such choices—as quickly as possible.

Notice that there is some connection between the obvious question and the tragic question, when citizens try to figure out what the acceptable threshold level of a central capability shall be. That is, asking what our options actually are, and figuring their costs and benefits, informs the process of reflection on the tragic question as well, by telling us that some ways of arranging or rearranging things are just impossible, or too costly, to be at all feasible as ways of thinking about basic entitlements. Suppose a certain religious group demands the right to withdraw its children from the entirety of compulsory education, saying that their free exercise of their religion requires this. Literacy and the associated capabilities are simply not a part of what they think children should have.[26] We think about what we should do here, and we reckon the costs and benefits. This process informs us that the alternative of allowing them to do this is probably extremely costly, not only for their own children and the state's interest in their education, but also for other citizens, who will seek similar exemptions, possibly destroying the entire system of education that is the basis for intelligent citizenship in a pluralistic democracy. Let us suppose this is what we think when we ask the obvious question. Now we turn to the tragic question: is this one of those instances where denying them this putative right is denying them a fundamental entitlement involved in the very notion of the freedom of con-

---

[26] A real-life case close to this is that of the Romanian gypsies, who insist that they should be exempt not only from compulsory education but also from laws prohibiting child labor and related forms of child abuse, because their culture requires a nomadic unlettered existence supported by begging and the use of small children in both begging and theft. All gypsies hold this, but only in Romania, where they form around 20 percent of the population, do they have sufficient political clout to maintain these views forcefully in the public sphere. Although the state does not accept their arguments, de facto they have prevailed so far, and the relevant laws are not generally enforced.

science, something that all citizens have a right to have? It seems clear that we will be inclined to say that it is not one of those cases: the answer to the question whether any of the available courses is morally acceptable is "yes." We can give people an acceptable level of liberty of conscience while insisting on compulsory primary education. We say this, in part, because we do not think freedom of religion in a pluralistic democracy can reasonably be interpreted to demand something that will erode the foundations of civic order. In that way we draw a connection between our two questions, and thinking about costs and benefits informs our inchoate deliberation about where to set the threshold for purposes of the tragic question.

We should not, however, take this connecting too far. My colleagues at Harvard might have concluded that changing the time of the colloquium would wreck the foundations of the social order; that indeed is how people are inclined to view many irritating changes in their habits. As recently as 1873, the U.S. Supreme Court held that to allow women to be lawyers would wreck the foundations of the social order and go against "the nature of things."[27] Knowing that we are not reliable judges of the meaning of change for the overall order of society, we should not hold fundamental entitlements hostage to current social possibilities. We should be skeptical of claims that the costs of securing a central capability to all citizens will be prohibitive: let us try first, we should say, and see how things go. And we should also be prepared to recognize that some very important social goods, which should remain on the capability list, are not available, or not available without prohibitive costs, in our current social environment. This gives us a motivation to design things better, so that we will be able to secure the capability to people at some future time. Setting the level too low, in response to current possibilities and impossibilities, may be a recipe for social lassitude.

Consider the case of compulsory education in India. All Indian states require primary education; in many cases, secondary education is compulsory as well. But literacy rates remain low: about 35 percent for women, 65 percent for men in the nation as a whole. Economic necessity is clearly involved in this distressing pattern: poor parents need to rely on the labor of their children, whether in the home or outside it. As I have noted above, many families would be at risk of going under completely if they were to send all their children to government schools. And yet there are also signs that intelligent planning can make a difference. The state of Kerala, a relatively poor state, has an adolescent literacy rate of 99 percent for both boys and girls. The difference has a great deal to do with state policies: aggres-

---

[27] Bradwell v. Illinois, 83 U.S. (16 Wall.) 130 (1873).

sive campaigning in favor of literacy; incentives to poor parents, in the form of a nutritious school lunch that goes some way to offsetting the losses to parents in child labor; and flexible multisession school hours.[28] If we look to states where literacy is particularly low, we find, correspondingly, an absence of intelligent planning. In some rural areas (in Andhra Pradesh, for example), there are neither schools nor teachers, since state government is corrupt and inefficient and has not bothered to make things happen. In many others areas, government schools fail to offer flexible hours that make schooling possible for working children; nongovernmental organizations sometimes fill the gap, but sometimes they do not.

All this suggests that there is some point to setting a high threshold with regard to education, in a way that gives education the moral force of a basic entitlement—even if the level set cannot currently be achieved in many areas. This is in fact what India is now doing: a proposal to amend the Constitution's list of Fundamental Rights to include a fundamental right of primary and secondary education has been introduced, and has broad support.[29] Obviously enough, amending the Constitution does not all by itself change the conditions I have described. But it does give education a new moral and legal emphasis: it is now a fundamental entitlement of all citizens, the deprivation of which constitutes a tragic cost. It will also be possible to litigate against states or other public actors that deprive children of this fundamental right through deficient planning. Raising the tragic question gives a new urgency to political planning.

Who should raise and who should answer the tragic question? In my analysis, the level of each basic entitlement is specified loosely in a constitution, and then spelled out further, as time goes on, through a combination of legislative and judicial action. Public deliberation can often contribute a great deal toward this process. When a choice is confronted that seems potentially tragic, institutional actors should not deliberate on their own, for the most part: they should turn to public deliberation and to legislative and/ or judicial deliberation—certainly for the Hegelian part of the process, planning for a future nontragic society, but also, often, for the determination

---

[28] See Jean Drèze & Amartya Sen, India: Economic Development and Social Opportunity (1995). Kerala's relative poverty, Drèze and Sen argue, is due to its bad economic policies: permitting unions to drive wages up very high has caused employment to shift to neighboring states. On the other hand, health and education have been well promoted in the absence of robust economic growth. (They use this example, among others, to illustrate the fact that, even in the absence of economic growth, one may achieve progress in these areas; on the other side, focusing only on economic growth—as other states have done—does not achieve progress in these areas.)

[29] See Archana Mehendale, Compulsory Primary Education in India: The Legal Framework, 13 From the Lawyers' Collective 4 (April 1998).

of whether a given situation is or is not tragic. Thus with compulsory education in India, the determination that this deprivation is a violation of a basic entitlement is being arrived at through a complex process of public deliberation about the proposed constitutional amendment. If the amendment is adopted, the right will be further interpreted by the courts. Usually the hard cases will not involve creation of a new constitutional right, but rather the determination of exactly how to demarcate an existing right. Those cases are typically hammered out through a combination of legislative and judicial action.

At times, an administrative agency may find itself having to make a decision that involves interpretation of a fundamental entitlement. In a nation that has a vaguely specified health right, or environment right, such agencies will have to make choices about which risks are acceptable, and I have said that they ought to do this invoking the tragic question. But their interpretation of basic entitlements should always be regarded as a tentative first step only. In other words, the minute it is clear that the tragic question has a point, and that one or more of the alternatives may violate a fundamental entitlement, public deliberation is called for and the agency should seek to initiate a deliberative democratic process.

III.   COST-BENEFIT ANALYSIS: ITS ROLE AND ITS LIMITS

Whenever the capabilities approach is presented to an audience containing economists and policy makers, the first question that is typically posed is, How do we make trade-offs when we cannot provide people with all the capabilities on the list? In other words, some kind of framework for cost-benefit analysis is requested. How much would such an analysis inform us, and what significant issues might be bypassed in the process of focusing on this approach?

For these purposes, I define cost-benefit analysis as a strategy for choice in which weightings are allocated to the available alternatives, arriving at some kind of aggregate figure for each major option. Although the most common way of doing this is the so-called willingness-to-pay approach, I shall not define cost-benefit analysis as equivalent to willingness to pay, because willingness to pay involves not only a commitment to numerical weighting and ranking but also a particular, and highly controversial, idea of how the weights are to be allocated—namely, in accordance with unrefined preferences. I believe, and have argued elsewhere,[30] that there are major and insoluble problems with any such approach. Preferences are the creation of experience and, therefore, also of laws and institutions. Willingness

---

[30] Nussbaum, *supra* note 15, ch. 2.

to pay does not even make the exclusionary moves that are by now common in the literature on social choice—for example, omitting preferences based on ignorance and haste, preferences deformed by malice, envy, resentment, or fear, and preferences that reflect adaptation to a bad state of affairs that is thought to be the only one possible.[31] Still less does it ask, or permit its users to ask, the deeper questions raised by Amartya Sen and Jon Elster, as to whether even corrected preferences could give us a reliable way of ranking social alternatives. So I think that there are devastating objections to be made against willingness to pay, quite independently of what I say here. But these objections do not disable cost-benefit analysis, since the weightings can always be assigned in some other way. Out of charity, then, I define cost-benefit analysis in a way that does not entail any particular way of assigning the weightings, although I do specify that there will be an aggregate number for each choice alternative.

Nor does cost-benefit analysis entail Utilitarianism, that is, the view that the aim of the exercise is to maximize social utility.[32] The aspects of choice we consider worth attending to in producing our weightings may be of many kinds; utility is only one thing that might occur on the benefit side. For, as I shall argue below, cost-benefit analysis does not entail the view that there is only one currency of value in all the heterogeneous material of choice.

Finally, cost-benefit analysis as construed here does not entail consequentialism, that is, the view that the right way of assessing alternatives in a choice situation is to look to the consequences they produce.[33] Some forms of nonutilitarian consequentialism are so elastic that they can include in the statement of consequences things that usually seem like fatal omissions in consequentialism: such as, the protection or violation of rights, and

---

[31] For a general discussion of these debates within welfarist social choice theory, see *id.;* some of the prominent examples of such corrections discussed there are Christopher Bliss, Lifestyle and the Standard of Living, in Nussbaum & Sen eds., *supra* note 23; John Harsanyi, Morality and the Theory of Rational Behavior, in Utilitarianism and Beyond 39–62 (Amartya Sen & Bernard Williams eds. 1982); and, from philosophy, Richard Brandt, A Theory of the Good and the Right (1979).

[32] See Amartya Sen & Bernard Williams, Introduction, in Sen & Williams eds., *supra* note 31, at 3–4; they show that Utiliarianism actually requires combining consequentialism with two other ideas: a focus on utility (or pleasure) as the source of value, and "sum-ranking," meaning that in sorting out the rankings of alternatives, we simply add up individual utilities or pleasures. Cost-benefit analysis clearly does not entail Utilitarianism's account of the source of value; whether it entails sum-ranking may be disputed, but I think, once again, we should say that it does not, if sum-ranking is taken to entail that we have rendered all the alternatives commensurable in terms of a single homogeneous measure of value: see below.

[33] For a similar definition, see *id.* at 3–4; also Consequentialism, at xiii (Philip Pettit ed. 1993).

the special value to agents of their own personal involvement in an action.[34] If consequentialism is construed so elastically, cost-benefit analysis as I construe it may seem closely linked to consequentialism. But often looking to consequences is contrasted with looking to something else, for example the intrinsic value of an action, or of the agent's role, or the overwhelming importance of the protection of rights. In this way of thinking of consequentialism, cost-benefit analysis does not entail consequentialism. We can look at any features of the choice situation we judge significant, and assign our weightings accordingly.

As should already be clear, I find cost-benefit analysis useful in answering the obvious question. It is not the only way of answering it: Krishna has a different strategy, one that forbids any weighting of diverse considerations where duty is involved. Many moral rigorists have followed Krishna here, arguing that an appeal to the totality of the factors can often lead moral thinking in the wrong direction. But here I think we should side with Arjuna: one thing we certainly need to know, before we act, is how the costs and benefits balance out, looking at the totality of the factors. Cost-benefit analysis provides a handy model, or group of models, for representing our practical thinking on complex questions of choice, where we must choose among plural and diverse goods and where our choices have complex consequences as well as involve complex issues of intrinsic value.

Nor would I object to cost-benefit analysis, as some have done, on the ground that it necessarily presupposes the homogeneity of all values, their commensurability on a single scale of value. This would be the case if all choice involving a comparison between diverse values necessarily involved a commensuration of all of them in terms of a single scale. Joseph Raz, for example, takes the line that we have two options only: total noncomparability, or commensurability, understood as comparability along a single linear scale of value, in which all the diverse values are imagined as reduced to a common coin.[35] But it seems to me that Henry Richardson is right: we often make comparisons among diverse values, and choices among options in-

---

[34] This is true, for example, of the form of consequentialism that Amartya Sen has advocated for some time: see Amartya Sen, Rights and Agency, 11 Phil. & Pub Aff. 3 (1982); Amartya Sen, Well-Being, Agency and Freedom: Dewey Lectures 1984, J. Philosophy 82 (1985); Amartya Sen, Rights, Duties and Consequences, The Heffers Lecture (Dep't Philosophy, Cambridge Univ., November 27, 1998). I discuss Sen's consequentialism, and the general problem of giving a demarcation of consequentialism, in such a way that it still represents a distinctive type of moral theory, in Martha Nussbaum, Goodness, Consequences, and Tragedy (2000), a reply to Judith Jarvis Thomson's Tanner Lectures (in press 2001).

[35] This appears to be the consequence of the definition of incommensurability as noncomparability, in Joseph Raz, The Morality of Freedom (1986), ch. 13, published previously in Proceedings of the Aristotelian Society 1986.

volving different values, without commensurating in this reductive way.[36] Often such choices involve judgments about what is better or worse overall: and the bare fact that we are able to make these comparisons of overall good and bad does not, it seems to me, imply that we have all along been reducing them to a single metric of value.[37] One way in which we standardly represent this weighting is to attach numbers to the alternatives, or even dollar amounts, as in willingness-to-pay and willingness-to-accept approaches.

To assign a monetary value to an option does not, however, imply that we have reduced the good so valued to nothing but the common coin of cash. The fact, for example, that most of us assign a certain monetary value to our intellectual labor does not mean that we believe that intellectual labor is just money and has no special qualities of its own.[38] One might certainly wonder whether assigning a monetary value to a good or a service might not ultimately change the way we value it, making us less sensitive to its distinctive value-qualities.[39] Clearly, we ought to worry about this possibility, and it would be a bad thing if it materialized. But whether such a shift in our modes of valuing is an inevitable consequence of assigning a monetary value is an empirical question, requiring empirical inquiry for its answer. There appears to be no good evidence that such a deep shift in mode of evaluation always, or even typically, occurs when a monetary value is assigned.[40] Certainly if we reflect about the way in which intellectual labor has developed since scholars began to get salaries, we have no reason to believe that all salaried scholars must be hacks, valuing their labor only as a certain amount of cash. As I have argued elsewhere, such claims sound all too much like claims that used to be made by the wealthy leisured classes in order to impugn the character of working-class people, Jews, and other nonlandowning types: they are just crass money-grubbing individuals, who have no appreciation of the finer things in life.[41]

Now admittedly, cost-benefit analysis does not seem to do any very pro-

---

[36] Henry Richardson, Practical Reasoning about Final Ends, chs. 5 & 6 (1994).

[37] See Nussbaum, Fragility, *supra* note 1, ch. 10.

[38] See Martha Nussbaum, "Whether from Reason or Prejudice": Taking Money for Bodily Services, 27 J. Legal Stud. 693 (1998); and also in Nussbaum, Sex and Social Justice, *supra* note 23, at 276–98.

[39] As is claimed, for example, by Elizabeth Anderson, Value in Ethics and Economics (1993); and Elizabeth Anderson, Is Women's Labor a Commodity? 19 Phil. & Pub. Aff. 71 (1990); Margaret Jane Radin, Market-Inalienability, 100 Harv. L. Rev. 1849 (1987); and, with a more nuanced view, Margaret Jane Radin, Contested Commodities: The Trouble with the Trade in Sex, Children, Bodily Parts, and Other Things (1996).

[40] See Scott Altman, (Com)modifying Experience, 65 S. Cal. L. Rev. 293 (1991).

[41] See Nussbaum, "Whether from Reason or Prejudice," *supra* note 38.

found work on its own: all the work of evaluating has to be done before-hand.[42] If the weightings are right, the analysis will give us good guidance concerning what we ought to choose. If the weightings are assigned badly, it will give us bad guidance. But cost-benefit analysis will not itself tell us how to assign the weightings—unless we construe cost-benefit analysis in terms of willingness to pay—which, as I have argued, we should not do, if we want to defend it as supplying plausible answers to the obvious question. At most, then, it is a useful technique of analysis for people who have already managed to assign plausible weightings to the alternatives before them. Nonetheless, that is not nothing; and there is no reason to think that the use of such a technique will lead us to perdition, as some would suggest.[43]

On the other hand, I think that there is something that we should be worried about in the ubiquitous use of cost-benefit analysis in public policy. This is, that we will focus on the obvious question, to which cost-benefit analysis is very well suited, and neglect the tragic question, to which it is not well suited at all. Cost-benefit analysis asks us to figure out, among the options open to us, which contains the largest net measure of good. But it does not encourage us to divide the alternatives into two distinct classes, those that involve serious ethical wrongdoing and those that do not. To continue with the capabilities approach, it does not encourage us to ask which options involve denying some citizens a central entitlement, one that they have a right to demand, and which options do not. Cost-benefit analysis does not pose the tragic question; if anything, it suggests that there is no such question, the only pertinent question being what is better than what.

Nor could we even represent the insights of the tragic question within the parameters of cost-benefit analysis. Let us see this by imagining how we might try to do so. Our most obvious strategy would be to assign a very large cost to the options that involve denying citizens some capability that they have a right to have: a kind of "tragedy tax," if you will. Notice that even to get this far we already have to pose the tragic question from without, so to speak: the question posed by cost-benefit analysis is not that question. And we also have to have some independent strategy by which to answer it: some independent ethical theory, for example, such as the capabilities list together with the theory of human dignity that supports it. So we will not even get to the point of assigning the tragedy tax unless we

---

[42] See Richardson, *supra* note 36, for an excellent discussion of this point.

[43] On the other hand, I am sympathetic to the worries raised in Henry Richardson's paper for this conference (The Stupidity of the Cost-Benefit Standard, in this issue, at 971–1003): even when used in this way, cost-benefit analysis does not embody some key virtues of practical intelligence, such as the ability to reformulate ends in the process of deliberation.

are already engaging in a form of ethical reasoning that is quite distinct from cost-benefit analysis and which cost-benefit analysis is likely to deter or obscure.

But even if we get this far, relying on our independent theory, the tragedy tax will not solve our problem. The tragedy tax says, for example, that depriving children of education is very, very costly. We can set that cost as high as we want it; we can make it so high as to be prohibitive. But representing things this way does not tell us what we need to know: that depriving children of their education is not just very, very costly but exacts a cost of a distinctive kind, namely, a cost that no citizen should be asked to bear, a cost that is incompatible with what human dignity requires. In today's India, giving children an education is, by anyone's analysis, very, very costly. So to show what is at stake in the choice between giving children an education and not giving them an education, we need to take a stand about people's basic entitlements, saying that some are just fundamental in a particular way, namely, things that people have a right to demand.

We could always set the tragedy tax so high that it will exceed every other cost. That would get us round the particular problem I have just identified. Of course it would not help us at all if we have a truly tragic situation on our hands, that is, one where there are no morally acceptable alternatives: for then we would just have to assign infinite cost to them all, so that none could possibly exceed any other. But let us imagine proceeding this way in a case in which (like Arjuna's second case) only one of the alternatives is morally unacceptable. Again: the proposed way of proceeding tells us a part, not the whole, of what we want to know: it tells us that the option is very very very costly, but not that it is a cost of a distinctive kind. Finally, notice that we get even this far only by asking the tragic question ourselves, independently of cost-benefit analysis, and answering it in some independent way, perhaps by using a theory of central human capabilities. We are in effect rigging things so that the cost-benefit analysis turns out the same way (or a way as close as possible to the same way) that an independent ethical analysis turns out. And that means that we really are not getting anything out of the cost-benefit analysis. It is just a crude and only partly adequate representation of what we have already figured out on our own.

Interestingly, the tragedy tax fails for a second reason as well. For it is not always true that it is very, very costly to deprive citizens of something that they have a right to have. In terms of standard willingness-to-pay models,[44] most U.S. citizens would probably demand only a small amount of

---

[44] Since my case actually involves willingness to accept, we should note that this may not always coincide with willingness to pay: see Richard Thaler, Quasi-Rational Economics (1993).

money to forfeit their right to vote at the next local election. (Many Indian parents think this way about education of their children, particularly female children. In fact, in many regions where women are traditionally secluded, you would probably need to pay parents to allow their daughters to be educated, rather than the reverse.)[45] The point that is brought home by the tragic question is not how much or how little people would demand to forfeit such a good; some people will not demand very much to forfeit a basic right, in some contexts. The point the tragic question makes is that this is a good of a particular sort, namely, one that all citizens are entitled to as part of a package of fundamental entitlements. It is something one simply should not be asked to forgo or trade off.

Now one could try to respond to this last point by saying that, no matter what actual people say about what they are willing to pay, we are always entitled to tack on the tragedy tax whenever, in our judgment, a fundamental right is at issue. But then we seem to have diverged from at least one very common type of cost-benefit analysis, which relies on actual preferences. More important, we have simply brought ourselves back to the first problem: for tacking on the tragedy tax is just not a very good way of representing the fact that these are losses of a distinctive kind, namely, losses that no citizen should be asked to endure. Finally, once again, we get this far only by asking and answering the tragic question for ourselves, together with an independent theory of value. We are just trying to rig things so that our cost-benefit analysis conforms to the results of our independent ethical inquiry.[46]

---

[45] Thus Gary Becker's proposal to give parents education vouchers for their girl children in developing countries, while it might work for some countries and for some parents, surely would not work in, say, rural Rajasthan, where the rate of female literacy is around 5 percent: parents would throw such vouchers down the toilet if they had toilets. Becker is to be applauded for seeing the crucial importance of female education for development, but (perhaps because he focuses on Latin America, where such a strategy will encounter less profound resistance) he underestimates the depth of the problem. See Gary S. Becker, Why the Third World Should Stress the Three R's, in The Economics of Life 67–68 (Gary S. Becker & Guity Nashat Becker eds. 1997).

[46] In his Response to Nussbaum, read at the American Philosophical Association Eastern Division Meeting, December 28, 1999, Philip Quinn points out that one can find a way of formally representing this aspect of tragic dilemmas: for one may associate with each alternative for choice an ordered pair. The first member of the pair will be the aggregate figure arrived at by ordinary cost-benefit analysis; the second member will be 1 in case the alternative does not involve a basic entitlement violation, and 0 in case it does. The decision rule will then take the following form: ''(1) If some of the alternatives have an associated ordered pair whose second member is 1, choose one of them associated with an optimal first member, breaking optimality ties randomly; and (2) If none of the alternatives has an associated ordered pair whose second member is 1, choose an alternative associated with an optimal first member and second member 0, breaking optimality ties randomly.'' I have no deep quarrel with this proposal; but I think it is a lot of fuss in order to tell us what we already know in

Once again, we may note that cost-benefit analysis can actually help us when we are in doubt about where to set the threshold of citizens' basic entitlements. In environmental and regulatory areas, for example, seeing the cost of various levels of protection is helpful when we consider exactly what level of protection is a basic entitlement: for we do not want to specify basic entitlements in an absurdly utopian or unworldly way. More generally, all rights have costs, so thinking about where to set the threshold level of any right is sensibly done with these costs in mind.[47] Once again, however, we should not take this worldliness too far: some things are exceedingly costly at the present time because of past injustice, or corruption, or laziness: such is the case with compulsory primary education in India; such is in manifold ways the case with the skyrocketing costs of medical care in the United States. So keeping our eyes on the costs should not be permitted to deter us from asking why something that seems quite important is, or has become, terribly costly: who has put the costs up so high? (To take just one example, ACT-UP is to be commended for forcing such questions onto the public agenda, where the inflated costs of AIDS medications are in question.) Costs may have a natural element, but they usually also have an element of human greed. We should not treat the greed as a given; we should exercise imagination in a free Hegelian spirit, asking what steps might be taken to produce a world that is free of some life-crushing contradictions.

Should a reasonable public order aim at the minimization or even the total removal of tragedy? For three very different reasons, I would oppose that goal. The first reason is relatively uninteresting: it is simply that some possibilities of tragedy that remain within a society are not very probable. If the likelihood of a tragic choice arising is very low—if, say, a given political order would give rise to tragic choices only in a case of civil war, and the society is a stable one—then it is surely not worthwhile expending effort to remove that possibility of tragedy.

The second reason is connected to my criticism of Creon: a sure way to remove tragedy is to have only one, or very few, basic entitlements. If tragedy removal were our salient goal, a very inadequate and unjust order might begin to seem more attractive than it is.

The third reason is connected to my point about the residuum of tragedy at the heart of human life: some rich and complicated aspects of life just are likely to be in tension with some other rich and complicated aspects,

---

ordinary language (as Hilary Putnam commented at the session). It also omits the Hegelian advice to work on rearranging things so that the conflict does not take a tragic form in future.

[47] See Stephen Holmes & Cass R. Sunstein, The Cost of Rights: Why Liberty Depends on Taxes (1999). On calculating environmental and regulatory costs, see Sunstein's paper for this conference (Cognition and Cost-Benefit Analysis, in this issue, at 1059–1103).

and even the wisest Hegelian will not be able to remove the possibility of tragedy—except by a radical simplification of the sphere of value that would be Creonic in its ruthlessness. Thus we could always remove tensions between religion and sex equality by doing everything in our power to get rid of religion. We could always remove tragic tensions between children's rights over their lives and parent's rights to control over their children—if we said, as for so long we have said, that children are simply their parents' property and have no rights. The appeal of the children-property idea surely derives in part from the fact that it does indeed make deciding hard cases very much easier. But that, like the discouragement of religion, is a Creonic course; it simply does not recognize what ought to be recognized. In that sense we have made progress by recognizing many cases in this sphere as involving tragedy, when we did not do so before—even if no Hegelian thinking will altogether remove the tension.

IV. TRAGIC *AUFHEBUNG* IN THE PUBLIC DOMAIN

When we see clearly that the tragic question is distinct from the obvious question, and that cost-benefit analysis does not answer it, or even enable us to represent well the asking of it, we see something further: that we badly need an independent ethical theory of basic entitlements to guide us in analyzing public policy choices. Whether we go for the capabilities approach or the (closely allied) human rights approach,[48] or whether we just consider our own Constitution and similar documents that describe the fundamental entitlements of citizens, we need to figure out, at least in a tentative and revisable way, what entitlements shall be treated as central and matters of tragedy should they be denied. Once we have gotten clear about this issue—or at least taken a stand for practical purposes on some plausible account of it—we will be able to analyze situations of conflict with Hegelian Aufhebung in our minds. That is, in addition to reckoning the costs and benefits, we will notice, like Arjuna and Bob Nozick, and unlike Creon, Antigone, and some Harvard philosophers, that some costs have a distinctive nature; they are bad in a distinctive way. No citizen should have to bear them. But then we will be spurred to use our imaginations, thinking how we might construct a world in which such conflicts do not confront citizens, or confront them as rarely as possible. With Hegel, I think this change in our consciousness would itself be progress.

---

[48] For the relationship between the two, see Nussbaum, *supra* note 15, ch. 1; and Nussbaum, Capabilities and Human Rights, *supra* note 23.

ON JUSTIFYING COST-BENEFIT ANALYSIS

ABSTRACT

This essay considers two problems in the justification of cost-benefit analysis. First, it argues that because cost-benefit analysis values policies, variation in imputed "values of life" are not, in theory, cause for concern. Second, it argues that the current framework of justification, which focuses on the moral justification of the formal theory of cost-benefit analysis, is inadequate because it ignores (1) the institutional context in which cost-benefit analyses occur, (2) the comparative nature of the justification, and (3) the fact that justification might be indirect rather than direct.

I. INTRODUCTION

COST-BENEFIT analysis occupies an unusual place in intellectual and practical life. On the one hand, cost-benefit analysis influences, if not controls, many public decisions of great import. Regulation of the environment and of health and safety in the United States often requires that the relevant agency conduct a cost-benefit analysis. On the other hand, although many scholarly commentaries acknowledge its relevance for at least some public decisions,[1] its justificatory foundations remain at best suspect and at worst in ruins. Despite these critiques, cost-benefit analysis remains an active area of research among both theoretical and applied economists.

The disjunction between public policy and theoretical justification, however, runs even deeper. Cost-benefit analysis is not the only criterion used or suggested in policy analysis. Maximization of the numbers of lives saved or the maximization of quality-adjusted life-years (QALYs), for example, have been suggested or used in some public policy areas. These criteria are less ambitious than cost-benefit analysis in that they permit one to deter-

* Engelberg Professor of Law, New York University. Research for this essay was supported by the Filomen d'Agostino and Max E. Greenberg Research Fund of the New York University School of Law. Matthew Adler, Mark Geistfeld, Liam Murphy, Eric Posner, and Richard Revesz commented on an earlier draft.

[1] See, for example, Matthew D. Adler & Eric A. Posner, Rethinking Cost-Benefit Analysis, 99 Yale L. J. 165 (1999); as well as Richard H. Pildes & Cass R. Sunstein, Reinventing the Regulatory State, 62 U. Chi. L. Rev. 1 (1995). Even Elizabeth Anderson, Value in Ethics and Economics (1993), at least nominally acknowledges its relevance.

[*Journal of Legal Studies,* vol. XXIX]

mine only how to allocate a fixed budget across policies, while cost-benefit analysis in principle can also determine how many resources to allocate to risk-reducing or environment-enhancing activities. Yet the justificatory foundations for these criteria do not seem notably sounder than those of cost-benefit analysis.[2] As in the case of cost-benefit analysis, however, these criteria often seem to improve the quality of decisions.

In this essay, I raise two concerns about the adequacy of attacks on the foundations of cost-benefit analysis. The first concern accepts the current framework within which debates over the foundations of cost-benefit analysis occur. I criticize two common (and related) critiques of cost-benefit analysis that I believe are misguided. These critiques, which I shall call the commodification critiques, charge that (*a*) cost-benefit analysis inappropriately commodifies relations or goods that ought not to be commodified[3] and (*b*) cost-benefit analysis, at least in practice, yields grossly inconsistent valuations of life.[4] I aim not to rehabilitate cost-benefit analysis so much as to eliminate two arguments I consider inadequate from other, more valid concerns that have been raised.

Second, and more tentatively, I raise questions concerning the framework of the debate over the foundations of cost-benefit analysis. The current framework largely focuses on the moral justifiability of what I call the formal theory of cost-benefit analysis. This assessment of the morality of cost-benefit analysis implicitly ignores the real context in which cost-benefit analysis takes place.

To begin, however, I must briefly describe cost-benefit analysis as both my critique of the commodification attacks on cost-benefit analysis and my

---

[2] The shakiness of the ethical foundations of a maximize (discounted) QALYs criterion would undoubtedly not surprise many critics of cost-benefit analysis because these foundations are grounded in a similar ethical concern for well-being and a similar economic methodology derived from expected utility theory. On the foundations of QALYs, see, for example, John Broome, QALY's, 50 J. Pub. Econ. 149 (1993), reprinted in John Broome, Ethics out of Economics (1999); and Graham Loomes & Lynda McKenzie, The Scope and Limitations of QALY Measures, in Quality of Life: Perspectives and Policy 84 (Sally Baldwin, Christine Godfrey, & Carol Propper eds. 1989). The criterion of maximization of lives saved has even shakier foundations. A welfarist approach would likely consider lives saved as a poor proxy for well-being. At least some deontological approaches contend that, at least in ethics, numbers should not count in the determination of one's obligation to save lives. Frances Kamm has sketched a procedure for allocating fixed resources and for determining the amount of resources to be allocated that she derives from her deontological account of morality (Frances Kamm, Deciding Whom to Help: Resource Prioritization, Population Health Measures and Disability (Working Paper No. 99.09, Harvard Sch. Pub. Health, Harvard Ctr Population Dev. Stud., July 1999)). Her suggestions, however, fall short of a fully defined decision procedure that can be compared to cost-benefit analysis.

[3] See Anderson, *supra* note 1.

[4] See, for example, John D. Graham & James W. Vaupel, The Value of a Life: What Difference Would It Make? 1 Risk Analysis 89–95 (1981).

discussion of the appropriate framework of justification rely on its machinery.

II. COST-BENEFIT ANALYSIS

As noted before, cost-benefit analysis is both a theory and a practice or, perhaps, a practice that is an applied theory. One may usefully decompose the practice of cost-benefit analysis into three parts: (i) a formal theory that derives relations between an individual's fundamental preferences and a ranking, in terms of money, of policies, (ii) a theory of measurement (or implementation theory) that identifies real-world correlates of the theoretical entities manipulated in the formal theory, and (iii) applications of the formal theory and theory of measurement to specific policy decisions.

The debate over the foundations of cost-benefit analysis largely concerns the moral justifiability of the formal theory, although some criticism, largely internal to the practice of cost-benefit analysis, criticizes the theory of measurement or attacks particular applications of cost-benefit analysis. Thus, a clear understanding of the formal theory is necessary to understand criticisms of cost-benefit analysis.

I focus on two elements of formal theory: its treatment of risk and its treatment of irreplaceable goods. I do so because the commodification critiques of cost-benefit analysis focus on the application of cost-benefit analysis to the analysis of risks to health, life, and the environment. Formal theory currently models these as irreplaceable commodities.

The term "cost-benefit analysis" often refers to a family of procedures for policy assessment. Broadly, one identifies some objective function for the policy maker and chooses the policy that does best on that criterion. More usually, however, cost-benefit analysis refers to a narrower class of procedures that evaluate policies in terms of the net benefits the policies provide to individuals. Benefits are then usually defined solely in terms of the change in individual well-being that the policy induces, and costs are generally measured in terms of the monetary costs of resources required to implement the project. Again, typically, individual well-being is understood as the satisfaction of subjective preferences; in practice these subjective values are inferred from market choices of individuals or are elicited through survey techniques. Comparison of costs and benefits thus requires that the cost-benefit analyst measure subjective benefits in monetary terms.

The foundations of the formal theory of cost-benefit analysis thus assume that each individual has well-defined preferences over policy outcomes. These preferences must satisfy a number of conditions, conditions sufficient to insure that one can assess not only policies with certain outcomes but also policies with risky and uncertain ones as well as ones that may implicate what I shall call irreplaceable commodities. In each of these four circumstances—certainty, risk with fungible commodities, uncertainty with fungible commodities, and risk (or uncertainty) with irreplaceable commodities—cost-benefit analysis allows an individual to represent her preferences over policies in monetary terms. I consider these four cases in turn.

1. *Certainty.* For certain outcomes, the procedure is straightforward and uncontroversial. Consider some representation of the agent's preferences, which are defined over all commodities, by a utility function, U.[5] Designate some commodity as the numeraire and label it as money. Consider the individual's assessment of her condition prior to the consideration of the new policy. It is $U(w, x)$, where w is her wealth and x is the vector of other commodities she possesses. A policy P' will change the bundle of commodities available to her from (w, x) to (w', x'). One may assign a dollar value to this policy by identifying the amount of money $m(P'; w, x)$ such that $U(w - m, x) = U(w', x')$. For a broad class of preferences, the numbers $m(P'; w, x)$ will be unique and thus represent the agent's preferences over policies because she prefers a policy P' to a policy P'' if and only if $m(P'; w, x) > m(P''; w, x)$.[6]

Complications arise when the analyst seeks to construct a measure of social value from the indices of individual well-being that each willingness to pay represents. For an aggregation of individual willingness to pay to be meaningful, the analyst must make two additional assumptions about each individual's $m(P'; w, x)$. First, the analyst must assume that $m(P'; w, x)$ carries more information than simply the agent's order of preference over policies. It must also provide information on how intensely an individual prefers policy P' to policy P''. Second, the analyst must assume that, for each two individuals j and k, the corresponding willingness-to-pay representations of their preferences—$m_j(P'; w, x)$ and $m_k(P'; w, x)$—are scaled equivalently so that they can be meaningfully added together. Under these

---

[5] A preference is simply a complete and transitive ordering over the commodity space. In addition, preferences must be continuous to be representable by a utility function.

[6] Notice that the status quo is simply a policy P that leaves (w, x) unchanged, and hence $m(P; w, x) = 0$. Uniqueness of $m(P'; w, x)$ requires (as a necessary but not sufficient condition) that the individual's preferences be monotonically increasing in w; that is, the agent must always prefer more wealth to less wealth. This requirement would be satisfied if wealth were intrinsically valuable or if the agent could always find some commodity in the bundle x that may be traded for money and of which she would prefer to have more. (The condition is not sufficient because it does not guarantee that there is an amount of additional wealth that could compensate for the loss of some particular good. This question is addressed further below.)

Notice that, in fact, there is another monetary amount $m'(P; w', x')$ that one might construct. It requires that $U(w, x) = U(w' - m', x')$.

conditions, the sum of the $m_j(P'; w, x)$ provide a ''utilitarian'' index of the value of different projects.[7]

2. *Fungible Commodities under Risk.*   I adopt the usual economic distinction between risk and uncertainty. Risk arises in a situation in which different outcomes are possible with known, fixed probabilities, while under uncertainty, probabilities are unknown.

The procedure for assigning a monetary value to a policy is easily seen in the context of an example. It will be helpful to have an example in mind. I use one adapted from other discussions of risk.[8] An agricultural region is threatened by drought. There are then two possible states of the world, wet (W) and dry (D). Wet years have probability q and dry years have probability $(1 - q)$. Each farmer cares only about his own income. The community proposes to build a dam that would provide few benefits in wet years but great benefits in dry years. In effect the proposed project reduces the variation in the farmer's returns. Specifically, suppose that in the absence of the dam, the farmer's income will be x_W in wet years and x_D in dry years, while with the dam, the farmer will earn y_W and y_D in wet and dry years, respectively. I assume that the dam is beneficial in both states—that is, $y_k - x_k > 0$ for $k = $ W, D—and that it reduces the risk of drought—that is, $y_W - y_D < x_W - x_D$.

Each farmer has preferences over policies: in this case building a dam or not. Because outcomes are uncertain in each policy, the farmer's preferences must exhibit more structure; assume that they satisfy the axioms of von Neumann–Morgenstern utility theory. Under risk, the willingness to pay is not uniquely defined. I consider two procedures for determining it. One might calculate each farmer's expected surplus from the dam or one might calculate her option price for the dam.

One can calculate the farmer's expected surplus from the dam on the assumption that his preferences can be represented by a utility function u that depends on his wealth in each state and on whether the dam is built or not. In wet years, the farmer's surplus S_W is $y_W - x_W$, while in dry years it is $S_D = y_D - x_D$. His expected surplus $E(S)$ is thus $qS_W + (1 - q)S_D = q(y_W - x_W) + (1 - q)(y_D - x_D)$. Note that the farmer's surplus in state k

---

[7] A further assumption is necessary to insure that total utility is independent of the prices that one uses to measure willingness to pay. If, for instance, $m_j(P'; w, x)$ is independent of w for every j, then this condition will be satisfied. Of course, when this independence condition is not met, it would be difficult to argue that the representations of j and k at the levels of wealth they happen to have are the appropriate choices for making interpersonal comparisons of well-being.

[8] Daniel A. Graham, Cost-Benefit Analysis under Uncertainty, 71 Am. Econ. Rev. 715 (1981); and Anthony E. Boardman *et al.*, Cost Benefit Analysis 215–18 (1996).

is simply what he would be willing to pay to have the dam rather than not; he would be willing to pay up to the amount of the additional income earned in the presence of the dam in that state.

Of course, the policy maker must decide whether to undertake the project knowing only the probabilities that the year will be dry rather than wet. The policy maker could thus ask the farmer for his ex ante willingness to pay. This ex ante willingness to pay might be described in various ways. One might ask the farmer before the project to state how much he would be willing to pay after the project in each state of the world. That is, one might describe his willingness to pay in terms of two ex post contingent payments, one in the event of a wet season and one in the event of a dry season.[9] The farmer is indifferent among all these schemes; in one of them, his payment is identical regardless of the weather. Call this identical payment the option price (OP).[10,11]

When the agent is risk averse, $OP > E(S)$.[12] Intuitively, the expected surplus simply measures the value of having the dam in each state, but the project has a second effect on the farmer's welfare because it reduces the variance in his returns. The expected surplus fails to measure this second benefit.[13]

Of course, in the presence of a perfect market for drought insurance, the farmer can eliminate completely the variance in his returns regardless of whether the dam is built. Then the expected surplus is the individual farmer's appropriate valuation of the dam because she can purchase insurance to eliminate any variation in returns across states. Moreover, if we allow the farmer to purchase insurance on the perfect market, her option price should equal the expected surplus. Often, however, insurance markets are imperfect either because of the presence of moral hazard or adverse selection in those markets or because of the difficulty of drafting appropriate

---

[9] Let m_W and m_D be the farmer's payments in the wet and dry events, respectively. The locus of willingness-to-pay pairs (m_W, m_D) is given by $qu(y_W - m_W) + (1 - q)u(y_D - m_D) = Eu(\text{no dam}) = qu(x_W) + (1 - q) u(x_D)$.

[10] Option price is fully ex ante in the sense that the farmer could make the payment OP prior to the construction of the dam.

[11] For a discussion of option price in cost-benefit analysis, see Graham, *supra* note 8; Daniel A. Graham, Public Expenditure under Uncertainty: The Net-Benefit Criteria, 82 Am. Econ. Rev. 822 (1992).

[12] See, for example, Boardman *et al.*, *supra* note 8.

[13] Notice that the expected surplus thus is not a representation of the agent's preferences over policies because two policies might yield identical expected surplus but differ in their risk characteristics. In the example the benefits to the project accrue to individuals; in some projects all benefits and costs might first flow to the government. In this latter instance, one might argue that individual attitudes toward risk should be ignored because the government, given its size, should act as a risk-neutral decision maker.

contingent claims contracts. In these circumstances, the expected surplus may not accurately represent the individual farmer's expected well-being.[14]

To evaluate the policy, the analyst must again aggregate the individual willingnesses to pay. Once more, the analyst must make further assumptions about the interpersonal comparability of the indices of well-being she has constructed.

3. *Uncertainty.* Consider now the case of uncertainty. In the example, uncertainty exists if the probability of a drought is unknown. Consequently, different farmers or a farmer and the policy maker may assess the risk of a drought differently. There are now four different ways to assess the value of the dam. As before, one might calculate the farmer's valuation of the dam either ex ante or ex post. But now one might use either the farmer's own assessment of the probability of drought to calculate the option price or expected surplus, or one might use the policy maker's assessment of the probability of a drought.

The prior subsection considered the role of insurance markets in this choice. I assume here that no insurance market exists and consider the two variants of option price only. The procedures thus differ over whose beliefs about the likelihood that different outcomes will be realized should be used. On some accounts, the analyst should use both the individual's actual valuations of certain outcomes (that is, her own preferences) and her actual beliefs about the likelihood of different outcomes or events. This procedure has been called variously ex ante,[15] actor assessed,[16] and unstructured.[17] An alternative procedure—called variously ex post, policy-maker assessed, or structured—would use the individual's actual preferences over outcomes but use the policy maker's assessment of the probabilities that each outcome will arise.

The agent-assessed option price and the policy-maker-assessed option price each assign a value to the effect of the policy on the risk to which the

---

[14] If expected surplus does not, in the absence of insurance markets, represent the agent's preferences over policies, why would the policy maker use it as an index? One might argue that the appropriate measure of the value of the project is not the farmer's expected well-being but the average of the actual well-being she would experience in each state. Phrased differently, the option price does represent the agent's preferences over risky policies; these preferences might be understood as based on expected well-being. The moral significance of expected well-being may be doubtful.

[15] Peter J. Hammond, Utilitarianism, Uncertainty and Information, in Utilitarianism and Beyond 5–102 (Amartya K. Sen & Bernard Williams eds. 1982).

[16] Lewis A. Kornhauser, Constrained Maximization: Corporate Law and the Maximization of Social Welfare, The Jurisprudence of Corporate and Commercial Law (Jody Kraus & Steven Walt eds., in press).

[17] John Broome, Structured and Unstructured Valuation, in Broome, Ethics out of Economics 183, *supra* note 2.

farmer is exposed. Unless the farmer and the policy maker have identical beliefs about the likelihood of drought, however, these valuations will differ. Of course, the actor-assessed option price captures the farmer's actual response to risk, while the policy-maker-assessed option price values the risk as the policy maker believes the farmer ought to assess the risk.

4. *Irreplaceable Commodities.*   Many regulatory policies have irreversible effects. Irreversible effects are common when considering environmental policies such as those concerning greenhouse gases and policies that will result in statistically certain deaths. Many of these irreversible harms also are irreplaceable in the sense that the agent cannot be restored to her preloss situation. Again, death and other physical injuries—such as blindness and quadriplegia—that result in permanent changes in the individual's functioning are often examples of this type.

A commodity might be more or less irreplaceable. In the weakest sense, irreplaceability means only that, for any given level of wealth, the individual would rather have the commodity than not. The loss of the commodity, however, might have two other effects on the agent's well-being. First, after the loss, a change in the agent's wealth may not have the same effect on the agent's well-being as it would have had in the absence of the loss.[18] For a given level of wealth, the agent might think the marginal utility of wealth in the postloss state either greater or less than its marginal utility in the preloss state. Second, one may not be able to restore the individual to her preloss level of well-being. Death clearly has this consequence; there is no amount of money one can transfer to the agent after death that will restore her to her preloss level of well-being.

Economic models of irreplaceable harms capture these senses of irreplaceability because they assume that the agent's assessment of her situation depends critically on whether she possesses the irreplaceable good. Describe any policy outcome by a triple, (s, w, x), where w is money as before, x represents other commodities, and when $s = 1$, the agent possesses the irreplaceable commodity, and when $s = 0$ she does not. Suppose that her preferences are representable by a utility function u.[19] Then a minimal requirement for the commodity to be irreplaceable is $u(1, w, x) > u(0, w, x)$

---

[18] In fact, one might evaluate the effect of a change in wealth in two different ways, yielding two different conceptions of irreplaceability. First, one might ask whether the agent's marginal utility for wealth is the same before and after the loss, measured at her preloss wealth. The agent's postloss marginal utility might be either greater or less than her preloss marginal utility for wealth, depending on the nature of the injury. Second, one might ask whether the agent's marginal utility for wealth before the loss (and measured at her preloss wealth) differs from her marginal utility for wealth after the loss, measured at that wealth (if it exists) that restores her to her preloss level of well-being.

[19] See Edi Karni, Decision Making under Uncertainty (1985), for a discussion.

for all w and x. (Call this the irreplaceability condition.) This representation captures the idea of an irreplaceable good: the agent always prefers to have the good than not to have it. Note that the irreplaceability condition does not imply that there is some $w' > w$ such that $u(1, w, x) = u(0, w', x)$; no amount of money might compensate the agent for the loss of the irreplaceable commodity.[20]

Much regulation concerns the reduction of risks that the agent will lose the irreplaceable good. Any regulation that affects the risk of death, for example, has this effect. An individual generally prefers a state of the world in which she is alive to a state of the world in which she is dead. Similarly, risks to health may have the same characteristic. Generally, one prefers being in good health to being in bad health regardless of one's material circumstances. Finally, one might model some attitudes toward the environment in this way; regardless of my wealth, I may prefer a world in which wilderness areas exist or biodiversity is preserved to a world without them.

The prior discussion of willingness to pay and the option price translates directly to the valuation of policies that affect risks to irreplaceable commodities. Suppose, for example, that an individual faces baseline risk p of loss of the irreplaceable commodity. One may value a policy that reduces the risk of loss by r with the option price as before: one finds the amount of money m such that $(1 - p)U(1, w, x) + pU(0, w, x) = (1 - p + r) U(1, w - m, x) + (p - r)U(0, w - m, x)$. In this instance, however, the willingness to pay $m(p, r, w, x)$ depends not only on wealth but also on the baseline risk p and the reduction in risk r induced by the policy. As I shall argue more fully in Section III below, this dependence of an agent's willingness to pay on features of the policy renders meaningless any inference of the value of a life from the valuations of policies.

III. A (PARTIAL) REPLY TO THE COMMODIFICATION CRITIQUE OF COST-BENEFIT ANALYSIS

Two common critiques of cost-benefit analysis concern its treatment of risks to health and safety, particularly to risks of death. The more fundamental of these critiques attacks formal theory directly, charging that cost-benefit analysis inappropriately treats risks to health and safety and to the environment as commodities. The second critique, that cost-benefit analysis yields wildly inconsistent values of life, is apparently directed at either the measurement theory or the practice of cost-benefit analysis. I argue below

---

[20] Similarly, it might be case that no x' is available such that $u(1, w, x) = u(0, w, x')$. When no w' or x' exists, the agent will be unwilling to sell her right to the irreplaceable commodity for any amount of money. Of course, she might still be willing to pay some amount to purchase the irreplaceable commodity.

that neither critique is valid because cost-benefit analysis values policies or very specific risks, not life itself; the theory itself is thus consistent with wildly varying estimates of the value of life.

A. The Critiques

In the course of an extensive argument that contends that the value theory in economics is misconceived, Elizabeth Anderson attacks cost-benefit analysis.[21] Her attack is wide-ranging and includes a general attack on welfarism as well as narrower critiques of potential compensation tests. Here I restrict attention to a critique fundamental to her nonconsequentialist approach to value: she claims that it inappropriately commodifies the risks to health and safety and to the environment that it seeks to regulate and to control.

On Anderson's account, cost-benefit analysis commodifies environmental, health, and safety risks in at least three ways. First, because it ranks alternatives in terms of money, cost-benefit analysis treats all goods as fungible with other goods.

Second, cost-benefit analysis uses a market measure of the value of (risks to) health and safety or the environment. Here Anderson might have three distinct criticisms in mind. The least interesting one concerns the theory of measurement that infers the individual's willingness to pay to avoid these risks from her actual market choices; Anderson might simply be arguing that this inference does not represent the true contribution to the agent's well-being of a reduction in these risks to agents. The second and third criticisms run against the formal theory of cost-benefit analysis. The second argues that a market measure of value implicitly uses an inappropriate standard for the interpersonal comparisons of well-being. As noted earlier, each individual's willingness to pay represents the individual's ordinal preference ordering accurately. Summation of these, however, assumes that each willingness-to-pay representation is not only ordinal but cardinal, and it assumes that individual A's willingness-to-pay representation is appropriately calibrated in terms of overall well-being with individual B's, regardless of the relative wealth of A and B. This assumption seems dubious. Anderson, however, probably has in mind a third criticism, which suggests that willingness to pay is meaningful only in the context of private (as opposed to public) goods; one cannot in principle represent the value of (risks to) health and safety or the environment in monetary terms.

---

[21] Anderson, *supra* note 1. Anderson in fact attacks consequentialist theories of value generally, not just welfare economics. For comments on another aspect of her critique of economic value theory, see Lewis A. Kornhauser, No Best Answer? 146 U. Pa. L. Rev. 1599 (1998).

Finally, Anderson argues that cost-benefit analysis commodifies risk because it assumes that the preferences that govern market choices should also determine public choices. Anderson notes that the reasons one has for public choices may differ from those one has for private choices.

The second, related critique of cost-benefit analysis arises from the widely variant valuations of life that have been attributed to various government policies. These range from roughly \$100,000 to \$5.7 billion.[22] Advocates of cost-benefit analysis argue that it would eliminate the radical inconsistencies observed in regulatory policies. To the extent that such variation arises from cost-benefit analysis itself, advocates would attribute the variation as a flaw in the theory of measurement or in the specific applications of cost-benefit analysis. Critics, by contrast, regard any variation in the valuations of life made by cost-benefit analysis as evidence that in principle one cannot price life. Neither position is tenable.

Here, I need only to sketch the method used to calculate these (implicit) valuations of life: one determines the amount of money x required to reduce the risk of death to one individual by the amount p. Then, according to this calculation, the governmental value of life implicit in the government policy is given by x/p. This calculation is justified by attributing to the government a von Neumann–Morgenstern utility function over ''life'' and money; if one assumes that the budget devoted to the reduction in risk is small, the formula follows directly.[23] This calculation may be challenged on a number of grounds;[24] below, however, I argue that it is inappropriate on the narrow terms of the formal theory of cost-benefit analysis itself because the individual's valuation of a change in the risk of loss of an irreplaceable good is not linear in the baseline risk or the size of the change.

B. Valuing Policies

A partial response to the commodification critique of cost-benefit analysis follows directly from the earlier exposition of the formal theory of op-

---

[22] The low number corresponds to a ban on unvented space heaters and the high number corresponds to the listing of wood-preserving chemicals as hazardous waste. Both numbers are drawn from a table that appears in Stephen G. Breyer, Breaking the Vicious Circle: Toward Effective Risk Regulation 24–27 (1993), and reprinted in Pildes & Sunstein, *supra* note 1, at 53--55. These disparate valuations do not result from cost-benefit analyses. Rather they are the imputed values of life that arise from actual or proposed federal regulations; the bases of the regulations or proposed regulations do not rest on cost-benefit analysis.

[23] It is derived using a first-order Taylor series expansion. For a discussion, see John Broome, The Economic Value of Life, 52 Economica 281 (1985).

[24] Broome, for example, argues that one cannot infer the value of life from valuations of risks of death. John Broome, Trying to Value a Life, 9 J. Pub. Econ. 91 (1978).

tion prices for policies that affect risks to irreplaceable commodities.[25] The basic argument simply observes that the commodification critique rests on a mistaken interpretation of the formal theory: cost-benefit analysis does not price life, the environment, or any other irreplaceable commodity. Rather, cost-benefit analysis places a value on specific policies offered in specific contexts. Given this contextual valuation of policies, there is no reason to expect consistency in the value of life nor to conclude that lives are treated as ordinary commodities.

In this context, cost-benefit analysis evaluates policies from a given status quo position defined by an agent's wealth and the baseline risk of loss of the irreplaceable commodity; it asks how much each individual is willing to accept to bear some increase in the risk of loss of the irreplaceable commodity by some given amount. If the individual receives that amount, she would be indifferent between the current situation in which she faces the baseline risk and the riskier situation with a higher wealth. The payment in some sense compensates her ex ante for the increased risk.[26] This willingness-to-accept valuation of the increased risk cannot be inferred from her behavior in the insurance market. An individual does not determine her insurance purchases by reference to her absolute level of well-being (or expected well-being); the insurance will not compensate her for the loss of the irreplaceable good in the sense that it will restore her to her preloss level of well-being. Rather, she selects a level of insurance so that her marginal utility for money in the state with the irreplaceable good equals her marginal utility for money in the state without it.

Suppose, for example, that an individual, Henry, faces some risk of going blind. The amount of blindness insurance that Henry purchases will depend on the relative marginal utility of money in the two states sighted and blind. It may be, at least for some range of initial wealth, that the marginal utility of money is higher in the blind state than the sighted state because Henry can use money in the blind state to purchase substitutes for sight. Henry has preferences over his total wealth conditional on the state of his vision.

On the other hand, it is possible that Henry would prefer to have more wealth in the sighted state than in the blind state.[27] Certainly, it is plausible

[25] A more complete response would address the general arguments of incommensurability that underlie many commodification critiques. I have argued elsewhere that arguments for incommensurability in ethics do not translate directly to the context of collective decision making. See Kornhauser, *supra* note 21. For an argument that incommensurability does not undermine cost-benefit analysis, see Matthew Adler, Incommensurability and Cost-Benefit Analysis, 146 U. Pa. L. Rev. 1371 (1998).

[26] That is, her expected well-being in the state with the baseline risk and her initial wealth equals her expected well-being in the state with the higher risk and the higher wealth.

[27] Many people may have this attitude toward death; they would rather have money while alive than while dead.

to believe that, for some people, and some irreplaceable commodities, the marginal utility of money is higher in the state in which the individual has the irreplaceable commodity than in the one in which he does not. If for instance, Henry, who is a bachelor and lives only for himself, faces some risk of death, money may have no value whatsoever in the event of death, and he would not buy any insurance against it.

One should not, of course, conclude from Henry's failure to purchase insurance that he valued his life at zero. More generally, regardless of whether Henry chooses to insure against the loss of an irreplaceable commodity or not, one should not equate the level of insurance purchased with Henry's valuation of the irreplaceable commodity. Rather, Henry values the irreplaceable commodity in the sense that he is willing to pay to reduce the risk that he will lose that commodity. This fact suggests that the value of the irreplaceable commodity to Henry is proportional to the amount he is willing to spend to reduce the risk of loss. Unfortunately, the amount Henry is willing to spend will depend on his level of wealth prior to loss, the baseline risk, and the amount of reduction he is asked to purchase.

One might try to circumvent the dependence of Henry's valuation of the irreplaceable commodity on the baseline risk and the degree to which the risk is reduced by comparing his well-being when he has the irreplaceable commodity for sure to when he certainly does not have the irreplaceable commodity. So, if Henry's preferences are represented by a utility function $u(s, w)$ with $u(\text{sighted}, w) > u(\text{blind}, w)$ for every w, then the value V of the irreplaceable commodity IC is given by $u(\text{no IC}, w + V) = u(\text{IC}, w)$. This procedure presents two, related problems. First, this valuation bears no relation to Henry's valuation of reductions in risk from baselines other than a certain risk of loss or for reductions from certain loss to less than certain possession. This valuation, then, does not help an agency to determine policy. Second, and related, for some functions or pair of functions $[u(\text{no IC}, -), u(\text{IC}, -)]$, no such V may exist. Yet, Henry would spend less than his full wealth to reduce the risk of loss by some small amount. This argument is plausible when the irreplaceable commodity is death and one might assume that $u(\text{no IC}, w)$ is less than the lower bound for $u(\text{IC}, w)$.[28]

Moreover, a given reduction of risk will depend on the baseline p from which the reduction occurs.[29] Suppose that the agent values money more in

[28] But the utility functions need not be so extreme as that. Suppose $u(\text{no IC}, w) = 1 - e - cw$ and that $u(\text{IC}, w) = b - e - cw$. Then if $b > 2$, there is no V that compensates the agent for the loss of IC.

[29] This discussion draws on John W. Pratt & Richard J. Zeckhauser, Willingness to Pay and the Distribution of Risk and Wealth, 104 J. Pol. Econ. 747 (1996); and Lewis A. Kornhauser, The Value of Life, 38 Clev. St. L. Rev. 209 (1990).

the state in which he has the irreplaceable commodity than when he does not. For very high probabilities of loss, wealth will be of little use to him. So he might as well spend it to reduce the loss by a given amount. This difference implies that the nature of the risk matters greatly.

Health policy presents a convenient context in which to consider these issues. Suppose that some population faces the threat of infection by a deadly disease: if an individual is infected, the probability p_1 of death is .8. On the other hand, the probability p of infection is reasonably low, say, .000125. The ex ante probability p_0 of death is thus .0001.

Assume everyone has identical preferences and identical wealth of $40,000 with the marginal and absolute utility of wealth higher when alive than dead for every possible (nonnegative amount of) wealth w. To be precise, let $u(\text{death}, w) = \ln(w + 1)$ and $u(\text{life}, w) = 5 + 5 \ln(w + 1)$. Consider two policies where each reduces the ex ante probability p_0 by 10 percent (that is, by .00001). Policy A accomplishes the reduction through a vaccine that is 10 percent effective; it reduces the probability of catching the disease from .000125 to .0001125. Policy B invests in a new treatment that will reduce the risk of death, conditional on infection, by 10 percent, that is, from .8 to .72. Ex ante, that is, prior to the possibility of exposure to the disease, these two policies have identical consequences. An individual is willing to pay $3.79 for the .00001 reduction in risk that each of these policies provides ex ante. Using the conventional method to calculate the value of the individual's life, we get a value of $379,000. Of course, if she were poorer, say, had a wealth of only $10,000, then her willingness to pay for this vaccine would fall to roughly $0.84 and the value of her life correspondingly falls to $83,694.

Suppose however, that the individual has been infected. Then she would be willing to pay $33,310 for the new treatment. This willingness to pay yields a value of life of $416,378. Of course, if the risk of death, conditional on infection, were even higher—say, .95—and the treatment were only marginally effective—say, reducing the probability of death .001—then the agent would still pay $1,543.77 for the treatment. This willingness to pay yields a value to life of $1,543,770.

Of course, one might say that these valuations are biased toward low estimates because the individual has a reasonably high marginal utility of money when dead. Moreover, if we treat her utility function as providing cardinal information, she is only roughly 5.5 times better off alive than dead. So suppose we say that she has constant well-being of 0 when dead. Then her willingness to pay for the initial vaccine rises to $4,639 and the value of life rises to $463,900. More impressively, if she is ill and faces a risk of death of .95, she will be willing to pay $8,135.66 to reduce that risk by .001; her valuation of this treatment yields a value to life of

$8,135,660.[30] This simple example thus yields a variation of roughly 100 in the imputed values of life.

A second example will suggest another way in which the valuation of policies is context specific and not a valuation of some disembodied risk. Consider a population of 1,000,000 smokers each of whom faces a(n) (independent) risk of lung cancer of .0001. Suppose further that the risk of death from lung cancer is .5. This group thus expects 50 deaths attributable to smoking.

Society must choose one of three policies to reduce this risk. Policy A reduces the risk that a smoker will contract lung cancer from .0001 to .00005. Policy B would cut the number of smokers to 500,000. Policy C would reduce the death rate from lung cancer to .25. Each of these three policies has the same effect on the expected number of deaths in the population: it cuts that number from 50 to 25.

A smoker might easily be willing to pay different amounts for each of these three policies. Consider first policy B. Some smokers may value the act of smoking very highly and be unwilling to abandon smoking. Their willingness to pay for policy A or C would therefore be higher than their willingness to pay for B. Similarly, a smoker may find it particularly troubling that her disease is attributable to her smoking. On this account, she would be willing to pay relatively more for policy A than for policy C. A cost-benefit analyst that regarded subjective preferences as the relevant measure of well-being would respect these different assessments of the three policies.

This example thus shows that cost-benefit analysis does not even provide a unique valuation of the value of the life an individual who smokes. Rather, cost-benefit analysis evaluates policies that have consequences for the survival prospects of individuals. It values policies, not irreplaceable commodities.

IV. THE STRUCTURE OF JUSTIFICATION OF COST-BENEFIT ANALYSIS

Cost-benefit analysis requires justification as an institutional practice for choosing among policies. The debate concerning the justification of cost-benefit analysis, however, typically assumes that cost-benefit analysis must be justified as a moral criterion. As a consequence, the debate over cost-benefit analysis focuses on the moral foundations of the formal theory with occasional attention to the theory of measurement. From this perspective,

---

[30] If she were wealthier—for example, had a wealth of $1,000,000—then she would be willing to pay $252,110 to reduce her .95 risk of death to .949. This yields a "value" of life of $252,110,000. Moreover, if the risk of death were even higher, she would be willing to pay disproportionately more.

one might attack cost-benefit analysis in several ways. Most fundamentally, one might reject the welfarism that underlies the most natural defense of cost-benefit analysis as a moral criterion. Arguably, the commodification critique discussed briefly above adopts this tack. Alternatively, one might accept that welfarism is the appropriate form of moral criterion for these public decisions but either reject the potential compensation criterion on which cost-benefit analysis rests or reject the conception of welfarism embodied in cost-benefit analysis.[31]

A justification of cost-benefit analysis as a moral criterion might suffice to justify cost-benefit analysis, but, fortunately, given the grave difficulties faced by welfarist justifications, it is not necessary.[32] As the insecurity of the foundations of cost-benefit analysis suggests, the defense of cost-benefit analysis as a moral criterion has proved inadequate. The prevalence of cost-benefit analysis as a public decision criterion and its grip on intuition as relevant suggest that some other tack of defense is required.

There are at least three difficulties with the moral criterion strategy of defense. First, this strategy defends cost-benefit analysis acontextually rather than contextually. That is, the strategy evaluates cost-benefit analysis in isolation from the institutional framework in which it is embedded. Second, the moral criterion strategy seeks a global, rather than a local, justification of cost-benefit analysis. The strategy seeks to defend cost-benefit analysis against all other possible decision criteria. In fact, however, many criteria are not, in some sense, feasible; cost-benefit analysis need only be better than the set of feasible criteria. Finally, the moral criterion strategy offers what one might call a direct defense of cost-benefit analysis; the formal theory must embody or manifest on its face the moral criterion that justifies it. One might defend cost-benefit analysis, by contrast, indirectly.

---

[31] I ignore consent justifications for cost-benefit analysis. They, like welfarist justifications, are flawed although, I think, in a more fundamental way because the formal theory lends itself most plausibly to welfarist interpretations. Any consent justification that runs through the formal theory infers consent from the structure of preference, but it is not obvious that consent follows preference in the appropriate way. Consequently, inferred consent is hypothetical rather than real consent, and the justification for cost-benefit analysis must actually rely on some substantive moral argument other than consent.

[32] The problems confronting a welfarist justification of cost-benefit analysis arise at virtually every level of argument. For instance, the appropriateness of welfarism as the sole public criterion of decision is often challenged. Most troubling, in my view, are the problems that arise in justifying cost-benefit analysis *within* a welfarist framework. The most grave of these arise from the observation made earlier that although for each individual the willingness-to-pay measure provides a representation of that individual's preferences, it is not clear that this representation is cardinal or interpersonally comparable to the representation of the preferences of others. Both of these are necessary to make sense of the aggregation of willingnesses to pay. Note that this problem does not result from concerns about the ability of a policy maker to determine the true (normative) preferences of an individual.

Cost-benefit analysis, on this account, is justified because it advances some moral value other than one that is embodied in its formal theory.

The discussion here suggests that it is inappropriate to evaluate cost-benefit analysis straightforwardly as a moral criterion. Matthew Adler and Eric Posner in a recent essay[33] have adopted a similar approach when they distinguish cost-benefit analysis as a moral criterion from cost-benefit analysis as a decision procedure (in light of a moral criterion). My account differs in that it suggests that a defense of cost-benefit analysis may be more indirect than the one they suggest. The discussion in Section IVC expands on the complexities of indirect justification.[34] They also seek a local, rather than global, justification of cost-benefit analysis. They do not seem to consider explicitly the problems presented by contextual evaluation.

A.   Cost-Benefit Analysis in Context

Administrative agencies use cost-benefit analysis to evaluate practical policies that affect, among other things, the health and safety of individuals and the quality of the environment. These agencies act within a complex institutional framework. In this context, it is inappropriate to consider cost-benefit analysis as a moral criterion meant to determine the structure of government or, without more, the morality of individual or public action. Justification, rather, must consider how cost-benefit analysis functions within the wider institutional framework within which administrative action occurs.[35]

Evaluation of particular agencies and specific agency actions tacitly acknowledges this point. No one thinks that the Environmental Protection Agency (EPA) has acted improperly because it has failed to improve the safety of automobiles even though a given expenditure that reduces the death rate from automobile accidents might improve welfare more or save more lives than the equivalent expenditure on air quality would. The task of regulating auto safety has been delegated to other government agencies.

---

[33] Adler & Posner, *supra* note 1.

[34] In fact, Adler and Posner may have a less radical defense of cost-benefit analysis in mind than the one suggested in Section IVC because one might understand their argument as driven by a recognition of problems in the theory of measurement rather than with the moral justification of the formal theory. For further comment, see Section IVC below.

[35] The justificatory debate over cost-benefit is thus akin to that over Richard Posner's proposal in the late seventies that common-law judges ought to maximize wealth. Posner in effect proposed a cost-benefit criterion for judicial decision and then attempted to justify that suggestion on general moral grounds. That justification largely failed, but one might attempt, as Louis Kaplow and Steven Shavell at one point did, to defend wealth maximization on institutional grounds. For a discussion, see Lewis A. Kornhauser, Wealth Maximization, in The New Palgrave Dictionary of Economics and the Law (Peter Newman ed. 1998).

This division of labor, however, is often forgotten in the attempts to justify cost-benefit analysis. Consider, for example, the objection that cost-benefit analysis fails as a welfarist moral criterion because, as a criterion based on a potential compensation test, it ignores distributional concerns. Cost-benefit analysis does in fact ignore distributional concerns,[36] but one might argue that administrative agencies that regulate health and safety ought not to take such distributional concerns into account; these concerns should be left to the relevant redistributional institutions in the society. Of course, the redistributional failings of cost-benefit analysis may seem more pressing if the redistributive institutions of society are inadequate, but the failure of cost-benefit analysis to make distributive judgments is not, given the complex institutional framework in which these analyses occur, per se a reason for rejection.

The argument here applies generally to the justification of government programs. It is not obvious that one can assess the fairness or morality of the Internal Revenue Code independent of other government action. Surely, the fairness of the tax structure depends not only on the distribution of burdens it imposes but also on the distribution of benefits that the government confers (as a result of its tax collection). Indeed, one cannot even assess the appropriateness of the total tax burden on the society without assessing the way in which tax receipts are spent.

More generally, the argument simply restates the distinction between the justification of a political structure and the justification of a rule or institution within that political structure. There is no reason to believe that every institution within a political structure must be justifiable in isolation on the same grounds that justify the entire political structure.

This observation, however, does not identify how one ought to justify cost-benefit analysis or any other government program. A justification of the use of cost-benefit analysis by the EPA, for example, must go beyond the simple observation that the use is mandated by a statute or was pursuant to lawfully promulgated regulations. After all, one wishes to assess whether the statutory mandate was desirable.

B. Cost-Benefit Analysis as Locally Justifiable

Commonly, a justification of cost-benefit analysis is global rather than local; one seeks to justify cost-benefit analysis against all other possible de-

---

[36] I have in mind here concerns about the distribution of income and wealth (or of general claims on resources) rather than concerns about the distribution of (risks to) health and safety generated by different policies. A theory of justice might restrict the set of socially acceptable distributions of risk even if that constraint entailed that society was subject overall to more risk. Even in this circumstance, however, it may remain inappropriate to evaluate the distributional effects of cost-benefit analysis policy decision by policy decision.

cision criteria. Cost-benefit analysis, however, need only be better than a much smaller set of feasible alternatives. In fact, the set of decision rules generally proposed to govern the evaluation of policies that affect risks to health, safety, or the environment is quite limited.[37] Moreover, the choice of decision criterion is constrained by a variety of second-best considerations that restrict severely the selection of a decision procedure.

A brief catalog of the constraints on the design of a decision procedure may help to identify some problems of justification. Some constraints are to a large extent technological. The public decision maker, for example, generally has radically incomplete information about the data relevant to a decision. In environmental regulation, the EPA may have only imprecise estimates of the health risks posed by certain chemicals, of the costs of reduction in emissions, or of the distribution of the chemicals in the environment (and how that distribution is related to the activities of individuals and corporations). Similarly, one might understand the theory of measurement in cost-benefit analysis as a formal and systematic response to the problems posed by the policy maker's lack of information about the well-being of citizens. All decision criteria must overcome these informational problems. One might ask both how a criterion responds to limited information and how sensitive its results are to informational imperfections.

Other constraints are political or social. Adler and Posner, for example, mention two such social/political constraints: the appearance of fairness and incentive compatibility.[38] A decision criterion that appears unfair will not long survive within a democratic polity. Incentive compatibility insures that, to the extent possible, it is in the interest of administrators to follow the decision procedure as outlined. These two concerns seem appropriate and unproblematic even if difficult to meet.

Other political constraints are more problematic. Not all decision procedures or institutional structures, for example, are politically feasible: a particular institution might lead to the implementation of the best outcomes yet be politically infeasible. Suppose, for instance, that justice requires radical redistribution of income, but society has not established institutions that will accomplish the necessary redistribution. More strongly, given the distribution of power within the society and the structure of its political institutions, one might conclude that the required redistribution will not occur within that political regime (within some reasonable time span). How does this injustice in the political institutions of society affect the justification of other institutions?

---

[37] Adler and Posner, for example, assess cost-benefit analysis relative to risk-risk analysis and to the use of quality-adjusted life-years.

[38] See Adler & Posner, *supra* note 1, at 218, where they elide perception and incentive compatibility under the idea of faithfulness.

The prior subsection suggested that in the presence of ideal redistributive institutions, the fact that cost-benefit analysis relied on potential compensation was not necessarily a valid objection to it as a decision criterion for the choice of policies affecting health and safety. Does the absence of ideal redistributive institutions resuscitate the redistributive objection to cost-benefit analysis? Certainly one might argue that in the absence of ideal redistributive institutions, a decision procedure for policies concerning risks to health and safety that was more attentive to distributional concerns would be preferable to one like cost-benefit analysis that ignored redistribution. Such an argument, however, must be more complex than the typical redistributive objection.

C. Self-Effacement

Justifications of cost-benefit analysis are not only acontextual and global, they are direct. That is, they assume that one must offer an interpretation of the formal theory that is justifiable in its own terms. As a theory of preference underlies the formal theory, it is natural to think that a moral justification of cost-benefit analysis requires that the formal theory be consistent with some morally justifiable account of well-being.

A justification, however, might be indirect; one might justify the practice not by justifying its theory but through justification of its results. One argues not that the principles from which one derives the specific elements of the practice are justified but that the results generated by the practice are justified. So, for example, one might defend cost-benefit analysis on the grounds that, in general—or more often than alternative procedures—it identifies the policy that maximizes well-being understood objectively. This justification is indirect to the extent that one interprets the formal theory as a theory of subjective well-being.[39] Notice that this strategy of justification would permit ignoring the formal theory; it may play no role in the success of cost-benefit analysis in achieving its ultimate end of maximizing objective well-being.

Indirect justification requires first that one identify the objective against which to evaluate the results of cost-benefit analysis. It also requires that

---

[39] Alternatively, one might say that the formal theory is one of objective well-being and that one has defended the theory of measurement indirectly. After all, the theory of measurement in cost-benefit analysis typically uses the actual choices of individuals as the measure of the well-being that a policy will generate for that individual. These actual choices depend on the individual's subjective interpretation of her welfare. Adler & Posner, *supra* note 1, seem to adopt this second route in their justification of cost-benefit analysis as a decision procedure rather than as a moral criterion. They argue for an interpretation of the formal theory as providing an account of well-being, but an account that is only imperfectly realized by the theory of measurement.

one be able to assess the success of cost-benefit analysis independently of the cost-benefit analysis. Both the content of the social objective of administrative action and the evaluation of these actions, however, are controversial.

V.   CONCLUDING REMARKS

In this essay, I have considered two very different problems in the justification of cost-benefit analysis. First, I considered the commodification critique of cost-benefit analysis. I argued, within the standard justificatory framework, that this critique was misconceived because it mistakenly assumes that cost-benefit analysis prices or puts a value on life, the environment, and other things that I have called irreplaceable commodities. In fact, cost-benefit analysis prices policies, not the consequences of those policies. This rebuttal of the commodification critique, of course, does not provide a substantive justification for cost-benefit analysis.

Next, I briefly suggested that the standard framework of justification of cost-benefit analysis is inappropriate. The standard framework assumes that cost-benefit analysis must stand on its own justificatory feet. By contrast, I argued that an appropriate justificatory framework must account for the fact that cost-benefit analysis occurs within a complex institutional structure. Moral evaluation cannot ignore the context in which cost-benefit analysis takes place. Consequently, many critiques of it are inapposite or incomplete.

Again, however, my observation of the inadequacy of the standard framework of justification does not indicate how justification should occur. After all, we have good reason to seek the justification of political practices in comprehensible pieces rather than in ungainly and unmanageable wholes.

COGNITION AND COST-BENEFIT ANALYSIS

*CASS R. SUNSTEIN**

ABSTRACT

Cost-benefit analysis is often justified on conventional economic grounds, as a way of preventing inefficiency. But it is most plausibly justified on cognitive grounds—as a way of counteracting predictable problems in individual and social cognition. Poor judgments, by individuals and societies, can result from certain heuristics, from informational and reputational cascades, from thinking processes in which benefits are "on screen" but costs are not, from ignoring systemic effects of one-shot interventions, from seeing cases in isolation, and from intense emotional reactions. Cost-benefit analysis serves as a corrective to these cognitive problems. In addition, it is possible to arrive at an incompletely theorized agreement on cost-benefit analysis—an agreement that does not depend on controversial arguments (for example, the view that willingness to pay should be the basis for all social outcomes) and that can attract support from a variety of reasonable views. There is discussion as well of the role of distributional weights and other equitable factors in cost-benefit analysis. The conclusion is that the best argument for cost-benefit analysis is rooted in cognitive psychology and behavioral economics.

> The American people have no doubt that more people die from
> coal dust than from nuclear reactions, but they fear the prospect
> of a nuclear reactor more than they do the empirical data that
> would suggest that more people die from coal dust, having coal-
> fired burners. They also know that more lives would be saved if
> we took that 25 percent we spend in the intensive care units in
> the last few months of the elderly's lives, more children would
> be saved. But part of our culture is that we have concluded as a
> culture that we are going to rightly, or wrongly, we are going to
> spend the money, costing more lives, on the elderly. . . . I think
> it's incredibly presumptuous and elitist for political scientists to
> conclude that the American people's cultural values in fact are
> not ones that lend themselves to a cost-benefit analysis and pre-

* Karl N. Llewellyn Distinguished Service Professor of Jurisprudence, University of Chicago Law School. I am grateful to Jill Hasday, Eric Posner, and Richard Posner for helpful comments on a previous draft; special thanks to Eric Posner for many helpful discussions. Brian Lehman and Brooke May provided excellent research assistance and valuable comments and criticisms.

[*Journal of Legal Studies,* vol. XXIX]

sume that they would change their cultural values if in fact they
were aware of the cost-benefit analysis.[1]

MANY people have argued for cost-benefit analysis on economic
grounds.[2] On their view, a primary goal of regulation is to promote economic efficiency, and cost-benefit analysis is admirably well suited to that
goal. Arguments of this kind have met with sharp criticism from those who
reject the efficiency criterion[3] or who believe that, in practice, cost-benefit
analysis is likely to produce a kind of regulatory paralysis.[4]

In this essay I offer support for cost-benefit analysis, not from the standpoint of conventional economics, but on grounds associated with cognitive
psychology and behavioral economics. My basic suggestion is that cost-
benefit analysis is best defended as a means of overcoming predictable
problems in individual and social cognition. Most of these problems might
be collected under the general heading of selective attention. Cost-benefit
analysis should be understood as a method for putting "on screen" important social facts that might otherwise escape private and public attention.
Thus understood, cost-benefit analysis is a way of ensuring better priority
setting and of overcoming predictable obstacles to desirable regulation,
whatever may be our criteria for deciding the hardest questions about that
topic.

Of course, much of the controversy over cost-benefit analysis stems from
the difficulty of specifying, with particularity, what that form of analysis
entails. None of the cognitive points made here supports any particular understanding of cost-benefit analysis. Certainly I do not mean to embrace the
controversial and indeed implausible proposition that all regulatory decisions should be made by aggregating private willingness to pay, as if economic efficiency is or should be the goal of all regulation.[5] I will attempt

---

[1] Joseph Biden, Confirmation Hearings for Stephen G. Breyer, to be an associate justice
of the United States Supreme Court, Senate Committee on the Judiciary, 103d Cong., 2d
Sess. 42 (July 14, 1994) (Miller Reporting transcript).

[2] See, for example, W. Kip Viscusi, Fatal Tradeoffs: Public & Private Responsibilities for
Risk (1992); W. Kip Viscusi, Risk Equity, in this issue, at 843.

[3] See Elizabeth Anderson, Value in Ethics and Economics (1993).

[4] See, for example, Thomas O. McGarity, Reinventing Rationality: The Role of Regulatory Analysis in the Federal Bureaucracy (1991).

[5] See Matthew D. Adler & Eric A. Posner, Rethinking Cost-Benefit Analysis, 109 Yale
L. J. 165 (1999); Cass R. Sunstein, Free Markets and Social Justice ch. 9 (1997); Amartya
Sen, The Discipline of Cost-Benefit Analysis, in this issue, at 931; Matthew D. Adler & Eric
A. Posner, Implementing Cost-Benefit Analysis When Preferences Are Distorted, in this is-
sue, at 1105. See, in particular, Amartya Sen, Rationality and Social Choice, 85 Am. Econ.
Rev. 1, 17 (1995) ("There are plenty of social choice problems in all this, but in analyzing
them, we have to go beyond looking only for the best reflection of given individual preferences, or the most acceptable procedures for choices based on those preferences").

instead to provide an understanding of cost-benefit analysis that is agnostic on large issues of the right and the good and that can attract support from people with diverse theoretical commitments or with uncertainty about the appropriate theoretical commitments.[6] In this sense I attempt to produce an incompletely theorized agreement on a certain form of cost-benefit analysis—an agreement on a form of cost-benefit analysis to which many different people, with diverse and competing views, should be willing to subscribe. This is partly an attempt to respond to the most natural objection to my principal claim here, an objection that would stress the possibility that cognitive problems would reappear in the values that end up being associated with various states of affairs.

The paper is organized as follows. In Sections I, II, and III, I seek to defend the general idea of cost-benefit analysis, not as embodying any sectarian conception of value, but as a way of overcoming predictable problems in understanding risks to life and health at both the individual and social levels. In Section IV, I briefly attempt to specify what cost-benefit analysis might be understood to entail. My goal is to show how this method, conceived in a particular way, might attract support from people with varying conceptions of the good and the right, including, for example, neoclassical economists and those who are quite skeptical about some normative claims in neoclassical economics, involving those who do and who do not take private preferences, and willingness to pay, as the proper foundation for regulatory policy. In other words, I try to show how a certain understanding of cost-benefit analysis might contain considerable appeal precisely because it overcomes problems in individual cognition, and I do so without taking a stand on controversial issues about the ultimate goals of regulation and law.

I. A TALE OF TWO TABLES

Let us begin with two simple tables. It is well known that there is a great deal of variability in national expenditures per life saved. Consider Table 1, which has come to define many discussions of these problems.[7]

This table should be taken with many grains of salt.[8] It does not contain nearly all of the benefits from regulation, including those that fall short of mortalities averted (including illnesses averted, benefits for animals, and

---

[6] See Adler & Posner, Rethinking Cost-Benefit Analysis, *supra* note 5, which is in the same general spirit as this essay, and from which I have learned a great deal.

[7] Based on data from Office of Management and Budget, Budget of the United States Government Fiscal Year 1992 pt. 2, at 370 tab. C-2 (1991).

[8] See Lisa Heinzerling, Regulatory Costs of Mythic Proportions, 107 Yale L. J. 1981 (1998).

TABLE 1

Cost Effectiveness of Selected Regulations: Cost per Life Saved

Regulation	Agency	Cost per Premature Death Averted (1990 $Millions)
Unvented space heater ban	CPSC	.1
Aircraft cabin fire protection standard	FAA	.1
Auto passive restraint/seat belt standards	NHTSA	.1
Steering column protection standard	NHTSA	.1
Underground construction standards	OSHA-S	.1
Trihalomethane drinking water standards	EPA	.2
Aircraft seat cushion flammability standard	FAA	.4
Alcohol and drug control standards	FRA	.4
Auto fuel system integrity standard	NHTSA	.4
Standards for servicing auto wheel rims	OSHA-S	.4
Aircraft floor emergency lighting standard	FAA	.6
Concrete and masonry construction standards	OSHA-S	.6
Crane-suspended personnel platform standard	OSHA-S	.7
Passive restraints for trucks and buses (proposed)	NHTSA	.7
Side-impact standards for autos (dynamic)	NHTSA	.8
Children's sleepwear flammability ban	CPSC	.8
Auto side door support standards	NHTSA	.8
Low-altitude windshear equipment and training standards	FAA	1.3
Electrical equipment standards (metal mines)	MSHA	1.4
Trenching and excavation standards	OSHA-S	1.5
Traffic alert and collision avoidance (TCAS) systems	FAA	1.5
Hazard communication standard	OSHA-S	1.6
Side-impact standards for trucks, buses, and MPVs (proposed)	NHTSA	2.2
Grain dust explosion prevention standards	OSHA-S	2.8
Rear lap/shoulder belts for autos	NHTSA	3.2
Standards for radionuclides in uranium mines	EPA	3.4
Benzene NESHAP (original: fugitive emissions)	EPA	3.4
Ethylene dibromide drinking water standard	EPA	5.7
Benzene NESHAP (revised: coke byproducts)	EPA	6.1
Asbestos occupational exposure limit	OSHA-H	8.3
Benzene occupational exposure limit	OSHA-H	8.9
Electrical equipment standards (coal mines)	MSHA	9.2
Arsenic emission standards for glass plants	EPA	13.5
Ethylene oxide occupational exposure limit	OSHA-H	20.5
Arsenic/copper NESHAP	EPA	23.0
Hazardous waste listing for petroleum refining sludge	EPA	27.6
Cover/move uranium mill tailings (inactive sites)	EPA	31.7
Benzene NESHAP (revised: transfer operations)	EPA	32.9
Cover/move uranium mill tailings (active sites)	EPA	45.0
Acrylonitrile occupational exposure limit	OSHA-H	51.5
Coke ovens occupational exposure limit	OSHA-H	63.5
Lockout/tagout	OSHA-S	70.9
Asbestos occupational exposure limit	OSHA-H	74.0
Arsenic occupational exposure limit	OSHA-H	106.9
Asbestos ban	EPA	110.7
Diethylstilbestrol (DES) cattlefeed ban	FDA	124.8
Benzene NESHAP (revised: waste operations)	EPA	168.2
1,2 dichloropropane drinking water standard	EPA	653.0
Hazardous waste land disposal ban (first, third)	EPA	4,190.4
Municipal solid waste landfill standards (proposed)	EPA	19,107.0
Formaldehyde occupational exposure limit	OSHA-H	86,201.8
Atrazine/alachlor drinking water standard	EPA	92,069.7
Hazardous waste listing for wood-preserving chemicals	EPA	5,700,000

Note.—CPSC: Consumer Protection Safety Commission; FAA: Federal Aviation Administration; NHTSA: National Highway Transportation Safety Administration; OSHA-S: Occupational Safety and Health Administration-Safety; EPA: Environmental Protection Agency; FRA: Federal Railroad Administration; MSHA: Mine Safety and Health Administration; OSHA-H: Occupational Safety and Health Administration-Health; FDA: Food and Drug Administration.

aesthetic and recreational gains). An adequate cost-benefit analysis would certainly take those benefits into account. (See the Appendix.) We will shortly see that the table depends on many contentious assumptions, above all involving the appropriate discount rate; modest changes in the discount rate can greatly reduce the expenditures and the disparities. But at the very least, the table creates a presumption that the current system of regulation suffers from serious misallocation of resources. It also suggests that with better allocations, we could obtain large gains. Indeed, a recent study finds that it would be possible to save the same number of lives that we now save with tens of billions of dollars left over—and that better priority setting could save 60,000 lives, and 636,000 life-years, annually at the same price.[9]

What is the source of the misallocations? Interest-group power undoubtedly plays a substantial role, because well-organized groups are able to obtain measures in their interest or to fend off measures that would harm them, and because poorly organized ones typically fail. Indeed, cost-benefit analysis might be defended partly as a corrective to interest-group power, operating as a kind of technocratic check on measures that would do little good or even produce net harm (and also on measures that do much less good than they should).[10] But officials are of course responsive not only to interest groups but also to general public pressures, and thus part of the answer must lie in the distinctive judgments of ordinary people, who do not assess risks through a well-informed cost-benefit lens. Indeed, divergences between expert and lay assessments of risks have been demonstrated in many places. Consider the comparison in Table 2.[11]

The Environmental Protection Agency (EPA) itself has found that EPA policies are responsive not to expert judgments but to lay assessments of risks.[12] Indeed, EPA policies track ordinary judgments extremely well.

If we put together these two tables, we can suggest a general hypothesis. The government currently allocates its limited resources poorly, and it does so partly because it is responsive to ordinary judgments about the magnitude of risks. A government that could insulate itself from misinformed judgments could save tens of thousands of lives and tens of billions of dollars annually. Let us attempt to be more specific about the cognitive problems that help account for current problems.

---

[9] See Tammy O. Tengs & John D. Graham, The Opportunity Costs of Haphazard Social Investments in Life-Saving, in Risks, Costs, and Lives Saved: Getting Better Results from Regulation 167, 172–74 (Robert W. Hahn ed. 1996).

[10] Of course it is possible that the content of the cost-benefit test will reflect interest-group power.

[11] Reprinted by permission from Stephen G. Breyer, Breaking the Vicious Circle: Toward Effective Risk Regulation 21 (1993).

[12] See id.

TABLE 2

RATING HEALTH RISKS

Rank by Public	Risk	EPA Experts' Rank
1	Hazardous waste sites	Medium to low
2	Exposure to worksite chemicals	High
3	Industrial pollution of waterways	Low
4	Nuclear accident radiation	Not ranked
5	Radioactive waste	Not ranked
6	Chemical leaks from underground storage tanks	Medium to low
7	Pesticides	High
8	Pollution from industrial accidents	Medium to low
9	Water pollution from farm runoff	Medium
10	Tap water contamination	High
11	Industrial air pollution	High
12	Ozone layer destruction	High
13	Coastal water contamination	Low
14	Sewage plant water pollution	Medium to low
15	Vehicle exhaust	High
16	Oil spills	Medium to low
17	Acid rain	High
18	Water pollution from urban runoff	Medium
19	Damaged wetlands	Low
20	Genetic alteration	Low
21	Nonhazardous waste sites	Medium to low
22	Greenhouse effect	Low
23	Indoor air pollution	High
24	X-ray radiation	Not ranked
25	Indoor radon	High
26	Microwave oven radiation	Not ranked

II.   SIX PROBLEMS IN THE PUBLIC DEMAND FOR REGULATION

For the moment, I attempt no controversial specification of cost-benefit analysis and understand the term broadly to refer to a regulatory method that calls for regulators to identify, and make relevant for purposes of decision, the good effects and the bad effects of regulation and to quantify those as much as possible in terms of both dollar equivalents and life-years saved, hospital admissions prevented, workdays gained, and so forth. (See the Appendix for examples from the EPA's regulation for ozone and particulates.) Let us also assume that cost-benefit analysis, thus understood, can accommodate distributional factors, by, for example, giving distributional weights to certain adverse effects, or by assuming uniform numbers for various goods (such as increased longevity) so as to ensure that they do not vary in accordance with wealth.

It is obvious that people, including government officials, often lack risk-related information; they may not know the nature of the health risks at issue or the adverse consequences of risk reduction. By itself this point argues for cost-benefit analysis, simply as a means of producing the relevant information. The public demand for regulation is often based on misunderstandings of facts.[13] But put this obvious point to one side. Why, exactly, might people's judgments about risk and risk regulation go badly wrong?[14] There are six points here.

A.   The Availability Heuristic

The first problem is purely cognitive: the use of the availability heuristic in thinking about risks.[15] It is well established that people tend to think that events are more probable if they can recall an incident of its occurrence.[16] Consider, for example, the fact that people typically think that more words, on any given page, will end with the letters "ing" than have "n" as the second-to-last letter (though a moment's reflection shows that this is not possible).[17] With respect to risks, judgments are typically affected by the availability heuristic, so that people overestimate the number of deaths from highly publicized events (motor vehicle accidents, tornados, floods, botulism) but underestimate the number from less publicized sources (stroke, heart disease, stomach cancer).[18] Similarly, much of the concern with nuclear power undoubtedly stems from its association with memorable events, including Hiroshima, Chernobyl, and Three-Mile Island.

To the extent that people lack information, or base their judgments on mental shortcuts that produce errors,[19] a highly responsive government is likely to blunder. Cost-benefit analysis is a natural corrective, above all because it focuses attention on the actual effects of regulation, including, in

[13] A colorful discussion is Barry R. Glassner, The Culture of Fear: Why Americans Are Afraid of the Wrong Things (1999).

[14] Some of these problems may infect market behavior as well, and when this is so there is a problem with using private willingness to pay as the basis for regulation, since private willingness to pay will (by hypothesis) be based on a misunderstanding of the facts. But markets contain some safeguards against these errors, through the budget constraint and opportunities for learning, and in any case the form of cost-benefit analysis that I support would not rest on mistaken factual judgments, as discussed in more detail below.

[15] See Roger G. Noll & James E. Krier, Some Implications of Cognitive Psychology for Risk Regulation, 19 J. Legal Stud. 747, 749–60 (1990).

[16] See Amos Tversky & Daniel Kahneman, Judgment under Uncertainty: Heuristics and Biases, in Judgment under Uncertainty: Heuristics and Biases 3, 11 (Daniel Kahneman, Paul Slovic, & Amos Tversky eds. 1982) (describing the availability heuristic).

[17] Amos Tversky & Daniel Kahneman, Extensional versus Intuitive Reasoning: The Conjunction Fallacy in Probability Judgment, 90 Psychol. Rev. 293, 295 (1983).

[18] Jonathan Baron, Thinking and Deciding 218 (2d ed. 1994).

[19] Other heuristics are likely to be at work, such as the representativeness heuristic, but availability is the most important source of distorted public judgments.

some cases, the existence of surprisingly small benefits from regulatory controls. To this extent cost-benefit analysis should be taken not as undemocratic but, on the contrary, as a means of fortifying (properly specified) democratic goals, by ensuring that government decisions are responsive to well-informed public judgments.

B. Aggravating Social Influences: Informational and Reputational Cascades

The availability heuristic does not, of course, operate in a social vacuum. It interacts with emphatically social processes and, in particular, with informational and reputational forces.[20] When one person says, through words or deeds, that something is or is not dangerous, he creates an informational externality.[21] A signal by some person A will provide relevant data to others. When there is little private information, such a signal may initiate an informational cascade, with significant consequences for private and public behavior, and with possibly distorting effects on regulatory policy.[22]

Imagine, for example, that A says that abandoned hazardous waste sites are dangerous or that A initiates protest activity because such a site is located nearby. B, otherwise skeptical or in equipoise, may go along with A; C, otherwise an agnostic, may be convinced that if A and B share the relevant belief, the belief must be true; and it will take a confident D to resist the shared judgments of A, B, and C. The result of this set of influences can be social cascades, as hundreds, thousands, or millions of people come to accept a certain belief simply because of what they think other people believe.[23] There is nothing fanciful to the idea. Cascade effects help account for the existence of widespread public concern about abandoned hazardous waste dumps (a relatively trivial environmental hazard), and in more recent years, they spurred grossly excessive public fears of the pesticide Alar, of risks from plane crashes, and of dangers of shootings in schools in the aftermath of the murders in Littleton, Colorado. Such effects recently helped produce massive dislocations in beef production in Europe in connection

---

[20] I draw in this section on Timur Kuran & Cass R. Sunstein, Availability Cascades and Risk Regulation, 51 Stan. L. Rev. 683 (1999).

[21] See Andrew Caplin & John Leahy, Miracle on Sixth Avenue: Information Externalities and Search, 108 Econ. J. 60 (1998).

[22] See Kuran & Sunstein, *supra* note 20, at 720.

[23] See David Hirshleifer, The Blind Leading the Blind: Social Influence, Fads, and Informational Cascades, in The New Economics of Human Behavior 188 (Mariano Tommasi & Kathyrn Ierulli eds. 1995).

with "mad cow disease"; they are currently giving rise to growing and apparently unfounded fears of genetic engineering of food.

On the reputational side, cognitive effects may be amplified as well.[24] If many people are alarmed about some risk, you may not voice your doubts about whether the alarm is merited, simply in order not to seem obtuse, cruel, or indifferent. And if many people believe that a certain risk is trivial, you may not disagree through words or deeds, lest you appear cowardly or confused. The result of these forces can be cascade effects, mediated by the availability heuristic. Such effects can produce a public demand for regulation even though the relevant risks are trivial. At the same time, there may be little or no demand for regulation of risks that are, in fact, quite large in magnitude. Self-interested private groups exploit these forces, often by using the availability heuristic. Consider the fact that European companies have tried to play up fears of genetically engineered food as a way of fending off American competition.

Cost-benefit analysis has a natural role here. If it is made relevant to decision, it can counteract cascade effects induced by informational and reputational forces, especially when the availability heuristic is at work. The effect of cost-benefit analysis is to subject a public demand for regulation to a kind of technocratic scrutiny, to ensure that the demand is not rooted in myth, and to ensure as well that government is regulating risks even when the public demand (because insufficiently informed) is low. And here too there is no democratic problem with the inquiry into consequences. If people's concern is fueled by informational forces having little reliability, and if people express concern even though they are not fearful, a governmental effort to cool popular reactions is hardly inconsistent with democratic ideals. Similarly, there is nothing undemocratic about a governmental effort to divert resources to serious problems that have not been beneficiaries of cascade effects.

C.   Dangers On-Screen, Benefits Off-Screen

Why are people so concerned about the risks of nuclear power, when experts tend to believe that the risks are quite low—lower, in fact, than the risks from competing energy sources, such as coal-fired power plants, which produce relatively little public objection? Why do people believe that small risks from pesticides should be regulated, even if comparatively small risks from X-rays are quite tolerable?

Suggestive answers come from research suggesting that for many activities that pose small risks but that nonetheless receive public concern, people

[24] See Kuran & Sunstein, *supra* note 20, at 727.

perceive low benefits as well as high risks.[25] For example, nuclear power itself is seen as a low-benefit, high-risk activity. Similar findings appear for some activities that are in fact relatively high risk: a judgment of low risk accompanies a judgment of high benefits. The very fact that activities are known to have high benefits skews judgment in their favor and hence makes people understate the costs as well.

The obvious conclusion is that sometimes people favor regulation of some risks because the underlying activities are not seen to have compensating benefits.[26] Thus for some activities, trade-offs are not perceived at all. Dangers are effectively on-screen, but benefits are off-screen. Note that this is not because such activities do not, in fact, have compensating benefits. It is because of a kind of perceptual illusion, a cognitive bias.

An important factor here is loss aversion. People tend to be loss averse, in the sense that a loss from the status quo is seen as more undesirable than a gain is seen as desirable.[27] In the context of risk regulation, the consequence is that any newly introduced risk, or any aggravation of existing risks, is seen as a serious problem, even if the accompanying benefits (a gain from the status quo and hence perceived as less salient and less important) are considerable.[28] Thus when a new risk adds danger, people may focus on the danger itself and not on the benefits that accompany the danger. And an important problem here is that in many cases where dangers are on-screen and benefits off-screen, the magnitude of the danger is actually quite low. Cost-benefit analysis can be a corrective here, by placing the various effects on-screen.

D.   Systemic Effects and Health-Health Trade-Offs

Often people focus on small pieces of complex problems, and causal changes are hard to trace. They "bracket" resulting issues. Consider an

[25] The fact that nuclear power and application of pesticides produce benefits as well as risks may not register on the lay viewscreen, and this may help produce a high-risk judgment. See Ali Siddiq Alhakami & Paul Slovic, A Psychological Study of the Inverse Relationship between Perceived Risk and Perceived Benefit, 14 Risk Analysis 1085, 1088 (1994).

[26] See Howard Margolis, Dealing with Risk (1996), for a detailed discussion of how this point bears on the different risk judgments of experts and lay people.

[27] See Richard H. Thaler, The Psychology of Choice and the Assumptions of Economics, in Quasi Rational Economics 137, 143 (Richard H. Thaler ed. 1991) (arguing that "losses loom larger than gains"); Daniel Kahneman, Jack L. Knetsch, & Richard H. Thaler, Experimental Tests of the Endowment Effect and the Coase Theorem, 98 J. Pol. Econ. 1325, 1328 (1990); Colin Camerer, Individual Decision Making, in The Handbook of Experimental Economics 665–70 (John H. Kagel & Alvin E. Roth eds. 1995).

[28] For some policy implications of loss aversion, see Jack L. Knetsch, Reference States, Fairness, and Choice of Measure to Value Environmental Changes, in Environment, Ethics, and Behavior: The Psychology of Environmental Valuation and Degradation 52, 64–65 (Max H. Bazerman et al. eds. 1997).

analogy. The German psychologist Dietrich Dörner has done some illuminating computer experiments designed to see whether people can engage in successful social engineering.[29] Participants are asked to solve problems faced by the inhabitants of some region of the world. Through the magic of the computer, many policy initiatives are available to solve the relevant problems (improved care of cattle, childhood immunization, drilling more wells). But most of the participants produce eventual calamities, because they do not see the complex, systemwide effects of particular interventions. Only the rare participant can see a number of steps down the road—to understand the multiple effects of one-shot interventions on the system.

Often regulation has similar systemic effects. A decision to regulate nuclear power may, for example, increase the demand for coal-fired power plants, with harmful environmental consequences.[30] A decision to impose fuel economy standards on new cars may cause a downsizing of the fleet, and in that way increase risks to life. A decision to ban asbestos may cause manufacturers to use less safe substitutes. Regulation of tropospheric ozone may control the health dangers of ozone, but ozone has various benefits as well, including protection against cataracts and skin cancer; hence regulation of ozone may cause health problems equal to those that it reduces.[31] Indeed, regulation of ozone will increase electricity prices, and because higher electricity prices will deprive poor people of air conditioning or lead them to use it less, such regulation may literally kill people.[32]

These are simply a few examples of situations in which a government agency is making health-health trade-offs in light of the systemic effects of one-shot interventions. Indeed, any regulation that imposes high costs will, by virtue of that fact, produce some risks to life and health, since "richer is safer."[33] A virtue of cost-benefit analysis is that it tends to overcome peo-

[29] See Dietrich Dörner, The Logic of Failure: Why Things Go Wrong and What We Can Do to Make Them Right (1996).

[30] See Stephen G. Breyer, Vermont Yankee and the Court's Role in the Nuclear Energy Controversy, 91 Harv. L. Rev. 1833, 1835–90 (1978). See generally Peter Huber, Electricity and the Environment: In Search of Regulatory Authority, 100 Harv. L. Rev. 1002 (1987).

[31] See Randall Lutter & Christopher Wolz, UV-B Screening by Tropospheric Ozone: Implications for the NAAQS, 31 Envtl. Sci. & Tech. 142A, 144A (1997) (estimating that the EPA's new ozone National Ambient Air Quality Standards (NAAQS) could cause 25–50 more melanoma skin cancer deaths and increase the number of cataract cases by 13,000–28,000 each year). See also Ralph L. Keeney & Kenneth Green, Estimating Fatalities Induced by Economic Impacts of EPA's Ozone and Particulate Standards 8 (Policy Study No. 225, Reason Public Policy Institute, June 1997) (calculating that if attainment of the new standards costs $10 billion annually, a number well within EPA's estimated cost range, it will contribute to 2,200 premature deaths annually). On the general phenomenon, see John D. Graham & Jonathan Baert Wiener, Risk versus Risk (1995).

[32] See C. Boyden Gray, The Clean Air Act under Regulatory Reform, 11 Tulane Envtl. L. J. 235 (1998).

[33] John D. Graham, Bei-Hung Chang, & John S. Evans, Poorer Is Riskier, 12 Risk Analysis 333, 333–35 (1992); Frank B. Cross, When Environmental Regulations Kill: The Role of

ple's tendency to focus on parts of problems, by requiring them to look globally at the consequences of apparently isolated actions.

E. Emotions and Alarmist Bias

A set of data now suggests that people are subject to alarmist bias.[34] The mere existence of discussions of new risks can aggravate concern, even when the discussions take the form of assurances that the risk level is relatively low. And when presented with information suggesting that a risk may range from A (low) to Z (high), the high risk number is especially salient, and it appears to have a disproportionate effect on behavior.

A recent paper by George Loewenstein et al. suggests that risk-related concerns are often based on feelings rather than judgments.[35] Thus risk-related objections can be a product not so much of thinking as of intense emotions, often produced by extremely vivid images of what might go wrong. This point is supported by evidence that reported feelings of worry are sometimes sensitive not to the probability of the bad outcome but only to its severity.[36] Vivid mental pictures of widespread death or catastrophe can drive a demand for risk regulation. Consider, for example, the motivations of those who press for regulation of airplane safety in the aftermath of an airplane crash, even though such regulation may increase travel risks on balance (by driving up the price of flying and causing a shift to driving, a more dangerous form of transportation).[37]

It is important to be careful with the relevant categories here. There is no sharp distinction between cognition and emotion.[38] Emotions are generally the products of beliefs, and hence an emotional reaction to risk—terror, for example—is generally mediated by judgments.[39] But this is not always true; sometimes the operation of the brain allows intense emotional reac-

---

Health-Health Analysis, 22 Ecology L. Q. 729 (1995); Ralph L. Keeney, Mortality Risks Induced by the Costs of Regulations, 8 J. Risk & Uncertainty 95 (1994); Aaron Wildavsky, Richer Is Safer, 60 Pub. Interest 23 (1980); Aaron Wildavsky, Searching for Safety 59–75 (1988).

[34] See W. Kip Viscusi, Alarmist Decisions with Divergent Risk Information, 107 Econ. J. 1657, 1657–58 (1997) (studying situations under which "[n]ew information about risks may generate alarmist actions that are not commensurate with the magnitude of the risks").

[35] See G. F. Loewenstein et al., Risk as Feelings (unpublished manuscript, Carnegie Mellon Univ., May 4, 1999).

[36] Id. at 12.

[37] See Robert W. Hahn, The Economics of Airline Safety and Security: An Analysis of the White House Commission's Recommendations, 20 Harv. J. L. & Pub. Pol'y 791 (1997).

[38] See Dan M. Kahan & Martha C. Nussbaum, Two Conceptions of Emotion in the Criminal Law, 96 Colum. L. Rev 269 (1996); Jon Elster, Alchemies of the Mind: Rationality and the Emotions (1999).

[39] Elster, supra note 38.

tions with minimal cognitive activity.[40] In any case the judgments that fuel emotions may be unreliable. We need not venture into controversial territory in order to urge not that emotions are free of cognition but that some risks produce extremely sharp, largely visceral reactions. These reactions can be impervious to argument. Experience with mass panics has shown exactly this structure, as assurances based on statistical evidence have little effect in the face of vivid images of what might go wrong.[41] Some fears even appear to have a genetic foundation; consider, as a possible example, fear of snakes, found in people who have no reason to think that snakes are dangerous.

The role of cost-benefit analysis is straightforward here. Just as the Senate was designed to have a cooling effect on the passions of the House of Representatives, so cost-benefit analysis might ensure that policy is driven not by hysteria or unfounded alarm but by a full appreciation of the effects of relevant risks and their control. If the hysteria survives an investigation of consequences, then the hysteria is fully rational, and an immediate and intensive regulatory response is entirely appropriate.

Nor is cost-benefit analysis, in this setting, only a check on unwarranted regulation. It can and should serve as a spur to regulation as well. If risks do not produce visceral reactions, partly because the underlying activities do not yield vivid mental images, cost-benefit analysis can show that they nonetheless warrant regulatory control. The elimination of lead in gasoline is a case in point.[42]

F. Separate Evaluation and Incoherence

Suppose that you are asked to say, without reference to any other problem, how much you would be willing to pay to protect certain threats to coral reefs. Now suppose that you are asked to say, without reference to any other problem, how much you would pay to protect against skin cancer among the elderly. Suppose, finally, that you are asked to say how much you would be willing to pay to protect certain threats to coral reefs and how much you would be willing to pay to protect against skin cancer among the elderly. Empirical evidence suggests that people's answers to questions taken in isolation are very different from their answer to questions when they are asked to engage in cross-category comparisons.[43] It appears that

[40] See Loewenstein et al., supra note 35.

[41] See the discussion of Love Canal in Kuran & Sunstein, supra note 20, at 691–98.

[42] See Economic Analyses at EPA: Assessing Regulatory Impact (Richard D. Morgenstern ed. 1997).

[43] See Daniel Kahneman, Ilana Ritov, & David Schkade, Economic Preferences or Attitude Expressions? An Analysis of Dollar Responses to Public Issues, 19 J. Risk & Uncertainty 203 (1999); Daniel Kahneman et al., Reversals of Judgment: The Effect of Cross-

when people assess problems in isolation, they do so by reference to other problems in the same basic category—and that this intuitive process is dramatically altered when people are explicitly told to assess problems from other categories as well. The result of assessing individual problems, taken in isolation, is to produce what people would themselves consider a form of incoherence.

The forms of regulatory spending shown in Table 1 undoubtedly reflect, in part, the kinds of irrationality that follow from judgments that are made without close reference to other problems from different categories. Incoherence is the natural result of the relevant cognitive processes. The argument for a form of cost-benefit analysis is straightforward: it operates as a built-in corrective to some of the distortions that come from taking problems in isolation. The point applies to contingent valuation assessments, but it operates more broadly with respect to expenditure decisions that otherwise risk incoherence, simply by virtue of the fact that they operate without looking at other problems, including those from other categories.

G.   General Implications

The cognitive argument for cost-benefit analysis is now in place. It is important but obvious to say that people lack information and that their lack of information can lead to an inadequate or excessive demand for regulation or a form of "paranoia and neglect."[44] What is less obvious is that predictable features of cognition will lead to a demand for regulation that is unlikely to be based on the facts. When people ask for regulation because of fears fueled by availability cascades, and when the benefits from the risk-producing activity are not registering, it would be highly desirable to create cost-benefit filters on their requests. When interest groups exploit cognitive mechanisms to create unwarranted fear or diminish concern with serious problems, it is desirable to have institutional safeguards. When people fail to ask for regulation for related reasons, it would be desirable to create a mechanism by which government might nonetheless act if the consequences of action would be good. Here too cost-benefit balancing might be desirable, as in fact it has proved to be in connection not only with the phase-out of lead but also with the Reagan administration's decision to phase out

---

Category Comparisons on Intendedly Absolute Responses (unpublished manuscript, Princeton Univ. 1999). See also Daniel Read, George Loewenstein, & Matthew Rabin, Choice Bracketing, 19 J. Risk & Uncertainty 171 (1999).

[44] See John D. Graham, Making Sense of Risk: An Agenda for Congress, in Hahn ed., *supra* note 9.

chlorofluorocarbons (CFCs), motivated by a cost-benefit analysis suggesting that the phaseout would do far more good than harm.[45]

A caveat: It is entirely possible that the public demand for regulation will
result from something other than cognitive errors, even if the relevant risk
seems low as a statistical matter. People may think, for example, that it is
especially important to protect poor children from a certain risk in a geo-
graphically isolated area, and they may be willing to devote an unusually
large amount to ensure that protection. What seems to be a cognitive error
may turn out, on reflection, to be a judgment of value, and a judgment that
can survive reflection. I will return to this point. For the moment note two
simple points. Whether an error is involved is an empirical question, subject, at least in principle, to empirical testing. And nothing in cost-benefit
analysis would prevent people from devoting resources to projects that they
consider worthy, even if the risk is relatively low as a statistical matter.

I have not yet discussed what cost-benefit analysis specifically entails,
and there are potentially serious controversies here. But it will be best to
discuss that question after dealing with some direct objections.

III.   OBJECTIONS: POPULISM, QUANTIFICATION,
AND RIVAL RATIONALITIES

The argument made thus far runs into three obvious objections. The first
involves democratic considerations; the second points to the limitations of
quantification; the third raises the possibility that ordinary people's judgments are based not on cognitive limitations but on a kind of "rival rationality."

A.   Populism

The first objection, populist in character, is captured by the opening quotation from Senator Biden. The objection would be that in a democracy,
government properly responds to the social demand for law. Government
does not legitimately reject that demand on the ground that cost-benefit
analysis suggests that it should not act. Any approach that uses efficiency,
or technocratically driven judgments, as a brake on accountability is fatally
undemocratic.

---

[45] See Morgenstern ed., *supra* note 42. See also Richard Elliot Benedick, Ozone Diplo-
macy: New Directions in Safeguarding the Planet 63 (1991) (Reagan administration supported aggressive regulation largely because cost-benefit analysis from the Council of Economic Advisers demonstrated that "despite the scientific and economic uncertainties, the
monetary benefits of preventing future deaths from skin cancer far outweighed costs of CFC
controls as estimated either by industry or by EPA").

The problem with this objection is that it rests on a controversial and even unacceptable conception of democracy, one that sees responsiveness to citizens' demands, whatever their factual basis, as the foundation of political legitimacy. If those demands are uninformed, it is perfectly appropriate for government to resist them. Indeed, it is far from clear that reasonable citizens want, or would want, their government to respond to their uninformed demands.

The analysis thus far suggests that the relevant demands are, in fact, uninformed or unreflective. If this is so, they should be subject to deliberative constraints of the sort exemplified by cost-benefit analysis. After that analysis has been generated, and public officials have taken it into account, democratic safeguards continue to be available, and electoral sanctions can be imposed on those who have violated the public will. The simple point is that if, once informed if the cost-benefit trade-off, people continue to seek some particular regulation, then democratic considerations require government to respect their choice.[46] At the very least, cost-benefit analysis should be an ingredient in the analysis, showing people that the consequences of various approaches might be different from what they seem.

B.   Quantification and Expressive Rationality

I have noted that the cost-benefit chart (Table 1) described above raised many questions. Those questions might be made into a thoroughgoing challenge to cost-benefit analysis. In an extensive discussion, Lisa Heinzerling has attempted to do precisely that.[47] Heinzerling argues that many of the values depend on controversial judgments of value and that the table itself masks those judgments. Her first point is that the table includes many regulations that were in fact rejected. Some of them were not issued on the ground that their costs would exceed their benefits. The table is also under-inclusive, for many regulations have been issued that impose dramatically lower costs than many of those included on the table. But by itself this is no indictment of cost-benefit analysis. Indeed, it provides support for cost-benefit analysis insofar as it suggests that the tool has resulted in a rejection of undesirable regulations.

But Heinzerling goes further. She contends that many of these numbers depend on controversial judgments about how to discount future benefits. Above all, the charts depend on a 10 percent discount rate, whereas the agencies tended to use a lower discount rate or not to discount at all. Heinz-

---

[46] At least assuming the decisions involve nothing peculiar or invidious, such as racial animus.

[47] See Heinzerling, *supra* note 8. Heinzerling's alternative table appears in *id.* at 2040 n.397.

TABLE 3

CORRECTED (?) TABLE ON COST EFFECTIVENESS OF REGULATIONS

Regulation	Agency and Year	Adjusted Cost Estimate (1995 $Thousands)
Asbestos	OSHA 1972	700
Benzene	OSHA 1985	2,570
Arsenic/glass plant	EPA 1986	6,610
Ethylene oxide	OSHA 1984	3,020–5,780
Uranium mill tailings/inactive	EPA 1983	2,410
Acrylonitrile	OSHA 1978	8,570
Uranium mill tailings/active	EPA 1983	3,840
Coke ovens	OSHA 1976	12,420
Asbestos	OSHA 1986	3,860
Arsenic	OSHA 1978	24,490
Arsenic/low-arsenic copper	EPA 1986	5,740
Land disposal	EPA 1986	3,280
Formaldehyde	OSHA 1985	31,100

NOTE.—OSHA: Occupational Safety and Health Administration; EPA: Environmental Protection Agency.

erling also suggests that the charts depend on downward adjustment of the agency's estimates of risk. Her own estimates result in Table 3, adjusted for inflation.

This table may be more accurate than Table 1; certainly there are problems with any approach that assumes a 10 percent discount rate. But even if Heinzerling's table is better, it offers an ironic lesson, serving largely to confirm the point that current regulatory policy suffers from poor priority setting. The disparities here are not as dramatic, and they certainly do not establish pervasive overregulation; but they do support the view that resources are being misallocated.

Heinzerling does not, however, conclude that this revised table is the appropriate basis for evaluating regulatory policy. Her aim is not to come up with a better table from which to reassess government behavior. On the contrary, she takes her argument to be a basis for rejecting cost-benefit analysis altogether. This, then, is a lesson about "the perils of precision."[48] Heinzerling also suggests that it "would be better if we left the picture blurry, and declined to connect the dots between all the confusing and sometimes conflicting intuitions and evidence."[49] She is concerned that "some, probably many, people will be fooled into believing that numerical

[48] *Id.* at 2042.
[49] *Id.* at 2069.

estimates of risks, costs, and benefits are impartial reflections of factual reality, in which case the likely result of increased reliance on quantification
in setting regulatory policy will be that the side that best obscures the value
choices implicit in its numbers will prevail.''[50]

There is considerable truth here; but I think that Heinzerling's lesson is
greatly overdrawn. Truth first: If an agency says that the cost of regulation
is $100 million, and the benefit $70 million, we still know much less than
we should. It is important to know who bears these costs and, if possible,
with what consequences. Will wages be lower? Whose wages? Will prices
be higher? Of what products? A disaggregated picture of the benefits would
also be important; what does the $70 million figure represent? Consider, for
example, a recent table explaining that the costs of skin cancer, from health
effects of reducing tropospheric ozone, are between $290 million and $1.1
billion, with dollar subtotals for skin cancers and cataracts.[51] By itself, this
table is insufficiently informative to tell people what they need to know.

Heinzerling is therefore on firm ground if she means to suggest that the
dollar numbers cannot substitute for a fuller inquiry into what is at stake.
Any cost-benefit analysis should include more than the monetary values by,
for example, showing what the values are about, such as life-years saved
and illnesses averted (see the Appendix for illustrations). But her own table
suggests that the general conclusion—that cost-benefit analysis can illuminate inquiry—remains unassailable. If regulation ranges from tens of thousands of dollars to tens of millions of dollars per life saved, at least there
is a presumptive problem. One of the functions of cost-benefit balancing is
to help show where limited resources should go. A regulation of particulates is hard to evaluate without knowing, for example, the number of
deaths averted and the range of consequences for morbidity: How many
workdays will be saved that would otherwise be lost? How many hospital-
izations will be avoided? How many asthma attacks will be prevented?
It could even be useful to attempt to describe these effects in terms of
"quality-adjusted life-years,"[52] knowing that here, too, a good analyst will
go back and forth between bottom lines and the judgments that go into their
creation.

I suspect that there may be theoretical claims behind Heinzerling's skepticism about quantification. She may believe that many of the goods at stake

[50] *Id.* at 2068.

[51] See Lutter & Wolz, *supra* note 31, at 145. In fairness to the authors, it should be noted
that a previous table in their essay describes adverse health effects in quantitative terms by
listing the numbers of cases averted.

[52] See Richard H. Pildes & Cass R. Sunstein, Reinventing the Regulatory State, 62 U. Chi.
L. Rev. 1 (1995); American Trucking Ass'n v. EPA, 1999 WL 300618 (D.C. Cir. May 14,
1999).

in regulation (human and animal life and health, recreational and aesthetic opportunities) are not merely commodities, that people do not value these goods in the same way that they value cash, and that cost-benefit analysis, with its reductionism, is inconsistent with people's reflective judgments about the issues at stake. Arguments of this sort have been developed in some philosophical challenges to cost-benefit analysis.[53]

Such arguments are convincing if cost-benefit analysis is taken to suggest a controversial position in favor of the commensurability of all goods— if cost-benefit analysts are seen to insist that people value environmental amenities, or their own lives, in the same way that they value a bank account, or if cost-benefit analysis is taken as a metaphysical claim to the effect that all goods can be aligned along a single metric, or as if five lives saved is seen as the same, in some deep sense, as $20–$30 million saved. Part of what people express, in their daily lives, is a resistance to this form of commensurability; some goods are believed to have intrinsic as well as instrumental value.[54]

The existence of qualitative differences among goods fortifies the claim that any bottom line about costs and benefits should be supplemented with a more qualitative description of the variables involved. But cost-benefit analysis should not be seen as embodying a reductionist account of the good, and much less as a suggestion that everything is simply a commodity for human use. It is best taken as pragmatic instrument, agnostic on the deep issues and designed to assist people in making complex judgments where multiple goods are involved. To put it another way, cost-benefit analysis might be assessed pragmatically, or even politically, rather than metaphysically.

We should conclude that the final number may provide less information than the ingredients that went into it and that officials should present cost-benefit analysis in sufficiently full terms to enable people to have a concrete sense of the effects of regulation. This is an argument against some overambitious understandings of what cost-benefit balancing entails. But it is not an argument against cost-benefit balancing.

C. Rival Rationalities

The final objection to the discussion thus far is the most fundamental. On this view, cost-benefit analysis is not desirable as a check on ordinary intuitions, because those intuitions reflect a kind of rival rationality. Ordinary people have a complex understanding of what it is that they want to max-

---

[53] See Anderson, *supra* note 3.
[54] See *id.*

TABLE 4

AGGRAVATING AND MITIGATING FACTORS IN RISK JUDGMENTS

Risk Traits	Aggravating	Mitigating
Familiarity	New	Old
Personal control	Uncontrollable	Controllable
Voluntariness	Involuntary	Voluntary
Media attention	Heavy media coverage	Ignored by media
Equity	Unfairly distributed	Equitably distributed
Children	At special risk	Not at risk
Future generations	At risk	Not at risk
Reversibility	Irreversible	Reversible
Identifiability of victims	Known	Identifiable
Accompanying benefits	Clear	Invisible
Source	Human origin	Created by nature
Trust in relevant institutions	Low	High
Timing of adverse effects	Delayed	Immediate

imize. They do not simply tabulate lives saved; they ask questions as well about whether the relevant risk is controllable, voluntary, dreaded, equitably distributed, and potentially catastrophic. Consider Table 4.

Some people suggest that to the extent that ordinary people disagree with experts, they have a ''thicker'' or ''richer'' rationality and that democracy should respect their judgments.[55] On a more moderate view, government's task is to distinguish between lay judgments that are products of factual mistakes (produced, for example, by the availability heuristic) and lay judgments that are products of judgments of value (as in the view that voluntarily incurred risks deserve less attention than involuntarily incurred ones).[56] In any case the ''psychometric paradigm'' is designed show how ordinary people's judgments are responsive to an array of factors other than lives saved.[57]

One problem with this view is that it may not be a criticism of cost-benefit analysis at all; it may suggest only that any judgment about benefits and costs (whether or not based on willingness to pay) will have to take account of people's divergent assessments of divergent risks. In principle, there is no problem with doing exactly that. There is, however, reason to question the now-conventional view that qualitative factors of this kind in

[55] See Paul Slovic, Baruch Fischhoff, & Sarah Lichtenstein, Regulation of Risk: A Psychological Perspective, in Regulatory Policy and the Social Sciences 241 (Roger G. Noll ed. 1985).

[56] See Richard H. Pildes & Cass R. Sunstein, Reinventing the Regulatory State, 62 U. Chi. L. Rev. 1 (1995).

[57] See Paul Slovic, Trust, Emotion, Sex, Politics and Science: Surveying the Risk Assessment Battlefield, 44 U. Chi. Legal F. 59 (1997).

fact explain people's disagreement with experts about certain risks of death. In fact, I do not believe that the psychometric paradigm can defend its own central claims. The first point is technical. In the relevant studies, the key factors—voluntariness, controllability, potentially catastrophic nature—have usually not been generated spontaneously or independently by subjects. Instead, those who conduct the relevant research ask people to rank risks along these dimensions. From this information it cannot be said that ordinary people think that these qualitative differences justify departing from the lives-saved criterion. The evidence is simply too indirect.

Now this does not mean that the rival rationalities view is wrong. There is independent evidence to suggest that people consider some deaths to be worse than others.[58] They are apparently willing to pay more, for example, to prevent a cancer death than to prevent an unforeseen instant death, and there is some evidence that voluntarily incurred risks receive less social concern than risks that are involuntarily incurred. Distributional judgments also appear to play some role in assessments about how to allocate scarce resources. But these points raise further questions.[59]

No doubt it is possible that people's judgments about risk severity are a product of some of the more qualitative considerations listed above; this idea leads to the widespread view that ordinary people have a richer rationality than do experts, since ordinary people look at the nature and causes of death, not simply at aggregate deaths at issue. But it is also possible that an apparently rich judgment that a certain risk is severe, or not severe, depends not on well-considered judgments of value, but instead on an absence of ordinary contextual cues, on a failure to see that trade-offs are inevitably being made, on heuristic devices that are not well adapted to the particular context, or instead on a range of confusing or confused ideas that people cannot fully articulate. When people say, for example, that the risk of nuclear power is very serious, they may be responding to their intense visceral concern, possibly based on (uninformed) statistical judgments about likely lives at risk and on their failure to see (as they do in other contexts) that the risk is accompanied by a range of social benefits. Thus it is possible that a judgment that a certain risk of death is unusually bad is not a rich qualitative assessment but an (unreliable) intuition based on a rapid balancing that prominently includes perceived lives at stake and the perceived presence of small or no benefits associated with the risk-producing activity.

Thus the question becomes whether citizen judgments that certain deaths

[58] Some of the data are collected in Cass R. Sunstein, Bad Deaths, 14 J. Risk & Uncertainty 259 (1997).

[59] I draw in the next several paragraphs from *id.*; Margolis, *supra* note 26, contains an excellent discussion of this point, from which I have learned a great deal.

are especially bad can survive a process of reflection. My conclusion is that understood in a certain way, the notions of dreaded deaths and unfairly distributed deaths are fully reasonable and deserve a role in policy. But the special concerns about deaths stemming from involuntarily run and uncontrollable risks raise serious doubts; as frequently invoked, they do not justify according additional concern to deaths that "code" as a product of involuntary or uncontrollable risks. At most, they suggest that government might spend more resources on deaths where the cost of risk avoidance is especially high and devote less attention to deaths where the cost of risk avoidance is especially low.[60]

1.   Dread

It is often said, on the basis of evidence like that outlined above, that especially dreaded deaths deserve special attention. Deaths from cancer and AIDS fall in this category. The underlying point is probably that the relevant deaths are especially grueling and hence there is a kind of "pain and suffering premium"—not merely a life lost, but an antecedent period of intense emotional and physical difficulty as well. This period of intense difficulty might impose costs on those with the illness and on friends and family members as well. Sudden, unanticipated deaths can be dreaded too—consider the extremely unpleasant idea of dying in an airplane crash. But the dread here stems from some factor (perhaps terror) different from and much shorter than the extended period of suffering that precedes some deaths. Thus it might be concluded that dreaded deaths deserve special attention in accordance with the degree of suffering that precedes them. A special problem with cancer deaths is that at least some of the time, people like to have upward-sloping utility. It is particularly bad to be in a situation in which things will constantly get worse.[61] With cancer deaths, the slope goes downward fairly consistently until the point of death.

2.   Voluntariness

People seem to perceive voluntarily incurred risks as less troublesome than involuntarily incurred risks. Consider diverse public reactions to airplane crashes and automobile crashes. Or consider the fact that tobacco is by far the largest source of preventable deaths in the United States. Why have we until recently not devoted much more of our regulatory effort to

---

[60] I borrow the next few pages from Sunstein, *supra* note 58.

[61] See George Loewenstein & Nachom Sicherman, Do Workers Prefer Increasing Wage Profiles? 9 J. Lab. Econ. 67, 71–75 (1991); George Loewenstein & Drazen Prelec, Negative–Time Preference, 81 Am. Econ. Rev. (Papers & Proc.) 347, 347 (1991).

reducing smoking? The reason seems to lie in a judgment that smoking is a voluntary activity, and hence the resulting deaths are less troublesome than other sorts of deaths. Here—it might be said—people have voluntarily assumed the relevant risks.

Puzzles: High Cost of Avoidance Rather than Involuntariness? A simple reference to voluntariness, if taken to suggest something special about "lay rationality," raises many puzzles. The most important problem is that it is not simple to know when a risk is voluntarily incurred. Voluntariness may be entirely absent in the case of an unforeseeable collision with an asteroid; but voluntariness is not, in the cases under consideration, an all-or-nothing matter. Instead, it is a matter of degree. Return to the conventional thought that airplane crashes are involuntary and automobile crashes more voluntary. Certainly it would be possible to see the risks from air travel as voluntarily run; people have a choice about whether to fly, and when they do fly, they pay a certain amount for a certain package, including risks of various sorts. The same is true of automobile safety—and it is not in any way less true, however disparate the two kinds of risks may seem. Perhaps people are responding to the perceived fact that they have no control over the pilot's behavior, whereas they have considerable control over automobile safety if they are themselves drivers. But airlines respond to market forces, including the market for safety, and many people injured in automobile accidents are not at fault. The difference between the two risks is hardly so categorical as to justify an assessment that they fall on poles of some voluntariness-involuntariness divide. Indeed, it is not clear even what is meant by the suggestion that one is voluntary and the other is not. Something else appears to underlie that suggestion.

Three Cases. To shed some light on the issue, let us consider three classes of cases. First, consider the question whether workers exposed to cancer risks are voluntarily or involuntarily so exposed. If workers do not know about such risks—if they lack relevant information—we seem to have an easy case of involuntariness. Thus it makes sense to say that risks are run involuntarily when the people running them do not know about them. Lack of adequate information provides a legitimate basis for a judgment of involuntary exposure to risk. But of course information itself can be obtained at some cost, pecuniary or otherwise. We are thus dealing, in cases of this kind, with high costs of risk avoidance, in the distinctive form of high costs of acquiring relevant information.

Second, suppose that people who are exposed to a certain risk are aware of the risk but are not in an actual or potential contractual relation with the risk producer. Many victims of pollution are in this position; recall that in surveys air pollution is a particular source of public concern. People in Los Angeles may well know that they face high levels of smog. Are they exposed involuntarily? If we conclude that they are, we may mean that a risk is incurred involuntarily in the sense that it is typically very expensive for people to avoid it—and when someone else can reduce the risks more cheaply. Here a claim that the risk is faced ''involuntarily'' may mean that those who run the risk can reduce it only at very high cost, at least compared to those who produce the risk. (The quotation marks are necessary for obvious Coasean reasons.) Or it is possible that we mean that on non-utilitarian grounds, the people exposed to the risk have a moral entitlement to be free from it, at least if they have not explicitly sold it.

But turn now to a third class of cases, involving a wage package or contract that does include compensation for the relevant risks. Assuming that point, we might want to distinguish between two different possibilities. In a case of a high-level scientist, knowledgeable about relevant risks and involved in work that he finds rewarding, people may well conclude that we have an instance of voluntariness. (In the same category can be found the case of an astronaut.) But people might not say the same about a low-level worker who does not like his work at all.[62] What distinguishes the two cases? If knowledge is present, or if the compensation package includes payment for the relevant risk, it is not clear how the two differ. The underlying judgment must be that the compensation is inadequate, perhaps because background inequality has produced a wage package that seems unfair even if voluntarily chosen by the parties.

From this discussion it seems reasonable to speculate that any judgment that a risk is run ''involuntarily'' is probably based on (1) a lack of knowledge of the risk or, more accurately, high costs of obtaining information about the risk; (2) a belief that, information to one side, it would be very costly for people to avoid the risk; or (3) a belief that the risk is unaccompanied by compensating benefits, notwithstanding their belief that the contract is in some sense worth signing. It may seem hard to make sense of point 3; what might be at work is a judgment that background inequalities are producing the relevant bargain (not by itself a good reason to disrupt the deal), or perhaps a belief that workers are competing to their collective detriment, and an agreement not to compete would be in their best interests. On this view, the question whether a risk is run voluntarily or not is often not a categorical one but instead a question of degree, associated with information cost, risk-reduction cost, and the existence or not of accompanying benefits. Of course there are interesting background questions about why and when a risk codes as voluntary or involuntary; undoubtedly the answer depends a great deal on heuristic devices and selective attention.

---

[62] Compare Anderson, *supra* note 3.

The Purpose for Which the Risk Is Incurred and Problems of Responsibility and Blame.   Death risks may seem voluntarily run when people do not approve of the purpose for which people run the relevant risks, and involuntarily run when people think that the purpose for which the risk is run is laudable. It is predictable that people will not want to pour enormous taxpayer resources into lowering the risks associated with skydiving, even if the dollars/life-years saved ratio is quite good. By contrast, it is doubtful that people think that it is wrong to spend enormous resources on the prevention of death from childbirth or being a police officer, even though the decision to have a child is (with appropriate qualifications) voluntary, and so too with the decision to become a police officer. People may think that when the appeal or purpose of the activity is associated with its very riskiness, resources should not be devoted to risk reduction. At least this is plausible when the risk is an independent good or part of the benefit of the activity. And it is easy to imagine a belief that some activities—unsafe sex, cigarette smoking—are like the skydiving case, perhaps because the risk is sometimes part of the benefit, perhaps because the risks are not incurred for a purpose that observers find worthy or valuable.

It might seem that this consideration—the purpose for which the risk is incurred—overlaps with or is even identical to the question whether there are high costs of risk avoidance. When the costs are low, as in skydiving, the purpose might seem inadequate. But on reflection the two ideas are hardly the same. It may well be that failing to sky dive, or skydiving with some safety-increasing technology, imposes high costs on sky divers. There seems to be an objective judgment, not necessarily connected with subjective costs, in the claim that some risks are voluntary, or deserve less attention, because they are run for inadequate purposes.

Relatedly, airplane accidents may seem different from automobile accidents not because the former are less voluntary, and not because of diverse costs of risk avoidance, but because the victims of airplane accidents are less blameworthy than the victims of automobile accidents, in the sense that the death is not a product of their own negligence or misconduct. In the case of an airplane disaster, weather conditions, mechanical failure, or pilot error are likely causes; in the case of an automobile accident, it is more likely (though not of course certain) that the victim could have avoided death through more careful driving. The point is crude, since many victims of automobile accidents are not drivers and many drivers in accidents do not behave negligently. But the perceived difference, in a significant number of cases, may underlie an apparent judgment of voluntariness that is really a judgment about responsibility and blameworthiness. In any case judgments are likely to be affected, and distorted, by the fact that drivers seem to be risk optimists—with 90 percent ranking themselves as safer than the average driver and less likely to be involved in an accident.[63] This is another place—illusions of control and risk optimism—where cognitive psychology argues in favor of cost-benefit analysis.

Underlying Questions and Assumption of Risk. We might therefore conclude that whether a risk qualifies as involuntary raises many of the questions raised by the question whether government should regulate the market at all. A risk might be characterized as involuntarily run because affected people lack relevant information, because the transactions costs of bargaining are high, because the risks should be seen to amount to externalities, because collective action problems make market outcomes unsatisfactory since (for example) workers are in a Prisoner's Dilemma best solved through law, or because some motivational or cognitive defect makes successful solutions through markets unlikely. These of course are among the conventional grounds for regulation in the first instance. When a risk seems voluntary, and not worthy of substantial regulatory resources, the term "voluntary" is serving as a placeholder for an argument that there is no sufficient ground for government action, because the accompanying benefits are high or the risk-reduction costs are low, and because market arrangements take adequate account of these facts.

Should voluntarily run risks of death receive no public attention, on the ground that the relevant people have already received compensation? We might imagine a death risk to be incurred voluntarily when an informed person decides to incur it in light of its costs and benefits. Suppose, for example, that someone purchases a small car with fewer safety features, or decides to become a boxer, an astronaut, or a police officer in a dangerous neighborhood. If a death results from such a choice, it might seem that the chooser has no legitimate ground for complaint; there has been ex ante compensation for the risk. But even in such cases, it is not clear that government lacks a role. If government can reduce a serious risk at low cost, and thus eliminate deaths, it should do so even if there was ex ante compensation for the relevant risk. There is a general point here. Sometimes observers confuse two quite different questions: (1) Should people be banned from running a certain risk, when they have run that risk voluntarily? (2) Should government attempt to reduce a certain risk, when people have run that risk voluntarily? A negative answer to question 1 does not answer question 2.

From this point we should conclude that a lay judgment that a risk is "voluntary" should not be decisive. A better understanding of what factors underlie and support that judgment should be used in regulatory policy.

---

[63] See Shelley E. Taylor, Positive Illusions: Creative Self-Deception and the Healthy Mind 10 (1994).

3.   Ripple Effects

The psychological evidence suggests, though it does not fully elaborate, an important and relevant fact: Some deaths produce unusually high externalities, in the sense that they generate widespread losses, including those stemming from empathy and fear, in a way that leads to predictable pecuniary and nonpecuniary costs. Consider, for example, the death of the president of the United States, a death that imposes a wide range of costs and that taxpayers invest significant resources to prevent. Part of the reason for allocating those resources is undoubtedly the greater risk that the president will be murdered; but the external costs associated with his death are undoubtedly important too. A parallel can be found in the relatively large level of resources devoted to prevent the assassination of many important public officials. But the point is hardly limited to the highest public officials. An airplane hijacking or crash, partly because it is likely to be well publicized, may produce large externalities in the form of empathy and fear. It may even deter air travel by making people unusually frightened of airplanes, simply because of heuristic devices (availability) and other predictable factors that make people's probability assessments go awry. This fear may be damaging because it is itself a utility loss and because it may lead people to use less safe methods of transportation, such as automobiles. Or an airplane crash might be especially disturbing because the sudden loss of dozens or hundreds of people seems so unusually and senselessly tragic, in a way that produces large empathetic reactions, or because it signals the further possibility of random, apparently inexplicable events in which large numbers of people die.

Special public concern about catastrophic events may reflect a judgment that certain kinds of deaths have ancillary effects, well beyond the deaths themselves. Consider in this regard the "Buffalo Creek Syndrome," documented several times in the aftermath of major disasters. Nearly 2 years after the collapse of a dam that left 120 dead and 4,000 homeless, psychiatric researchers continued to find significant psychological and sociological changes; survivors were characterized by a loss of direction and energy, other disabling character changes, and a loss of communality.[64] One evaluator attributed this loss of direction specifically to "the loss of traditional bonds of kinship and neighborliness."[65]

These various points raise a number of questions. We do not yet have a

---

[64] Daniel J. Fiorino, Technical and Democratic Values in Risk Analysis, 9 Risk Analysis 293 (1989).

[65] Id. at 295. See also J. D. Robinson, M. D. Higgins, & P. K. Bolyard, Assessing Environmental Impacts on Health: A Role for Behavioral Science, 4 Envtl. Impact Assessment Rev. 41 (1983).

full understanding of the basis for special public concern with catastrophes. Moreover, the argument for devoting special resources to deaths with externalities is strongest when the externalities do not reflect irrationality or cannot be reduced through other means. For example, some of the fear that follows certain widely reported deaths is based on confusion or ignorance about actual probabilities; if it is possible to dispel the confusion, the fear should dissipate as well. Here the question is whether government can legitimately spend extra resources to avert the harms associated with irrational public attitudes. Perhaps information-based strategies would be preferable to allocating additional resources to deaths whose occurrence produces widespread panic. On the other hand, there are undoubtedly instances in which information is ineffective, and there are also cases in which high externalities, in the form of special fear, are not a product of factual ignorance. In such cases government is justified in giving additional resources to death prevention.

4.   Inequitable Distribution

Some risks might be, or be thought to be, inequitably distributed, above all because the victims are disproportionately members of socially disadvantaged groups. Certain deaths might, for example, be concentrated among poor people, African-Americans, or homosexuals. Consider the risk of lead paint poisoning suffered by inner-city children, or the risk of AIDS, faced disproportionately by African-Americans as well as homosexuals. Citizens or elected representatives may think that inequitably distributed risks of death deserve special attention from government.

When such social concern exists, and when it is not objectionable on constitutional or other grounds, it is entirely legitimate for officials to respond.[66] Thus regulators should be permitted to use a uniform number per life or life-years saved; this is itself a (modest) redistributive strategy, because wealthy people (simply because they are wealthy) are willing to pay more to reduce risks than nonwealthy people. Regulators might also be permitted to give distributional weights to risks whose distributional incidence is especially troublesome.[67] These weights might take a technical form (through adding numbers to the ones that would otherwise be used) or appear via the official judgment about how to proceed after the cost-benefit

---

[66] It is inadequate to respond that potential compensation could be made to losers in the context of efficient programs; if the compensation is only potential, the concern remains.

[67] See the critical comments about willingness to pay in Sen, The Discipline of Cost-Benefit Analysis, *supra* note 5, and in Adler & Posner, Implementing Cost-Benefit Analysis, *supra* note 5.

analysis has been supplied (through deciding in favor of a strategy not strictly suggested by the numbers). The distributional concern supports special efforts to control AIDS; environmental risks like asthma, which are concentrated among inner-city children; and perhaps the spread of diseases whose incidence is concentrated among women. My minimal claim is that if there is a public judgment in favor of according a distributional weight to a certain death-reduction policy, and if that judgment is not unconstitutional or otherwise illegitimate, policy makers should not be barred from respecting that judgment.

5. No Rival Rationality

I conclude that there is no rival rationality and that people are willing to depart from the lives-saved criterion for reasons that cast a clearer light on what it is that they are attempting to maximize. More particularly, I suggest the following:

People Are Willing to Pay a Premium to Avoid Deaths That Involve a High Degree of Pain and Suffering. At least presumptively, this desire, or judgment, should be respected by government regulators; the presumption might be rebutted if, for example, the premium seems so high as to suggest that some kind of irrationality is at work.

People Are Willing to Devote More Resources to Protect Children. This judgment may depend on a belief that children are typically more vulnerable to risk, in the sense that they cannot protect themselves, or on a belief that more life-years are at stake when children are in jeopardy. In either case, this judgment too deserves respect.

People Are Willing to Pay a Premium to Avert Catastrophes. This may depend on a belief that catastrophes have ripple effects that outrun lives actually lost. A plane crash killing 100 people may be worse than 100 deaths from poor diet, if the consequence of the former is to create pervasive fear and anxiety. A shooting in a high school may warrant special attention, keeping lives saved constant, if only in order to ensure that students and parents are not constantly fearful about the safety of schools. These ripple effects qualify as social costs and at first glance seem to deserve special attention. The major qualification is that it may be possible to address them directly, rather than to cater (pander?) to them. Suppose, for example, that education can assure the public that flying is generally quite safe. If information can accomplish this end, it is better to provide it than to engage in regulation that is costly and that has no purpose other than to reassure.

People Are Willing to Devote More Resources to Protect against Dangers When the Costs of Risk Avoidance Are High. Perhaps people do not have information about certain risks, and perhaps information is costly to obtain. Perhaps third parties are in danger, and perhaps it is costly for them to avoid the danger. This point may involve fairness; it may involve efficiency. It involves fairness if people believe that those who bear high costs from risk avoidance should not, in principle, have to bear those costs. If this is the underlying belief, then it may follow that those who can easily avoid the cost of some risk should, in principle, do exactly that. The point involves efficiency if the judgment is that the best means of reducing aggregate costs (public as well as private) is to regulate the entity that is imposing the relevant risk.

People May Believe That It Is Especially Important to Protect Vulnerable or Traditionally Disadvantaged Groups against Certain Risks. If, for example, AIDS is concentrated among African-Americans and homosexuals, there may be a special reason to devote resources to its prevention, even if quantitatively identical risks receive less attention.

These various points suggest that there is no rival rationality. The question is whether people believe that some dangers deserve more attention than (quantitatively identical) others and, if so, whether that belief can survive critical scrutiny. But these points also suggest that it is wrong to think that policy should follow the judgments of experts focused on the single question of "lives at stake."[68] This is not the social maximand for reflective citizens. Such citizens have a different view about what their government ought to be doing. That different view does not embody any exotic conception of rationality.

IV. AN INCOMPLETELY THEORIZED AGREEMENT ON COST-BENEFIT ANALYSIS?

A. *Problems with Aggregated Willingness to Pay*

Thus far I have suggested that cost-benefit analysis is a sensible approach to cognitive problems faced by ordinary people in the assessment of risk. I have also suggested that there is no democratic objection to using cost-benefit analysis as an ingredient in decisions, even a crucial ingredient, and that cost-benefit analysis can be understood in a way that responds to reasonable concerns about quantification and about the idea that the only thing to be maximized is total lives saved (or, somewhat better, life-years saved).

But none of this deals with the general question how cost-benefit analysis should be understood. In the least contentious formulation—the formula-

---

[68] This is the apparent recommendation in Margolis, *supra* note 26.

tion that I have used here—cost-benefit analysis is simply a form of open-ended consequentialism, an invitation to identify the advantages and disadvantages of regulation,[69] without saying anything about appropriate weights. The virtue of this formulation is that it is uncontentious; the vice is that it is vacuous. People can agree with it, but it does not mean anything. In its most contentious formulation, cost-benefit analysis depends on asking people how much they are willing to pay for various goods and making decisions depend on the resulting numbers.[70] Problems with this approach lie in a possible lack of private information, possible distributional unfairness (since willingness to pay depends on ability to pay), potential differences between private willingness to pay and public aspirations,[71] and collective action problems of various sorts that might draw into doubt the privately expressed amounts.[72] It will be worthwhile to spell out these points in a bit more detail.

Willingness to pay is a simple way to capture people's valuations, and for this reason it has practical advantages. Indeed, it is a good place to start, especially in the absence of anything better. But it also suffers from several problems. First, willingness to pay may be a product of cognitive and motivational distortions of various kinds. Willingness-to-pay judgments may be insufficiently informed or reflective with respect to both facts and values. For example, people may overstate the risks that receive disproportionate media attention. If this is so, it seems odd to base government policy on those judgments. It is also possible that people will be willing to pay little to avoid some bad X simply because they are used to it and their preferences have adapted accordingly.[73] Preferences based on lack of information or adaptation to deprivation are hardly a good basis for regulatory policy. They need not be taken as given and translated into law. In any case, private preferences may be a product of social norms over which individuals have little control, by which they live, but which they would like to change if they could. If people are willing to pay little to avoid some risk (for example, of smoking) because of prevailing norms that they would wish

---

[69] See Sen, The Discipline of Cost-Benefit Analysis, *supra* note 5; compare the notion of cost-benefit analysis as a decision procedure in Adler & Posner, Rethinking Cost-Benefit Analysis, *supra* note 5.

[70] See Richard A. Posner, Economic Analysis of Law (5th ed. 1998).

[71] See Daphna Lewinsohn-Zamir, Consumer Preferences, Citizen Preferences, and the Provision of Public Goods, 108 Yale L. J. 377 (1999); Sunstein, *supra* note 5, ch. 2.

[72] See Lewinsohn-Zamir, *supra* note 71; Amartya Sen, Environmental Evaluation and Social Choice: Contingent Valuation and the Market Analogy, 46 Japanese Econ. Rev. 23, 29 (1995).

[73] See Jon Elster, Sour Grapes: Studies in the Subversion of Rationality (1983).

changed, willingness to pay is unjustified as a basis for policy, since the norm could be changed through collective action.[74]

Second, willingness to pay is imperfectly correlated with utility; at best the first is a proxy for the second, and the two should not be confused in principle. Poor people are willing to pay less than wealthy people simply by virtue of being poor, and their willingness to pay for something (for example, a reduced mortality risk) is crudely connected with the utility that they would gain from it. In the face of disparities in wealth, willingness to pay should not be identified with expected utility or with the value actually placed on the good in question.[75]

Third, there is a purely distributive concern.[76] Because poor people have less money than wealthy people, they are willing to pay less for equivalent goods (such as reduced risks to life). The result of the use of willingness to pay would be to produce greater expenditures to protect wealthy people than poor people, a controversial result to say the least.[77]

Fourth, the willingness-to-pay criterion will produce losers as well as winners, and many of the losers will go uncompensated; it is scant comfort to say that they could be compensated with side payments or a system of optimal taxation. Hence an attempt to defend cost-benefit analysis by reference to the efficiency criterion, as measured by private willingness to pay, runs into great difficulties, at least unless steps are taken to ensure against distributional bias.[78]

Fifth, and finally, there may be differences between the choices people make as consumers and the choices that they make as citizens, and it is not clear that the former should be preferred. The context of citizenship may evoke other-regarding or altruistic values that are not reflected in private choices. This is partly because aggregating private willingness to pay can

[74] See Sunstein, *supra* note 5, ch. 2.

[75] This seems to me a mistake in Viscusi's illuminating discussion: Viscusi, Risk Equity, *supra* note 2.

[76] This is a standard point in economic discussions of cost-benefit analysis, though it is ignored in many discussions by economic analysts of law. See, for example, Richard W. Tresch, Public Finance: A Normative Theory 541 (1981): "In our opinion the distributive question is the single most important issue in all of cost-benefit analysis." Tresch discusses how distributional considerations might be incorporated. See also A. Allan Schmid, Benefit-Cost Analysis 157–90 (1989), with a discussion of distributive weights at 170–72.

[77] At least unless poor people are compensated for any losses via side payments.

[78] There are some complexities here. Of course markets are ordinarily based on willingness to pay, and poor people are willing to pay less for safety, simply because they have less. Poor people are willing to pay less, as a class and other things equal, for safer cars, safer neighborhoods, and so forth. The aggregated willingness-to-pay approach simply generalizes this phenomenon; there is nothing unusual about it. Thus a system that assigns uniform values to life embeds a kind of subsidy to people with relatively less resources or, more precisely, to people with less willingness to pay.

replicate various collective action problems faced in the private domain; people may be willing to pay more simply because they know that other people are contributing as well.[79] If this is so, it makes no sense to base policy on private willingness to pay, where the collective action problem arises.

In any case we might think that government policy should be based on the reasons given for one or another outcome, and the fact that people are willing to pay a lot or a little for some outcome tells us too little about whether good reasons exist. Before discussion, for example, people may be willing to pay a fair bit to discriminate on the basis of sex, and they may be willing to pay little to protect large populations of animals that are at risk. These judgments may change as a result of reason giving in the public domain. In other words, government is a place for exchanging reasons for one or another course or action. It is not simply a maximizing machine, taking private willingness to pay as the foundation, whatever the source or the grounds of prediscussion preferences.

A particular problem here is that people may not want to spend a great deal to protect (for example) environmental amenities because they seek to protect their (relative) financial position.[80] A regulatory program supported by all might maintain relative position, which may be what people care about. Current willingness-to-pay numbers do not take account of this possibility. We have an empirical speculation here, one that suggests that current numbers are far too low. Much further work remains to be done to test whether people would in fact be willing to spend more for safety, or for environmental amenities, if the result would be significant decreases in absolute income but the same relative income.

Nor would it be sensible to disregard the presence of tragic choices, as when cost-benefit analysis leads to a choice of course A over course B, but course A leads to uncompensated losers (a group whose members may suffer from serious illnesses and even death).[81] Perhaps it is possible, in such cases, to restructure social arrangements so as to reduce or eliminate the tragedy. But even if this is so, a cost-benefit analysis, of the sort to be described, can help inform a decision about what tragedy-reducing course to take and whether such a course is worthwhile at all.

[79] See Robert H. Frank, Choosing the Right Pond: Human Behavior and the Quest for Status (1985); Lewinsohn-Zamir, *supra* note 71; Sunstein, *supra* note 5.

[80] See Frank, *supra* note 79; Robert H. Frank & Cass R. Sunstein, Cost-Benefit Analysis and Relative Position, U. Chi. L. Rev. (in press, 2001).

[81] See Martha C. Nussbaum, The Fragility of Goodness: Luck and Ethics in Greek Tragedy and Philosophy (1983); Martha C. Nussbaum, The Costs of Tragedy: Some Moral Limits of Cost-Benefit Analysis, in this issue, at 1005.

B.   Incomplete Theorization: Cost-Benefit Analysis
as Political, Not Metaphysical

Often it is possible to resolve hard questions of law and policy without
resolving deeply contested issues about justice, democracy, or the appropriate aims of the state.[82] Often it is possible to obtain an incompletely theorized agreement on a social practice. In many areas of law and public policy, people can reach closure about what to do despite their disagreement
or uncertainty about why, exactly, they ought to do it. Thus people who
disagree about the purposes of the criminal law can agree that rape and
murder should be punished, and punished more severely than theft and tres-
pass. Thus people can support an Endangered Species Act amidst disagreement about whether the protection of endangered species is desirable for
theological reasons, or because of the rights of animals, plants, and species,
or because of the value of animals, plants, and species for human beings.
A great advantage of incompletely theorized agreements is that they allow
people of diverse views to live together on mutually advantageous terms.
An even greater advantage is that they allow people of diverse views to
show one another a high degree of both humility and mutual respect.

I believe that an incompletely theorized agreement is possible here. For
reasons just discussed, it would be difficult to obtain agreement on the view
(which seems to me implausible) that all questions of regulatory policy
should be resolved by asking how much people are willing to pay for various social goods.[83] But it should be possible for diverse people to agree on
presumptive floors and ceilings for regulatory expenditures. A great deal
can be done without confronting the hardest theoretical questions raised by
contentious specifications of cost-benefit analysis.

An obvious question here is, Who could join this incompletely theorized
agreement? Who would reject it? My principal claim is that the agreement
could be joined by a wide range of reasonable people, including utilitarians
and Kantians, perfectionist and political liberals, and those who accept and
those who doubt the idea that private willingness to pay is the appropriate
foundation for regulatory policy. There is room here for deliberative democrats who emphasize the need for government to reflect on private preferences, rather than simply to translate them into law.[84] A prime purpose of

---

[82] See Cass R. Sunstein, Legal Reasoning and Political Conflict (1996); Cass R. Sunstein,
One Case at a Time (1999).

[83] See Adler & Posner, Rethinking Cost-Benefit Analysis, *supra* note 5.

[84] Absolutists of various kinds might refuse to join an agreement on these principles. Perhaps their refusal would be most reasonable in the case of the Endangered Species Act, where
nothing said below explains why millions of dollars should be spent (at least in opportunity
costs) to save members of ecologically unimportant species. It would be possible, however,
to imagine a kind of ''meta'' cost-benefit analysis that would point in this direction, perhaps

the approach is to ensure more in the way of reflection; cost-benefit analysis, as understood here, is a guarantee of greater deliberation, not an obstacle to it. Nor is the approach rigid. Under the proposed approach, agencies have the authority to abandon the floors and ceilings if there is reason for them to do so. If, for example, agencies want to spend a great deal to protect African-American children from a risk disproportionately faced by them, they are entitled to do so, as long as they explain that this is what they are doing, and so long as what they are doing is reasonable.

C. Eight Propositions

Here, then, are eight propositions, offered in the hope that they might attract support from diverse theoretical standpoints. I do not attempt to defend them in detail here. The goal is to provide a starting point for the effort to anchor cost-benefit analysis in an incompletely theorized agreement about regulatory policies.

1. *Identify and Quantify.*   Agencies should identify the advantages and disadvantages of proposed courses of action and also attempt to quantify the relevant effects to the extent that this is possible. When quantification is not possible, agencies should discuss the relevant effects in qualitative terms and also specify a range of plausible outcomes—for example, annual savings of between 150 and 300 lives, or savings of between $100 million and $300 million, depending on the rate of technological change. The statement should include the full range of beneficial effects. The Regulatory Impact Statement involving the EPA's particulates and ozone regulation provides considerable help in this regard. (See the Appendix.) The problem of particulates and ozone regulation poses some serious difficulties to challengers to cost-benefit analysis (CBA); if the EPA is not to do a form of CBA, what is it to do, concretely?

2. *Provide Quantitative and Qualitative Descriptions.*   The quantitative description should supplement rather than displace a qualitative description of relevant effects. Both qualitative and quantitative descriptions should be provided. It is important to know the nature of the relevant effects—for example, lost workdays, cancers averted, respiratory problems averted. To the extent possible, the qualitative description should give a concrete sense of who is helped and who is hurt—for example, whether the beneficiaries are mostly or partly children, whether the regulation will lead to lost jobs, higher prices, more poverty, and so forth. Where the only possible informa-

---

on the ground that it greatly simplifies decision without imposing high costs overall. For the regulatory issues dealt with here, an absolutist approach seems hard to justify, not least because there are dangers to life and health on both sides of the equation.

tion is speculative, this should be noted, along with the most reasonable speculations.

3. *Convert Nonmonetary Values.*   Agencies should attempt to convert nonmonetary values (involving, for example, lives saved, health gains, and aesthetic values) into dollar equivalents. This is not because a statistical life and (say) $5 million are the same thing, but to promote coherence and uniformity and to ensure sensible priority setting. There is nothing magical or rigid about the dollar equivalents; the conversion is simply a pragmatic tool to guide analysis and to allow informed comparisons.

4. *Establish Presumptive Floors and Ceilings.*   Agencies entrusted with valuing life and health should be controlled, by statute or executive order, via presumptive floors and ceilings. For example, a statute might say that a statistical life will ordinarily be valued at no less than $2 million and no more than $10 million. Evidence of worker and consumer behavior, suggesting a valuation of between $5 million and $7 million per statistical life saved, is at least relevant here. The fact that the willingness-to-pay numbers are in this range is hardly decisive, but it is supplemented by the fact that similar numbers appear to represent the midpoint of agency practice. Thus both market and governmental measures point in the same basic direction.[85] The Office of Management and Budget should establish presumptive floors and ceilings for various regulatory benefits. If an agency is going to spend (say) no more than $500,000 per life saved, or more than $20 million, it should have to explain itself. Actual agency practice reveals a mixed record. The EPA now values a life at $4.8 million; some agencies go as high as $5.6 million or as low as $1 million; and some agencies do not provide specific numbers at all.

5. *Adjust Ceilings and Floors.*   Agencies should be permitted to adjust the ceilings and floors, or to choose a low or high end of the range, on the basis of a publicly articulated and reasonable judgment that such an adjustment or such a choice is desirable. Perhaps adjustments could be made if, for example, poor people are especially at risk. There should be no adjustments downward for poor people; in other words, the fact that poor people are willing to spend less to protect their own lives (because they are poor) should not call for correspondingly lower expenditures by government. The principal danger here is that well-organized groups will be able to use equitable arguments on behalf of their preferred adjustments. It is important to ensure a degree of discipline here, and perhaps the dangers of interest-group manipulation are serious enough to suggest that uniform numbers or ranges

---

[85] Note, however, that if relative position is what matters, these numbers may be too low, for reasons stated above. See Frank & Sunstein, *supra* note 80.

might be used or that the presumptions are strong and rebuttable only in the most compelling cases.[86]

6. *Adjust According to Qualitative Factors.* Agencies should be permitted to make adjustments on the basis of the various qualitative factors discussed above. For example, they might add a pain and suffering premium or increase the level of expenditure because children are disproportionately affected or because the victims are members of a disadvantaged group. It would be reasonable to conclude that because AIDS has disproportionate adverse effects on homosexuals and poor people, special efforts should be made to ensure against AIDS-related deaths. To the extent possible, agencies should be precise about the nature of, and grounds for, the relevant adjustments, especially in light of the risk that interest-group pressures will convert allegedly qualitative adjustments in illegitimate directions.[87]

7. *Respond to Social Fear.* The appropriate response to social fear not based on evidence, and to related ripple effects, is education and reassurance rather than increased regulation. Sometimes public concern about certain risks is general and intense, even though the concern is not merited by the facts.[88] The best response is educational; the government should not expend significant resources merely because an uninformed public believes that it should. But if education and reassurance fail, increased regulation may be defensible as a way of providing a kind of reassurance in the face of intense fears, which can themselves impose high costs of various kinds. Consider, for example, the possibility that people afraid of risks of plane crashes will shift to driving, a more risky method of transportation; consider also the fact that the fear is itself a cost.

8. *The Role of Courts.* Unless the statute requires otherwise, judicial review of risk regulation should require a general showing that regulation has produced more good than harm, on a reasonable view about valuation of both benefits and costs.[89] On this view, courts should generally require agencies to generate and to adhere to ceilings and floors. But they should also allow agencies to depart from conventional numbers (by, for example, valuing a life at less than $1 million or more than $10 million) if and only if the agency has given a reasonable explanation of why it has done so. The

---

[86] See Viscusi, Risk Equity, *supra* note 2.

[87] See *id.;* see also James T. Hamilton & W. Kip Viscusi, Calculating Risks? The Spatial and Political Dimensions of Hazardous Waste Policy (1999) (showing that allegedly equitable shifts are driven by political pressures not mapping onto any sensible conception of equity).

[88] See Kuran & Sunstein, *supra* note 20.

[89] See Margolis, *supra* note 26.

ultimate task would be develop a kind of common law of cost-benefit analysis, authorizing agencies to be law-making institutions in the first instance.[90]

V. Conclusion

I have suggested that cost-benefit analysis, often defended on economic grounds, can be urged less contentiously on cognitive grounds. Cost-benefit analysis, taken as an inquiry into the consequences of varying approaches to regulation,[91] is a sensible response not only to interest-group power but also to limited information and to predictable problems in the public demand for regulation. These problems include the use of the availability heuristic; social amplification of that heuristic via cascade effects; a failure to see the benefits that accompany certain risks; a misunderstanding of systemic effects, which can lead to unanticipated bad (and good) consequences; and certain emotional reactions to risks. In all of these areas, an effort to identify costs and benefits can properly inform analysis.

These points do not show how cost-benefit analysis should be specified. Here I have raised questions about the willingness-to-pay criterion and suggested that, at least in principle, it would be obtuse to attempt to assess regulatory proposals via a uniform number for lives saved; but I have also suggested that presumptive ranges, for life as well as other beneficial effects on health and other values, would be an excellent way to clarify and order regulatory policy, in a way that should lead to both greater consistency and more overall protection. If ordinary market behavior and ordinary government behavior point to a similar basic range (for example, $3 million to $7 million per life saved), that is an excellent place to start.

My ultimate hope is for a form of cost-benefit analysis that is a pragmatic instrument that ought not to be terribly contentious—a form of cost-benefit analysis that does not take a stand on highly controversial questions about what government ought to do and that promises to attract support from people with diverse conceptions of the right and the good. I have suggested here that the most promising source of such an agreement is not only or even mostly neoclassical economics, but also behavioral economics and cognitive psychology.

---

[90] This has started to happen in various areas. See the development of a common law of risk significance under the Occupational Safety and Health Administration, discussed in Cass R. Sunstein, Is the Clean Air Act Unconstitutional? 98 Mich. L. Rev. 303, 352–53 n.243 (1999).

[91] There is no alternative to regulation. What is sometimes described as deregulation, or a failure to regulate, is actually regulation via the common law.

APPENDIX

All tables are taken from Environmental Protection Agency, Innovative Strategies and Economics Group, Regulatory Impact Statement for Particulates and Ozone Regulation (1997).

TABLE A1

PROPOSED PM_{10} STANDARD (50/150 g/m^3) 99th PERCENTILE:
NATIONAL ANNUAL HEALTH INCIDENCE REDUCTIONS

Endpoint[a]	Partial Attainment Scenario
$PM_{2.5}$(g/cm^3):	
Annual	50
Daily	150
*1. Mortality:[b]	
Short-term exposure	360
Long-term exposure	340
*2. Chronic bronchitis	6,800
Hospital admissions:	
*3. All respiratory (all ages)	190
All respiratory (ages 65+)	470
Pneumonia (ages 65+)	170
COPD (ages 65+)	140
*4. Congestive heart failure	130
*5. Ischemic heart disease	140
*6. Acute bronchitis	1,100
*7. Lower respiratory symptoms	10,400
*8. Upper respiratory symptoms	5,300
Shortness of breath	18,300
Asthma attacks	8,800
*9. Work loss days	106,000
*10. Minor restricted activity days	879,000

NOTE.—Estimates are incremental to the current ozone and particulate matter (PM) National Ambient Air Quality Standards (year = 2010). Numbers may not completely agree because of rounding. COPD = chronic obstructive pulmonary disease.

[a] Only endpoints denoted with an asterisk are aggregated into total benefits estimates.

[b] Mortality estimates must be aggregated using either short-term exposure or long-term exposure but not both because of double-counting issues.

TABLE A2

OZONE: NATIONAL ANNUAL HEALTH INCIDENCE

	PARTIAL ATTAINMENT SCENARIO		
ENDPOINT[a]	.08 5th Maximum High-End Estimate	.08 4th Maximum Low- to High- End Estimates	.08 3rd Maximum High-End Estimate
Ozone health:			
*1. Mortality	80	0–80	120
Hospital admissions:			
*2. All respiratory (all ages)	280	300–300	420
All respiratory (ages 65+)	2,300	2,330–2,330	1,570
Pneumonia (ages 65+)	860	870–870	600
COPD (ages 65+)	260	260–260	200
Emergency department visits for asthma	120	130–130	180
*3. Acute respiratory symptoms (any of 19)	28,510	29,840–29,840	42,070
Asthma attacks	60	60–60	90
Minor restricted activity days	620	650–650	920
*4. Mortality from air toxics	1	1–1	2
Ancillary PM health:			
*1. Mortality:[b]			
Short-term exposure	60	0–80	110
Long-term exposure	180	0–250	340
*2. Chronic bronchitis	400	0–530	690
Hospital admissions:			
*3. All respiratory (all ages)	70	0–90	120
All respiratory (ages 65+)	50	0–60	80
Pneumonia (ages 65+)	20	0–20	30
COPD (ages 65+)	10	0–20	20
*4. Congestive heart failure	10	0–20	20
*5. Ischemic heart disease	10	0–20	20
*6. Acute bronchitis	290	0–400	530
*7. Lower respiratory symptoms	3,510	0–4,670	6,190
*8. Upper respiratory symptoms	320	0–430	570
Shortness of breath	800	0–1,220	1,660
Asthma attacks	4,210	0–5,510	7,200
*9. Work loss days	38,700	0–50,440	66,160
*10. Minor restricted activity days	322,460	0–420,300	551,300

NOTE.—Estimates are incremental to the current ozone National Ambient Air Quality Standards (year = 2010). COPD = chronic obstructive pulmonary disease.

[a] Only endpoints denoted with an asterisk are aggregated into total benefits estimates.

[b] Particulate matter (PM) mortality estimates must be aggregated using either short-term exposure or long-term exposure but not both because of double-counting issues.

TABLE A3

WILLINGNESS-TO-PAY (WTP) ESTIMATES (Mean Values)

Health Endpoint	Mean WTP Value per Incident (1990 $)
Mortality:	
Life saved	$4.8 million
Life-year extended	$120,000
Hospital admissions:	
All respiratory illnesses, all ages	$12,700
Pneumonia, age 65+	$13,400
COPD, age 65+	$15,900
Ischemic heart disease, age 65+	$20,600
Congestive heart failure, age 65+	$16,600
Emergency visits for asthma	$9,000
Chronic bronchitis	$260,000
Upper respiratory symptoms	$19
Lower respiratory symptoms	$12
Acute bronchitis	$45
Acute respiratory symptoms (any of 19)	$18
Asthma	$32
Shortness of breath	$5.30
Sinusitis and hay fever	Not monetized
Work loss days	$83
Restricted activity days:	
Minor	$38
Respiratory	Not monetized
Worker productivity	$1 per worker per 10% change in ozone
Visibility:	
Residential	$14 per unit decrease in deciview per household
Recreational	Range of $7.30–$11 per unit decrease in deciview per household
Household soiling damage	$2.50 per household per g/m^3

TABLE A4

PROPOSED PM$_{10}$ STANDARD (50/150 g/m^3) 99TH PERCENTILE:
NATIONAL ANNUAL MONETIZED HEALTH BENEFITS
INCIDENCE REDUCTIONS

Endpoint[a]	Partial Attainment Scenario High-End Estimate
PM$_{2.5}$(g/cm^3):	
Annual	50
Daily	150
*1. Mortality ($):[b]	
Short-term exposure	1.7
Long-term exposure	1.6
*2. Chronic bronchitis ($)	1.8
Hospital admissions ($)	
*3. All respiratory (all ages)	.002
All respiratory (ages 65+)	.006
Pneumonia (ages 65+)	.003
COPD (ages 65+)	.002
*4. Congestive heart failure	.002
*5. Ischemic heart disease	.003
*6. Acute bronchitis ($)	0
*7. Lower respiratory symptoms ($)	0
*8. Upper respiratory symptoms ($)	0
Shortness of breath	0
Asthma attacks	0
*9. Work loss days ($)	.009
*10. Minor restricted activity days ($)	.034
Total monetized benefits ($)	
Using long-term mortality	3.4
Using short-term mortality	3.5

NOTE.—Estimates are incremental to the current ozone (.12 ppm, 1 hour) (1990 $billions; year = 2010). Numbers may not completely agree because of rounding. COPD = chronic obstructive pulmonary disease.

[a] Only endpoints denoted with an asterisk are aggregated into total benefits estimates.

[b] Mortality estimates must be aggregated using either short-term exposure or long-term exposure but not both because of double-counting issues.

OZONE: NATIONAL ANNUAL MONETIZED HEALTH BENEFITS

ENDPOINT[a]	PARTIAL ATTAINMENT SCENARIO		
	.08 5th Maximum High-End Estimate	.08 4th Maximum Low- to High- End Estimates	.08 3rd Maximum High-End Estimate
Ozone health:			
*1. Mortality	.370	.000–380	.570
Hospital admissions:			
*2. All respiratory (all ages)	.004	.004–.004	.006
All respiratory (ages 65+)	.029	.029–.029	0
Pneumonia (ages 65+)	.014	.014–.014	.010
COPD (ages 65+)	.004	.004–.004	.003
Emergency department visits for asthma	.001	.001–.001	.002
*3. Acute respiratory symptoms (any of 19)	.001	.001–.001	.001
Asthma attacks	0	0–0	0
Minor restricted activity days	0	0–0	0
*4. Mortality from air toxics	.003	.006–.006	.011
Ancillary PM health:			
*1. Mortality:[b]			
Short-term exposure	.300	0–.400	.520
Long-term exposure	.870	0–1.210	1.640
*2. Chronic bronchitis	.110	0–.140	.180
Hospital admissions:			
*3. All respiratory (all ages)	.001	0–.001	.001
All respiratory (ages 65+)	.001	0–.001	.001
Pneumonia (ages 65+)	0	0–0	0
COPD (ages 65+)	0	0–0	0
*4. Congestive heart failure	0	0–0	0
*5. Ischemic heart disease	0	0–0	0
*6. Acute bronchitis	0	0–0	0
*7. Lower respiratory symptoms	0	0–0	0
*8. Upper respiratory symptoms	0	0–0	0
Shortness of breath	0	0–0	0
Asthma attacks	0	0–0	0
*9. Work loss days	.003	0–.004	.005
*10. Minor restricted activity days	.012	0–.016	.020
Total monetized benefits:			
Using short-term PM mortality	.790	.056	1.300
Using long-term PM mortality	1.400	1.785	2.400

NOTE.—Estimates are incremental to the current ozone NAAQS (.12 ppm, 1 hour) (1990 $billions; year = 2010).

[a] Only endpoints denoted with an asterisk are aggregated into total benefits estimates.

[b] Particulate matter (PM) mortality estimates must be aggregated using either short-term exposure or long-term exposure but not both because of double-counting issues.

TABLE A6

OZONE: SUMMARY OF NATIONAL ANNUAL MONETIZED HEALTH AND WELFARE BENEFITS

CATEGORY	PARTIAL ATTAINMENT SCENARIO		
	.08 5th Maximum High-End Estimate	.08 4th Maximum Low- to High-End Estimates	.08 3rd Maximum High-End Estimate
Health benefits	1.4	.06–1.76	2.4
Welfare benefits	.25	.32–.32	.5
Total monetized benefits	1.6	.4–2.1	2.9

NOTE.—Estimates are incremental to the current ozone and particulate matter National Ambient Air Quality Standards (1990 $billions; year = 2010).

TABLE A7

COMPARISON OF ANNUAL BENEFITS AND COSTS OF PM ALTERNATIVES IN 2010

PM$_{2.5}$ Alternative (g/m^3)	Annual Benefits of Partial Attainment[a] (1990 $Billions) (A)	Annual Costs of Partial Attainment (1990 $Billions) (B)	Net Benefits of Partial Attainment (1990 $Billions) (A − B)	Number of Residual Non-attainment Counties
16/65 (high-end estimate)	90	5.5	85	19
16/65 (low-end estimate to high-end estimate)	19–104	8.6	10–95	30
15/50 (high-end estimate)	108	9.4	98	41

NOTE.—All estimates are measured incremental to partial attainment of the current PM$_{10}$ standard (PM$_{10}$ 50/150, 1 expected exceedance per year). The results for 16/65 and 15/50 are only for the high-end assumptions range. The low-end estimates were not calculated for these alternatives.

[a] Partial attainment benefits based on postcontrol air quality as defined in the control cost analysis.

COMPARISON OF ANNUAL BENEFITS AND COSTS OF OZONE ALTERNATIVES IN 2010

Ozone Alternative (ppm)	Annual Benefits of Partial Attainment (1990 $Billions)[a] (A)	Annual Costs of Partial Attainment (1990 $Billions) (B)	Net Benefits of Partial Attainment (1990 $Billions) (A − B)	Number of Residual Non-attainment Areas
.08 5th Maximum (high-end estimate)	1.6	.9	.7	12
.08 4th Maximum (low-end estimate to high-end estimate)	.4–2.1	1.1	(.7)–1.0	17
.08 3rd Maximum (high-end estimate)	2.9	1.4	1.5	27

NOTE.—All estimates are measured incremental to partial attainment of the baseline current ozone standard (.12 ppm, 1 expected exceedance per year). The results for .08, 5th maximum and .08, 3rd maximum are only for the high-end assumptions. The low-end estimates were not calculated for these alternatives.

[a] Partial attainment benefits based on postcontrol air quality estimates as defined in the control cost analysis.

IMPLEMENTING COST-BENEFIT ANALYSIS WHEN PREFERENCES ARE DISTORTED

MATTHEW D. ADLER and ERIC A. POSNER*

Abstract

Cost-benefit analysis is routinely used by government agencies in order to evaluate projects, but it remains controversial among academics. This paper argues that cost-benefit analysis is best understood as a welfarist decision procedure and that use of cost-benefit analysis is more likely to maximize overall well-being than is use of alternative decision procedures. The paper focuses on the problem of distorted preferences. A person's preferences are distorted when his or her satisfaction does not enhance that person's well-being. Preferences typically thought to be distorted in this sense include disinterested preferences, uninformed preferences, adaptive preferences, and objectively bad preferences; further, preferences may be a poor guide to maximizing aggregate well-being when wealth is unequally distributed. The paper describes conditions under which agencies should correct for distorted preferences, for example, by constructing informed or nonadaptive preferences, discounting objectively bad preferences, and treating people differentially on the basis of wealth.

COST-BENEFIT analysis (CBA) is widely and increasingly used by government agencies, yet academic debate about CBA is in disarray. Defenders of CBA traditionally conceptualize it as a technique for implementing either Pareto efficiency or Kaldor-Hicks efficiency, two criteria that many welfare economists take to be normatively basic. They also traditionally define Pareto efficiency, Kaldor-Hicks efficiency, and CBA in terms of a person's actual, as opposed to informed or otherwise undistorted, preferences. A project is (1) Pareto efficient relative to the status quo if at least one person actually prefers it to the status quo and no one prefers the status quo or (2) Kaldor-Hicks efficient relative to the status quo if there is a hypothetical

* University of Pennsylvania Law School and University of Chicago Law School, respectively. We thank Andrei Marmor, Cass Sunstein, Adrian Vermeule, and participants at this conference and at workshops at the University of Southern California and the University of Toronto, for helpful comments, and Kate Kraus and Bruce McKee for valuable research assistance. Posner also gratefully acknowledges the financial support of the John M. Olin Fund, the Sarah Scaife Foundation Fund, and the Ameritech Fund in Law and Economics.

[*Journal of Legal Studies*, vol. XXIX]

costless redistribution from those who prefer the project to those who do not that would make the project Pareto efficient. A project is a CBA improvement over the status quo if the sum of compensating variations for the project is a positive number, where P's compensating variation (CV) for a project is the dollar amount paid to or from him in the project world such that, given P's actual preferences, he is indifferent between that world and the status quo. The academic critics of CBA argue that actual preferences are a poor basis for governmental policy. They further argue that the link between CBA and Pareto efficiency is tenuous and that the link between CBA and Kaldor-Hicks efficiency, although tighter, does not justify CBA, because Kaldor-Hicks itself lacks normative significance.

The critics are right, up to a point. The traditional defense of CBA is a failure. Where the critics go wrong is in thinking that this is a failure of CBA, rather than merely of a particular argument in its favor. As we have elsewhere tried to show, CBA is properly conceptualized as a welfarist decision procedure. The proper link is to the normative criterion of overall well-being, rather than to Pareto efficiency or Kaldor-Hicks efficiency, where overall well-being refers to the satisfaction of certain restricted preferences, rather than all actual preferences. (We will discuss the restrictions below.) By overall well-being we mean to include the large family of welfarist (but not necessarily utilitarian) moral and political theories, that is, those that hold that a policy's effect on people's welfare is a morally relevant, though not necessarily conclusive, consideration. The link between CBA and overall well-being is rough, not perfect: sometimes a project will be picked out by CBA as an improvement over the status quo and yet, in fact, be welfare inferior to the status quo. But CBA is sufficiently accurate in tracking overall well-being and has sufficient other procedural virtues— it is relatively cheap to implement, relatively easy to monitor by oversight bodies, and relatively undemanding of agency expertise—that it is plausibly the welfare-maximizing procedure for agencies to employ, in a significant fraction of their choice situations, compared to available alternative procedures.

The problem with the traditional definition of CBA in terms of actual preferences is that satisfaction of actual preference and maximization of well-being are not equivalent. But we think that the failure of the actual-preference view of well-being need not undermine CBA. In the course of defending this position, we will use the following vocabulary. Cost-benefit analysis can be redefined as the sum of welfare equivalents (WEs) rather than the sum of CVs, where P's WE is the amount of money such that— paid to or from him in the project world—he is just as well-off as in the status quo, on the correct theory of well-being. Thus defined, CBA is agnostic across theories of well-being and, in particular, is not committed to the view that welfare and actual-preference satisfaction are equivalent. Because of this, when we discuss WEs, we will often not have a fixed number or formula in mind; the concept of WE (unlike the concepts of CV and equivalent variation, for example) is used as a placeholder to describe what dollar amount would be necessary under a given theory, or cluster of theories, of well-being. Nonetheless, even without making strong assumptions about the right theory of well-being, we will be able to derive some restrictions on how WEs are determined.

The concept of WE is necessary because the actual-preference theory of CBA must be abandoned. Actual preferences are not necessarily constitutive of welfare because they can be distorted, in various ways. For example, P may prefer the project to the status quo because he is uninformed; with fuller information, he would prefer the status quo. Or P's preference for the project may not track relevant criteria of objective value. The project harms innocent children; P, who is a sadist, prefers the project just because it does that, and he retains this despicable preference under full information. In these kinds of cases, traditional CBA equates the welfare impact of the project upon P to his CV, which is a positive number. Yet most people would agree that the ignorant or sadistic P, who prefers the project only in virtue of his ignorance or his sadism, should not be counted as a project beneficiary, who helps tip the cost-benefit scale in the project's favor. But how should the project's welfare impact upon P be calculated? At first glance, the correct agency response to the problem of distorted preferences seems to be to ask what P would hypothetically be willing to pay or accept if his preferences were relevantly undistorted (well-informed, nonsadistic) and use that number rather than P's CV in the cost-benefit calculus. The problem here is that P continues to have his actual preferences, not his hypothetical preferences, and his actual preferences—on the right theory of well-being—may have a significant effect on his welfare. If P remains ignorant and continues to prefer the project to the status quo, then the fact that he would (under full information) have a valuation of, say, −$100 for the project hardly means that the actual welfare effect of the project is −$100, and similarly for the sadistic P.

So agencies face a dilemma. On the one hand, CVs defined in terms of actual preferences deviate from welfare, when such preferences are distorted. On the other hand, hypothetical valuations in light of undistorted preferences may not capture the real welfare impact of projects either. This article takes a stab at solving that dilemma. The glib answer is that agencies should aggregate WEs, not CVs or hypothetical CVs. But this glib answer is really just a promissory note, because it remains to be seen how actual and undistorted preferences interact, for various kinds of distortions, to produce WEs. A further problem, which also needs to be confronted, is that the sum of WEs can deviate substantially from overall well-being because the marginal utility of dollars depends upon the wealth of the person affected. (This is a well-known problem for conventional CBA based on CVs; the use of WEs does not by itself solve this problem.) The glib response here is that WEs should be weighted by a factor inversely proportional to wealth. As we discuss in more detail below, that response overlooks the point that rich and poor people behave in accordance with their actual wealth, not their hypothetical wealth.

Section I of the article lays out, in compressed form, our view of CBA as a welfarist decision procedure and further clarifies the idea of a WE.[1] Section II surveys agency practice and demonstrates that agencies performing cost-benefit analysis do, in fact, adjust valuations to correct for various kinds of preference distortions. Section III analyzes how agencies should adjust valuations to correct for preference distortions. We focus upon the five most important scenarios in which traditional CBA (the sum of unweighted CVs) and overall well-being may diverge: disinterestedness, poor information, adaptation to circumstances, objectively bad preferences, and wealth effects. For the first four scenarios, we discuss in detail how WEs can diverge from CVs and how WEs should be calculated; for the last scenario, wealth effects, we analyze various subtle problems associated with the form of CBA that weights WEs or CVs to reflect the declining marginal utility of income. Section IV addresses some institutional issues. Section V summarizes our views and presents concrete recommendations as to when agencies should depart from traditional CBA.

I. COST-BENEFIT ANALYSIS: THE TRADITIONAL DEFENSES, AND A NEW ONE

Cost-benefit analysis is traditionally linked to the familiar economic criteria of Pareto efficiency or Kaldor-Hicks efficiency. A project is Pareto efficient, relative to the status quo, if no one loses from the project and at least one person gains. A project is Kaldor-Hicks efficient, relative to the status quo, if there is a hypothetical costless lump-sum redistribution in the project world, from winners to losers, such that this amended project world is Pareto efficient relative to the status quo.[2] The concepts of welfare loss

---

[1] Section I is based on Matthew D. Adler & Eric A. Posner, Rethinking Cost-Benefit Analysis, 109 Yale L. J. 167 (1999), which contains further details and citations to the literature.

[2] Technically, there is a difference between Kaldor efficiency, Hicks efficiency, and Kaldor-Hicks efficiency. A project is (1) Kaldor efficient relative to the status quo if there is a hypothetical lump-sum redistribution in the project world, from project winners to project losers, such that this amended project world is Pareto efficient relative to the status quo; (2) Hicks efficient relative to the status quo if there is no hypothetical lump-sum redistribution in the status quo world, from project losers to project winners, such that this amended status quo world is Pareto efficient relative to the project; and (3) Kaldor-Hicks efficient if

and gain, as referenced by these criteria, are standardly cashed out in terms of preference satisfaction. P gains from a project, and loses from the status quo, if and only if he prefers the project. There are real difficulties in the equation of preference satisfaction and welfare, which we shall discuss in a moment. But even apart from such difficulties, the putative link between CBA and economic efficiency—either in the Pareto sense or in the Kaldor-Hicks sense—is one that needs to be broken.

Pareto efficiency has genuine normative import. An agency does the right thing, everything else equal, by approving a Pareto-efficient project. But the connection between CBA and Pareto efficiency is elusive. An individual project will be chosen by CBA over the status quo even though the project is not Pareto efficient relative to the status quo, as long as the aggregate CVs of those who gain from the project exceed the aggregate CVs of those who lose. The very idea behind CBA is to commensurate winners' gains and losers' losses, such that the project can be identified as better or worse even though neither option is Pareto efficient relative to the other. Nor can CBA be justified in light of Pareto efficiency by claiming (1) that project winnings will be redistributed through the tax system to project losers, since agencies employ CBA in many scenarios where no such redistribution will take place; (2) that a general policy of CBA is Pareto efficient for all affected, since agencies regularly employ CBA to impose losses sufficiently grave (for example, death or injury) that the persons thus affected would be better off in a world with no such policy;[3] and (3) that persons would choose a general policy of CBA if they were choosing ex ante and under conditions of uncertainty, since there are good arguments that persons in such circumstances would choose a different policy.[4]

As for Kaldor-Hicks efficiency, that criterion lacks genuine normative import. The fact that the project winners could compensate the project losers entails nothing of normative significance about the project. A project can be a Kaldor-Hicks improvement, relative to the status quo, without increasing overall well-being—for example, if the project produces a large

---

the project is Kaldor efficient and Hicks efficient. (The last criterion is also called the Scitovsky criterion.) For purposes of exposition, we adopt a simpler definition of Kaldor-Hicks efficiency in the text and focus upon what is, technically, Kaldor efficiency. Our arguments readily carry over to Hicks efficiency and to Kaldor-Hicks efficiency in the technical sense; none of the three criteria has genuine normative import.

[3] Note further that, because CBA inflates the welfare effect of projects on rich persons and deflates the welfare effect on poor persons, poor persons might also be better off in a world without the practice of CBA.

[4] John Harsanyi famously argued that persons choosing ex ante and under conditions of uncertainty would choose a policy of welfare maximization. See John C. Harsanyi, Morality and the Theory of Rational Behavior, in Utilitarianism and Beyond 39 (Amartya Sen & Bernard Williams eds. 1982). But welfare maximization is different from CBA.

increase I in the resource endowment of richer persons and a smaller decrease D in the resource endowment of poorer persons, such that $I > D$ (making the project Kaldor-Hicks efficient), but the welfare impact of I is less than the welfare impact of D. Nor should Kaldor-Hicks be thought to have normative significance apart from welfare maximization. For example, any normative link to the powerful notion of consent is vitiated by the crucial point that it is hypothetical winner-to-loser compensation, not actual winner-to-loser compensation, that makes a project Kaldor-Hicks efficient. The fact that the losers would or should consent to the efficient project, if the redistribution from winners to losers were performed, does not mean that the losers do or should consent to the project where no such redistribution actually takes place.

In short, the fact that a project with a positive total sum of CVs, relative to the status quo, is Kaldor-Hicks efficient relative to the status quo does not explain why the agency ought to choose the project. Further, it turns out that—for technical reasons—a project can have a positive, total sum of CVs relative to the status quo and not be Kaldor-Hicks efficient.[5]

Cost-benefit analysis needs to be reconceptualized. The way to do so is twofold. First, CBA itself must be recognized to lack normative significance.[6] The fact that a project has a positive sum of CVs does not mean that it is a genuine moral improvement over the status quo.[7] Rather, CBA is a decision procedure. It is a technique used by agencies for choosing between options, a technique whose justifiability must be evaluated in light of normative criteria with which CBA is only contingently connected.

Second, there is a genuine normative criterion that does plausibly justify the use of CBA, and that is the criterion of overall well-being. It is this criterion, not Pareto efficiency or Kaldor-Hicks efficiency, that provides the normative foundations for CBA. Overall well-being is one of the several normative criteria bearing upon governmental choice; it is morally relevant

[5] See Robin W. Boadway, The Welfare Foundations of Cost-Benefit Analysis, 84 Econ. J. 926 (1974).

[6] Perhaps it is an exaggeration to describe this particular element of our view of CBA as a "reconceptualization." Sophisticated contemporary defenders of CBA, within welfare economics, view it as a decision procedure that imperfectly implements either Pareto efficiency or Kaldor-Hicks efficiency. But our overall view of CBA clearly is a reconceptualization; and seeing CBA as a decision procedure rather than a bedrock normative criterion is an important component of our overall view.

[7] The reason that CBA lacks normative significance is parallel to the reason that Kaldor-Hicks efficiency does. A project may produce gains for the rich (whose CVs are inflated by their wealth) and losses for the poor (whose CVs are deflated by their poverty), such that it is counted as an improvement by CBA even though the project decreases overall well-being. So CBA is not equivalent to the welfare criterion. And, as with Kaldor-Hicks efficiency, it is very hard to see how CBA could have moral significance by tracking or constituting some moral criterion other than the welfare criterion.

to, if not conclusive of, government's choice between a project and the status quo. Thus we disagree with classical utilitarianism, which is the view that overall well-being is the sole criterion bearing on governmental choice. Our view is that the government should choose a welfare-improving project unless other considerations, such as deontological or egalitarian considerations, justify rejecting the welfare-improving project and choosing the status quo instead. How such nonwelfarist considerations should be operationalized at the agency level is a complicated matter. It may be the case that an institutional division of labor obtains, where agencies focus solely on the welfare criterion and courts and legislatures then revise agency choices in light of deontological criteria, egalitarian criteria, and the like. In any event, we do not mean to suggest that CBA is a superprocedure, which implements all the moral considerations bearing upon governmental choice. Rather, CBA is plausibly justified in light of a particular moral criterion— overall well-being—and thus is plausibly one part of the set of procedures and institutions comprising government.

Note that our view, albeit nonutilitarian, does entail a commitment to the possibility of interpersonal welfare comparisons. It was once a widely held view within welfare economics that such comparisons are impossible—that Pareto-noncomparable states are welfare noncomparable. That view has changed and, in any event, is wrong. Consider a project that causes minor headaches to a few people, but averts many premature deaths. The project is Pareto noncomparable with the status quo, but surely it increases overall well-being. In our ordinary lives, as family members or citizens, we routinely judge that the positive (or negative) welfare effect of an option on some person or persons is large enough to outweigh the negative (or positive) welfare effect of the option on others. Any theory of well-being that does not license such comparisons is, on those very grounds, an unreasonable theory.[8]

Granting the moral relevance of overall well-being and the possibility of interpersonal welfare comparisons, why think that CBA is a decision procedure justified in light of overall well-being? There are a variety of possible decision procedures by which agencies might choose between their options. One such procedure is CBA; another procedure is the direct implementation

---

[8] Skeptics of interpersonal welfare comparisons sometimes point out that it is not practicable for government to make such comparisons. We agree. But this is not the same as saying that interpersonal comparisons are impossible. To think otherwise is to conflate decision procedures and normative criteria. Although actual agencies should not choose between project and status quo by attempting to perform a comparison of the winners' welfare gains with the losers's losses—because that procedure is too expensive, and so on—there remains, or may remain, a right answer to the question, Are the winners' welfare gains larger than the losers' losses?

of the welfare criterion, where agencies actually attempt to judge whether overall well-being is greater in the project world or the status quo; yet another procedure is one where agencies pick a single dimension bearing upon welfare (such as longevity, or aesthetic experience, or employment) and choose options by maximizing along that single dimension. Or an agency might eschew maximization and aggregation entirely, as agencies do when they make choices by looking to social norms. Why think that CBA, by contrast with these other procedures, is the best procedure for agencies to use—the procedure the use of which maximizes overall well-being? Our view is actually a bit more qualified: although there are some scenarios in which agencies should not employ CBA (for example, where the project's likely impact on overall well-being is too small to warrant the expense of CBA), CBA is welfare justified in a significant fraction of agency choice situations. By contrast with unidimensional and nonaggregative procedures, CBA is relatively accurate—although not perfectly accurate—in tracking overall well-being. By contrast with direct implementation of the welfare criterion, CBA is cheaper to perform, less prone to agency error, and more readily monitored by oversight bodies such as legislatures or the Office of Management and Budget (OMB).

These are surely contestable and (to some extent) empirical claims, which bear further examination and debate. But at a minimum it is clear to us what the debate about CBA should concern: it should concern whether, as compared with other possible agency procedures, CBA is the procedure by which the welfare criterion is best implemented. Again, it is welfare, not efficiency, that figures here, and it must be kept firmly in mind that although CBA itself lacks normative import, its use as a decision procedure may be better justified in light of some genuine normative criterion than the direct implementation of that criterion.

The reader, by this point, may have noticed one large lacuna in our sketch of the welfarist justification for CBA. That concerns the link between CBA and actual preferences. Cost-benefit analysis is traditionally defined as the sum of CVs, and CVs in turn are defined in terms of actual preference. P's CV is the dollar amount such that, paid to or from him in the project world, he is indifferent—given his actual preferences—between that world and the status quo. But there are many reasons to think that an actual-preference account of welfare is wrong. At a minimum, that account is wrong because it treats disinterested or morally motivated preferences as welfare relevant. A preference is simply a particular kind of ranking (specifically, a ranking by P that has some explanatory connection to P's choices). But if P prefers (ranks) the project over the status quo simply because he believes the project to be morally required, then surely the occurrence of the project need not benefit P. To think otherwise is to confuse the totality of factors that influence P's rankings and choices—including his moral views, his special commitments to family and friends, and so forth—with one such factor, namely, P's welfare.[9]

An example might help make the point. Imagine that the project, which would be implemented in Montana, involves eliminating an endangered species located in that state. P, who lives in New York, believes that this is morally wrong because he believes that endangered species have intrinsic value. P has no other involvement with the species or Montana. He has never been to that state and never plans to go. His professional work has nothing to do with the environmental movement, and he has no particular nonprofessional involvement either: he does not devote large amounts of his time, or resources, or attention to environmental issues. Still, he has been persuaded (after reading a book on environmental ethics) that there are strong moral grounds against eliminating endangered species. He therefore rejects the project; he ranks it below the status quo, and this ranking is connected to his choices, in the sense that it leads him (let us imagine) to take certain steps to help the species, such as sending a $100 check to the Sierra Club. This hardly entails that P personally benefits from the status quo—that the project harms his own welfare. After all, P himself would deny that claim, and it would run afoul of our commonsense intuitions about welfare. P rejects the project not because he believes it harms him but because he believes that the project is morally wrong; and there is nothing driving P's preference, no personal or professional connection, other than this belief. Thus P's act of sending the check to the Sierra Club is disinterested: it is an action that diminishes P's own well-being (because he loses $100) and that he takes to do so, but that is motivated by considerations other than P's own well-being. If welfare and preference satisfaction are equivalent, then the concept of disinterested action is incoherent.

We therefore adopt a restricted preference-based account of well-being. A project is a welfare improvement for P only if P prefers the project and only if this preference is properly restricted to P's own interests, concerns, and welfare. Providing a precise account of this restriction is difficult, but it is clear that some such amendment to the actual-preference account of welfare is needed—as the case of morally motivated preferences shows.

More generally, there are a variety of factors, other than actual preference, that may bear upon P's welfare. These factors include the following:

---

[9] Sen distinguishes preferences based on "commitment"; Harsanyi distinguishes "ethical preferences." See Amartya K. Sen, Rational Fools, 6 Phil. & Pub. Aff. 317 (1977); John G. Harsanyi, Cardinal Welfare, Individualistic Ethics, and Interpersonal Comparisons of Utility, 63 J. Pol. Econ. 315 (1955). Other works defending the view that only a restricted set of preferences are relevant for well-being—that some preferences can be disinterested—are cited in Adler & Posner, *supra* note 1, at 197–204.

Information.   P prefers the project. However, with fuller information, P would prefer the status quo. Arguably, P is not benefited by the project, or at least not benefited as much as he would be if his fully informed preferences were in favor of the project.

Objective Good.   P prefers the project. However, the status quo is objectively much better for P, in light of objective welfare goods such as friendship, knowledge, aesthetic experience, or accomplishment. Arguably, P is not benefited by the project, or at least not benefited as much as he would be if the objective value of the project were greater.

Adaptive Preference.   P prefers the status quo because that is the world in which his preferences were formed. However, P's preferences are misshapen by various unjust features of the status quo. (Imagine that the status quo is a world in which P lacks wealth, or self-respect, or a basic education, and in which his preferences have been shaped by these deficits.) If the project is implemented, P's preferences may change—such that he now prefers the project, not the status quo—or the preferences may be sufficiently entrenched that they do not change. In either event, there may be good grounds for thinking that P benefits from (or at least is not harmed by) the project even though he prefers or once preferred the status quo.

Affect and Experience.   P prefers the project. However, if the project were implemented, he would not enjoy it. Or, if the project were implemented, he would not experience—become aware of—that fact. (Note that P's preference for a state of the world is satisfied if the state of the world occurs; it is a further and contingent matter whether P experiences the occurrence of the state of the world.) Arguably, P cannot be benefited by a project that he does not enjoy or experience.

We are not sure that the actual-preference view of well-being needs to be modified in all the ways just listed. These are plausible proposals, but we find them somewhat less compelling than the earlier point that morally motivated and other unrestricted preferences are welfare irrelevant. On the other hand, we are hardly confident that the right theory of well-being omits reference to P's information, to the objective goods that he realizes, to the adaptive cast of his preferences, or to his affect and experience. Thus we need to provide a defense of CBA that is consistent with such amendments to an actual-preference view of welfare.

One defense returns to the point that CBA is a decision procedure, not a normative criterion. P's CV does not perfectly capture the welfare effect of the project upon him, given the disjunction between the actual-preference view of welfare and the correct view—a restricted-preference view that may further incorporate factors such as information, objective goods, adaption, and affect or experience. But perfect capture is not needed. Compensating variations are sufficiently accurate in tracking welfare impacts and sufficiently easy to implement and monitor by agencies that CBA as tradi-tionally defined is welfare justified in light of the right theory of welfare, notwithstanding the disjunction from the actual-preference view. Or so the argument in favor of traditional CBA might go.

This argument may be persuasive, at least in part. There may well be scenarios in which traditionally defined CBA is indeed the welfare-maximizing decision procedure for agencies to employ. But it is important to see that the welfarist defense of CBA is not limited to the argument just sketched. Cost-benefit analysis need not be defined in the traditional way, as the sum of CVs. The valuation concept at the core of CBA can be amended. As we noted earlier, CVs might be replaced with welfare equiva-lents, or WEs, where P's WE is the amount of money paid to or by him in the project world such that—on the right theory of well-being—P is just as well-off there as in the status quo. Note that CBA, defined as the sum of WEs, automatically corrects for the disjunction between the actual-preference view and the right theory, whatever that theory happens to be. For example, imagine that the view is a hybrid view, such that P benefits from the project if and only if (1) he actually prefers it and (2) he would prefer it under full information. In the case where ignorant P prefers the project but fully informed P would prefer the status quo, P's CV is a posi-tive number but—on the theory at hand—the welfare impact of the project upon him is nil. And so P's WE is also nil, because that concept (by con-trast with the simpler concept of the CV) makes reference to the full and correct welfare theory.

To be sure, the accuracy of the WE in tracking the right welfare theory is, from another point of view, a defect. Compensating variations are rela-tively easy to calculate; WEs may not be. Telling agencies to aggregate WEs rather than CVs may give them additional scope for shirking and er-ror. But we are confident that, at least in some cases, CBA defined as the sum of WEs (or something like that) will be welfare maximizing, as com-pared to traditional CBA and other procedures. Cost-benefit analysis can, to some extent, be modified in a way that corrects for the failings of an actual-preference view of welfare and that still leaves in place a practicable choice procedure. At a minimum—since the traditional version of CBA cannot just be assumed to be the welfare-maximizing version—economists, lawyers, and philosophers need to begin considering what a sum-of-WEs approach would involve. That is the task to which we turn in the remainder of this article.

One final and significant point bears mention here. We have criticized an actual-preference theory of welfare for making P's preferences the sole constituents of his welfare. The right theory adds additional elements—re-strictions, information, objective goods, to name some plausible candidates—beyond sheer preference. But preference cannot be dispensed with entirely. The right theory of well-being, in our view, is one that gives preference[10] a partial and constitutive role; theories that fail to do so, so-called objective or hedonic theories, are therefore mistaken. If P prefers the status quo to the project, and would do so (and continue to do so) even if the project were implemented, then P is not benefited by the project. The fact that P hypothetically would approve the project under full information, or that it is objectively good, may be necessary conditions for the project's benefiting P, but they are not sufficient conditions. To think otherwise is to give too little weight to P's own point of view; it is to think, implausibly, that P can made better off by an option in the teeth of P's actual and continuing aversion to it. This will be of much importance in thinking about how agencies should modify CBA.[11]

II.   How Government Agencies Correct
for Distorted Preferences

A preference distortion arises when a person's CV for a project does not accurately measure the extent to which the project improves his welfare, properly understood. The previous section argued that preference distortions may have diverse causes. A person's CV for a project is inaccurate if it reflects his disinterested preferences rather than his self-interested preferences. Further, a person's CV for a project may be inaccurate if his preferences are uninformed, adaptive, or objectively bad. Finally, a person's CV for a project is inaccurate if it is inflated by his relative wealth or deflated by his relative poverty.

The preference distortions identified in the prior section may seem more theoretical than real. However, in this section we argue that government agencies act in ways that reflect concerns about preference distortions, and they therefore deviate from what we call "textbook CBA"[12] (by which we

[10] More precisely, the right theory of well-being is one that gives preference or some other pro-attitude a partial and constitutive role. Thus in our earlier paper, see Adler & Posner, *supra* note 1, at 197–204, we characterize ourselves as adopting a restricted desire-based view, where desires are, generically, pro-attitudes, including, specifically, preferences. This is a point of detail that need not be pursued here.

[11] More precisely, P can only be intrinsically benefited by a project if he prefers it or comes to prefer it. Clearly, P can be instrumentally benefited absent a conforming preference, for example, in the case where P prefers a pill that he believes to be a health-causing vitamin, when in fact it is a death-causing poison. The "project" of keeping the pill from P benefits him notwithstanding his unchanging belief that the pill is a vitamin. See Adler & Posner, *supra* note 1, at 202 n.97.

[12] We acknowledge that CBA textbook authors sometimes discuss these distortions. By "textbook CBA," we mean the kind of CBA that is generally espoused by its advocates, that is, the sum of unweighted CVs based upon actual preferences. Citations to the economic literature on CBA, and in particular to the literature advocating CBA, are provided by Adler & Posner, *supra* note 1, at 187–94.

mean, again, the sum of unweighted CVs based on actual, unrestricted preferences).

In Section III below, we will evaluate these administrative actions and propose modifications of the ways in which agencies deal with preference distortions. We should stress at the outset that we do not approve of all, or even many, of the government's approaches to these problems; we spend time on them in order to show that these problems are real and pose important practical difficulties.

A. Disinterested Preferences: The Problem of Existence Value

Textbook CBA reduces moral commitments to valuations. Consider, for example, the recent debate over the use of contingent valuation methods to value environmental goods. Textbook CBA, as generally understood, directs agencies to translate people's moral attitudes about the environment into CVs for the existence of environmental goods that they do not directly enjoy, usually called "existence value" or "nonuse value."[13] These CVs are then added to the balance of costs and benefits of a project, like any other CV.

Until recently, agencies did not calculate existence values and use them in order to evaluate regulations. The earliest sustained discussion of existence values by an agency that we have found occurred in 1986 and involved the Department of Interior's guidelines on valuing environmental damage caused by a discharge of oil or a hazardous substance. But the rule itself did not involve the calculation of an existence value.[14] The first use of existence values in rule making was, as far as we have found, by the Environmental Protection Agency (EPA) in 1991,[15] and the practice of measuring existence values has only recently become common. For example, the EPA's recent CBA for effluent regulations included existence valuations for "benefits to wildlife, threatened or endangered species, and biodiversity benefits."[16] Thus, the use of existence values by government

---

[13] Existence value is the value from knowing that some good exists; it is sometimes used interchangeably with nonuse value, but nonuse value also is understood to include the option value of having some good in the future, which we exclude from our analysis.

[14] See Department of the Interior, Natural Resource Damage Assessments, 51 Fed. Reg. 27,674 (1986).

[15] See Environmental Protection Agency, Approval and Promulgation of Implementation Plans: Revision of the Visibility FIP for Arizona, 56 Fed. Reg. 5173 (1991).

[16] Environmental Protection Agency, Effluent Limitations Guidelines, Pretreatment Standards, and New Source Performance Standards for the Transportation Equipment Cleaning Point Source Category, 63 Fed. Reg. 34,686, 34,724 (1998). See also Environmental Protection Agency, Lead Fishing Sinkers: Response to Citizens' Petition and Proposed Ban, 59 Fed. Reg. 11,122, 11,135 (1994) (endorsing use of existence values). The use of the methodology has been approved by the D.C. Circuit, see Ohio v. U.S. Dep't Interior, 880 F.2d 432, 474–81 (D.C. Cir. 1989).

agencies has lagged the widespread use of cost-benefit analysis by about a decade.

One reason for hesitation about calculating existence values was no doubt methodological. Existence values cannot be inferred from market behavior, but must be derived from costly and controversial surveys. Another reason for hesitation might have been politics. But it is also likely that agencies have been uncertain about the conceptual soundness of using existence values. If not, they should have been—as we argue in the next section.

Whether or not we are correct about the reasons for the delay in using existence values in environmental regulation—namely, that existence values do not constitute morally relevant information, either with respect to overall well-being or with respect to other moral criteria—we think these reasons do explain why existence values are not used outside environmental regulation. The Food and Drug Administration (FDA) does not ask Christian Scientists whether they care about the existence of people using commercial drugs. The U.S. Department of Agriculture (USDA) does not ask animal rights activists whether they care about the existence of slaughterhouses. The U.S. Postal Service does not ask individuals whether they care about the existence of pornography in the mail. One might be able to point to some factors that distinguish these cases from environmental regulation. The Constitution bars the government from implementing religious views. Concerns about the treatment of farm animals are not as widespread or deep as concerns about the environment. But there is no conceptual reason for distinguishing among these different contexts. If people's disinterested preferences are worthy of consideration in CBAs, then disinterested environmental preferences are not the only ones that matter. All such attitudes—including attitudes toward abortion, the death penalty, medical research, family structure, the treatment of children, and the appropriateness of government intervention—should be quantified, monetized, and weighed against opposing costs and benefits when agencies implement projects.

B. Uninformed Preferences

Either textbook CBA ignores the problem of uninformed preferences (by assuming that all persons have perfect information), or it recognizes the problem but purports to solve it by conceptualizing information as yet another good. Individuals know that they lack information and are willing to pay for more information if and only if the expected gain exceeds the cost. So an individual who is partly uninformed about a given project is rationally uninformed, and his CV for the project should be calculated based upon his uninformed preferences.[17]

---

[17] In particular, the individual's CV would be set equal to the expected value of the project or to the single ex post payment in all the project states of the world such that (given the

Government agencies' treatment of uninformed preferences is, in fact, more complex. At the outset, it is worth distinguishing between the effect of information on (i) instrumental preferences and on (ii) intrinsic preferences. In the first case, information has the effect of changing persons' judgments about the causal link between the project and those states of affairs that they intrinsically value or disvalue. P opposes a project to fluoridate drinking water because he falsely believes that fluoridation causes cancer and does not help teeth. In the second case, information changes intrinsic valuations. P's CV for an arts project is low because he has not been fully informed about the aesthetic qualities of the project.

Agencies frequently refuse to use CVs that reflect uninformed preferences. Sometimes, agencies supply people with information when asking them for their CVs. Before asking them about air quality over the Grand Canyon, the EPA showed survey respondents photographs of the site with different levels of pollution.[18] The EPA's goal was presumably to provide information on environmental aesthetics, about which respondent's intrinsic preferences were uninformed. For a regulation involving labeling of meat and poultry products, the USDA relied on CVs for health benefits people would enjoy if they altered their behavior in response to the labels, rather than people's CVs for nutrition disclosure.[19] The agency appeared to take the intrinsic preference (for health) as a given and to circumvent the problem of imperfectly informed instrumental preference (for nutritional disclosure). Instrumental preferences are constructed; people are assumed to have preferences for whatever means will best satisfy their intrinsic preferences, even if they are misinformed about these means—even if, in our example, some people would oppose labeling because they (falsely) think it will confuse them.

The premise of modern workplace regulation is that workers are uninformed about risks. If this premise is false, then wages and workplace safety procedures reflect rational trade-offs made by workers, and regulations simply interfere with the satisfaction of their preferences. It would make no sense, for example, for the Occupational Safety and Health Administration to restrict workers' exposure to ethylene dibromide, a carcinogenic chemical used in various industries,[20] because any restrictions suffi-

---

individual's information) he is indifferent between the project and the status quo. Lewis Kornhauser's contribution to this symposium provides a more detailed discussion of how textbook CBA calculates CVs when actors are not fully informed. See Lewis A. Kornhauser, On Justifying Cost-Benefit Analysis, in this issue, at 1037.

[18] See Leland B. Deck, Visibility at the Grand Canyon and the Navajo Generating Station, in Economic Analysis at EPA 267 (Richard D. Morgenstern ed. 1997).

[19] Department of Agriculture, Nutrition Labeling of Meat and Poultry Products, 56 Fed. Reg. 60,302 (1991).

[20] See Department of Labor, Occupational Exposure to Ethylene Dibromide, 48 Fed. Reg. 49,959 (1983).

ciently cheap that workers are willing to pay for them have voluntarily been implemented by employers. More risk-averse workers would move to safer, lower paying jobs; more risk-preferring workers would take the more dangerous, higher paying jobs. In such a labor market, regulations would be costlier than their safety benefits warrant. The denial that this market prevails is implicit in all regulation of contractual relations; agencies occasionally are explicit about it.[21]

In sum, agencies do not always take uninformed preferences as they find them. Instead, they sometimes evaluate projects by using the preferences people would have if they were informed.

C. Adaptive Preferences

Textbook CBA does not recognize the existence of adaptive preferences. Preferences that are the result of adaptation are treated the same as preferences that are not the result of adaptation.

As noted in Section I, people may psychologically adapt to an unjust or otherwise unfavorable environment, so that their CV for eliminating a risk or irritant is less than what it would be if they did not adapt. An overburdened housewife might rationalize her position and so not be willing to pay in order to have her burdens removed.[22] Or a person in a bad environment might feel sour grapes toward someone in a pleasant environment and refuse to pay for an improvement in his own environment because he has convinced himself that the pleasant environment is really worse. Or a person might adapt to the status quo, so while he will oppose any project, if the project were nevertheless implemented, he would oppose a further project that would reverse the first.[23]

Many agency programs assume that people's preferences are distorted by psychological problems. For example, programs to reduce drug use assume that drug addicts would be benefited by restrictions on drugs, not harmed by them, even though their preferences may well be the opposite. In justifying regulations governing antidrug programs for the employees of private air carriers, the Department of Transportation (DOT) did not take into account the preferences of the drug users, even though these people may well be hurt by the regulations on an actual-preference account of CBA.[24] In justi-

---

[21] See, for example, Department of Labor, Occupational Exposure to Bloodborne Pathogens, 56 Fed. Reg. 64,004, 64,087 (1991) (arguing that workers do not know about many risks and are unable to analyze them correctly).

[22] Amartya Sen, On Ethics and Economics 45 (1987).

[23] Cass R. Sunstein, Free Markets and Social Justice 252–53, 256–58 (1997); Jon Elster, Sour Grapes: Studies in the Subversion of Rationality (1983).

[24] Department of Transportation, Anti-drug Program for Personnel Engaged in Specified Aviation Activities, 53 Fed. Reg. 47,024 (1988).

fying mandatory drug tests for drivers of commercial vehicles, the DOT did not take account of the cost to drivers who derive pleasure from the use of alcohol and illegal drugs.[25] Yet in these same regulations, the agencies did take account of preferences that are not considered adaptive, such as preferences for time or money.

However, several qualifications are necessary. First, agencies do not generally assume that preferences are defective in these ways unless directed by a statute. Second, it is not clear whether the preferences of drug users are ignored because they are adaptive or because they are considered objectively bad (see below) or distorted in other ways.[26]

D. Objectively Bad Preferences

Textbook CBA assumes that objectively bad preferences should receive the same weight as morally neutral preferences. An agency should presumably count the preferences of a person who hates children, and is willing to pay $1,000 to prevent a children's vaccine program, or the preferences of a person who hates homosexuals, and is willing to pay $1,000 to prevent AIDS research.

Agencies routinely ignore sadistic preferences and other objectively bad preferences. For example, the FDA's cost-benefit analysis of a regulation designed to curb distribution of cigarettes to children did not include as a cost the lost profits to industry, "because most of this profit stems from illegal sales to youths."[27] Nor did it count the children's lost consumer surplus. It is hard to believe that agencies would count a preference that homosexuals not be helped through AIDS research, no matter how widespread that preference may be. And, as we saw above, the DOT's refusal to count the preferences of drug users may reflect an evaluative judgment (on the

---

[25] See Department of Transportation, Federal Motor Carrier Regulations; Controlled Substances and Alcohol Use and Testing; Commercial Driver's License Standards, Requirements and Penalties; Hours of Service of Drivers, 57 Fed. Reg. 59,567 (1992).

[26] Rather than being adaptive or objectively bad, it might be the case that a drug user's preference is (1) uninformed, in the sense that she is mistaken about the consequences of drug use (health consequences, the risk of addiction); (2) akratic, in the sense that the drug user prefers not to use drugs, given their consequences (of which she is aware), but nonetheless irrationally continues to use them; (3) conflicted, in the sense that she has a first-order preference for drug use but a second-order preference not to have this first-order preference; or (4) coerced, in the sense that the drug addict has a preference for drug use only because she will experience miserable withdrawal symptoms if she stops using drugs. Compare Douglas N. Husak, Drugs and Rights (1992) (considering, but rejecting, possible grounds for regulating recreational drug use).

[27] Food and Drug Administration, Regulations Restricting the Sale and Distribution of Cigarettes and Smokeless Tobacco to Protect Children and Adolescents, 61 Fed. Reg. 44,396, 44,593 (1996).

part of Congress) rather than, or in addition to, a concern that the preferences are adaptive.

As another example, consider a Federal Aviation Administration (FAA) program for airline security, which refused to use profiling on the basis of race, national or ethnic origin, and other possibly relevant but morally suspect factors. Although the FAA performed a CBA, it did not consider the possibility that a discriminatory system might be less costly than the system that it endorsed[28] or that some people (white supremacists, racially biased airline travelers) might have strong tastes for discrimination and therefore have significant, positive CVs for a discriminatory system.

In sum, agencies depart from textbook CBA by refusing to weigh certain kinds of objectively bad preferences. This practice is not as obvious as other adjustments are, because we are not accustomed to thinking that satisfying preferences for discrimination, suffering, and other morally bad outcomes will benefit the holders of the preferences. Thus the agencies' practice seems natural. But that is only because in this significant respect textbook CBA deviates from common moral intuitions.

E.   Wealth Distortions

Textbook CBA does not adjust for distortions caused by the distribution of wealth. A wealthy person is willing to pay more to reduce the risk of death than is a poor person with identical preferences, but it does not follow that the agency maximizes welfare by placing dangerous projects in poor neighborhoods rather than in rich neighborhoods. On the contrary, it seems reasonable to assume that premature death has the same effect upon overall well-being, whether the person who dies prematurely is wealthy or poor. Note that this distortion is different from the other three. The others arise because of the disjunction between preference satisfaction and well-being; relatedly, they cause (or may cause) a deviation between CVs and WEs. By contrast, the wealth distortion described just now arises because CVs and WEs are calculated in terms of dollars, which do not accurately reflect relative well-being when endowments differ. This distortion would exist even if actual and undistorted preferences did not diverge, and (where they do diverge) even if agencies were able to costlessly and accurately calculate WEs.

Agencies correct for wealth distortions in various ways. They use a constant figure for the monetized value of life.[29] They rely on quality-adjusted

---

[28] Department of Transportation, Security of Checked Baggage on Flights within the United States, 64 Fed. Reg. 19,220 (1999).

[29] See U.S. General Accounting Office, Regulatory Reform: Agencies Could Improve Development, Documentation, and Clarity of Regulatory Analysis 26–27 (GAO/RCED-98-142,

or -nonadjusted life-years, which is a number that is invariant with wealth.[30] The Department of Health and Human Services, for example, said that the benefit of its organ transplant rule was the saving of 297–1,306 life-years.[31] They quantify other benefits without monetizing them. The EPA, for example, noted that a regulation of certain heavy-duty engines would reduce nitrogen oxide emissions by 593,000 tons, without attaching a value to this amount.[32] In all these cases, the benefits of the regulation are invariant to the wealth of those affected by them. Of course, as the agencies depart farther and farther from the use of CVs, the basis of evaluation becomes increasingly obscure.

Agencies also correct for wealth distortions in more broad-gauged ways. Regulation of pesticides and lead-based paint may have been influenced by a desire to benefit, on distributional grounds, low-income farm workers, in the first case, and low-income inner-city residents, in the second.[33] Agencies also pay attention to whether a regulation will "threaten the existence" of an industry, that is, have substantial, concentrated impacts.[34] Indeed, Clinton-era executive orders that require consideration of "environmental justice" and equity appear to require attention to the distributional consequences of regulations.[35] The original executive order directing agencies to use CBA says: "When an agency determines that a regulation is the best available method of achieving the regulatory objective, it shall design its regulations in the most cost-effective manner to achieve the regulatory objective. In doing so, each agency shall consider incentives for innovation, consistency, predictability, the costs of enforcement and compliance (to the

---

1998). More precisely, they use a range, but they do not make their choice within the range depend on the wealth of the victims.

[30] See Department of Health and Human Services, Regulatory Impact Analysis of the Proposed Rules to Amend the Food Labeling Regulations, 56 Fed. Reg. 60,856, 60,871 (1991) ("dying of a heart attack at age 80 is posited to be of less societal concern than dying in a car accident at age 35"). Yet the 80-year-old might have a higher CV than the 35-year-old.

[31] Office of Management and Budget, Draft Report to Congress on the Costs and Benefits of Federal Regulations, 63 Fed. Reg. 44,034, 44,048 (1998). See also *id.* at 44,052–53, on the FDA and other agencies.

[32] *Id.* at 44,048.

[33] Louis P. True, Jr., Agricultural Pesticides and Worker Protection, in Economic Analysis at EPA 324 (Richard D. Morgenstern ed. 1997); Environmental Protection Agency, Lead: Identification of Dangerous Levels of Lead, 63 Fed. Reg. 30,302, 30,305 (1998); Department of Housing and Urban Development, Office of Lead-Based Paint Abatement and Poisoning Prevention; Requirements for Notification, Evaluation and Reduction of Lead-Based Paint Hazards in Federally Owned Residential Property and Housing Receiving Federal Assistance, 61 Fed. Reg. 29,170, 29,202 (1996).

[34] See, for example, Department of Labor, *supra* note 21, at 64,082.

[35] See Exec. Order No. 12,898, 59 Fed. Reg. 7629 (1994) (environmental justice).

government, regulated entities, and the public), flexibility, *distributive impacts, and equity.*"[36]

One might doubt whether these instructions have had much impact. On the one hand, agencies typically publish, alongside the CBA, a discussion of distributive impacts. On the other hand, these discussions are usually formulaic and inconclusive. But they do show that distributive issues have some prominence, contrary to the prescription of textbook CBA.[37]

F.   Some Objections

Agency practice diverges in many ways from the requirements of textbook CBA. We argue that these practices reflect, in a loose and mostly unarticulated way, our concerns about the moral foundations of CBA.

An alternative hypothesis is that the divergence between agency practices and textbook models reflects either attempts to economize on decision costs or political constraints.

Neither of these alternatives is plausible. Agencies economize on decision costs in many ways, but what needs to be explained is a more complex pattern of behavior. Often agencies do expend considerable resources to determine what people's CVs are, and often they do not; the question is, why do they expend resources sometimes and not at other times? Consider agencies' refusals to determine the CVs of drug users when a project increases the cost of using drugs or their refusals to determine the CVs of racists for a project that involves racial profiling. Calculating these CVs is no more costly than calculating CVs in other contexts—for example, the CV of someone who is harmed by airplane noise or the CV of someone who experiences an increased risk of cancer. When agencies face high decision costs, they are usually quite candid about this problem. They will say that data are unavailable or too costly to acquire. They will make estimates based on a small sample. It is impossible to imagine an agency saying that the only reason that it did not calculate the CVs for drug use or racial discrimination is that data were unavailable.

The political argument might be that interest group politics result in the divergences that we have discussed. But there are interest groups on both

---

[36] Exec. Order No. 12,866, 58 Fed. Reg. 51,735 (1993) (emphasis added). Guidelines issued by OMB say, "When benefits and costs have significant distributive effects, these effects should be analyzed and discussed, along with the analysis of net present value." Office of Management and Budget, Guidelines and Discount Rates for Benefit-Cost Analysis of Federal Programs, Circ. No. A-94, Rev. (October 29, 1992), available from Westlaw in the database "OMB-circular."

[37] Ironically, the one thing that agencies do not do is use explicit weightings of CVs on the basis of marginal utilities of money, which is the most popular approach in CBA textbooks.

sides of virtually every regulation. A more plausible political account of agency practice is that agencies fear public outrage. Agencies hesitate about using wealth-dependent valuations of life, or respecting preferences for drug use, or attaching dollar values to environmental amenities, because these practices may produce public outrage. Public outrage may reflect ignorance, or herding, or strategic behavior,[38] but we think that it also reflects a conviction that deep moral intuitions are being ignored. If this is the case, the political argument is no different from our moral argument.

Defenders of textbook CBA will more likely regret the divergence between textbook CBA and agency use of CBA than explain it away. But we think that the divergence justifies attention to the problems with textbook CBA and provides support for our view that unrestricted preferences should not always be the basis of agency action. Nonetheless, the agency practices we have discussed raise questions.

First, as we have already pointed out, it is improper for agencies to correct for the fact that actual preferences may be distorted by shifting wholesale to undistorted preferences and calculating CVs based on those. What kind of shift should be made is a subtle problem and will vary depending on the source of distortion. Second, the modifications risk making CBA less transparent, cheap, and reliable. When agencies are told that the preferences relevant for CBA are different from the preferences people actually hold, they obtain a degree of freedom that will interfere with review by hierarchical superiors. Finally, there is no generally accepted means for correcting for wealth distortions. The balance of the article examines these problems in detail.

III. How Agencies Should Respond to Distorted Preferences

A. Disinterested Preferences

Many people criticize agencies' use of contingent valuation techniques to measure existence values, but these criticisms are for the most part methodological. Critics argue that contingent valuation techniques do not yield reliable results. Defenders argue that the techniques are adequate or improving. They argue that if surveys were conducted more carefully, or with certain controls, then inconsistencies and intransitivities would disappear.[39]

---

[38] See Eric A. Posner, The Strategic Basis of Principled Behavior: A Critique of the Incommensurability Thesis, 146 U. Pa. L. Rev. 1185 (1998).

[39] See the essays in Valuing Environmental Preferences: Theory and Practice of Contingent Valuation in the US, EU, and Developing Countries (Ian J. Bateman & Kenneth G. Willis eds. 1999); Using Surveys to Value Public Goods: The Contingent Valuation Method (Robert Cameron Mitchell & Richard T. Carson eds. 1989).

However, as several economists have acknowledged, the main problem with contingent valuation of environmental goods is conceptual, not methodological.[40]

When people are asked for existence values, they often respond in strange ways. They refuse to answer surveys on environmental goods or, by way of protest, register a zero valuation or unrealistically high valuations that agencies must ignore. They provide valuations that are invariant across large and small parcels of wilderness or quantities of wildlife or that are inconsistent or intransitive. Their answers depend on the order in which questions are asked and are sensitive to the wording of the questions.[41]

Although one might hope for improvements that will eliminate inconsistencies, it is clear that no amount of methodological refinement will eliminate protest responses in the form of unrealistically high or low valuations or refusals to answer. But these responses must reflect something. When people give valuations of zero or infinity, these responses should be interpreted as an assertion that the question does not make sense, not as an assertion that the respondent would give nothing to save the environmental good (in the first case), or everything (in the second case), or is acting strategically (in either case) since he must know that his response will be disregarded. This is even more clearly true when people refuse to respond to the surveys.

What about reasonable CVs for environmental goods when people do not directly enjoy them? When people have no direct experience of environmental goods and claim to be willing to pay just for their existence, then (aside from the option value for possible use) this CV cannot reflect the goods' contribution to well-being. The dollar amounts in the survey responses should be interpreted as a valuation of the violation of a moral commitment, not as a valuation of an environmental amenity. To the extent the dollar amounts thus reflect moral commitments, aggregating them does not give one information about the effect of the project upon overall well-being or upon other moral criteria.

Why should agencies not pay attention to valuations people attach to violations of moral commitments? To see why, suppose that P believes that he will gain $100 from the construction of a dam as a result of lower electricity bills, but believes that construction of a dam is immoral. Q would lose $125

[40] See, for example, Charles R. Plott, Contingent Valuation: A View of the Conference and Associated Research, in Contingent Valuation: A Critical Assessment 470–73 (Jerry A. Hausman ed. 1993); Donald H. Rosenthal & Robert H. Nelson, Why Existence Values Should *Not* Be Used in Cost-Benefit Analysis, 11 J. Pol'y Analysis & Mgmt. 116 (1992). But compare Gardner M. Brown, Jr., Economics of Natural Resource Damage Assessment: A Critique, in Valuing Natural Assets (Raymond J. Kopp & V. Kerry Smith eds. 1993).

[41] See Plott, *supra* note 40, at 471–73, for a brief summary of the literature.

as a result of higher fish prices, but believes that construction of a dam is a moral obligation ("the march of progress"). P would pay an additional $50 to see his moral commitment vindicated, and Q would pay an additional $100 to see her moral commitment vindicated. These additional payments are, we suggest, morally irrelevant; they neither change the effect of the project on overall well-being (which is negative) nor change the moral status of the project in some other regard. The project is either moral or immoral or morally controversial; its morality does not depend on how much people are willing to pay to vindicate their moral views. If P receives a large inheritance, and so is willing to pay another $200 to see the project stopped, and this increase reflects his moral values, then it is false to say that the moral status of the project switches back from positive to negative, just because P's inheritance now enables him to outbid Q. Now it might be the case that an agency should take account of people's disinterested moral views when it decides whether to implement a project. We discuss this possibility below. The point to understand is that even if an agency should, it should not try to monetize these disinterested preferences, and should not include them as part of a CBA.

How then should environmental commitments (as well as other disinterested preferences) be recognized? There are two possibilities. The first is that agencies should have the minimal task of determining the effect of projects on overall well-being, and different political actors—Congress, the courts—should enforce moral commitments. No one asks agencies to decide whether to implement such "projects" as abortion legalization and capital punishment. In the political arena controversial issues are resolved not by cost-benefit analysis, but instead by political and moral debate through which people find common ground. Congress and the courts can erect constraints that bind agencies. These constraints prevent agencies from approving projects that, among other things, involve racial discrimination, the use of fetal tissue, and experimentation on people who do not give their consent—regardless of the extent to which the benefits of these projects outweigh their costs.[42]

The second possibility is to allow agencies to take into account the full range of moral considerations bearing upon projects and not simply the criterion of overall well-being. We have no objection to this alternative, in theory, as long as it is understood that the agency should not resolve a question of fairness, or deontological rights, or distributive justice—say, the use of fetal tissue in medical research—by engaging in cost-benefit analysis. The use of fetal tissue might be morally correct, or wrong, or morally con-

---

[42] See Department of Transportation, *supra* note 28.

troversial, but the resolution does not depend on whether one side of the debate is willing to pay more than the other side of the debate, in order to see its views embodied in the law. In any event, we suspect that agencies should not be given this authority, because they are not generally well positioned to make moral decisions other than decisions regarding welfare maximization.

Finally, it bears emphasis that the case of morally motivated preferences is arguably just the most extreme example of disinterested (non-welfare-relevant) preferences. Consider the case where P prefers the project not because it matters to his own well-being, but also not because he takes it to be morally obligatory; rather, P's preference is motivated by some kind of group loyalty. Or consider the case where P prefers the project out of a sense of obligation to his children. If we had a full and persuasive theory of how preferences should be restricted—of how the distinction between disinterested and welfare-relevant preferences should be drawn—then we might suggest that agencies should ignore *any* kind of disinterested preference or preference-motivating consideration in calculating WEs. But no such theory is yet at hand. The case of morally motivated preferences is, for now, the only case in which it is (1) clear that CVs can be disinterested and therefore can diverge from WEs and (2) practicable to enjoin agencies that they should adjust CVs so as to eliminate the effect of disinterested preferences.[43]

B.   Lack of Information

Suppose that an agency is considering whether to construct a park. A person P has no knowledge about the advantages of parks, so his CV may diverge from his WE. Specifically, let us imagine that P's CV is $-\$10$: when asked how much he would pay or require to be paid in the project (park) world so as to be indifferent between the park and the status quo, he answers that he would require to be paid \$10.

Further, let us define P's CV-I as his hypothetical willingness to pay, given complete information: the amount that, if P were fully informed, he would pay or require to be paid in the project (park)[44] world so as to be

[43] Compare David Sobel, Well-Being as the Object of Moral Consideration, 14 Econ. & Phil. 249 (1998), which provides a critical overview of philosophical attempts to distinguish between disinterested and welfare-relevant preferences.

[44] For the remainder of this article, unless otherwise noted, it should be assumed that all payments to or from persons are made in the project world. This is a basic feature of the CV. That construct—by contrast with the so-called equivalent variation, or EV—is defined in terms of the amount that persons would pay or require to be paid in the project world, not the status quo world. Similarly, all the variations on the concept of CV that we shall develop here, such as the WE, or the CV-I, shall be based on project world payments. Each of these variations can be matched with an analogous variation on the concept of the EV; but since

indifferent between the park and the status quo. Assume that CV-I is $100. (Note that CV-I, not CV, is the number that an agency elicits when respondents to valuation surveys are provided with detailed information about projects, such as in the Grand Canyon study.) Which number should the agency use in its CBA of the park? In particular, what is P's WE? Is it −$10, $100, or something else?

The answer depends on the nature of the project. Let us distinguish several possibilities.

First, people might costlessly and rapidly acquire the relevant information when the project is completed. P's CV is low (−$10) because he thinks that park views are ugly; in fact, they fill him with joy. His belief is wrong because he has never seen a well-maintained park. If P held the correct belief, he would be willing to pay $100, his CV-I; and if the park is implemented, his actual valuation will change to $100. Under these conditions WE is equal to CV-I rather than CV, and P's valuation should be treated as though it were $100.[45]

Second, people might never acquire the relevant information. P might undervalue the park, because he thinks it is full of common and easily cultivated plants, when in fact they are rare and difficult to grow—something P never learns. So P's actual valuation of the park remains −$10, even after the park is implemented. This is one type of case where correcting for preference distortion by looking to undistorted preferences (CV-I) turns out to be a mistake. Although CV-I is $100, P's WE cannot be greater than $0. As we have elsewhere argued in greater detail, it is a necessary condition for a person to benefit from a project that (at some point) she prefer that project to the status quo; actual preferences have at least *that* role on the correct theory of well-being, however idealized. This premise, a quite basic one, has the immediate implication that P cannot benefit from the project just described—in other words, that his WE must be $0 or negative.

A harder question is whether P's WE should be equated here with his CV (−$10), or set at 0, or given yet another (negative) value. That question

---

cost-benefit analysts in practice use CVs, not EVs, our focus will be upon the CV and its refinements.

[45] As we explained in Section I, we do not have a general theory as to how fully informed preferences and uninformed preferences interact, to produce well-being. But we are reasonably convinced that, in the particular case at hand, WE is equal to CV-I rather than CV. What if a period of time must pass during which P learns to appreciate parks? The simple solution is to discount to present value the amount he would pay once informed. P's CV should not be treated as though it were $100 but as though it were $100 discounted to present value. However, this simple solution is merely a suggestion on our part; the propriety of discounting future benefits and harms is a controversial issue that we do not have space to discuss here. See generally Richard L. Revesz, Environmental Regulation, Cost-Benefit Analysis, and the Discounting of Human Lives, 99 Colum. L. Rev. 941 (1999).

cannot be answered without a particular view as to how uninformed and fully informed preferences interact to produce well-being. On one view, WE is properly −$10 because it is P's uninformed preferences that constitute (and continue to constitute) P's view of the world. On another view, both types of preferences have a coequal role in shaping welfare; P cannot be made better off by a project that he never comes to actually prefer, but neither can he be harmed by a project that, if fully informed, he would prefer. Thus he neither truly gains, nor truly loses, and his WE is neither his CV nor his CV-I but $0. We confess to being swayed by the view that equates WE and CV (in the case at hand), but it is beyond the scope of this paper to take a definitive stand on that.

Several variations on this second case should be mentioned. One is where CV and CV-I have the same sign, but differ in amount. P barely likes the park, and would like it more if he knew about it; or he detests it, and would slightly dislike it if better informed. Note that the premise we invoked above—actual preference is a necessary condition for benefit—does not here help in deciding where WE lies in the range between CV and CV-I. A different variation on the second case is where information changes P's behavior. For example, a well-informed P would go into the park (and CV-I is based on the prediction that he would thus behave), but in fact P never learns something significant about the park and never goes in. In this particular example, P is not made better off by the park because he does not use it; his WE is not greater than $0, even though CV-I is $100. Generalizing from the example is hazardous, but it at least seems clear that WE can differ from CV-I by virtue of the behavioral impact of imperfect information.

Finally, the second case can be varied by having the information change instrumental judgments rather than intrinsic valuations. The project is not a park, but an air quality project, which P values (and would value under full information) in light of the effect of air quality on his longevity. He believes, incorrectly, that the cleanser used by the project would actually reduce his longevity, so CV = −$10. In fact, the cleanser improves air quality, so CV-I = $100. Here, the case for setting WE equal to CV-I even if P remains uninformed about the project once implemented seems stronger.

To turn now to a third case: people might acquire the relevant information only if the agency feeds it to them. The agency might have to distribute leaflets describing the benefits of parks or invest in television commercials. These activities are costly and should be included in the cost of the project. If the cost of disseminating information is high enough that the project has negative value once that cost is taken into account, then we have the second case, above. Otherwise, the agency performs an educative function as well as implementing the project.

C. Objectively Bad Preferences

Suppose some people support or oppose projects because their actual as well as fully informed preferences are sadistic. A person might favor a park because he wants to see a neighbor's beloved home demolished in order to make way for the park, or he may oppose the park because he does not want his neighbors to benefit from higher property values. Or a person might oppose AIDS research because he dislikes homosexuals and drug users with whom he is acquainted and does not want to see their suffering relieved. Or, suppose some person prefers a way of life that is clearly worthless. Person P wants to spend his days in an opium-induced haze, rather than working, developing relationships, accomplishing intellectual or practical goals, starting a family, or doing anything else; and this preference is wholehearted, in the sense that it conflicts with no second-order preference of P's[46] and does not change under full information.

The sadism and drug fixation[47] examples show that objective criteria are sometimes plausibly relevant to agency decisions and CBA.[48] The simplistic account of their relevance runs as follows: If the status quo is bad for person P in light of objective criteria, and the project is better for P in light of objective criteria, then the move from the status quo to the project improves P's welfare, regardless of P's actual preferences. But this simplistic account is incorrect, given the role of actual preference as a constituent (if not the sole constituent) of well-being. If the project is objectively better for P than the status quo, but P prefers (and would continue to prefer) the status quo, then his WE for the project cannot be larger than 0. This is parallel to the point we made in Section IIIA, about the size of WE given a deviation between actual and fully informed preferences.

So how should WE be calculated where criteria of objective welfare value and actual preferences diverge? In theory, we could think of the interaction between preference and value, to produce WE, along the following lines: Define a new measure, CV-O, as the amount that P would be willing

[46] See Harry G. Frankfurt, Freedom of the Will and the Concept of a Person, 68 J. Phil. 5 (1971) (discussing second-order preferences).

[47] The opium user's case is a case of drug fixation, not addiction, since his preference for drug use is fully informed, wholehearted, and (let us assume) otherwise autonomous. Government might plausibly prohibit the fully autonomous use of drugs just because that activity is thought to be objectively worthless.

[48] For arguments to the effect that objective values are a component of welfare, see, for example, John Finnis, Natural Law and Natural Rights (1980); Martha C. Nussbaum, Nature, Function, and Capability: Aristotle on Political Distribution 145 (Oxford Studies in Ancient Philosophy, supp. vol., Julia Annas & Robert Grimm eds. 1988); George Sher, Beyond Neutrality: Perfectionism and Politics (1997).

to pay or be paid for the project if his preferences perfectly tracked considerations of objective value; and then set WE depending upon the divergence between CV-O and CV. For example, P is willing to pay $10 for a new art museum, but if his preferences tracked objective values, he would be willing to pay $50; WE would be some amount between $10 and $50, depending on how exactly actual preferences and objective values interact under the right theory of well-being.

But this suggestion is not practicable. Calculating CV-O would be a hopelessly difficult task for agencies that were sincerely trying to measure WEs. Further, instructing agencies to determine CV-O would significantly increase the opacity of CBA and thus the extent to which agencies can pursue their own agendas rather than sincerely attempting to perform CBA. We are less sanguine about integrating considerations of objective value into agency decision making than we are about integrating the informational considerations discussed in Section IIIA—what P would prefer under full information, as against what he actually prefers—given that claims of objective value are highly contestable and not amenable to empirical testing.

A simpler and more practicable approach would be for objective values to bear upon agency valuations like this: If P is so perverse as to prefer a project that is clearly[49] objectively bad, or to disprefer a project that is clearly objectively good, then P's WE should be taken by the agency to be $0. Otherwise (except in the case of changing preferences, to be considered momentarily), objective values should be ignored.[50]

A plausible supplement to this proposal is to use objective values as a tool for choosing between different sets of actual preferences, where those preferences change over time. Suppose that P prefers the status quo but would prefer the project if it were implemented. Specifically, suppose that P's CV for the project based upon status quo world preferences is −$20, while his CV for the project based upon his project world preferences is $15.[51] In this sort of case, textbook CBA has no resources for assigning P

---

[49] "Clear" is an attempt to sort between value choices sufficiently uncontestable not to give rise to serious problems of transparency, and so on, and other sorts of value choices. It might not work.

[50] It is plausible that objective values are one component of well-being, but—as we stated in Section I—we are unsure whether this plausible suggestion is really correct. Thus the recommendation advanced in the text is a contingent one: If the designer of administrative procedures takes objective values to be a component of well-being, then he should instruct agencies to calculate WEs as recommended. The recommended use of objective values as a tiebreaker for choosing between different sets of actual preferences, set forth immediately below, is similarly contingent.

[51] This distinction between status quo world and project world preferences should not be confused with the quite separate distinction between CVs and EVs. (As we have already explained, textbook CBA generally uses CVs, not EVs, and the analysis in this paper is similarly focused upon CVs.) The CV/EV distinction concerns where dollar payments occur: P's

a unique project valuation. Both the status quo world and the project world preferences are actual-preference sets of P; given the view of welfare traditionally associated with cost-benefit analysis, namely, the unalloyed actual-preference view, there are no grounds for picking one set or the other as the unique basis by which to measure P's valuation of the project. Thus the textbook approach (at least in theory) would be to calculate two aggregate CV measures for the project described here, one assigning P a CV of −$20 and the other assigning her a CV of $15. This could, in turn, produce an indeterminacy at the level of aggregate CV and, thus, in the overall cost-benefit evaluation of the project. For example, if the project described here affects no one else in the world but P and Q, and Q's CV for the project is −$10, then one aggregate CV measure of the project (−$20 + −$10 = −$30) counts it as worse than the status quo, while another aggregate CV measure of the project ($15 + −$10 = $5) counts it as better.

However, a more sophisticated account of welfare may enable us to choose between conflicting sets of actual preferences and, thus, to assign a unique WE to persons whose preferences change over time. If P's status quo preferences are distorted in some way, while his project world preferences are undistorted, then plausibly P should be assigned a unique WE based upon his undistorted, project world preferences. This is, in effect, what we argued above where the distortion at hand was P's lack of information: where the project would increase P's information, such that his (uninformed) status quo preferences and (informed) project world preferences are different, agencies should use the latter in calculating P's WE. The same is plausibly true where the distortion at hand is the deviation between P's preferences and criteria of objective value. If the project is clearly better for P than the status quo, and if P's project world preferences favor the project while his status quo preferences do not, then the agency does have a basis for choosing between the two sets of preferences, and it is willingness to pay based upon project world preferences that the agency should use to calculate a unique WE for P.

D. Adaptation

Suppose people are not willing to pay for parks because they have adapted to a world without parks. Or they have persuaded themselves that

---

CV is the hypothetical dollar payment in the project world that would counterbalance the project's effect on him, while his EV is the hypothetical dollar payment in the status quo world that would counterbalance the project's effect on him. If P has unchanging preferences, then his EV and CV can still differ, but his CV will be a single, unique amount. By contrast, if P has different preferences in the project and status quo world, then this can give rise to two different values for his CV. That is our concern here.

only rich people need parks, because rich people are effete and weak. Merely informing people about the benefits of parks, then, will not cause people to change their preferences. Indeed, to keep the example as clear as possible, we will assume that people are well informed.

One should distinguish two kinds of adaptation. In the first case, people's adaptive preferences never change. Whether or not the agency creates a park, P will always oppose parks because of his impoverished childhood. For the same reason that agencies should not implement projects that benefit people only if they obtain information that will forever elude them, agencies should not implement projects only because the projects are ranked higher by idealized (''nonadaptive'') preferences[52] that will never become actual. Where P prefers and continues to prefer the status quo (given his actual, adaptive preferences), the project cannot be welfare improving for him—his WE for the project cannot be greater than $0—even if P's idealized, nonadaptive preferences point in favor of the project.

To see why, imagine that the overburdened housewife discussed by Sen[53] opposes a project to create a well near her home, preferring the long walk to the river (which, let us assume, the well project will make inaccessible to her). If her preferences truly cannot be expected to change in response to the project—if she will use the well with regret, continuing to prefer the world in which she walked to the river—then it is hard to say how the project would make her better off. The project might be supplemented with educational efforts, in the hope that the housewife will develop different preferences as a result of education. But in the limiting case where the housewife's preferences are irrevocably entrenched, by virtue of upbringing, her WE for the project is no greater than $0.

As with the information case, the issue remains whether the housewife should be counted as being hurt by the project or instead be given a WE of $0. If the answer is $0, then the housewife is in effect ignored by the agency in its cost-benefit analysis of the well project even though her actual valuation of that project is negative. If the answer is to set WE equal to CV, then the agency would simply not take account of the fact that the housewife's preferences are adaptive. This might be the right answer, because the third alternative—to choose a number between $0 and the CV that properly reflects the degree of adaptiveness—is unpalatable. The problem with this alternative is its excessive difficulty. The problem here is even more difficult than the problems posed by lack of information. One can

---

[52] Everything we say in this section holds true regardless of the specifics of a theory for deciding when preference are inappropriately adaptive and for constructing idealized, nonadaptive preferences.

[53] See note 22 *supra*.

more easily imaginatively construct informed preferences out of uninformed preferences than nonadaptive preferences out of adaptive preferences. If the housewife prefers the walk because she was abused as a child, can we imagine what her preferences would be if she had not been abused? If she prefers the walk because she has unconsciously absorbed the views of her neighbors, can we imagine what her preferences would be if she has not unconsciously absorbed these views? We doubt that these questions can be answered, and we are sure that administrative agencies are in a poor position to answer them.

One possible solution to the problem is to use criteria of objective value. This is the solution we tentatively recommend. Sometimes adaptive preferences will also be clearly objectively bad. Perhaps this is true of the well case: perhaps it is clearly objectively better for the housewife to use the well than to walk to the river. If so, our suggested rule for the case of objective value would come into play,[54] and the housewife's WE would be set at $0. Sometimes, however, a person P can have an adaptive preference for the status quo—that preference can be rooted in some injustice or other deficiency of the person's background—even though the status quo is not objectively bad, relative to the project.[55] Imagine that P prefers one kind of recreation to another, that P continues to do so under full information, and that this recreation is not objectively harmful for P, but that P would prefer the second recreation had not the first been the only recreation available to him during an impoverished childhood. In this sort of case, we suggest, WE should be set equal to CV.

In the second variation on the case of adaptive preference, people's preferences change over time. P has an actual preference for the status quo, rooted in some unfortunate feature of his background, while his nonadaptive or idealized preference is in favor of the project. But P's actual preference is not fixed; if the project were implemented, he would come to prefer it. So P's CV based upon status quo world preferences is, say, −$55, while his CV based upon project world preferences is, say, $25. In this sort of case, at least in theory, criteria of adaptiveness could be used for choosing between P's conflicting sets of actual preferences, even where the project and the status quo are objectively fine and thus criteria of objective value provide no basis for making the choice. The agency could assign P a unique WE equal to $25 on the grounds that his actual project world preferences are nonadaptive while his actual status quo preferences are adaptive. But

[54] See Section IVC.

[55] Compare L. W. Sumner, Welfare, Happiness and Ethics 156–71 (1996) (distinguishing between the view that preferences must be objectively good to be welfare constitutive and the view that preferences must be autonomous to be welfare constitutive).

given the especial malleability of the concept of adaptive preferences (even as compared to the notion of an objectively "good" or "bad" way of life, which seems to have more commonsense resonance), we are quite skeptical that agencies should be instructed to use adaptiveness as a tiebreaker when status quo and project world preferences are different.

To sum up: Adaptiveness is a separate way in which preferences can be distorted, distinct from the lack of information and the lack of objective value. P's preference for the status quo can be adaptive, even if this prefer- ence is fully informed and even if the status quo is not clearly objectively worse than the project. Thus, in theory, adaptiveness could be a separate basis for agencies to reject CVs and a separate ingredient in the calculation of WEs. However, this suggestion strikes us as impracticable. In some cases, P's adaptive preference will also be uninformed, or objectively bad, or both, and in such a case a WE will appropriately be calculated for P based on considerations of full information or objective value. But adap- tiveness per se should not, we think, be a component of agency decision making. If P's preference is distorted solely because it is adaptive, and in no other way, then agencies should stick to textbook CBA and use P's CV as the measure of the project's welfare impact upon him.

E.   Wealth Distortions

Cost-benefit analysis is inaccurate, quite apart from the divergence be- tween CVs and WEs, by virtue of the fact that both measures reduce wel- fare impacts on project winners and losers to dollars—which are, in turn, differentially productive of welfare in different persons. In particular, the marginal utility (strictly, marginal increase in overall well-being) of a dollar expended by a person poor in total wealth is generally larger than the mar- ginal utility of a dollar expended by a rich person. The apparent solution is for agencies to weight WEs by the marginal utility of money. There are technical problems in constructing the right weighting factor; there may also be problems in transparency and reliability. But quite apart from tech- nical and implementation difficulties, the proposal that agencies correct for the distorting effect of endowments by weighting WEs raises the subtler issues of (1) market adjustment (where rich and poor effectively undo the project picked out by weighted CBA, since their behavior is driven by un- weighted preferences);[56] (2) the possible welfare superiority of money transfers to agency projects; and (3) the redistributive objection, which points out that weighted WEs (or CVs) would cause agencies to seek out

---

[56] Similar phenomena are widespread and much discussed—for example, the possibility that safety regulations cause consumers to take less care. See, for example, W. Kip Viscusi, Fatal Tradeoffs: Public and Private Responsibilities for Risk 223–27 (1992).

redistributive projects rather than projects that solve market failures. These are the issues we will focus upon here.

Suppose that an agency must decide whether to construct a park in a wealthy neighborhood or a poor neighborhood.[57] All people have the same preferences, which include a desire for more park space. More people live in the poor neighborhood than in the wealthy neighborhood, but the wealthy people are willing to pay more for the park because of their lower marginal utility of money. The agency, however, adjusts CVs using the marginal utility of money and relies upon the adjusted CVs to justify placement of the park in the poor neighborhood.

The result of the agency's action is that the property values in the poor neighborhood will rise relative to the property values in the rich neighborhood. If the poor people are renters, landlords might terminate their leases, convert to condominiums, and sell the condominiums to rich people. The rich people move out of the old rich neighborhood, and the poor people move out of the old poor neighborhood. Perhaps they simply switch places. Far from benefiting poor people, the agency's project benefits landlords, who are likely to be relatively wealthy, while causing a large welfare loss as people engage in unnecessary migration. It would be better to give the park to the rich neighborhood.[58]

This is an extreme version of what might happen. Another possibility is that some poor people own their own homes. These people would benefit from the increase in property values. But they would presumably sell to rich people, so the result of the agency decision to place the park in the poor rather than rich neighborhood is a transfer of wealth from rich people and poor people who do not own their homes to poor people who do own their homes. The rich people lose because they must pay to move to a new neighborhood, likewise, the poor people without homes. The poor people with homes gain because of the increase in property values.

In this second case, the project of building the park in the poor neighborhood is welfare inferior to the project of building the park in the rich neighborhood plus arranging a lump-sum payment from the rich people to the

---

[57] So the two outcomes being compared by CBA are "park in wealthy neighborhood" and "park in poor neighborhood." One would then be designated the status quo world, the other the project world, for purposes of calculating CVs. The discussion that follows does not depend upon which outcome, "park in wealthy neighborhood" or "park in poor neighborhood," is in fact designated as status quo.

How is the park funded? The funding scheme (for example, a scheme for funding the park through taxes) might well affect the welfare of persons in the "park in wealthy neighborhood" world, as compared to the "park in poor neighborhood" world. But we ignore this complication.

[58] See Sunstein, *supra* note 23, at 283.

poor people (or poor people with homes), which would not necessitate the uprooting and migration of large populations. However, agencies do not have the authority to order lump-sum payments. The agency's choice, then, is between benefiting some poor people through a project that diminishes the welfare of other poor people and a few rich people or benefiting a few rich people and some poor people at the expense of other poor people. Both are welfare inferior to the option of building the park in the rich neighborhood plus a transfer.

Suppose finally that people cannot move and that, therefore, property values do not adjust. The rich people will stay in the rich neighborhood and the poor people will stay in the poor neighborhood. Suppose that the rich people's aggregate CV is $1,000 and the poor people's aggregate CV is $500. If the park is placed in the poor people's neighborhood, they will obtain a value of $500. And this is true even of the very poor people who do not own their homes. One might argue that a better project would be the construction of the park in the rich neighborhood with a transfer, of say $600, from rich to poor.[59]

What should the agency do in these three cases? In the first case, by virtue of market adjustment, placing the park in the rich neighborhood turns out to be welfare superior to placing the park in the poor neighborhood. Here, it seems straightforward to us that the park should be placed in the rich neighborhood.[60] In evaluating the project, the agency should take account of market adjustment; if market adjustment undermines the value of a superficially attractive project, the project should not be implemented. Because placing the park in the poor neighborhood does not, after market adjustment, increase overall well-being, the welfare criterion counts against the park's placement there.

The second and third cases are more difficult. The fact that a third project—placing the park in the rich neighborhood and transferring wealth from rich to the poor—is welfare superior to the projects under consideration hardly seems relevant when that third project is not available to the agency. We know of no agency in the U.S. government that has the authority to order wealth transfers, and there are many good reasons for denying them this authority.

---

[59] See Louis Kaplow & Steven Shavell, Why the Legal System Is Less Efficient than the Income Tax in Redistributing Income, 23 J. Legal Stud. 667 (1994). Note, however, that an even better project than that might be constructing the park in the poor neighborhood and transferring $600 or a larger amount from rich to poor.

[60] This seems straightforward to us, insofar as the agency is solely concerned with overall well-being. If the agency is instructed to consider both overall well-being and other moral criteria, it might have grounds for placing the park in the poor neighborhood, although, in the particular example at hand, it is hard to see what those grounds could be.

Assume that this does not change and that in the second and third cases the only options available to the agency are the simple ones. What should the agency do? There is a plausible case that the agency should just choose the option identified by marginal utility weighted CBA, namely, placing the park in the poor neighborhood.[61] After all, this is welfare superior to placing the park in the rich neighborhood; weighted CBA is accurate, to this extent. To be sure, it might be the case that welfare-improving transfers through the tax and welfare system are not made because Congress has other things on its mind, and not because the optimal distribution of wealth has been achieved. But the agency has identified a way of increasing overall well-being and should implement it, and if this result is welfare inferior to an alternative that is politically impossible, that is irrelevant.

One might object to the approach suggested here because it would give agencies a license to search for projects that have differential impacts on rich and poor, and then approve them not because of their public good aspects, or because they satisfy other standard market failure rationales for government intervention,[62] but because of their redistributive effects. Agencies will implement projects in poor neighborhoods until people in those neighborhoods are as rich as people in rich neighborhoods. Weighted CBA gives agencies a license to undertake projects that increase overall well-being just by changing the distribution of wealth. This is the redistributive objection to weighted CBA.

The redistributive objection is a cogent one. There may be good, principled reasons against authorizing agencies to approve projects that are welfare increasing merely in virtue of their redistributive effects—because such a practice produces a disincentive to the accumulation of wealth, thereby decreasing overall well-being in the long run; or because, at some point, it invades the property rights of the rich; or perhaps for some other reason. But if this conclusion is correct, then the appropriate response of agencies is not to return to conventional CBA, with unweighted CVs (or WEs). There is no reason to think that a simple cost-benefit comparison of a project and the status quo, which uses unweighted CVs (or WEs), should generally reach the same result as a sophisticated cost-benefit comparison of a project and the status quo, which uses weighted CVs (or WEs) and also integrates market adjustment effects and incentive effects into the outcomes being compared.

---

[61] For purposes of the discussion, we shall assume that in the second case the option of placing the park in the poor neighborhood is indeed superior, using weighted CBA (and taking account of market adjustment), to the option of placing the park in the rich neighborhood.

[62] See, for example, Stephen G. Breyer, Regulation and Its Reform (1982) (presenting market failure rationales); Anthony Ogus, Regulation: Legal Form and Economic Theory (1994) (same).

Rather, we see two possible responses to the redistributive objection. First, as we suggested above, in theory agencies should count as costs perverse incentives that might result where CVs are weighted to correct for the declining marginal utility of wealth, that is, in inverse proportion to total wealth, thus producing a long-run disincentive to the accumulation of wealth. They should also include costs that would result from market adjustments, like the migration between neighborhoods discussed in the example above. Without consideration of market adjustments and perverse incentives, the placement of the park in the poor neighborhood looks better (using weighted CBA) than the placement in the rich neighborhood. With consideration of market adjustments but not perverse incentives, the placement of the park in the poor neighborhood looks better (using weighted CBA) than the placement in the rich neighborhood if rich and poor cannot move (the third case described above) but not necessarily if they can (the first and second cases). Finally, with consideration of both market adjustments and perverse incentives, the placement of the park in the poor neighborhood may not look better (using weighted CBA) than the placement of the park in the rich neighborhood even in the case where rich and poor cannot move.

To see how perverse incentives might be factored into agency decision making, consider once more the case of immobile neighbors and assume the following. Rational Rick, in response to the park's placement in the rich neighborhood, will pursue one employment plan, E1. In response to the park's placement in the poor neighborhood, he will pursue another plan, E2, that earns him less wealth (because he has less incentive to earn wealth if he thinks that the park agencies and other agencies will weight his CVs in inverse proportion to his wealth). Assume further that Rick's CV for E1, as against E2, is $200. Then $200, as weighted for Rick's marginal utility of wealth, could be added to the rich persons' CVs ($1,000, again appropriately weighted) in determining the monetized benefits of placing the park in the rich neighborhood.

A second possible response to the redistributive objection is for agencies to rely upon a rule of thumb. The problem with the first suggestion is that it may be impossible to calculate the ancillary costs—work disincentives, market adjustment—created by a project and by the particular technique that the agency uses to evaluate it. This is similar to the problem of calculating objective values. A possible rule of thumb is that agencies should avoid projects that produce large and concentrated losses, even on wealthier segments of society, and that provide minimal benefits, even to poorer segments of society. The EPA might rely on such a rule of thumb,[63] although

---

[63] See True, *supra* note 33, at 324.

it has not given its reasons, and one might suspect that the EPA avoids such projects simply because their high visibility makes them politically dangerous. Nevertheless, there is a rationale for this rule of thumb, and that rationale is that as losses associated with the project decline, and as the number of people affected declines, the magnitude of the project's perverse effect on work incentives and the danger of market adjustment also decline.

IV. SOME INSTITUTIONAL CONSIDERATIONS

Administrative agencies make decisions within a political structure and have important political purposes. They are agents of Congress, the president, and the people. If they are not supervised, they may regulate in a way that does not serve the public interest. The capture theory of regulation, according to which regulated industries bend agencies to their will, identifies one kind of agency problem. More broadly, an agency might serve the interests of its administrator, or of its bureaucracy, or of influential citizens or groups, rather than the interests of hierarchical superiors in the political branches or the general public. This danger might lead Congress, the president, or the courts to supervise agencies very closely. But if agencies are supervised too closely, then the various advantages that flow from specialization and division of labor are lost. Some balance must be struck between deference and supervision.

One technique for supervising agents (and agencies) is to require them to disclose information about their behavior. This is the political advantage of cost-benefit analysis: it forces agencies to be clear about the basis of their decisions, and this facilitates monitoring by other actors. Agencies that engage in direct welfare evaluation of projects may get the evaluation right or wrong, but it is very difficult for other actors to evaluate the agencies unless the agencies quantify or monetize costs and benefits. Analysis of some agency actions in fact suggests that agencies do not get it right. Agencies that do not use cost-benefit analysis make inconsistent assumptions about valuation of life.[64] Even agencies that use cost-benefit analysis make inconsistent assumptions about valuation of life, discount rate, and no doubt much else (see the Appendix), but it is easy to identify these inconsistencies and ask the agencies to justify them.[65] If an agency assumes a high valuation of life when justifying a regulation that injures one industry, while assuming a low valuation of life when rejecting a regulation that injures an-

---

[64] See Viscusi, *supra* note 57, at 264; John F. Morrall III, A Review of the Record, 10 Regulation 13, 30 (1986).

[65] See U.S. General Accounting Office, *supra* note 29.

other industry, and the regulations are in other respects identical, suspicions will be aroused that the second industry has captured the agency.[66]

Appendix Tables A1 and A2 show that agencies have tremendous freedom in choosing discount rates and valuations of life, despite efforts by OMB to impose some order.[67] An agency can apparently use a discount rate of 0.03 and a valuation of life of $5.8 million in one regulation and a discount rate of 0.1 and a valuation of life of $1.5 million in another regulation. That means that the agency could assert that a regulation that, say, saves 10 lives per year for 5 years produces benefits of as much as $266 million, or as little as $57 million. Cost-benefit analysis constrains agencies, but not as much as its proponents might hope.

Given that CBA currently imposes little constraint on agencies—at least, when the regulation will produce statistical deaths over a long period of time—one might hesitate about giving agencies more freedom by allowing them to correct for preference distortions. If agencies are permitted to modify CVs in order to account for distortions in preferences, then (1) inconsistencies in assumptions will be difficult to identify, and indeed (2) agencies may be able to conceal improper goals. This is a serious possibility, but the harm can be limited if agencies are required to explain deviations from CV baselines and use uniform adjustments. If an agency adjusts CVs to account for wealth differences, for example, it should be required to explain what the wealth differences are and what weightings are used to make the adjustments. The agency's argument for the adjustment will have to be reasonable, and, more important, it will have to be consistent across regulations, so that the agency cannot opportunistically change assumptions in order to justify some regulations and not others.

V. CONCLUSION: SOME PROPOSALS FOR REFORM

Cost-benefit analysis poses a number of difficult conceptual problems. We have discussed five; these are the treatment of disinterested preferences, of preferences distorted by lack of information, adaptation, and objective badness, and of preferences whose influence is inflated or deflated by relative wealth. If agencies did not face information and decision costs and were not subject to political constraints, they could maximize overall well-being in several straightforward ways:

---

[66] This is an interpretation of Corrosion Proof Fittings v. EPA, 947 F.2d 1201, 1222–23 (5th Cir. 1991), which criticized the EPA for defending a regulation on the basis of a valuation for lives saved that is higher than that used to reject other regulations.

[67] See Office of Management and Budget, Benefit-Cost Analysis of Federal Programs: Guidelines and Discounts, 57 Fed. Reg. 53,519 (1992).

1. They would ignore disinterested preferences or else treat widespread moral commitments as (nonmonetized) constraints on projects.
2. They would use informed preferences when persons will become informed as a result of the project or when preferences are instrumental rather than intrinsic; they would otherwise rely, at least to some extent, on uninformed preferences; and they would consider information dissemination as a potential supplement to the project, with its own benefits and costs.
3. They would discount adaptive preferences, and rely to some extent on idealized, nonadaptive preferences in calculating WEs—if, for example, such preferences will become actual as a result of the project and even, perhaps, if adaptive preferences are entrenched.
4. They would ignore objectively bad preferences.
5. They would adjust for wealth distortions by weighting for marginal utility.

But agencies do face information and decision costs. Such fallible agencies must use whatever decision procedure minimizes the sum of these costs and the cost of error. Although it is hard to generalize, a number of comments can be made.

Even fallible agencies can successfully ignore objectively bad preferences when preferences violate widespread, uncontroversial intuitions about valuable and worthless behavior. Moreover, fallible agencies can successfully ignore disinterested preferences in certain situations: they should not use existence values for environmental entities. However, the appropriate response is not always so straightforward. A person might have a high CV for, say, a public commuter train both because of a self-interested preference for convenient transportation and because of a disinterested preference for environmentally sound transportation. A person might have a high CV for a bridge both because it reduces his cost of transportation and because it annoys his neighbors. These CVs would be reflected in market behavior as well as in survey results. In such cases of mixed preferences, the ideal agency would sort them out, but a real agency probably cannot. The real agency might plausibly choose to rely on traditional CVs on the theory that self-interested preferences tend to have much greater influence on CVs, except in domains where it seems likely that disinterested preferences dominate. The most important such domains are ones where the actual CVs are low, because in such cases the direct impact of the project is small and moral feelings are relatively powerful. Environmental regulation is such a domain, and that is why existence values should be ignored.

Real agencies are, we suspect, unlikely to be able to distinguish adaptive preferences from nonadaptive preferences. Accordingly, we think that agencies should ignore this category. It is likely that most extreme cases are better handled as objectively bad preferences. For example, preferences of drug addicts, whether or not adaptive, are generally considered objectively bad. Indeed, the fact that agencies would ignore the preferences of nonaddicted drug users suggests that objective value is the more appropriate category.[68]

When preferences are uninformed, agencies should sometimes make adjustments. If projects that are based on informed preferences actually improve well-being, either because people do not need information in order to receive the benefit or because they are likely to obtain information after the project is implemented, then there is a good case for constructing informed preferences. However, when uninformed people do not become informed as a result of the project, matters are more complex, as we discussed in Section III.

We are more optimistic about restricting preferences on the basis of information than on the basis of adaptation for two reasons. First, it is easier for agencies to derive informed preferences from uninformed preferences, than nonadaptive preferences from adaptive preferences. One can, for example, compare the behavior of people who are informed about nutrition and people who are uninformed about nutrition; one can observe changes in behavior as people obtain information; and so on. But it is, even as a conceptual matter, hard to distinguish adaptive preferences from nonadaptive preferences. Many influences contribute to the formation of preferences; distinguishing "corrupt" from "pure" influences may be impossible or even meaningless. Second, it is easier to give people information than it is to change their preferences. Indeed, people will seek out information because it can help them satisfy their desires, but people commonly resist efforts to change their preferences. The first requires education; the second requires brainwashing.

Finally, when CVs are distorted because of wealth differences, real agencies might use distributive weights and then make further corrections to deal with the problems of market adjustment and perverse incentives. We have outlined how these corrections could be made. But the more practicable course, we think, is for agencies to rely upon the rule of thumb suggested above—to avoid projects that have a large impacts upon the distribution of wealth.

Further, it is unclear whether the basic idea of distributive weighting is itself a feasible one. It may be just too complicated for Congress or OMB to specify a methodology for weighting CVs, in inverse proportion to total

---

[68] See note 47 *supra*.

wealth or income, that is reasonably accurate (in compensating for the declining marginal utility of wealth) and that agencies can use with reasonable success. The feasibility of distributive weighting has been much debated, without a clear resolution, by welfare economists. If distributive weighting is not feasible, then agencies should probably use unadjusted CVs when the distribution of wealth among the winners does not differ much from the distribution among the losers. When the distributions differ greatly, an agency could refrain from implementing the project. One possible alternative route would be to inform Congress and hierarchical superiors in the executive branch; these officials might be willing to arrange for compensation of the losers or some other politically desirable outcome. Finally, an agency could use a procedure other than CBA for comparing the project and status quo[69]—in effect, a procedure that reaches the same kind of results as weighted CBA but is more feasible—but this would lead back to the problem of market adjustment and perverse incentives. We are skeptical that agencies can really take account of these.

A comment about this last point should be added. Supporters of CBA have traditionally argued that it avoids distributional judgments and allows agencies to focus on efficiency improvements that their expertise puts them in a position to identify. Critics of CBA have pointed out that distributional judgments cannot be avoided. The efficiency of a project is a function of its distributive effects. Unadjusted CVs are unacceptable because they reward people on the basis of wealth, yet wealthy people are on average likely to value a dollar on the margin less than poor people are. Properly adjusted CVs would result in possibly massive redistribution to the poor as agencies implemented projects that tax the rich (because their marginal dollars are worth little to them) and benefit the poor (who can then use valuable marginal dollars for other purposes). Our view is that in theory agencies should take account of the costs of market adjustments and work disincentives, and if they could do this, then properly adjusted CBA would not result in a massive redistribution of wealth. In practice, agencies are unlikely to be able to calculate these costs, so certain broad constraints—against projects that have large impacts on the distribution of wealth, for example—might be justified. This may be a rough description of agency practice, but there is much room for improvement.

[69] See Adler & Posner, *supra* note 1, at 229–33 (discussing multidimensional assessment).

APPENDIX

TABLE A1

VALUATIONS OF LIFE

Regulation	Value ($Million)
Department of Transportation, Federal Aviation Administration, Proposed Establishment of the Harlingen Airport Radar Service Area, TX, 55 Fed. Reg. 32,064 (1990)	1.5
Department of Agriculture, Food Safety and Inspection Service, Pathogen Reduction: Hazard Analysis and Critical Control Point Systems, 61 Fed. Reg. 38,806 (1996)	1.6
Department of Health and Human Services, Food and Drug Administration, Regulations Restricting the Sale and Distribution of Cigarettes and Smokeless Tobacco to Protect Children and Adolescents, 61 Fed. Reg. 44,396 (1996)	2.5
Department of Transportation, Federal Aviation Administration, Aircraft Flight Simulator Use in Pilot Training, Testing, and Checking and at Training Centers, 61 Fed. Reg. 34,508 (1996)	2.7
Environmental Protection Agency, Protection of Stratospheric Ozone, 53 Fed. Reg. 30,566 (1988)	3.0
Department of Health and Human Services, Food and Drug Administration, Proposed Rules to Amend the Food Labeling Regulations, 56 Fed. Reg. 60,856 (1991)	3.0
Department of Transportation, Federal Aviation Administration, Financial Responsibility Requirements for Licensed Launch Activities, 61 Fed. Reg. 38,992 (1996)	3.0
Department of Agriculture, Food and Nutrition Service, Proposed National School Lunch Program and School Breakfast Program, 59 Fed. Reg. 30,218 (1994)	1.5, 3.0
Environmental Protection Agency, National Ambient Air Quality Standards for Particulate Matter, 62 Fed. Reg. 38,652 (1997)	4.8
Environmental Protection Agency, National Ambient Air Quality Standards for Ozone, 62 Fed. Reg. 38,856 (1996)	4.8
Department of Health and Human Services, Food and Drug Administration, Medical Devices: Current Good Manufacturing Practice, 61 Fed. Reg. 52,602 (1996)	5.0
Department of Health and Human Services, Public Health Service, Food and Drug Administration, Quality Mammography Standards, 62 Fed. Reg. 55,852 (1997)	5.0
Environmental Protection Agency, Requirements for Lead-Based Paint Activities in Target Housing and Child-Occupied Facilities, 61 Fed. Reg. 45,778 (1996)	5.5
Environmental Protection Agency, National Primary Drinking Water Regulations: Disinfectants and Disinfection Byproducts, 63 Fed. Reg. 69,390 (1998)	5.6
Environmental Protection Agency, Radon in Drinking Water Health Risk Reduction and Cost Analysis, 64 Fed. Reg. 9560 (1999)	5.8

TABLE A2

Discount Rates

Regulation	Discount Rate (Costs/Benefits)
Environmental Protection Agency:	
Emission Standards for Locomotives and Locomotive Engines (1997)	7/7
Requirements for Lead-Based Paint (1996)	3/3
Nuclear Regulatory Commission, License Term for Medical Use Licenses (1997)	7/not quantified
Occupational Safety and Health Administration:	
Respirator Protection (1998)	7/not quantified
Indoor Air Quality (1994)	10/not quantified
Food and Drug Administration:	
Food Labeling Regulations (1993)	5/not quantified
Regulations Restricting the Sale and Distribution of Cigarettes and Smokeless Tobacco to Protect Children and Adolescents (1996)	Not quantified/3
Federal Aviation Administration, Aircraft Operator Security (1997)	7/7
National Highway Transportation Safety Administration, Federal Motor Vehicle Safety Standards; Lamps, Reflective Devices and Associated Equipment (1997)	2–10/2–10
Consumer Product Safety Commission, Requirements for Labeling of Retail Containers of Charcoal (1996)	5, 10/5, 10

Source.—Edward R. Morrison, Judicial Review of Discount Rates Used in Regulatory Cost-Benefit Analysis, 65 U. Chi. L. Rev. 1333, 1364–69 (1998).

A COMMENT ON THE CONFERENCE ON COST-BENEFIT ANALYSIS

GARY S. BECKER*

ABSTRACT

This comment discusses the importance of politics in understanding cost-benefit analysis. Economists frequently rely on a social planner model, under which cost-benefit analysis has a straightforward role, but a better model is the interest group competition model. In this model, cost-benefit analysis can be used to explain why some regulations are adopted and others are not. Further, cost-benefit analysis may also be useful for undermining misleading claims of self-interested political pressure groups.

EVER since the workshop by Eric Posner and Matthew Adler last spring,[1] I have become convinced that an understanding of government behavior is essential for motivating a useful cost-benefit analysis of government programs. Although the relevance of cost-benefit depends crucially on the political process, political issues have been almost entirely neglected in the conference papers and most of the discussion. To concentrate on these issues, I sidestep interesting questions raised at the conference, such as which goods and activities can be included in utility, or whether discounting of future utilities is rational.

I evaluate cost-benefit analysis from the perspective of two polar interpretations of political behavior. The first is the social planner model; the second is the interest group competition model.

THE SOCIAL PLANNER MODEL

An all-powerful social planner lies behind many discussions by economists of political choices. This planner chooses regulations, taxes, and subsidies that maximize perhaps a highly nonlinear function of individual utili-

---

* University of Chicago. This is a reaction to the conference presented informally. I appreciate the comments of Casey Mulligan and Eric Posner on the written version.
[1] See Matthew D. Adler & Eric A. Posner, Rethinking Cost-Benefit Analysis, 109 Yale L. J. 165 (1999).

[*Journal of Legal Studies*, vol. XXIX]

ties. If the planner can redistribute income with lump-sum taxes and subsidies, then the cost-benefit criteria for evaluating any project or program become very simple and powerful. Total benefits equal the sum of dollar benefits to different individuals, and total costs equal the sum of dollar costs. A program should be undertaken if aggregate benefits exceed aggregate costs, regardless of the program's size or its effects on the poor and rich.

If benefits exceed costs, everyone would be made better off by the program, regardless of its initial incidence. For the planner would redistribute away from any adverse initial incidence, until everyone is made better off (assuming all individual utilities are normal goods in the social welfare function).

The assumption of lump-sum redistributions simplifies the analysis, but it is obviously not realistic. A better approach recognizes that all redistributions affect incentives and in this way produce deadweight costs (DWCs). With DWCs, the appropriate calculation of benefits and costs becomes more complicated, although it is still clear in principle. Instead of simply adding all benefits and costs, they should be weighted by the inverse of the marginal DWCs of redistributing to or away from each individual.

Moreover, since DWCs tend to rise as redistribution increases, these weights would not be constant, but would be different for large and small programs. However, the locally relevant weights in principle could be backed out by estimating the DWCs of the taxes, subsidies, or regulations that affect incomes. Note that it is still not necessary to know much about the content of the social welfare function. The assumption that a planner is maximizing a stable welfare function of individual utilities is sufficient to allow a backing out of the weights attached to different utilities in the vicinity of the planner's equilibrium position.

In the social planner model, cost-benefit analysis remains relevant even with the more realistic assumption of DWCs. Moreover, the principle is easy to implement, although in practice it would often be difficult to estimate the relevant weights applied to the gains and losses of different individuals.[2]

Still, even with DWCs, the social planner approach is a fairy tale and is not relevant to understanding which regulations, taxes, and subsidies get implemented. A better model of the political process is required to judge the value of cost-benefit analysis.

---

[2] See, for example, Arnold C. Harberger, Basic Needs versus Distributional Weights in Social Cost-Benefit Analysis, 32 Econ. Dev. Cultural Change 455 (1984).

THE INTEREST GROUP COMPETITION MODEL

A good start is the interest group competition model promoted in the past couple of decades by many political scientists, and also by economists, such as George Stigler, Sam Peltzman, Casey Mulligan, myself, and others.

In this approach, the political power of different groups determines which regulations, taxes, and subsidies are adopted. Since redistributions of income induced by powerful interest groups are not likely to be socially "optimal" in the sense used in the social planner model, cost-benefit analysis may seem to be irrelevant. But an analysis that weights equally benefits and costs to all individuals is still useful in explaining actual political programs.

The programs implemented by the political process obviously depend on the political power of different groups, such as farmers, steelworkers, automobile companies, and others. Cost-benefit analysis does not tell us much about many determinants of political power. However, the magnitude of the benefits from a program to a political group determines the maximum amount that this group would be willing to spend on campaign contributions, on advertising, and in other ways in order to have that program adopted. Similarly, the cost of a program to any group determines the maximum amount that group would spend to prevent the program from being implemented.

Therefore, the larger the difference between the benefits and costs of a program, the greater tend to be political expenditures by supporters compared to political spending by opponents. That is, even when all interest groups are completely selfish, regulations, taxes, and subsidies are more likely to be adopted when they produce larger benefits compared to costs.[3]

Put differently, programs with relatively small DWCs are more likely to be adopted than those with relatively large DWCs. Political power held constant, programs with benefits that exceed costs—those with negative DWCs—have the best chances of being implemented. Similarly, policies tend to be abandoned when their DWCs grow sharply over time. Peltzman bases his explanation of the deregulation movement in the 1970s and early 1980s on the growth over time in DWCs from airline, financial, telecommunication, and other regulations.[4]

So benefits and costs remain an important factor in determining actual regulations, taxes, and subsidies even in models of competition among

[3] Gary Becker, Public Policies, Pressure Groups, and Dead Weight Costs, 28 J. Pub. Econ. 329 (1985).

[4] Sam Peltzman, The Economic Theory of Regulation after a Decade of Deregulation, in The Political Economy of Privatization and Deregulation (Elizabeth E. Bailey & Janet Rothenberg Pack eds. 1995).

selfish interest groups. To be sure, no cost-benefit criterion is necessary or sufficient for the political implementation of policy. But the difference between aggregate benefits and costs helps explain which policies are adopted. Moreover, thousands of potential policies never muster sufficient political support because they have large costs relative to benefits. Cost-benefit analysis, then, is a useful tool for the political economist who wishes to explain why some policies are adopted and others are not.

Calculations of the benefits and costs produced by different programs sometimes also influence which programs are rejected or accepted. Very small interest groups, such as sugar growers, may be successful because voters have little incentive to become informed about the effects of complicated policies. Effective groups are able to persuade enough voters to support policies that favor these groups, even when they badly hurt many others.

Cost-benefit analysts may be in a battle against misleading information spread by self-interested political pressure groups. Still, these analysts can influence political outcomes by making enough voters aware of the true effects of different policies. For this information sometimes raises the opposition by voters to programs with large DWCs. For example, I believe the timing of the deregulation movement mentioned earlier was affected by the economists and lawyers who showed how much harm resulted from the regulation of airlines, banking, trucking, securities, and telecommunications.

CONCLUSION

Cost-benefit analysis has a strong and clear place in a social planner model of political choices. But that model is of little value in explaining actual regulations, taxes, and subsidies. Yet, even when political decisions result from competition among interest groups, benefits and costs help explain which policies are adopted. Moreover, information about the true benefits and costs of different programs sometimes determines whether policies muster enough political support.

COST-BENEFIT ANALYSIS: DEFINITION, JUSTIFICATION, AND COMMENT ON CONFERENCE PAPERS

*RICHARD A. POSNER**

ABSTRACT

In this comment on the conference papers, Judge Posner argues for a pragmatic construal and defense of cost-benefit analysis, demonstrating the benefit of such analysis; responding to specific criticisms of, and suggested changes in, the analysis; and emphasizing that the value of such analysis as an evaluative and decision tool for social and economic policy making does not depend on the resolution of philosophical problems.

THE term "cost-benefit analysis" has a variety of meanings and uses. At the highest level of generality, which we encounter at the outset of Amartya Sen's paper,[1] it is virtually synonymous with welfare economics, that is, economics used normatively—used, that is, to provide guidance for the formation of policy, either public (the more common domain of the term) or private.[2] At the other end of the scale of generality, the term denotes the use of the Kaldor-Hicks (wealth maximization rather than utility maximization) concept of efficiency to evaluate government projects, such as the building of a dam or the procurement of a weapons system; government grants, such as grants for medical research; and government regulations, including not

---

* Chief Judge, U.S. Court of Appeals for the Seventh Circuit, and Senior Lecturer, University of Chicago Law School. I was asked to comment on the papers presented at the conference Cost-Benefit Analysis: Legal, Economic, and Philosophical Perspectives, held at the University of Chicago Law School on September 17–18, 1999. This is the revised text of my oral comment given at the end of the conference; I have made further revisions in response to changes made by the authors in revising their papers for publication. I thank Paul Choi for his very helpful research assistance; Gary Becker and Eric Posner for their very helpful comments on a previous draft; and the conference participants themselves, some of whose oral comments I have appropriated.

[1] Amartya Sen, The Discipline of Cost-Benefit Analysis, in this issue, at 931.

[2] As in Guido Calabresi's theory of strict liability, which emphasizes the effect of strict liability in inducing potential injurers to compare the costs and the benefits of their accident-causing activities.

[*Journal of Legal Studies*, vol. XXIX]

only administrative regulations dealing with health, the environment, and other heavily regulated activities but also statutes and common-law doctrines and decisions. The last—the common law—has been the focus of my own interest in cost-benefit analysis; I have long argued that cost-benefit analysis in the Kaldor-Hicks sense is both a useful method of evaluating the common law and the implicit method (implicit, for example, in the Learned Hand formula for determining negligence) by which common-law cases are in fact decided—and rightly so in my opinion. I do not, however, claim that it is usable for all questions of public policy; I do not know how it could be used to deal with Martha Nussbaum's example of whether to permit Amish parents to keep their children out of school.

What I just said about the common law suggests additional distinctions. It suggests, consistent with Gary Becker's oral comment at the conference, that cost-benefit analysis has value as positive as well as normative analysis. That is, it can be used to explain and predict some government decisions, especially decisions that are relatively insulated from the operation of interest group politics, which is true of most courts (though of the U.S. Supreme Court least of all) and of some administrative agencies in some areas.

Along a different axis of definition, the term cost-benefit analysis can refer to a method of pure evaluation, conducted wholly without regard to the possible use of its results in a decision; or to an input into decision, with the decision maker free to reject the results of the analysis on the basis of other considerations; or to the exclusive method of decision. When used in the last sense, as in my advocacy of the use of cost-benefit analysis to guide common-law decision making, the Kaldor-Hicks approach (if that is the form of cost-benefit analysis used) must be defended because of its well-known normative inadequacies. But when cost-benefit analysis is merely an input into decision, and even more clearly when it is a pure exercise in scholarship, there is no need to insist on its adequacy as a normative principle, provided that efficiency in the Kaldor-Hicks sense is accepted as a social value, albeit not the only social value.

What the Kaldor-Hicks concept particularly leaves out of normative consideration is distributive justice; it treats a dollar as worth the same to everyone. This omission will trouble even some economists who think of economic welfare as synonymous with utility in the utilitarian sense, for it is well known that the marginal utility of income (and perhaps the inframarginal utility of income as well) is different for different persons. But to the extent that distributive justice can be shown to be the proper business of some other branch of government or policy instrument (for example, redistributive taxation and spending) and that ignoring distributive considerations in the particular domain of decision making that is under consideration will not have systematic and substantive distributive consequences, it is possible to set distributive considerations to one side and use the Kaldor-Hicks approach with a good conscience. This assumes, as I have said, that efficiency in the Kaldor-Hicks sense—making the pie larger without worrying about how the relative size of the slices changes—is a social value. But in our society it clearly is, and not merely for "base" materialistic reasons.[3] I think that even Sen, who is more skeptical about free markets than I, agrees and that even Henry Richardson, who is, I would guess, more skeptical about free markets than Sen, agrees also.

In the discussion at the conference John Broome offered as a counter-example to the claim that efficiency in the Kaldor-Hicks sense is a social value the forced uncompensated transfer of a table from a poor person to a rich person. I agree that allowing the transfer would not improve social welfare in any intelligible sense. But it would not be Kaldor-Hicks efficient when one considers the incentive effects, on rich and poor alike, of allowing such transfers and the alternative of forcing the rich person to transact with the poor person. The typical project or policy to which Kaldor-Hicks cost-benefit analysis is applied does not have the features that make Broome's example unpalatable. It is true that judgment, for example in the choice of a discount rate for a project that will yield costs or benefits over a substantial period of time, is unavoidable in cost-benefit analysis and that the need for it cannot be entirely sidestepped by using ranges of estimates rather than point estimates. But this is a reason not for embracing but for resisting the introduction of additional subjective considerations, such as distributive justice, that are not unavoidable, provided, as I say, that one is willing to accept that social wealth, however distributed, is a social value. I would, however, use willingness to accept rather than willingness to pay as the value measure when the policy the costs and benefits of which are being measured takes away property rights, as in the case where farmland will be flooded as a result of the building of a dam. Willingness to accept provides better protection for property rights, which have an important economizing role in a market economy.

I do not want to stake my all on a defense of the Kaldor-Hicks concept of efficiency. For me the ultimate test of cost-benefit analysis employing that concept is a pragmatic one: whether its use improves the performance

---

[3] And for reasons that go considerably beyond the materialistic. See Richard A. Posner, Equality, Wealth, and Political Stability, 13 J. L. Econ. Org. 344 (1997).

of government in any sense of improvement that the observer thinks appropriate.

Throughout this comment, when I use the term cost-benefit analysis without qualification it is in the Kaldor-Hicks sense, but it may refer to any of the three uses of cost-benefit analysis that I have identified—as pure evaluation, as an input into decision, or as the decision rule.

That in a nutshell is my own position on cost-benefit analysis, and it will provide the framework for my commentary on the conference papers. For convenience I divide them into four groups. The first, consisting of the papers by Robert Hahn, Lewis Kornhauser, Cass Sunstein, and Kip Viscusi,[4] are primarily concerned with defending cost-benefit analysis against its critics, as was Gary Becker's comment on the papers. The next group—Robert Frank, and Matthew Adler and Eric Posner[5]—wish to alter it in significant ways, while in the third group, consisting of Broome, Nussbaum, and Richardson,[6] doubt about the validity and utility of cost-benefit analysis is the dominant chord, although none of the papers in this group, not even Richardson's, I shall argue, rejects cost-benefit analysis entirely. Finally, there is Sen's paper,[7] which seems perfectly balanced between the second and third groups, and which I shall discuss last.

I shall be a dutiful commentator and comment on each of the papers, but I want first to make several general observations. The first, repeating what I have already said, is that in my view the ultimate criterion should be pragmatic; we should not worry whether cost-benefit analysis is well grounded in any theory of value. We should ask how well it serves whatever goals we have. So if we are particularly interested in the welfare of minority groups, we should ask whether cost-benefit analysis serves or disserves their interests; on the evidence of Viscusi's paper, it serves them. Notice that it is possible, although I think unlikely, for cost-benefit analysis to pass the pragmatic test even if Kaldor-Hicks efficiency has no social value but turns out simply to be a convenient instrument.

---

[4] Robert W. Hahn, State and Federal Regulatory Reform: A Comparative Analysis, in this issue, at 873; Lewis A. Kornhauser, On Justifying Cost-Benefit Analysis, in this issue, at 1037; Cass R. Sunstein, Cognition and Cost-Benefit Analysis, in this issue, at 1059; W. Kip Viscusi, Risk Equity, in this issue, at 843.

[5] Robert H. Frank, Why Is Cost-Benefit Analysis So Controversial? in this issue, at 913; Matthew D. Adler & Eric A. Posner, Implementing Cost-Benefit Analysis When Preferences Are Distorted, in this issue, at 1105.

[6] John Broome, Cost-Benefit Analysis and Population, in this issue, at 953; Martha C. Nussbaum, The Costs of Tragedy: Some Moral Limits of Cost-Benefit Analysis, in this issue, at 1005; Henry S. Richardson, The Stupidity of the Cost-Benefit Standard, in this issue, at 971.

[7] Sen, *supra* note 1.

Second—and I have also touched on this point—the utility of cost-benefit analysis as a decision rule is a function of the degree to which a particular type of governmental decision process is insulated from political influence, and many such processes are so insulated, to a greater or lesser degree.

Third, the supporters of cost-benefit analysis have made a persuasive pragmatic case, focused principally on risk regulation, that cost-benefit analysis can improve the quality of governmental decision making. Sunstein, who puts this point very well, saying that cost-benefit analysis is "best taken as [a] pragmatic instrument, agnostic on the deep issues and designed to assist people in making complex judgments where multiple goods are involved,"[8] argues that its practical value is especially great because of cognitive quirks that he believes make it difficult for people to think straight and therefore require the kind of rational discipline that cost-benefit analysis imposes on decisions. Sen also refers approvingly to the disciplinary benefit of insisting on explicitness in valuation. When cost-benefit analysis is applied to the regulation of risks to health and safety by different federal regulatory agencies, bizarre anomalies that no one would defend—that none of the critical papers at the conference, certainly, attempted to defend—are discovered. This discovery alone is worth, as it were, the price of admission.

Next, I believe that those papers that accept the essential validity of cost-benefit analysis but seek to improve its normative flavor by modifying or even rejecting the Kaldor-Hicks assumption gain less in normative plausibility than they lose in complication and uncertainty. Better to accept that cost-benefit analysis cannot be the only decision rule used by government and that it can have value when used as an input into decision, as the risk regulation studies show. This may seem a cop-out, as it leaves the government without a decision rule and fails to indicate how cost-benefit analysis is to be weighted when it is merely a component of the decision rule. On this score I am content to say that cost-benefit analysis performs the usual normative role of economics, which is that of compelling the decision maker to confront the costs of a proposed course of action,[9] and further I am content to allow the usual political considerations to reinforce or override the results of the cost-benefit analysis. If the government and the tax-

---

[8] Sunstein, *supra* note 4, at 1077.

[9] "Cost-benefit analysis was intended from the beginning as a strategy for limiting the play of politics in public investment decisions." Theodore M. Porter, Trust in Numbers: The Pursuit of Objectivity in Science and Public Life 189 (1995). He is discussing the use of cost-benefit analysis by the U.S. Army Corps of Engineers, which began using such analysis on proposals for dams, harbors, and other public works in the 1920s.

payer and the voter all know—thanks to cost-benefit analysis—that a project under consideration will save 16 sea otters at a cost of $1 million apiece, and the government goes ahead, I would have no basis for criticism.

My last general point is that none of the papers that considers cost-benefit analysis an unacceptable procedure to use on the issues in which the author is most interested has suggested a superior alternative for evaluating public policies. I doubt that any of them would favor an uninformed political judgment. I conclude that cost-benefit analysis is inescapable across a large range of policy decisions.[10] I shall amplify some of these points in relation to particular papers.

Hahn's paper might be thought pessimistic. He finds that the trend toward requiring cost-benefit analysis at the state level has achieved little in the way of more efficient regulation. He remarks in passing that "more than half (57 percent) of the federal government's regulations would fail a strict benefit-cost test using the government's own [dubious, self-serving] numbers"[11] and that "a reallocation of mandated expenditures toward regulations with the highest payoff to society could save as many as 60,000 more lives a year at no additional cost."[12] These are shocking figures, at least if one suppresses the heartless thought that not all those 60,000 lives may be worth saving. The successes for cost-benefit analysis that Hahn recites, of which my favorite are the repeal of one regulation barring hearses from certain (I assume scenic) parkways and another, a regulation of school signs, that had been adopted at the suggestion of a schoolchild, are modest. Politics, and no doubt (although Hahn does not emphasize this) bureaucratic inertia and self-seeking, have proved major impediments to cost-benefit analysis at all levels of government.

But his pessimistic outlook overlooks three important points. First, as significant as the failures of cost-benefit analysis is how fashionable the technique has become at all levels of government. The theoretical objections to cost-benefit analysis, the sort of objections that are found in a number of the papers at this conference, have crumbled at the practical level—they have retreated to the academy. The spread of cost-benefit analysis, even when it takes the form merely of lip service to the principles of effi-

---

[10] "Those who oppose the use of benefit-cost analysis of course, are seldom completely faithful to their 'health-only' creed. They talk about economic feasibility rather than cost; they countenance lax enforcement; they create exemptions for special classes of polluters; they encourage—indeed, sometimes even demand—delay, lest the consequences of their general policy become too apparent." R. Shep Melnick, The Politics of Benefit-Cost Analysis, in Valuing Health Risks, Costs, and Benefits for Environmental Decision Making: Report of a Conference 23, 25 (P. Brett Hammond & Rob Coppock eds. 1990) (footnote omitted).

[11] Hahn, *supra* note 4, at 892–93 (footnote omitted).

[12] *Id.* at 893 (footnote omitted).

ciency, confirms an international trend toward free markets. Cost-benefit analysis is, after all, primarily an effort to introduce market principles into government, or to induce government to simulate market outcomes, or in short to make government more like business. There is an ideology of free markets; it has some influence on specific governmental decisions; and the growing popularity of cost-benefit analysis is both an effect and, to a small degree, a cause of this ideology.

Second, Hahn may underestimate the degree to which foolish administrative decisions are undone in the compliance phase of administrative proceedings or circumvented by adroit exploitation of loopholes by the regulated firms. And third, and at least a partial response to Gary Becker's suggestion in the discussion that the conduct of cost-benefit analyses by government agencies as opposed to outsiders has little value, Hahn overlooks the significance of judicial review of administrative action in keeping agency cost-benefit analysis honest. When government regulations are based on cost-benefit analysis however inept or tendentious, persons subject to the regulation are armed in challenging it in court to point out the respects in which the analysis was unreasonable and their own cost-benefit analyses superior. It is more difficult to challenge a regulation that rests entirely on nebulous equity grounds.

Kornhauser's paper makes the essential pragmatic defense of cost-benefit analysis—that it "often seem[s] to improve the quality of decisions,"[13] a proposition for which the other papers in this first group provide empirical support. He reinforces this point with a useful distinction between evaluating cost-benefit analysis by reference to a global moral criterion and evaluating it by reference to the feasible alternatives; the latter is surely preferable. It is not helpful to be told that cost-benefit analysis violates some moral desideratum, if there is no feasible alternative method of dealing with a problem or if the only feasible alternatives yield results that even moral philosophers would think worse. My only reservation, and it is little more than a point of personal privilege, is that my own justification for using cost-benefit analysis in common-law decision making is based primarily, consistent with Kornhauser's approach, on what I claim to be the inability of judges to get better results using any alternative approach.[14]

My only area of serious disagreement concerns Kornhauser's discussion of the value of life. He makes an important point, which I shall come back to, that cost-benefit analysis does not really attempt to value lives. But he does not make it as clearly as he could, and, worse, he defends it with an

---

[13] Kornhauser, *supra* note 4, at 1038.

[14] See, for example, Richard A. Posner, The Problems of Jurisprudence 387–88 (1990).

example that he claims, I believe mistakenly, shows that "cost-benefit analysis does not even provide a unique valuation of the value of the life [of] an individual who smokes."[15] Let me begin with that example. Kornhauser points out correctly that smokers need not be indifferent among three policies each of which is expected to reduce the expected number of deaths from lung cancer by one-half—making cigarettes safer, reducing the number of smokers, and reducing the lethality of lung cancer. He infers from this that there is no unique value of life even for smokers. But it is not the value of life that varies in these examples; it is the other consequences of smoking. In the first example, the smoker gets to have his cake and eat it, while in the second he loses whatever utility he obtains from smoking, and in the third he incurs the cost of lung cancer, although it is a lower cost because he has a better chance of surviving.

What Kornhauser should have said about the value of life is that cost-benefit analysis values risks, and the so-called value of life that cost-benefit analysts refer to is just a mathematical transformation. Suppose that it is discovered by studies of people's behavior that the average person would be willing to incur a maximum cost of $1 to avoid the one-in-a-million chance of being killed by some hazard that a proposed project would eliminate. And suppose that 2 million persons are at risk from this hazard and that the proposed project (which for simplicity I will assume has no other benefits) will cost $3 million. Since each of the persons benefited (in an expected sense) by the policy would pay only $1 to avoid the hazard, for a total of $2 million, the benefits are less than the costs. An equivalent way of putting this is that the life-saving project can be expected to save the lives of only two people, each of whom "values his life" at "only" $1 million ($1/.000001), and so the total benefits are only $2 million and are less than the costs. As I said, this is just an arithmetical transformation of an analysis that values risks rather than lives.

Broome offered an example that illustrates the pitfalls of attempting to value lives rather than risks. Two projects each of which will result in the death of one person have the same cost (assuming all their other costs are the same), he argued, even if the death in the first project is the result of imposing a one-in-a-million risk of death on each of a million people and the death in the second project is the result of imposing a one-in-a-thousand risk of death on each of a thousand people. The cost is the same in an ex post sense, but evaluating the projects ex ante requires consideration of the ex ante costs, and they are not the same. The second project is more costly ex ante, because people are much more reluctant (plausibly more than a

[15] Kornhauser, *supra* note 4, at 1051.

thousand times as reluctant) to be subjected to the higher risk. If the 1 million would pay less in the aggregate to avert the risk to them than the 1 thousand would pay to avert the respective risk to them, the second project is more costly.

Sunstein's paper is particularly striking for a point that he does not make, which is that he is inverting one of the standard criticisms of cost-benefit analysis, and of economic thinking more generally: that it undervalues "soft" variables. These critics argue that people give too much weight to factors that can be quantified, and if so this is a good illustration of the availability heuristic in action. Sunstein is arguing that cost-benefit analysis can be used to combat that heuristic and promote rationality in public policy. In so arguing, however, he risks circularity, since if the cognitive quirks that concern him infect market behavior, the prices on which cost-benefit analysis is based will not be a dependable tool for disciplining thought.

I have some other reservations about Sunstein's paper. One, which is more of a quarrel with behavioral economics than a comment on cost-benefit analysis, is his lack of clarity about those cognitive quirks that he believes impede rational thinking. First and least, he classifies the distortions caused by "vivid mental pictures of widespread death or catastrophe"[16] under the heading "Emotions and Alarmist Bias,"[17] yet it seems a prime example of the availability heuristic. More important, some of his quirk categories seem rational, such as that people think better when they are given a context rather than asked to solve a problem in isolation. Preference reversal comes about not because people are inconsistent, but because when they are prodded to recall information that helps them deal with the problem of valuation they give better answers. Likewise, it seems rational to be more fearful about novel risks, such as that of nuclear power, than about old risks, such as that of pollution caused by the burning of coal, since when a risk is novel its mean and variance are difficult to estimate. Viscusi joins Sunstein in thinking fear of novel risks irrational; I disagree with both of them. When some new horror occurs, like the first mass shooting of schoolchildren by fellow students, there is a natural concern that this may be the beginning of a trend, rather than an isolated occurrence; and in that particular case there is also a concern with the possibility of imitation, another legitimate source of alarm.

Second, some of Sunstein's examples can be analyzed in simpler terms than he uses. For example, I do not think the concept of "voluntariness" is necessary or useful for explaining our different reactions to investing in

---

[16] Sunstein, *supra* note 4, at 1070.
[17] *Id.*

the reduction of deaths in skydiving accidents compared to deaths in child-birth. In the former but not the latter case we realize that a low-cost mea-sure of saving lives is for sky divers to switch to safer sports, whereas we do not think that the cheapest way of avoiding deaths in childbirth is a zero birthrate. This is a point that students of strict liability have made in distin-guishing between changes in activity or activity level, as distinguished from changes in care levels, as methods of accident avoidance; sometimes the cheapest method is to abandon the dangerous activity. Similarly, an impor-tant economic consideration in choosing a level of protection against assas-sination of public officials is that they are much more likely to be attacked than the average person, so we may be able to dispense with dread as the explanatory variable.

Third, and related to the problem of circularity that I mentioned earlier, Sunstein hedges on whether to accept or combat misperceptions in de-termining costs and benefits. If property values will plummet because of an irrational fear of contagion from patients in a hospital, should that count as a cost in deciding where to locate the hospital? On the one hand, to accept the market's irrational valuation reduces the advantage of cost-benefit anal-ysis that he stresses, which is that it promotes more rational thinking. If the hospital is built, and neighbors do not become infected, irrational fears of contagion will tend to dissipate. On the other hand, the costs to people of their irrational fears are real costs in the sense of making them unequivo-cally worse off. Thus, in the example given, the decline in property values is a tangible cost, and incidentally one that will be incurred by property owners who do not have irrational fears (but it is a benefit to fearless buyers of their property). In principle, the best solution to the dilemma is Adler and Posner's—weight the irrational fears if but only if they are unlikely ever to be dissipated. For in that case, overriding the fears will not produce Sunstein's hoped-for benefit of getting people to think straighter. But this solution both is difficult to implement, because it is often unclear whether a fear is irrational, and does nothing to prevent the loss in property values that irrational fears can generate. I am not much troubled by the second point, however, because the values will be restored once the irrational fears dissipate. The winners and losers will be different people, but that is a purely distributional concern, which I exclude from my conception of a proper cost-benefit analysis.

Fourth, I do not agree with Sunstein's remarks on distributive justice. He suggests, although only in passing, that the poor, women, and homosexuals should all be entitled to a thumb on the scale in weighting the benefits of programs. So far as the poor are concerned, the objections made by Viscusi, Frank, and Adler and Posner seem decisive, and I shall not repeat them. I am particularly puzzled by the suggestion that women and homosexuals should receive favored treatment in matters of health policy. Women after all outlive men by a considerable margin, and so they might actually benefit, to the extent they value male companionship, from a reorientation of government spending on medical research designed to bring male longevity closer to female, in order to reduce the stark imbalance between the number of elderly women and the number of elderly men. As for the homosexual population, expenditures on finding a cure for a disease that is avoidable through behavioral modification (I am thinking of course of AIDS, which is the principal health concern of the male homosexual qua homosexual) are often a poor investment from an overall social standpoint. For unless the cure is so effective that it causes the disease to disappear, a reduction in its cost will lead to an increase in its incidence—precisely the experience with syphilis after penicillin was discovered to be an effective cure for it. The recent dramatic advances in the treatment of AIDS, advances resulting from heavy government spending on AIDS research, have led to an increase in the incidence of unsafe sex between homosexual men.

I agree with Sunstein, however, that certain private benefits should be excluded from cost-benefit analyses done by government agencies, such as the cost of unwanted race "mixing." In a multiracial society government must be sensitive to the sensitivities of minorities, who would be offended to learn that the government considered bigotry a source of social benefits.

As in the case of Sunstein, my reservations about Viscusi's article concern secondary points. There is first a confusion in the paper over risk in the sense of danger. Viscusi distinguishes among "heterogeneity in individual riskiness, heterogeneity in individual willingness to incur risks, and differences in preferences for activities that pose risks."[18] In the first category he places the higher death rates of men than of women from accidents and homicides. Surely these examples belong in the second category, differential willingness to incur risks. Men do not get killed in accidents, or get murdered, because they are clumsy or weak, but because they engage in riskier activities than women do, on average. In addition, Viscusi's typology leaves out an important fourth category of heterogeneity in the individual valuation of risk, that of a pure taste for danger. Dangerous sports, and dangerous occupations such as fighting fires, are valued by their participants in part for the danger, the confronting of which enhances the participant's sense of self-worth.

I also think Viscusi too cavalier in recommending the dissemination of information about health and safety hazards by government in order to dispel misinformation that drives a wedge between subjective and objective

---

[18] Viscusi, *supra* note 4, at 847.

costs (or irrational and rational fears). Among serious criticisms of public information programs, none of which he discusses (either specific programs or specific criticisms), are the following:

1. Such a program will often lack credibility because government policies are known to be subject to political influence.
2. The program may have a substitution effect: it may reduce private efforts to disseminate information by reducing the impact of those efforts once the government program is in effect; as a result, the net increase in information may be slight. Put differently, Viscusi overlooks the fact that while information is a classic public good, much information is nevertheless produced privately. Precisely because it is a public good, in the sense that its social benefits are difficult to appropriate privately, the supply of it is likely to shrink when government offers a substitute.
3. Information is costly to absorb, so that flooding the public with information about hazards may cause people to become less well informed about some other and equally important matter.
4. Informing the public about a subset of hazards may cause people to underestimate the significance of other hazards, thinking that if they were substantial the government would inform the public about those hazards as well.

I also do not think that Viscusi devotes enough attention to the issues involved in measures for saving lives. It is too simple to say that "efforts that save very little in terms of life expectancy divert resources from programs that could have a major life expectancy effect."[19] The assumption that saving the life of a 50-year-old must be more beneficial than saving the life of an 80-year-old because the former will normally have a longer life expectancy may seem obvious; but if the usual ex ante perspective is taken, it may not be correct. People's valuation of their remaining life generally does not decline with age, for at no age do most people consider themselves to have any good alternatives to living. Thus they will spend as much to gain a few years of life as to gain many, because the expenditure has (to exaggerate slightly) no opportunity cost to them even if they are not protected by private or social insurance. Maybe the ex post perspective is proper here, but this has to be argued rather than assumed; Viscusi does not mention the point.

I want to make two additional points about his paper. The first, which may however be implicit in it, is that when the issue is not curing a disease

---

[19] *Id.* at 859.

of the elderly but merely reducing risk, willingness to pay may indeed be inverse to age, since the older you are, the smaller the expected benefit of reducing the risk. Second, saving an old person is a disease subsidy. Diseases compete to kill people, and so if you save a person from one disease you increase the likelihood of his being killed by another. The older the person, the more vigorous the competition and the less it is dampened by eliminating one of the competitors. That is why, for example, a complete elimination of cancer would have only a modest effect on longevity. Most cancer victims are old, and if they are spared by cancer it increases the opportunities for the other diseases of the old. A related point is that saving an old person increases his expected medical costs and that altering the age composition of a society can have substantial although not necessarily bad consequences of both an economic and a political character.

Viscusi raises but lets drop the difficult question of whether to discount consequences for future populations, asking, "Should risks [that will materialize] at least 100,000 years from now merit the same concern as risks to current populations?"[20] One argument against giving them the same concern and thus for discounting is that people are so likely to be much wealthier in the distant future as a result of continued scientific progress, and, specifically, to be much better able to eliminate risks to safety and health, that for us to devote our resources now to heading off those risks would produce a grave maldistribution of wealth across time. The decisive argument, however, is that we cannot project risks 100,000 years in advance.

I move now to the second group of papers and begin with Robert Frank's. Frank, like Sunstein, is favorably disposed toward behavioral economics but, unlike Sunstein, sees the behavioral insights as posing problems rather than opportunities for cost-benefit analysis. Before getting to that, however, let me note Frank's variant of Viscusi's "100,000 years from now" conundrum. Without quite endorsing the view that "if failure to adopt more stringent air quality standards today means that respiratory illnesses will be more common a generation from now, those illnesses should receive roughly the same weight as if they were to occur today,"[21] Frank seems quite sympathetic to it. But if there is some likelihood that a generation from now most respiratory illnesses will be easily and cheaply curable and therefore less costly than today, some discounting would be warranted.

My general reservations about behavioral economics resurface when I read Frank's paper. He gives one of Richard Thaler's examples of risk aversion, and as it happens I have recently, in a paper coauthored with Gertrud

[20] *Id.* at 865.
[21] Frank, *supra* note 5, at 916.

Fremling,[22] discussed essentially the same example appearing in a different paper by Thaler. Here is Thaler's example that Fremling and I discuss; it differs only trivially from the one that Frank discusses: "Two survey questions: (a) Assume you have been exposed to a disease which if contracted leads to a quick and painless death within a week. The probability that you have the disease is 0.001. What is the maximum you would be willing to pay for a cure? (b) Suppose volunteers were needed for research on the above disease. What is the minimum payment you would require to volunteer for this program? (You would not be allowed to purchase the cure.)"[23] Thaler reports that the typical response to question a is only $200 but to question b it is $10,000. No doubt with college students, who are the usual experimental subjects for behavioral economics, a liquidity effect can explain part of the discrepancy. But a more interesting possibility is that being put in a situation (in question b) of being deliberately exposed to a disease is degrading, as it resembles experiments on laboratory animals, prisoners of war, and inmates of prisons and insane asylums—all "persons" of low status. There is no comparable connotation to refusing to purchase an expensive cure. So while the probability of death is the same in questions a and b, the latter involves an additional cost, that of signaling willingness to undergo a degrading experience. The signal suggests masochism, lack of self-esteem, or poverty and desperation—all things that would make other people less likely to engage in advantageous personal or commercial transactions with the signaler.

Frank puts so much weight on income as a positional good as to make it doubtful that he could defend his claim that increases in average income increase the size of the social pie. He argues that "[m]easuring the social value of a consumption good by summing what individuals spend on it is similar to measuring the social value of military armaments by summing the amounts that individual nations spend on them."[24] In other words, striving to increase one's income is a move in an arms race, which is a zero-sum game. There is something to this. If people use consumption goods to signal desired traits such as neatness, respect, and dignity, a general increase in the income level may result in substituting more costly goods as signals with no gain in information. But there are three reasons to doubt whether that is the only or principal effect of higher incomes. First, relative income is important as a signal of how well one is doing. If your boss is paying you a lot less than someone who does similar work, something is

[22] Gertrud Fremling & Richard A. Posner, Market Signaling of Personal Characteristics (unpublished manuscript, Univ. Chicago Law Sch., January 22, 2000).

[23] Id. at 22.

[24] Frank, supra note 5, at 923.

wrong, unless you have decided to substitute nonpecuniary for pecuniary income. Evening out all incomes would thus deprive people of a great deal of information about their status and prospects.

Second, relative income is important in bidding for scarce goods. One's ability to buy a fine painting, for example, depends more on one's relative than on one's absolute income. Frank may be misinterpreting the result of the survey that asked graduate students whether they would rather earn $50,000 when others were earning $25,000 or $100,000 when others were earning $200,00 and that found that a majority preferred the first state. If average personal income were half of what it is today, other than as the consequence of some catastrophe such as another great depression or a major war, prices would probably also be half what they are today, so that the $50,000 earner in the first state would be as well off as the $100,000 earner in the second state, which means better off in terms of my first two points. That first point, incidentally, about the informational significance of relative income, also explains the second finding in the survey, that the students were much less interested in relative vacation time than in relative income. The length of one's vacation is an ambiguous indicator of "how one is doing"; a longer vacation may just indicate that one has an undemanding job.

Third, a striving for income-conferred status has desirable incentive effects, at least in a well-ordered society, that may explain much of America's prosperity. Anthropologists distinguish between "black" and "white" envy. If your neighbor builds a new barn and you are envious and want to burn it down, this is "black" envy: restoring parity by reducing your competitor's income. If instead you seek to assuage your envy by working harder so that you can build an even better barn, this is "white" envy. It benefits society as a whole to the extent that you are not able to capture the entire social product of your harder work as private product. In sum, vying for higher incomes is not a zero-sum game.

I could go on and discuss Frank's example of hyperbolic discounting, which shows nothing more than that people have a much clearer idea of how they would spend $100 next week and $105 a week from now than they have of how they would spend these sums in adjacent weeks a year from now. But I am straying from the topic of cost-benefit analysis. What is most disappointing about Frank's paper is that after first defending cost-benefit analysis in principle, and then reciting objections that behavioralists might advance to it, he leaves us without a recommendation. Should we jettison cost-benefit analysis? Should we use it unflinchingly in order to combat the cognitive quirks? Or should we build them into the design of our cost-benefit analyses? And could we? And if not, then what?

The Adler and Posner paper seeks to preserve cost-benefit analysis with a few modifications intended to accommodate some of the common criticisms of it. In effect, they want to align it more closely with its utilitarian foundations. In my view the justification for cost-benefit analysis, and the criterion for modifying it, should as I have said be pragmatic rather than foundational, and I worry that modifications designed to make it a better measure of average utility (or, as Adler and Posner prefer, overall well-being) will simply make it more complicated and subjective. Their theoretical points are often well taken—for example, as I suggested earlier, their point that irrational preferences or aversions should be taken as givens because they are unlikely to be alterable by the policy recommended by a cost-benefit analysis that ignored irrationality. But I do not think these insights should affect how cost-benefit analysis is done, although they should sometimes affect how it is used; here the distinction between cost-benefit analysis as a method of evaluation and as a decision rule becomes critical. The difference between complicating cost-benefit analysis in order to align it more closely with its desideratum, and keeping it simple while acknowledging its normative incompleteness, is like the difference in accounting between what goes in the text, and affects the bottom line directly, and what goes in the footnotes, reflecting subjective judgments that if introduced into the income statement and balance sheet proper would make their interpretation opaque.

I am puzzled by Adler and Posner's decision to exclude moral commitments, even when monetizable, in calculating the benefits or costs of a policy. I understand the difference between acting from a sense of duty and acting to increase one's happiness. But in cases in which the cost of not being able to fulfill a duty can be monetized, why exclude it? Suppose someone who does not expect to benefit from preserving the existing number of species nevertheless believes, perhaps as a matter of religious conviction, that it is wrong to allow a species to become extinct as a consequence of human activity; and he backs up his conviction with his money by making charitable contributions from which his implicit, and positive, valuation of species preservation can be inferred and even monetized with adequate objectivity to be incorporated into a cost-benefit analysis. Arguably, at least (the counterargument is made by Sen, and I shall come to it later), such a person incurs a real cost if a policy measure causes the extinction of a species, and it is not a sufficient reason for excluding this cost from the cost-benefit analysis of the measure that it falls outside Adler and Posner's definition of overall well-being.

But the deeper problem is that what the contingent values used in environmental cost-benefit analysis measure are not well described, for the most part, as moral commitments having the curious properties that trouble the authors. People can love wild animals or wilderness and want them to be preserved without either feeling a moral commitment to them or wanting to meet them, as it were. The enjoyment of these things is a type of consumption activity that is distinguishable from keeping pets or a garden only by the greater difficulty of measuring the value of the enjoyment. There is no difference in principle, and hence no paradox, in asserting that a person's utility would be reduced more by the extinction of the striped cheetah than by a flood that damaged the person's carpet. The problem is measurement, as with the sound principle advocated by Adler and Posner that uninformed (plus adaptive) preferences should be excluded when one is confident that the preferences would change as a result of the policy's being adopted. Similarly, I agree with them that it would be infeasible to weight costs or benefits by the marginal utility of income. But this is not because interpersonal comparison of utilities is unsound in principle, but because the measurement problem is insoluble and if overcome still would result in a bottom line that would be a confusing mixture of efficiency and equitable considerations.

I disagree with the suggestion that government agencies should "ignore objectively bad preferences when preferences violate widespread, uncontroversial intuitions about valuable and worthless behavior."[25] This may be correct as a matter of decision making, but it is dubious as a matter of evaluation. As between two equally effective drug treatment programs, costing the same amount, one of which gave drug addicts the same pleasure that they had derived from an illegal drug and the other of which did not, the first would be preferable from a utilitarian standpoint.

I turn now to the severe critics of cost-benefit analysis, as I shall call Broome, Nussbaum, and Richardson. Broome says that because cost-benefit analysis is a method of evaluation (although it can also be a decision rule), "it needs to be founded on a theory of value."[26] This strikes me as little better than a play on words (value-valuation). Cost-benefit analysis need be "founded" on nothing deeper or more rigorous than a showing that it has consequences that we like. In this connection let me give just two examples of the pragmatic merit of cost-benefit analysis in the simple Kaldor-Hicks sense that I defend. The first is antitrust law, and the second is risk regulation. The modern rationale for antitrust law, which commands a social consensus, is that cartelizing and other anticompetitive practices reduce welfare. This conclusion follows from a simple cost-benefit analysis. A cartel, to take the simplest example, both reduces the value of output (this is the "deadweight loss" caused by a supracompetitive price) and foments rent seeking, which has the wasteful aspects of an arms race. In making this

---

[25] Adler & Posner, *supra* note 5, at 1143.
[26] Broome, *supra* note 6, at 954.

judgment—which, as I have said, provides an uncontroversial basis for modern antitrust law—antitrust policy gives no weight either to the compensation of the losers from antitrust law or to distributive considerations. No attempt, in short, is made to show that antitrust law is Pareto efficient or utility maximizing. All values are computed on the assumption that a dollar is worth the same to everyone and that welfare is increased when a policy inflicts a dollar loss on the losers from it and confers a dollar and five cents gain on the winners even though the losers are not compensated.

As for risk regulation, perhaps the most important contribution of cost-benefit analysis in recent years has been to demonstrate, in the writings of Stephen Breyer, Viscusi, Sunstein, and others, that federal regulation of hazards to safety and health is a crazy quilt and in particular that many of the regulations are bad specifically because they flunk a cost-benefit test. This is increasingly accepted, and reform is progressing, albeit haltingly, even though the analysts in this field have implicitly rejected Broome's claim that "to do cost-benefit analysis properly, we need a theory about the value of a life."[27] It does not help Broome's case that he is unable to come up with such a theory.

His attempt to do so, however, is interesting. He argues that on the one hand bringing or not bringing a person into existence does not make the person better off or worse off than he would otherwise have been, because he would not have *been* otherwise; there is no other state with which to compare the person's state of existence; and so adding a person (by birth, not immigration) to a society cannot be said to create more benefits than costs, or more costs than benefits, excluding effects on other people. But on the other hand we can imagine this person being added to two different societies and (this is the only relevant difference) his being better off in one than in the other. The society in which he is better off will have, therefore, a higher level of overall utility than the other and so is to be preferred—which means that the bringing of a new person into existence *can* create additional benefits. Broome shows that this is a genuine paradox. But this will not surprise anyone who has eavesdropped on the debate over whether average or total utility should be the utilitarian maximand. It is absurd to think that we should immiserate ourselves to create a vastly increased human (and perhaps animal) population that will have a greater total utility although average utility is low. But it is equally absurd to think that we should destroy a large part of the population (in a way they would not notice, so they would suffer no pain) if that would maximize average utility. Broome's fuzzy neutral range results from such uncertainties about what it

---

[27] *Id.* at 958.

means to evaluate social well-being from the nonpersonal standpoint (the point of view of the universe, as he describes it) that he believes unavailable in dealing with the unborn.

These paradoxes of utilitarianism reflect one of the fundamental and seemingly insoluble problems of that philosophy, which is its inability to specify the community whose utility is to be maximized. Should it be just the living? Should it be just human beings? Just Americans? Should it include fetuses? The human population 100,000 years from now? Sentient animals (which as Martha Nussbaum suggested would add a new layer of complication to environmental cost-benefit analysis)? These questions are not answerable, at least within utilitarianism and probably not at all. But I will make one suggestion. Suppose that adding 1,000 people to society would have no effect on the welfare of the existing population; there would be no congestion or other negative externalities (or for that matter positive externalities). But suppose further that of these 1,000 people, although their lives would be "mediocre" in Broome's term, none of them would want to commit suicide; that is (I am setting aside any religious scruples or other costs to suicide), each of them would derive a positive utility from being born. This would mean that the addition of the 1,000 people would be Pareto efficient, which is a strong normative principle. It is true that the average utility of the society would be less (assuming the average life of the members of the existing population was above the "mediocre" level), but total utility would be greater and no person would be worse off. To the extent that any concrete issue of population policy approximates this example, we can I think make a relatively uncontroversial normative judgment in favor of the unborn when they do not impose negative externalities.

Which leaves us with the problem of global warming, the vehicle for Broome's speculation about the welfare effects of adding population. In his discussion of this problem and these effects, he makes the mistake of claiming that by killing people through flooding, global warming will reduce the future population "because some of the people it kills would later have had children."[28] The implicit assumption is that the number of children a person has is fixed, rather than being a matter of choice. The assumption has led in other contexts to such erroneous predictions as that the number of births is reduced by the number of abortions. The reduction in births is smaller because abortion is in part a matter of the timing of births rather than the number of births. If a woman wants to have two children, aborting her first pregnancy is unlikely to induce her to have only one child. And likewise if many people are killed in floods, other people may decide to have more

[28] *Id.* at 969.

children. A couple who loses a child in a flood may decide to have another child, which they would have had if the child had lived; here the analogy to abortion (or, even better, to miscarriage) is very close. But in addition, by raising the ratio of land to people, the killing floods may increase the incomes of the survivors, and this may (or may not) increase the number of children that the survivors decide to have.

Since it is wholly uncertain how many people global warming will kill, and since the effect of an increased death rate on future populations is uncertain, and since the benefits and costs associated with larger or smaller future populations are uncertain even apart from the paradox explored by Broome, I should think the proper approach to cost-benefit analysis of global warming would be simply to ignore population effects, as in Samuel Fankhauser's careful study, which finds substantial social costs of global warming without considering population effects.[29] I wonder whether Broome would agree with Fankhauser's approach or would suggest that cost-benefit analyses of global warming not be conducted at all, and if so what mode of analysis or response he would suggest instead for dealing with global warming.

Nussbaum's paper is concerned with tragedy and tragic choice. She illustrates these terms with reference both to Sophocles' play *Antigone* and to her own difficulties as a junior faculty member in balancing professional and family obligations. (She gives some other examples, but these are the clearest.) Her conception of tragedy is best seen in the implicit comparison of herself to Antigone; her minor tragedy[30] has a happy ending, and she suggests that if only Thebes had adopted something like the religion clauses of our First Amendment, Sophocles' play (or rather the legend on which it is based) could have had a happy ending too. This notion of tragedy seems to me both too broad and too shallow. Nussbaum exaggerates the tragic domain even when she says, a little more plausibly than in her own case, that "not to have the freedom of speech . . . is always a tragedy."[31] Was it a tragedy that Shakespeare wrote plays in a society in which the theater was heavily censored?

To me the real point of tragedy, both as a literary genre and as a concept distinct from that of the hard or painful choice—and it is a point well illustrated, as it happens, by *Antigone*—is to show that some conflicts cannot

[29] Samuel Fankhauser, Valuing Climate Change: The Economics of the Greenhouse (1995). Earlier cost-benefit analyses of global warming are summarized in Fankhauser, *supra,* at 121–23.

[30] I do not mean to belittle the tensions and pressures that women experience in trying to balance a job with motherhood, but merely to suggest that it cannot be equated to Antigone's situation, which resulted in her being executed.

[31] Nussbaum, *supra* note 6, at 1023.

be solved; they do not yield to cost-benefit analysis however generously construed; they are genuine no-win situations. Let me amplify Nussbaum's sketch of the play a bit. Creon is ruling Thebes in succession to the disgraced and exiled, but charismatic, Oedipus. One of Oedipus's sons, Eteocles, is the commander of Thebes's army. The other son, Polynices, revolts against Creon and Thebes, and in the ensuing battle both Eteocles, heroic defender of the city, and Polynices, the traitor, the rebel, are killed. Creon gives Eteocles a hero's funeral but orders that Polynices be left unburied, to be food for vultures—a terrible punishment in Greek mythology. Antigone, Oedipus's daughter and thus the sister of the slain brothers, disobeys Creon's order and buries Polynices. Creon had specified capital punishment for anyone who disobeyed the order, and he orders Antigone executed. Creon believes it essential to the preservation of civic order that the traitor be treated in death in a fashion that differentiates him from the loyal brother and that the traitor's sister who disobeyed his order be punished for that disobedience. Without these measures, his authority would erode and the civic values that he personifies (including the rule of law) would be subordinated to the potentially subversive religious and familial values personified by Antigone. She believes, in contrast, that those values have transcendent significance. There is no via media between these two value systems; that is what makes the play a tragedy rather than a plea for working out compromises.

Nussbaum wants to annul tragedy (although she denies this, it is plainly the spirit of her paper) by "imagin[ing] what a world would be like that did not confront people with such choices."[32] This would be a world in which all conflicts, all public conflicts anyway, are resolved by balancing the competing interests or, as we might say, comparing the costs and the benefits. Such a conception of what is possible to achieve in the way of resolving conflicts should make her friendlier to cost-benefit analysis than she is. She does not reject it, but she qualifies it to the point where its utility as a tool for public policy is greatly diminished. For example, she argues that in the case of basic constitutional rights, the costs of infringement should be regarded not as subject to being offset by benefits but instead as wrongs that no citizen should be required to bear. But constitutional rights are to a large extent determined by a balancing of costs and benefits. Think of all the limitations on the constitutional right of freedom of speech—for example, it does not prevent suits for defamation or prosecutions for threats and criminal solicitations. And cost-benefit analysis is unavoidable when the question is how many resources to devote to the enforcement of a con-

[32] *Id.* at 1013.

stitutional right, as Nussbaum implicitly acknowledges later in her paper by pointing out that all rights have costs.

The heaviest thumb that she wants placed on the cost-benefit balance is what she calls a "tragedy tax," designed to reflect the special indignation that particular costs should in her view engender in the analyst. I shall explain my disagreement with this suggestion with the help of her example of girls' education in the Third World. We now have a good deal of information about the return to investments in human capital, and we can use that information to conduct cost-benefit analyses of proposals to expand education in poor countries. We can compare the benefits of adding a year of high school for boys to, say, the benefits of adding 2 years of elementary education for girls, in societies in which boys are favored in education. (I shall assume for simplicity that the costs are the same.) Suppose the economy of the country is such that quite apart from any religious or customary inhibitions on the employment of women (because I want also to abstract from concerns with irrational and adaptive preferences), the potential demand for women in the job market is limited. The reason might be the infeasibility of child-care arrangements that would enable women to work full time in the market. In such a case, the added education for girls might be less productive than that for boys. Or might not, for one would have to consider the increased productivity of children (when they become adults), which might be considerable, if their "stay at home" mothers were educated. This is a difficult calculation, but not impossible.

After conducting such a cost-benefit analysis and finding as one might that giving the boys the extra education would be more valuable than giving extra education to the girls, the decision maker might still decide that equality was more important than the benefits in greater productivity. But at least he would have a clear idea of what would have to be given up in order to achieve the desired equality. To inject the tragedy tax into the cost-benefit analysis would merely occlude the cost of equality.

Richardson's paper is the one most critical of cost-benefit analysis. He makes two valid points. The first is that cost-benefit analysis will not by itself pick out the projects or policies to be evaluated or compared. The second is that explicit cost-benefit analysis is not required for all rational decisions. These points establish valid limits to the utility of the analysis. But they do not make it "stupid." Often, as Broome pointed out in the discussion of Richardson's paper, the project or policy is a given and the only task remaining is to compare it with doing nothing. And if the project or policy is complex, the kind of seat-of-the-pants reasoning that we often quite satisfactorily employ in everyday life may yield results that no one wants.

In calling cost-benefit analysis "stupid," Richardson particularly overlooks the distinction between evaluation and decision. He thinks it a stupid decision rule yet implicitly commends it as a method of evaluation and indeed as an input into decision, by saying that we ought certainly to collect information about willingness to pay in order to help us make good decisions: "I in no way mean to downgrade the importance of collecting information about the benefits and costs of alternative proposals. To the contrary, this is the first step in any intelligent process of deliberation."[33] But collecting that information is what is meant by cost-benefit analysis as an evaluative tool, indeed as anything less than the exclusive decision rule. It is not the equality or inequality sign that marks analysis as cost-benefit but the collection and display of costs and benefits. If the analyst finds that the benefits of some project would be $10 million and the costs $12 million, the analysis is complete; he does not have to add, "And therefore the costs exceed the benefits."

Richardson's real criticisms are thus of the use of cost-benefit analysis as a decision rule. One of them is that a consideration of alternative ways of achieving a given end often leads us to change that end, a possibility that he claims cost-benefit analysis precludes. We might wish to be clothed, and therefore consider alternative means of clothing; but "[i]f the only available covering was poison ivy, I, for one, would feel justified in going naked."[34] But this is not a problem for cost-benefit analysis. The method of covering that produces the greatest surplus of benefits over costs is nudity. Nudity produces zero benefits, but zero benefits are greater than negative benefits, which is what poison ivy, the only alternative to nudity, produces. (And likewise, in his later example, burning down the house to cook pork produces negative benefits compared to the alternative of simply going without cooked pork—of course the balance might change if starvation loomed.) Alternatively, the analyst's goal is misspecified: not what is the best covering, but what choice with regard to covering is best. In the division of intellectual labor, the cost-benefit analyst may not be the one who adds alternatives or respecifies goals. But his analysis may still produce information that leads someone else in the decision-making chain to modify the original design of the analysis.

A better example of the limitations of cost-benefit analysis than the poison ivy example, but one that is subject to the same response that I gave to it, is the case in which the maximand is hopelessly vague ("I want to be a success"). Before embarking on a cost-benefit analysis in such a case, the analyst will ask whoever commissioned the analysis for clarification. No

---

[33] Richardson, *supra* note 6, at 973.
[34] *Id.* at 979 (footnote omitted).

one denies, for example, to skip ahead to Richardson's brief discussion of negotiated rule making, that discussion and deliberation may help to get a better fix on what the costs or benefits or a proposal are, or what alternative proposals ought to be considered. If anything, his example of the vague maximand points up an additional benefit of cost-benefit analysis; for it is the inability to do the analysis without greater specification of the maximand that may induce reflection on its vagueness. Snags in the conduct of a cost-benefit analysis will lead the analyst to seek further guidance from the decision maker, and this will aid the decision maker in his Richardsonian deliberation.

Richardson is correct that in the process of implementing a means toward some end one may discover that the means is an end in itself, as in his ballet example. This point is the same as that of Sunstein and others concerning the proper design of cost-benefit analysis in the face of uninformed preferences; if the ballet dancer had known how much she would enjoy the ballet lessons, she would have attached a greater benefit to the lessons than merely better posture. This is a legitimate point, but it merely identifies a problem of information, which would plague any decision rule.

I cannot tell from Sen's paper what he really thinks about cost-benefit analysis, although if I had to guess I would guess that he thinks it a generally valuable but very often misused policy tool. He discusses the principles and pitfalls of cost-benefit analysis[35] but does not discuss actual cost-benefit analyses, and so it is difficult to tell, until he begins discussing environmental evaluation at the end of the paper, how often he thinks it goes wrong. He does not indicate, for example, what human costs the Indian dam that he mentions had omitted and how he would have rectified the omission. He mentions as an alternative approach to assessing cost-benefit analysis one that he does not follow in his paper, however, although he does not disapprove of it: a "bottom-up" approach in which the actual practice of cost-benefit analysis would be examined and a critique evolved from that examination. I wish he had followed that approach, because it is impossible to tell from his discussion of principles how he would like to alter the practice, and it is the practice that I am interested in. I would have liked to see him discuss the Indian dam, of which he obviously disapproves, and point out what principles guided the cost-benefit analysis that supported the project and what principles should have guided analysis.

But toward the end of the paper Sen does get concrete, raising a powerful objection to measuring environmental values by asking people what they

---

[35] This has been the subject of an immense literature. See, for good introductions, Richard Layard & Stephen Glaister, Cost-Benefit Analysis (2d ed. 1994); Robert Sugden & Alan Williams, The Principles of Practical Cost-Benefit Analysis (1978).

would pay to save a member of an endangered species, say, when the purchase of that good is not in fact an option for the person questioned. To put Sen's objection in the simplest possible form, we do not buy endangered species the way we buy toothpaste, and so while asking a person what he would pay for a tube of toothpaste will elicit a meaningful answer, asking him what an endangered species is worth to him will not; the weird answers that these surveys elicit may reflect not a cognitive quirk, as the behavioralists believe, but the remoteness of the inquiry from the context in which people encounter the price system. The question, then, which Sen however does not address, is what to do. (So his paper has an analogous trajectory to Broome's.) One possibility is to limit cost-benefit analysis to the market consequences of the proposed policy (an environmental protective policy, I will assume) and leave to the political process a determination of whether the net costs (if the costs exceed the benefits) override the pressures brought to bear by environmental groups. As a preliminary to assessing this possibility, I suggest that someone compare the environmental evaluations that are elicited in the questionable surveys with the rankings of environmental projects implicit in the lobbying activities of the leading environmental groups. Perhaps the valuations, although worthless as prices, measure an intensity of emotion that becomes translated into and can be measured by the amount and intensity of political advocacy by environmentalists.

INDEX

Accountability: demands of, 99; Regulatory Accountability Provision (1996, 1997, 1998), 55; strengthening, 52-53; transparency increases, 49

Adaptation: adaptive preferences, 278, 284–85, 297–300; in agency decision making, 297–300

Adler, Matthew, 217, 219, 326, 331–33

Allen, George, 72, 73, 75

Anderson, Elizabeth, 210

Antitrust law, 333–34

Aristotle, 143

Arrow, Kenneth, 113, 146–47

Availability heuristic: cascade effects mediated by, 231, 236; judgment of risk using, 229–30, 242, 325

Becker, Gary S., 323

Benefits: of cost-benefit analysis, 224–37; with deadweight costs, 314; exclusion of private, 327; in interest group competition model, 315–16; measured by cost-benefit analysis, 102–5, 203; measured by willingness to pay, 17–18; measurement of, 81–92; of saving life in cost-benefit analysis, 120–26. *See also* Costs

Biden, Joseph, 223–24, 237

Blackorby, Charles, 129, 130

Bossert, Walter, 130

Bradwell v. Illinois (1873), 190

Breyer, Justice Stephen, 28

Broome, John, 141, 319, 324, 333–36

Bush, George H. W., 51

Bush administration, Council on Competitiveness, 51

California: Economic and Fiscal Impact Statement, 61–62; regulation reform initiatives, 57–62; Regulation Review Unit, 59, 62; Regulation Review Unit (RRU), 59, 62; required economic analysis in Executive Order (1997), 60–62; Trade and Commerce Department Regulation Review Unit (RRU), 59

California Administrative Procedures Act (CAPA): California Environmental Protection Agency under, 58–59; Office of Administrative Law (OAL) under, 58–59; requirements for assessment and review under, 57–58; requirements for proposed regulations, 61

Cartel: in antitrust law, 333; as deadweight loss and cause for rent seeking, 333–34

Carter, Jimmy, 50

Carter administration, 18; Regulatory Analysis Review Group, 50; Regulatory Council, 50

Cascades: availability, 231, 236; informational and reputational, 230–31

Chiles, Lawton, 63